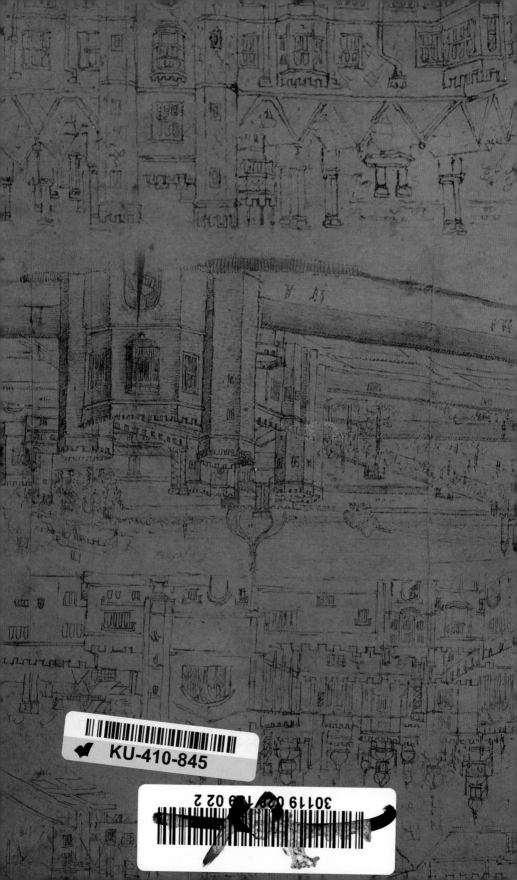

HOUSES OF POWER

Also by Simon Thurley

The Royal Palaces of Tudor England: Architecture and
Court Life, 1460–1547

Hampton Court: A Social and Architectural History

Whitehall Palace: An Architectural History of the
Royal Apartments 1240–1698

Somerset House: The Palace of
England's Queens 1551–1692

Men from the Ministry: How Britain Saved Its Heritage

The Building of England: How the History of
England Has Shaped Our Buildings

Houses *of* Power

The Places That Shaped
the Tudor World

SIMON THURLEY

BANTAM PRESS

LONDON · NEW YORK · TORONTO · SYDNEY · AUCKLAND

TRANSWORLD PUBLISHERS
61–63 Uxbridge Road, London W5 5SA
www.penguin.co.uk

Transworld is part of the Penguin Random House group of companies
whose addresses can be found at global.penguinrandomhouse.com

First published in Great Britain in 2017 by Bantam Press
an imprint of Transworld Publishers

A CIP catalogue record for this book
is available from the British Library.

ISBN 9780593074947

Maps and plans redrawn by Liane Payne.

Typeset in 11.75/16 pt Minion Pro by Jouve (UK), Milton Keynes
Printed and bound in Great Britain by Clays Ltd, Bungay, Suffolk

Penguin Random House is committed to a sustainable
future for our business, our readers and our planet. This book
is made from Forest Stewardship Council® certified paper.

For my mother, who gave me my love of history

CONTENTS

INTRODUCTION

IN 1972, ON A FAMILY HOLIDAY in Brittany, I was taken to see the Château of Largoët deep in the woods of Elven near Vannes. Although it is now an ivy-covered ruin, the colossal soaring tower that still stands shows that it was once a powerful place. I didn't know it at the time, but between 1474 and 1476 the five-storey Tour d'Elven was home to the Earl of Richmond, the future king Henry VII of England. Henry, confined in a stone chamber on the fifth floor, was the 'guest' of Francis II, Duke of Brittany. The seventeen-year-old Henry's rather tenuous claims to the English throne through his mother and, less so, through his father, led to an attempt in 1483 to put him on the throne and, as a result, he became a magnet for disaffected Lancastrians and a target of intense hostility for the ruthless usurper King Richard III.

The Tour d'Elven shows just how unpromising Henry Richmond's situation was in 1476. Spartan, secure and impossibly remote from London,

The Tour d'Elven at the Château of Largoët, where Henry, Earl of Richmond, the future Henry VII, was held for nearly two years.

it epitomized his isolation and political irrelevance. Few at the time, including Henry himself, could have predicted that this penniless young aristocrat would successfully bring to an end the Wars of the Roses, the dynastic squabbles that had dominated fifteenth-century England. But by the time of his death in 1509, when he handed the throne on to his teenage son, this is exactly what he had achieved.

When Henry VII won the throne in 1485 the English monarchy was 500 years old. As king, he inherited both a well-developed system of government and an extensive network of residences. These ranged from mighty castles such as Pontefract, Kenilworth and Dover to elegant riverside retreats such as Sheen and Greenwich. Royal houses differed from those of the aristocracy because it was from them that the king ruled. They were much like 10 Downing Street today, in that executive power was exercised in a domestic context, the private and political completely and inextricably mixed.

What was different from today was the all-pervading importance of etiquette, and not in the trivial sense of forbidding elbows on the table. By the Tudor period royal etiquette was a complex and subtle series of written rules and regulations governing the way people at the heart of power did things. This protocol affected the way royal buildings were designed and the way they were lived in. As a result, royal residences were a special type of building uniquely providing the setting for ceremonial and power.

Over the centuries royal buildings have been appreciated and admired in different ways: most often as supreme examples of this architectural style or that; but more recently people have begun to be interested in what royal buildings can tell us about monarchs' lives. In 1984 I became fascinated by this interaction between power, protocol and architecture, by the way that royal buildings contained evidence which, if it could be unravelled, would reveal a great deal about the way kings and queens lived and governed.

The problem was that most Tudor royal houses were gone. A bit of Tudor Hampton Court survived and some of St James's Palace; many royal castles still remained, ruined, but few of the parts where monarchs lived were still standing. So understanding royal houses first required a reconstruction of how they once were. In trying to do this there were two important tools: the first was archaeology, because many royal houses have been excavated over the years; the second was the financial accounts prepared for the building maintenance and furnishing as well as the occasional surviving plan or drawing. Using these tools I found that it was possible, in many instances, to draw accurate plans of what Tudor royal houses were once like.

Over the last thirty years I have had the chance to work on the archaeology of at least a dozen Tudor royal houses and have hunted down the documents that make sense of the jumble of brick walls and fragments of stone. For others, where everything has gone, or where digging has yet to happen, some good guesses can still be made based on the English obsession for bureaucracy. As a result, we now have a huge body of information on how Tudor royal houses looked and what went on inside them. But most of my work, and the work of others, has been published in obscure academic journals or in expensive monographs too heavy to hold in one hand; more importantly, nobody has put it all together and asked what does it mean, what does it tell us about our most famous reigning dynasty?

This book, for the first time, tells the story of the Tudors through what they built and where they lived. It is not just a catalogue of who built what, although it does do that; more importantly, it sets out to show that, as Tudor royal life changed so did the buildings that they inhabited. So, if you can work out the way that the buildings developed, you can, by deduction, tell the story of the Tudor monarchy from the inside.

My starting point is at the oldest royal house we still have standing, one founded by William the Conqueror, and a place I knew well for eight years as its curator: the Tower of London.

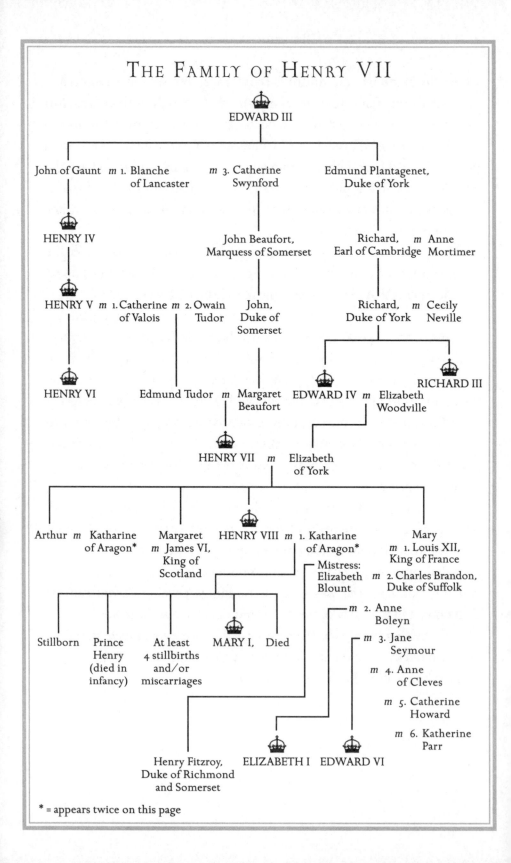

THE FAMILY OF HENRY VII

EDWARD III

John of Gaunt *m* 1. Blanche of Lancaster — *m* 3. Catherine Swynford — Edmund Plantagenet, Duke of York

HENRY IV

John Beaufort, Marquess of Somerset

Richard, Earl of Cambridge *m* Anne Mortimer

HENRY V *m* 1. Catherine of Valois *m* 2. Owain Tudor

John, Duke of Somerset

Richard, Duke of York *m* Cecily Neville

HENRY VI

Edmund Tudor *m* Margaret Beaufort

EDWARD IV *m* Elizabeth Woodville

RICHARD III

HENRY VII *m* Elizabeth of York

Arthur *m* Katharine of Aragon*

Margaret *m* James VI, King of Scotland

HENRY VIII *m* 1. Katharine of Aragon*

Mistress: Elizabeth Blount

m 2. Anne Boleyn

m 3. Jane Seymour

m 4. Anne of Cleves

m 5. Catherine Howard

m 6. Katherine Parr

Mary *m* 1. Louis XII, King of France *m* 2. Charles Brandon, Duke of Suffolk

Stillborn

Prince Henry (died in infancy)

At least 4 stillbirths and/or miscarriages

MARY I, Died

Henry Fitzroy, Duke of Richmond and Somerset

ELIZABETH I

EDWARD VI

* = appears twice on this page

• I •

A GRAND INHERITANCE

THE ROYAL CROWN

THE TOWER OF LONDON IS OF London but not in it. It actually sits outside the square mile and always has done. This is because, in the aftermath of the Norman Conquest, it was built to overawe and subdue Londoners, to terrify England's richest and most populous town through its size and its might. It was always a fortress, a place where monarchs kept their military hardware and to which they retreated at times of great trouble or moment; but until the reign of Elizabeth I it was also a residence, with fine rooms with sophisticated decoration and luxurious facilities overlooking the river. As time went on, many other functions were attracted there: it became the headquarters of the Mint, of the Royal Observatory, of the Ordnance Survey – and of course for long periods it was used as a prison and a place of execution.

For eight years in the 1980s and 1990s I was the curator of the Tower and often experienced its cold walls out of hours. Somehow these hard stone faces seemed to have absorbed the essence of the events they had encircled and they radiated back to me both the misery and the magnificence of England's past. There are many places in the Tower where that history is so thick that it takes little imagination to be transported back into it. Most powerful of all is the basement of the White Tower, the oldest part of the castle, where you can still visit the rooms once known as the Black Hall and the Black Chamber.

Utterly secure and lit only by the narrowest of slits, these were once part of the King's Wardrobe – his repository of valuable chattels. They led to a third room, a small barrel-vaulted chamber with an apse at its east end and walls almost 15 feet thick. It was entered through a narrow opening barred by a door of massive thickness and with many locks. Without a lantern you could see nothing more than the bulky outlines of the enormous iron-bound chests that lined the walls. This room, sunk beneath the Chapel of St John above, contained the king's most valued possessions. First amongst these were the crown, sword, sceptre, ritual comb, spoon and chalice, plus a collection of vestments, that made up the coronation regalia of the English monarchy. By legend many had belonged to Edward the Confessor, who reigned 1042–66, but in reality, apart from the crown itself, most were made subsequently. So valuable were these sacred relics, entombed in the depths of the kingdom's safest chamber, that they rarely saw the light of day.

Kings needed to wear crowns as a symbol of their majesty and so, as well as the regalia, each monarch had his personal crown, which could be brought out and used at great religious feasts and on other state occasions. These were generally kept not at the Tower, but at the Palace of Westminster – in the Middle Ages the king's principal residence – in a specially constructed safe-house known as the Jewel Tower.

The Jewel Tower, Westminster Palace, one of the few remaining fragments of England's most important medieval royal residence. Built in around 1365 to safeguard Edward III's treasure, it was still in use as a jewel house in the fifteenth century.

This structure, one of the last surviving fragments of the once great palace, stands just to the west of the House of Lords near a patch of grass used today by television commentators for political interviews. The ground floor is a room of great architectural pretension, covered with a many-ribbed vault with carved bosses. This was the office of the 'keeper of the jewels and gold and silver vessels', who controlled access to the narrow stair that led to the two upper floors. The entrance to the second-floor room is through one of the original two massive iron-studded oak doors, behind which the king's jewels were secured under heavy lock and key.[1]

It was from the Jewel Tower that, on 12 May 1485, the Yorkist King Richard III took his crown and a large amount of treasure as he left to direct the nation's defences against Henry, Earl of Richmond, who was known to be preparing an invasion from France. Richard's heavy baggage train made its way to Windsor, Berkhamsted Castle in Hertfordshire and then, via Nottingham Castle, to Leicester, where chests of coin, plate and the all-important crown were secured.[2]

Theatre is a fundamental ingredient of monarchy and Richard must have known that, win or lose, there would be a moment when wearing his crown would be essential. And indeed that moment came. In the heat of the Battle of Bosworth on 22 August, with his army deserting him, Richard called for his crown from its travelling chest. His helmet was designed so it could take the crown securely and, with the gold band glinting in the sun, Richard rose up amongst his troops and rode, with his elite knights, directly towards Henry. Richard would probably have been the victor had not Sir William Stanley, who had thus far committed to neither cause, joined on Henry's side with 3,000 men. Richard's inner circle were pushed sideways into a marsh, where the king was cut down and killed in the mud. His helm was retrieved and the crown placed on the head of the man who was now King Henry VII.[3]

Bosworth had been the closest-fought battle imaginable. But the transfer of the royal diadem from one man to another on a blood-soaked field was seen not only as the victory of might, but as the enactment of the will of God. As Henry gave thanks to his maker, so all the rights, powers and privileges of kingship passed to him, and with them the duties and responsibilities of the monarch before God.

The same crown that had left Leicester on King Richard's head now returned to that city worn by King Henry. Leicester was the location of a great Lancastrian shrine, the College of the Annunciation in the Newarke, founded in 1330 by Henry, Earl of Lancaster as an act of piety and transformed in the 1350s under his son, also Henry, into a splendid family mausoleum. In the collegiate church the kin of the Lancastrian kings Henry IV and V were buried and to it had flowed bounty from the royal coffers. It might have been a relatively small building, but it was very lavish and Henry's arrival at his ancestral vaults as the inheritor of the Lancastrian royal mantle was symbolic, if coincidental.[4]

A Capital Reception

Time, though, was precious. Henry needed to make his way to London, and soon. The City had been thrown into a state of anxiety by news of his victory and the Lord Mayor had imposed a curfew while preparations were made for the reception of the new king. Henry needed to consolidate his rule and show himself to the people of his capital. When he made his entry on 3 September, the streets were packed with citizens fighting to get a glimpse of their twenty-eight-year-old king. This was a man many had never heard of, let alone seen, and so he was an object of extreme curiosity. As he rode through the City Henry revealed himself as a tall, lean but strong man with dark, shoulder-length hair; he had blue eyes, and anyone close enough could see that while one wandered the other fixed its gaze on you.

The City of London was central to the successful exercise of kingship. As well as being the source of victuals, luxury goods, manpower and finance for the court, it was also the theatre of royal power and everyone expected showy pageantry. At its centre was old St Paul's. More than a place of worship, it was the royal arena of the nation, the place where monarchs made public their triumphs in the sight of God and, more importantly, in front of the people. On this day Henry's cavalcade made straight for the cathedral and, in front of the altar, he laid his three standards from Bosworth – great flags depicting the Cross of St George, the Dragon of Wales and the Dun Cow of Warwick, this last a symbol of the king's descent from the Lancastrian line.

It might have been expected that from St Paul's Henry would have made his way to the Tower of London. This, after all, was the great royal fortress bursting with arms, armour and supplies of gunpowder, and there the regalia was waiting to be claimed by the new king. From there Henry could have commanded his new capital, but for most Londoners in 1485 the Tower was tarnished by some of the most grisly and despicable events of the fifteenth-century struggle for the English Crown that we know as the Wars of the Roses. In here Henry VI had been murdered in 1471, as had been the sons of Edward IV, the Princes in the Tower, twelve years later. So Henry adopted an alternative strategy and remained at St Paul's.

While the Tower of London sat low by the river to the east of the City, old St Paul's was a hilltop citadel. Sited on Ludgate Hill, one of the two highest points in the City, it was completely enclosed by a high wall and entered through one of four stout gates. The precinct formed a city within a city (see map, pages 10–11), with a population of 300 or more and, at its heart, the largest and most comfortable house in London – the house of the Bishop of London. This stood at the west end of the nave occupying most of the precinct's north-west corner, and was linked, by a private door, to the north aisle of the cathedral.[5]

To stay here was a calculated choice: not only was it the best house in town, it was in the heart of the City, well protected but accessible to everyone, and basking in the daily endorsement of the Church. It was here that Henry VI, in moments of extreme crisis, had stayed to show himself to his people, and it was here that Henry VII now threw his first party, distributing largesse to all and publicly celebrating his God-given victory. After a few days, probably exhausted by his exertions, the king moved from the bishop's house and established himself nearby at Baynard's Castle, which had been prepared for him.

Medieval London – which was still crammed into a square mile enclosed by walls – was a city of precincts. Packed in amongst the tall, timber-framed houses of the citizens and merchants were the walled enclaves of over twenty monastic institutions. These were like mini cathedral closes, approached via gatehouses on the street and protected by tall walls on all sides. And just as the Church had enclaves in the City, so did the Crown – two of them. One was the Tower of London, perched just outside the City's eastern administrative boundary, while in the west was another that included Baynard's Castle, a large riverside mansion built by Humphrey, Duke of Gloucester in the late 1430s. From the street all that could be seen of this was a massive wall with a gatehouse at one end, but inside was a spacious courtyard and fine rooms overlooking the river. This was a place rich in symbolism for Henry, because in March 1453 the house had been granted to his father, Edmund Tudor, who was Henry VI's half-brother.[6]

The grant of Baynard's Castle can be said to have marked the founding of the Tudor dynasty, for that year Henry VI had ennobled his two half-brothers, Jasper as Earl of Pembroke and Edmund as Earl of Richmond. At an investiture at Greenwich they became the premier earls of England, a turn of events that nobody had expected. At the time the two brothers were virtually penniless and entirely dependent on the generosity of the king. This turned out to be very great – vast lands in Pembrokeshire came the way of Jasper, while the huge and valuable estates of Richmond in Yorkshire were given to Edmund. In London, Edmund was granted the fine residence at Baynard's Castle to enable him to sustain his position at court.[7]

That position did not last long. In 1455, Henry VI was forced by parliament to withdraw most of the grants he had made since becoming king, so Baynard's Castle was taken away from Edmund and soon became the property of Richard, Duke of York. From this moment the house became the unofficial London headquarters of the Yorkists – the place where the crown was offered to two of the Duke of York's sons: in 1461 to Edward IV and then, in 1483, to Richard III.

Of the Baynard's Castle occupied by Henry VII in those early days we know little, but we do know that it was part of a wider royal enclave in that part of the City. Immediately to its north was an aristocratic mansion converted in the 1360s to form the headquarters of the Great Wardrobe.

This was quite different from the King's Wardrobe, already mentioned, that stored goods in the White Tower. The Great Wardrobe was the supply department of the royal household; here everything, other than food, that a monarch could ever need was either purchased or made. It was deliberately near Cheapside, the main shopping street of the capital; here Great Wardrobe staff could easily purchase luxury goods, especially huge orders of textiles for royal clothes, the liveries of the household, bedding, table linen and furnishings, including tapestries. Outdoor equipment – such as horse trappings, dog collars and tents – was also bought and stored here.[8]

To the west of the Great Wardrobe, and connected to it by a long narrow gallery, was the London Blackfriars, one of the largest monasteries in the City. It had long enjoyed royal patronage and the chancel of the monastery church was full of the tombs of English royalty – including the heart of Edward II. The friary was frequently used by the royal family, parliament met there, high-status guests were lodged in its residential buildings and court events were staged in its great hall; I shall be mentioning it many times in this history.[9]

It was in this environment, then, on the edge of the City, close to a royal church and to the Great Wardrobe, that Henry first began to attend to the business of rule.

Up to this point Henry's first-hand experience of kingship had been extremely limited. His father had died in his mid-twenties with Henry still in his mother's womb and Henry became a ward of the Crown, the fate of young aristocrats who were minors when their fathers died. He lived deep in the English and Welsh provinces, mostly in south Wales, and his only exposure to the English court had been on a single trip to London as a thirteen-year-old in 1470. That year Henry's mother, Lady Margaret Beaufort, saw an opportunity to renegotiate the terms of her son's wardship and decided to petition King Henry VI directly.

This was an unstable and anxious time in the capital and Henry VI's court was fragile and precarious, presided over by a bewildered king. When, in 1421, he had come to the throne, only eight months old, he was the youngest monarch ever. Unfortunately he never became equal to the huge challenges he faced, and his naivety was compounded in 1453 by the onset of catatonic schizophrenia, which left him periodically incapable of governing. In 1459 civil war broke out and two years later Henry was deposed and Edward of York, a grandson of King Edward III, was declared king in his stead. Edward IV, as he became, was himself unseated and exiled in 1470 and, for a brief year, Henry VI returned to the throne. It was this moment of Lancastrian glory that Lady Margaret Beaufort seized to improve the prospects of her son.

The young Henry's uncle, Jasper, brought him to London, where he joined his mother at her house in the City. On the morning of 27 October Henry was rowed to Westminster, where, for the first time, he entered the gates of an English royal palace; a few minutes later he was in the presence of King Henry VI.[10] We do not know for how long Lady Margaret and Henry saw the king, or exactly where in the Palace of Westminster the meeting took place, or indeed what the outcome was, but this fleeting experience, and the dinner he had afterwards with the king's chamberlain, Sir Richard Tunstall, was the sum total of Henry Tudor's experience of the English court and, indeed, of London before he himself became king.

This atypical experience of monarchy was not his only one. In 1484, at the end of his fourteen-year exile, and in preparation for his assault on Richard III's England, Henry had fled, with his small group of close supporters, from Brittany to France. The French king was the fourteen-year-old Charles VIII. He took Henry to Paris, where he and his companions were Charles's guests for around a month in February 1485. In early March he moved with the French court first to Evreux and then to Rouen before sailing for England on 1 August. During his time with the court Henry certainly visited the Louvre, Charles's principal residence in the centre of Paris, and he witnessed a number of royal events, including the French king's formal entry into Rouen.[11] It is likely that this brief time at the court of France, witnessing its operation and setting, made a greater and more lasting impression on him than the fleeting glimpse of Westminster Palace he had had as a young teenager.

In 1485, now king and installed at Baynard's Castle with virtually no knowledge or understanding of the workings of the English court, Henry

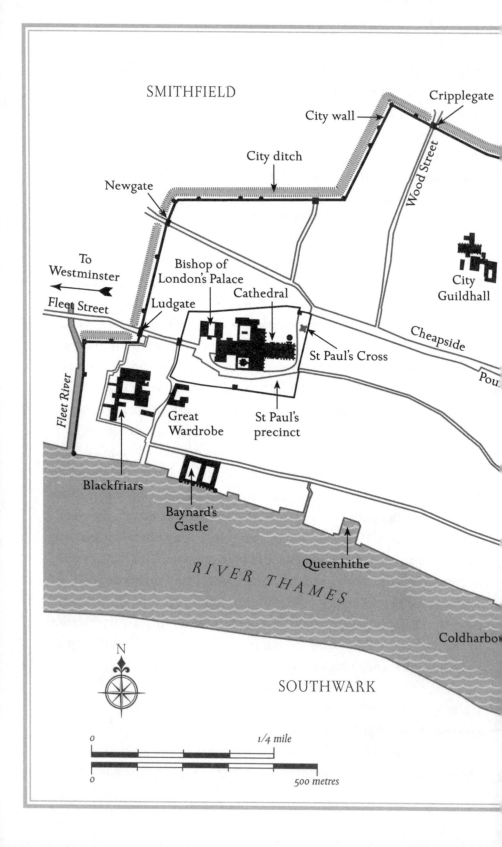

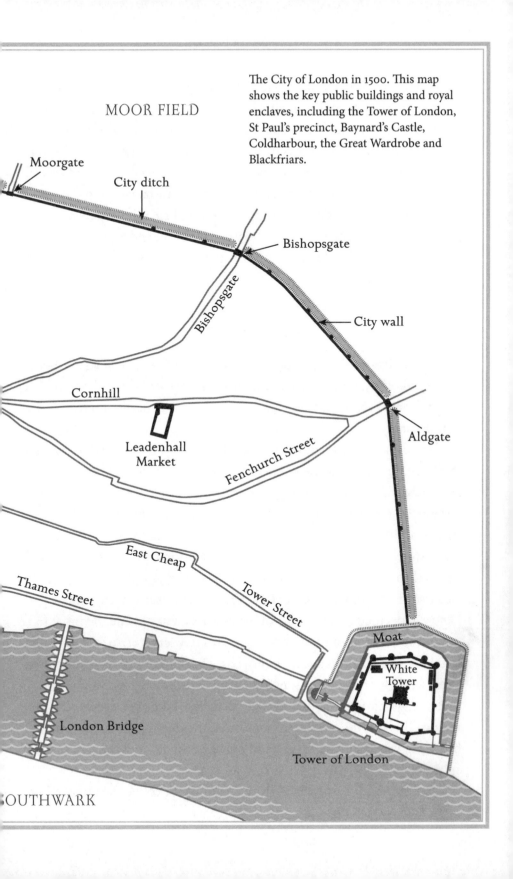

The City of London in 1500. This map shows the key public buildings and royal enclaves, including the Tower of London, St Paul's precinct, Baynard's Castle, Coldharbour, the Great Wardrobe and Blackfriars.

MOOR FIELD

Moorgate

City ditch

Bishopsgate

Bishopsgate

City wall

Cornhill

Leadenhall
Market

Fenchurch Street

Aldgate

East Cheap

Thames Street

Tower Street

Moat

White
Tower

London Bridge

Tower of London

SOUTHWARK

had to take his first decisions. Hundreds of grants were made rewarding friends, supporters and kin, while writs were issued to call parliament. For parliament to meet he had to be crowned, so a date was set – Sunday, 30 October. Planning, however, was as far as Henry got before he was forced to leave London in a hurry. In the wake of his triumphant arrival had come a trail of vagabonds, mercenaries and hangers-on. Some of them carried the dreaded sweating sickness and soon London was in the grip of a terrible epidemic. Henry boarded his barge and travelled upriver, moving first to Guildford in Surrey then on to Sheen, modern-day Richmond upon Thames.[12]

TAKING STOCK

Henry's arrival at Sheen, a place he had never been, was, again, laden with symbolism, for it was here that his predecessor Henry V had built a magnificent new house as the spiritual and dynastic home of the Lancastrians.

In the second half of the fourteenth century, Edward III expanded the Norman manor house of Sheen (or Shene), which had been used by both Edward I and Edward II, and made it into a royal residence that became a favourite retreat. The place was equally favoured by his successor, Richard II, but he hysterically razed it to the ground after his wife, Anne of Bohemia, died of plague there in 1394. Thus, when Henry V decided to build a riverside retreat at Sheen in 1414 he was making a clean start. Or almost. Edward III's manor had sat within a moat and Henry V decided to build part of his new residence inside the moat too, around 100 feet from the river's edge. This new enterprise was designed to be a home for the Lancastrian dynasty in the hour of its triumph – a 'great work', for the idea was to build a house around which would cluster three religious foundations dedicated to the king, his family and the nation. This was the most ambitious monastic foundation ever attempted by an English king, one that would put the monarchy at the heart of the spiritual life of the nation.[13]

On the south bank of the river, to the north of the new house, was

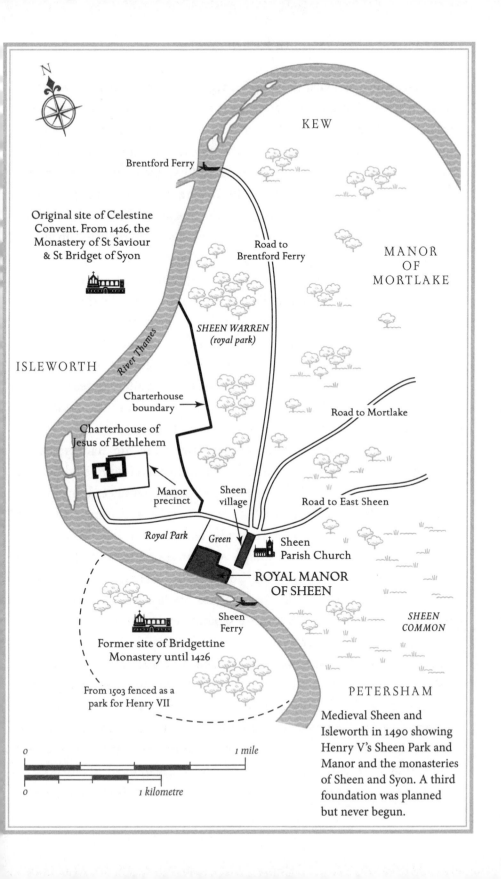

N

KEW

Brentford Ferry

Original site of Celestine Convent. From 1426, the Monastery of St Saviour & St Bridget of Syon

Road to Brentford Ferry

MANOR OF MORTLAKE

SHEEN WARREN (royal park)

ISLEWORTH

River Thames

Charterhouse boundary

Road to Mortlake

Charterhouse of Jesus of Bethlehem

Manor precinct

Sheen village

Road to East Sheen

Royal Park

Green

Sheen Parish Church

ROYAL MANOR OF SHEEN

Sheen Ferry

SHEEN COMMON

Former site of Bridgettine Monastery until 1426

PETERSHAM

From 1503 fenced as a park for Henry VII

Medieval Sheen and Isleworth in 1490 showing Henry V's Sheen Park and Manor and the monasteries of Sheen and Syon. A third foundation was planned but never begun.

0 ——————— 1 mile

0 ——————— 1 kilometre

to be a Carthusian charterhouse of thirty monks; opposite it on the north bank at Isleworth, and named Syon (or Zion), was to be a Bridgettine monastery designed for up to eighty-five monks and nuns; and a third monastery of Celestines was projected but never begun.[14] These were to be powerhouses of prayer for the king and his family, past, present and future, rather like the College of the Annunciation in the Newarke in Leicester which he had also paid to complete. These foundations enveloped his new residence so that their bells could be heard from the royal house as they tolled the liturgical hours.

There were two parts to the manor of Sheen: a large, mainly timber-framed house with a great hall, a chapel and rooms for the king and queen. Near to this, but surrounded by its own moat, was what we would today call a castle. Measuring only around 140 × 123 feet, it was built of stone and had a small courtyard at its centre. An image of it, drawn much later, shows it in the reign of Elizabeth after domes had been added to the tops of the towers (see plate section). With these removed it can be seen for what it was – a pocket pleasure-castle, the perfect retreat for a warrior king, where he could withdraw from the main residence and be with his closest family and companions. But Henry V did not live to enjoy it: he died suddenly in 1422 and it was completed, in fits and starts, under his son, Henry VI.[15]

Masons at the courts of Henry V and VI were an international bunch; many had worked in France and some had seen the Louvre, as Henry V himself had. In the 1360s King Charles V of France had encrusted the royal lodgings there with turrets and towers and in the inner courtyard was the great circular drum tower, a separate residence soaring above all, crowned with a steep conical roof. Here again was a pocket palace, a small castle in its own moat, just as Sheen was to become (see plate section). Closer to home (though not much) was another example of a separate stone-built lodging tower – this was Warkworth Castle in Northumberland, where a separate tower of great elaboration was built for the Earl of Northumberland some time in the 1380s. This was not much smaller than the tower at Sheen, and as ingeniously planned.[16]

In the autumn of 1485 Henry VII spent four days at Sheen, and it is likely that he was joined there by his mother. For Lady Margaret Beaufort, her son's victory at Bosworth and his arrival in London was the triumphant culmination of twenty years of plotting, and their reunion, after fifteen years of separation, must have been emotional. Apart from the coronation, the most pressing topic of conversation was no doubt Henry's marriage, which his mother had promoted behind the scenes while he was in exile. His bride was to be Elizabeth, the eldest child of Edward IV and his queen, Elizabeth Woodville. This was a dynastic alliance, not a love match; the idea of the marriage was to bring together the blood lines of York and Lancaster, so ending their longstanding rivalry for the throne. Henry had never met Elizabeth and the priority was now to bring her to London and prepare her for marriage.

It was decided that Lady Margaret should be granted Coldharbour, Elizabeth Woodville's former residence in the City. This was another great riverside mansion, not far from Baynard's Castle and, like it, originally the home of a super-rich merchant. It could be approached from the street through a great gatehouse, or by barge via a landing stage on the riverfront. A chapel and a great hall overlooked the Thames and above there was a great chamber; near this was a chamber for Elizabeth of York and a wardrobe below for her possessions.[17]

Henry's mother was a guiding light in those early years and was given semi-regal status. At many royal houses she had rooms adjacent to those of the king. But soon Henry was also to enjoy confidence in his wife. Elizabeth of York had been born at the Palace of Westminster and was daughter, sister, niece and wife to four successive monarchs – Edward IV, Edward V, Richard III and Henry VII. Both Henry's mother and his wife thus had the courtly experience he lacked and brought into his circle some of Edward IV's former courtiers.

Westminster Palace

In early October 1485, a month after his arrival in the capital, Henry finally made his entry into Westminster Palace. This had been one of the most important royal houses since Saxon times, but had been transformed into England's principal royal residence during the reign of Henry III. It was he who had decided, in 1245, to rebuild Westminster Abbey and establish the cult of the royal saint Edward the Confessor there. His reconstruction of Westminster Palace at the same time as the abbey transformed it into the premier house of the realm. Indeed it was the only royal house ever described at that time as a palace – *Palatium regium*. The term derived from the residence of the Roman emperors on the Palatine Hill in Rome and, as 'palace' meant principal residence, there could be only one of them. All the king's other residences were known as houses, castles or, more usually, manors. In this book I shall follow the contemporary usage and not indiscriminately call all royal residences 'palaces'.[18]

Westminster was a place of great antiquity and magnificence, and it was another enclave. A wall with gatehouses and bell towers completely enclosed what was, in effect, a gravel island next to the Thames. On this stood Westminster Abbey with all its ancillary buildings and, in an inner enclosure, the royal palace.

Westminster Palace was entered from King Street, modern Whitehall, through a great gatehouse that led into an outer court. Here, facing visitors, was the north front of Westminster Hall – an elevation that appeared as if it were the front of a cathedral, but in reality faced up the end of a colossal great hall built by William Rufus from 1097 and re-roofed in 1393–1401. This was the ceremonial hub of the kingdom, where great public events took place. It was here that Henry VII, like his predecessors, was to celebrate his coronation feast at a huge marble table set on a dais beneath giant carved and gilded oak angels that represented the heavens above his head.

Adjoining Westminster Hall to the south was a suite of smaller rooms, including the White Hall, which served as the everyday audience

The Palace of Westminster in 1500. Apart from Westminster Hall, the Jewel House and the undercroft of St Stephen's Chapel, none of the buildings shown here remains today. The diligent work of Georgian and Victorian antiquarians plus a small collection of drawings, paintings and prints have informed this reconstruction. The details have been filled in using the building and repair records of the medieval Office of Works.

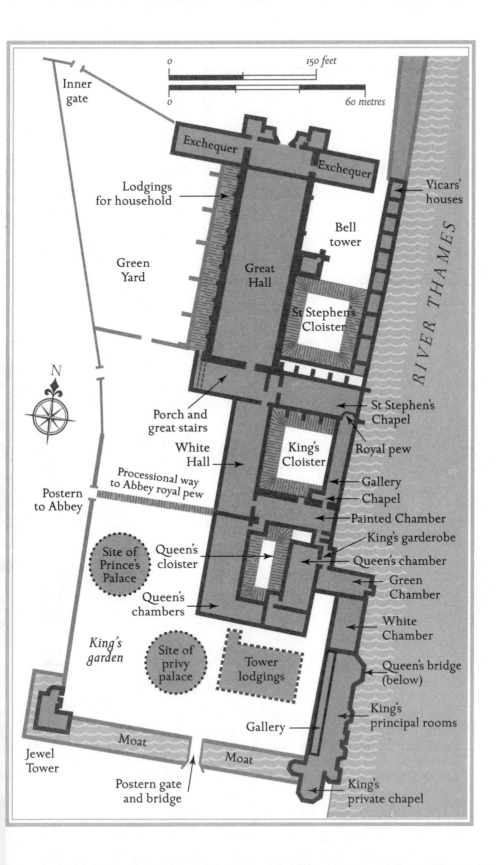

Inner gate

0   150 feet

0   60 metres

Exchequer

Exchequer

Vicars' houses

Lodgings for household

Bell tower

Green Yard

Great Hall

St Stephen's Cloister

RIVER THAMES

Porch and great stairs

St Stephen's Chapel

Royal pew

N

White Hall

King's Cloister

Gallery

Processional way to Abbey royal pew

Chapel

Painted Chamber

Postern to Abbey

King's garderobe

Site of Prince's Palace

Queen's cloister

Queen's chamber

Green Chamber

Queen's chambers

White Chamber

King's garden

Site of privy palace

Tower lodgings

Queen's bridge (below)

King's principal rooms

Jewel Tower

Moat

Gallery

Moat

King's private chapel

Postern gate and bridge

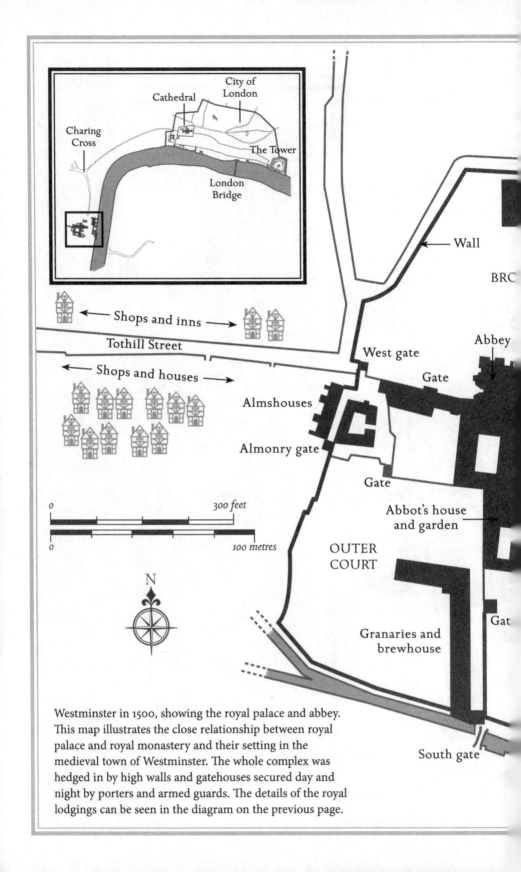

City of London

Cathedral

Charing Cross

The Tower

London Bridge

Wall

BRC

Abbey

Shops and inns

Tothill Street

West gate

Gate

Shops and houses

Almshouses

Almonry gate

Gate

0   300 feet

0   100 metres

Abbot's house and garden

OUTER COURT

N

Gat

Granaries and brewhouse

South gate

Westminster in 1500, showing the royal palace and abbey. This map illustrates the close relationship between royal palace and royal monastery and their setting in the medieval town of Westminster. The whole complex was hedged in by high walls and gatehouses secured day and night by porters and armed guards. The details of the royal lodgings can be seen in the diagram on the previous page.

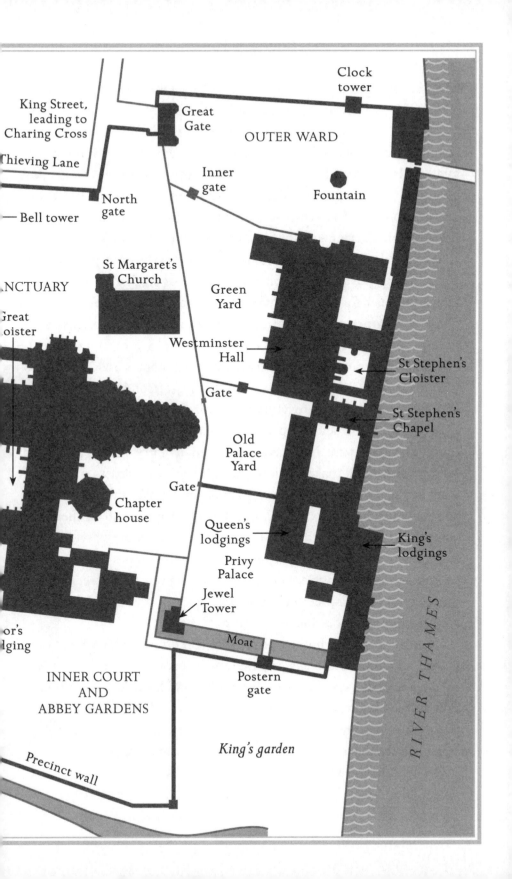

King Street, leading to Charing Cross

Thieving Lane

— Bell tower

Clock tower

Great Gate

OUTER WARD

Inner gate

Fountain

North gate

SANCTUARY

St Margaret's Church

Green Yard

Great Cloister

Westminster Hall

St Stephen's Cloister

Gate

St Stephen's Chapel

Old Palace Yard

Gate

Chapter house

Queen's lodgings

King's lodgings

Privy Palace

…or's …dging

Jewel Tower

Moat

Postern gate

INNER COURT AND ABBEY GARDENS

King's garden

Precinct wall

RIVER THAMES

hall, and, at right angles to this, the king's chamber, richly painted and gilded with murals and known as the Painted Chamber, which contained his bed in a curtained enclosure. Beyond this were the king's chapel and the queen's chamber and chapel. Under King Henry III this was the sum total of the accommodation, but in the early fourteenth century his grandson King Edward II added a third room, the Green Chamber, a new bedroom that looked over the river.[19] This southern part of the palace, further extended by both Edward III and Edward IV, became the zone in which the royal family lived. Next to it was the privy palace, privy just meaning private. This contained a maze of smaller rooms for the king and queen, for which we have no evidence. The privy rooms looked out on to a garden and, in a tower at the south-west corner of this, as we have already seen, the king kept his jewels.

Henry's entrance to Westminster was a big moment, and not one to be thrown away. While he had been in the City of London and at Sheen, various branches of the royal household had been busy preparing the palace for him and setting up a ceremonial entry. There is no record of this momentous event, but a herald recorded his entry into the palace the following year and makes it clear that this was more or less a re-run of what had happened in 1485. Henry left Sheen for Westminster by barge and was met at Putney by the Lord Mayor, aldermen and all the livery companies aboard their barges. They escorted him to the palace landing stage, where they disembarked and, dressed in their robes and furs, lined his route through the palace precincts. The king was then greeted by the priests of the royal College of St Stephen, part of the royal palace, who escorted him in procession to his rooms.[20]

For Henry VII, who as we have seen had only ever been there for a couple of hours as a teenager, this was a lot to take in. But he was accompanied by expert guides – his mother and his wife-to-be, who not only showed him round the palace room by room but became his tutors in the all-important issues of court etiquette. Henry very quickly had to learn how to make his royal residences work for him and this meant understanding the arcane workings of the English court.[21]

THE ROYAL COURT

There is an important difference between a household and a court. The household was the organization that made possible the monarch's existence, containing everything he needed for everyday life and for the normal business of ruling. The court is a more amorphous concept, because it had no static membership but contained the people who were, at that time, welcomed by the king as part of his daily round of life. They might be his friends, they were certainly his supporters and they were part of the setting of kingship – ornaments to the king's power. So there was a sense of spectacle to the court, while the household was the machinery that made that spectacle possible.

A crucial component of a court is courtliness, a code of manners and behaviour to which its members subscribe. The early medieval kings simply didn't have this; their closest attendants were usually tough soldiers geared to military action. The court of King Edward I, who reigned from 1239 to 1307, for example, was a business-like household, full of military men and administrators. Those who had the greatest status were his fifty household knights – the royal bodyguard, in effect a sort of elite standing army. Their friendship and loyalty had been forged in blood and battle and they set the militaristic tone of the king's entourage. Everyone below them, from pages and grooms to cooks and tailors, had a military role to play when the household was at war. The camaraderie and bonhomie of the soldier brought an informality of tone in which the king and his subjects mixed freely during everyday exchanges and even on special occasions.[22] During the fourteenth century, such royal war bands gradually became more interested in the arts – in tapestry, painting, poetry, sculpture and music. Macho aversion to such things gradually gave way to an appreciation of artistic accomplishment. At the same time, more women were admitted into the everyday mix of people surrounding the monarch.

Although some of these things can be discerned in England as early, perhaps, as the reign of Henry III (1216–39), all of them become a marked feature in the time of Richard II (1377–99). In fact, a royal court in a sense recognizable to us today begins to exist in England from his reign.[23] Richard's was a court that expressed an interest in culture, that comprised women to a much greater degree than previously, that could portray itself magnificently and that had a sense of hierarchy expressed in degrees of status and deference. Richard loved to wear his crown, presiding imperiously, and enthroned, over banquets, religious feasts and audiences. He was preoccupied by ceremony and his court festivities became more formalized and ceremonious. He loved expensive clothes, priceless personal jewellery, rich food and enjoyed having himself portrayed by painters.[24]

Richard II's household was not alone in becoming less militaristic and more ceremonious in character. Royal households across Europe were growing more formalized, partly, perhaps, in reaction to waves of violent unrest across the continent. The most notable English expression of this was the Peasants' Revolt of 1381, which perhaps caused a stiffening in Richard's determination to appear majestic. Richard's upbringing and character were important too, as was his interest in the court of France and later his sense of rivalry with it.[25] There were significant architectural implications in this shift from a household to a court and the foundations for this were in fact laid under Richard's predecessor, his grandfather Edward III (1327–77).

Under Edward III some major architectural changes began to be introduced at Westminster. For his predecessors it had been enough to live in the White Hall, the Painted Chamber and the Green Chamber – the three great rooms of the palace. But Edward decided that he wanted more space for himself, his family and his closest companions. So on to the Green Chamber he added a two-storey block comprising two rooms – the White Chamber and an inner chamber – and these led, at their far end, to another building containing a private chapel. These rooms overlooked the river and had no windows on the landward side; this was because, unlike earlier royal rooms, which led into each other, these had a gallery at their rear so that they could be serviced and accessed discreetly when necessary. These were buildings for comfort and pleasure. The richly hung rooms had their own integral garderobes (WCs), while beneath the White Chamber was the royal bathroom and below the inner chamber the king's wardrobe.

WINDSOR CASTLE

At Westminster, Edward III was adding to a pre-existing building; at Windsor, where some of his work actually survives, he started anew. Edward was born at Windsor Castle in 1312 but, as a young king, showed little interest in the place. In 1344, however, in an attempt to drum up knightly recruits for war against France, he decided to hold a great tournament there. After three days of combat the king and his team emerged as the victors and, in celebration, Edward announced that he would be founding an order of chivalry based on King Arthur and his knights of the round table. The order, he decided, would have its own circular building, 200 feet in diameter, which would contain a round table: not a disc, but a ring which the knights sat at facing inwards.[26]

The king lost interest in this extraordinary (and short-lived) structure, but the idea of a chivalric order based at Windsor lived on and, at another tournament in 1348, Edward founded the Order of the Garter. The order was to be supported, at Windsor, by a new college of priests attached to the existing chapel in the lower ward; at the same time a similar college was founded at Westminster Palace – the College of St Stephen.

Edward's extraordinary military success in France, and in particular his capture of King John II, transformed his financial situation; the French king's ransom alone, paid over a period of years, was worth more than £250,000. This wealth changed Edward's ambitions for Windsor. From 1350 to 1368 he rebuilt much of the castle at a cost of £51,000. The most important part of this was the £44,000 he spent between 1357 and 1368 on building himself the largest and most magnificent residence yet constructed by any English monarch.

Edward swept away the timber buildings of his predecessors and embarked on constructing a heroic structure designed and executed in a single campaign. It had no precedent in English or French architecture in size, formality or plan. The building relied on proportion to impress: this wasn't a fancy building; its impressiveness lay in its restraint and austerity – characteristics suitable for a great military hero.

The main façade was nearly 390 feet long and incorporated two gatehouses, one leading to the kitchens, the other to the king's lodgings. These were dominated by a colossal great hall and a chapel nearly as large. They were approached by a long, wide, stone stair, large enough to ride a horse up.

As at Westminster, the great hall was a ceremonial space and the king's own rooms were located at a little distance from it. The layout of his Windsor lodgings was directly copied from Westminster. Arranged in an 'L' shape, at their core was the Great Chamber, about the same size as the Painted Chamber at Westminster, off which was a private tower containing some smaller rooms for the king's pleasure. Then came an audience chamber, later known as the presence chamber (where you were ushered into the sovereign's presence). On the north front, partially within a large canted tower, was the king's bedchamber looking out over the spectacular landscape of the Thames valley to Eton and beyond. Beyond the bedchamber was a private chapel with a closet in it where the king could hear Mass, a lesser bedchamber and a study. Meanwhile,

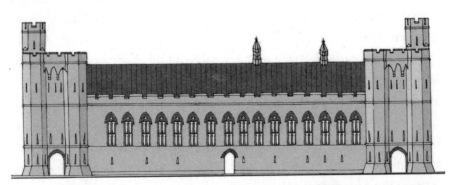

Reconstruction of the principal façade of Edward III's royal lodgings in the upper ward at Windsor, c.1370. The regular façade gives no clue as to the functions of the rooms behind. The tower to the left was the entrance to the royal lodgings, that on the right gave access to the kitchens. To the right of the central door on the first floor was the great hall, to the left was the chapel. The tower on the far left-hand side contained the king's private closet.

preceding the Great Chamber was a sort of antechamber, presumably for people to wait in. We know that Edward's queen, Philippa of Hainault, had a suite of rooms here too. Her outer chamber was called her Dancing Room, the next room was covered in mirrors and, like the king's, her bedchamber had a little chapel next to it.[27]

Edward III's Windsor was an extraordinary building, entirely new in its architectural ambition, in its sophistication of planning and in the way the great rooms of state were juxtaposed with spaces for the leisured enjoyment of the monarch. It was built to respond to the changing requirements of Edward's lifestyle.

In the fourteenth century the restless, peripatetic lives of English monarchs began to settle into a more sedate pattern. The royal household grew in size from perhaps only 150 to over 500 followers and this larger, more cumbersome organism moved less frequently between houses. Meanwhile, some of the routine administration that had always been executed from wherever the king happened to be staying was settled in Westminster, which, by 1350, had become the administrative headquarters of the realm. As Edward retired from the battlefield he grew more sedate and liked to spend time closeted away privately with his friends and family.[28]

These changes in royal behaviour underlay the architectural changes at both Westminster and Windsor. A larger household needed bigger houses, with more accommodation and larger kitchens. The king's desire for more leisure meant increased private space, including a private bedroom and bathroom. These are the key features of Edward III's and Richard II's building works at Westminster, Windsor and elsewhere.

In the century following Richard II's death, the size, splendour and influence of the English court waxed and waned depending on the character and preferences of the sovereign, his resources and circumstances.[29] Edward IV set great store by the maintenance of a magnificent court, and visitors remarked upon the richness of the trappings of his houses and the formality and ceremoniousness of his courtiers.[30] These were the expectations that Henry VII inherited, and those that he set out to fulfil. For Henry immediately laid great stress on the magnificence and

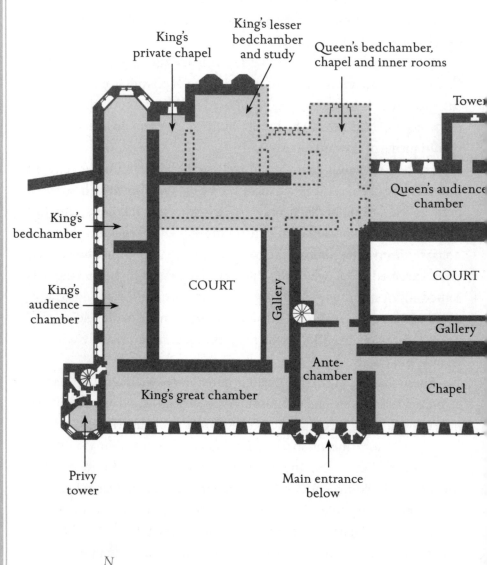

King's lesser bedchamber and study

King's private chapel

Queen's bedchamber, chapel and inner rooms

Tower

Queen's audience chamber

King's bedchamber

King's audience chamber

COURT

Gallery

COURT

Gallery

Ante-chamber

Chapel

King's great chamber

Privy tower

Main entrance below

N

0   75 feet

0   25 metres

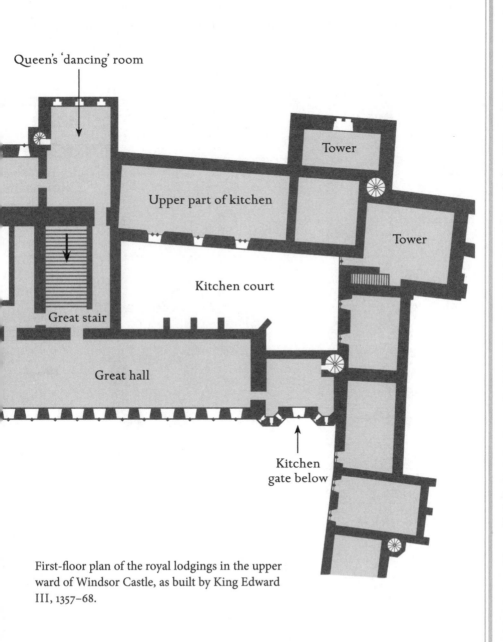

Queen's 'dancing' room

Tower

Upper part of kitchen

Tower

Kitchen court

Great stair

Great hall

Kitchen
gate below

First-floor plan of the royal lodgings in the upper
ward of Windsor Castle, as built by King Edward
III, 1357–68.

formality of his court, on the lavish dispersal of hospitality and of court spectacle and ceremony. What we do not know is whether this was an instinctive reaction as a ruler; whether it was a consequence of his long, penniless exile; or whether his wife and mother schooled him in the arts of courtly magnificence. In reality, it was probably a blend of all three.

◆ II ◆

THE LABOURS OF
HERCULES

Modus Vivendi

For a man who had been a virtual prisoner for his first twenty-eight years, Westminster and Windsor must have been bewildering in scale and blinding in magnificence. These were amongst the largest royal houses in northern Europe, and arranged quite unlike those of the French king that Henry had briefly experienced before Bosworth. There the king's and queen's rooms were stacked up in great towers, not spread out in a parade as in England. Access to the king of France was free and easy for all; in England, a more controlled and exclusive system operated. To gain access to the magnificent enfilade of state chambers you had to pass the scrutiny of the royal guards, who excluded people who were unknown or not important enough.[1]

Richard III never thought that he would lose his crown to the upstart Henry Tudor and, as he left Westminster and Windsor to dispose of this rebel, he had every reason to expect he would return victorious. So when Henry entered London the two great ancestral piles, which were now his, were still furnished with the personal possessions of Richard III. Though these great residences were, by the 1480s, a century old and, externally, may have looked old-fashioned, internally they contained furnishings collected by the Yorkist kings in the latest international taste.

Although perched on the northern periphery of Europe, England was no cultural backwater. From its eastern seaboard a network of trading relationships stretched across the North Sea to northern Europe and the Baltic. The Low Countries were a lot closer and more accessible to London than many parts of northern and western England, and huge quantities of imported goods flowed into the capital's port. Hundreds of

Flemings and other lowlanders came to work in London in the late fifteenth century. As the craft guilds had created a system of closed shops within the City itself, they settled on the periphery, in Westminster and Southwark, out of range of the City's trade monopoly.[2]

The monarch sometimes bought furnishings directly from foreign merchants, sometimes from alien traders, but mainly procured goods through the Great Wardrobe in the City. The King's Wardrobe of the Beds would order linen, the Wardrobe of the Robes, clothes for the king's person; his Master of the Horse, saddles and horse harness; his librarian would get his books bound there; and the clerk of his chapel would obtain vestments and incense. When items were no longer in use they were returned to the Great Wardrobe where they were stored in specially made trunks, cupboards and drawers. There, in rooms swept, dusted and regularly fumigated with frankincense, the monarch's goods were guarded by the keeper and his staff.[3]

A change of monarch meant a lot of work. Although Henry VII's personal tastes were probably not very different from those of Richard III or Edward IV, in 1485 the royal houses and their furnishings were encrusted, at every turn, with the heraldic devices of the Yorkists. From the moment Henry arrived in London, painters and embroiderers from the Great Wardrobe worked overtime expunging the white roses and sunbursts of Edward IV, the boar of Richard III and the falcons and fetterlocks of their father, and replacing them with the double Tudor rose, the Beaufort portcullis and Henry's heraldic supporters, the dragon and the greyhound. Instructions (called warrants) could be issued to the Great Wardrobe by only a few people, chief amongst these the monarch himself. So refurnishing the royal houses in the 1480s would have largely been ordered by the king.

Interior decoration was not the only thing on Henry VII's mind in his first years in power; however, he knew, or had been taught, that the glue that stuck a monarch to the throne was magnificence. Magnificence was the art of being a king, the art of transmitting the confidence and power of monarchy through your physical surroundings. This included gargantuan houses furnished with rich textiles, with sideboards buckling

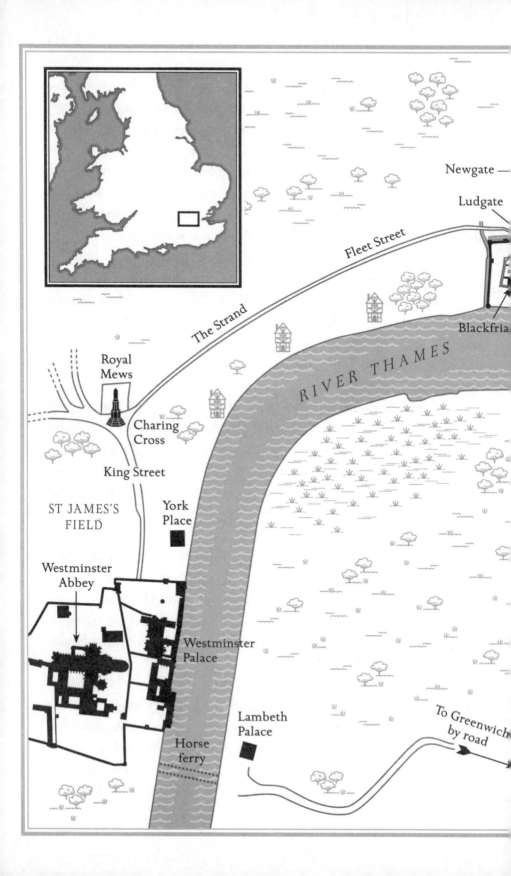

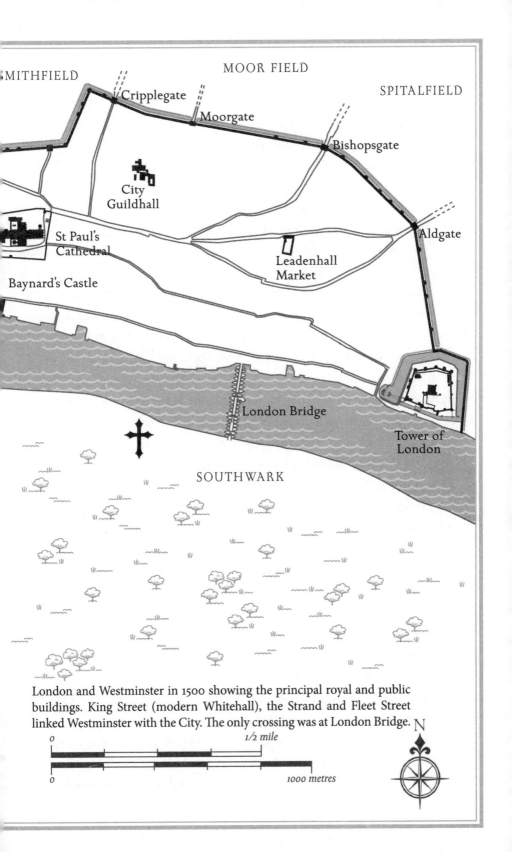

MITHFIELD · MOOR FIELD · SPITALFIELD

Cripplegate
Moorgate
Bishopsgate
City Guildhall
Aldgate
St Paul's Cathedral
Leadenhall Market
Baynard's Castle
London Bridge
Tower of London
SOUTHWARK

London and Westminster in 1500 showing the principal royal and public buildings. King Street (modern Whitehall), the Strand and Fleet Street linked Westminster with the City. The only crossing was at London Bridge. N

0   1/2 mile
0   1000 metres

under the weight of gold plate; but it also included the size and splendour of your stable, the sleekness of your barges, the stock in your parks, the flowers in your gardens, the size of your stags and the speed of your hounds. It included the breastplates of your bodyguard, the furs of your chamberlain and the liberality of a sensationally well-provisioned table. It embraced the music of your chapel, the numbers of friars who prayed for you and the quality of the masons building your mausoleum. So all these were concerns for Henry from his early days as king.

We know that within weeks of ascending the throne he received one of the Grenier family in London. Pasquier Grenier was a merchant from Tournai who had become Europe's leading tapestry merchant and taste-maker. He was not a weaver, but an impresario who seduced clients, procured designs, commissioned the work and took the money. In late 1486 Henry ordered an eleven-piece set depicting the story of the Trojan War. This was one of the grandest, most expensive and spectacular hundred yards of tapestry available in Europe at the time and work started on weaving it immediately. At Michaelmas 1488 the set arrived at court, personalized with the king's badges and arms. The pieces graphically depicted the bloodthirsty wars of Troy with scenes familiar to those who had fought at Bosworth, but they also showed Henry as a scholar aware of the stories as told in French and Latin texts.[4] This purchase was the first of many designed to establish him as a magnificent king.

The king who sat and discussed tapestry with Grenier was also the man who was myopically focused on securing his throne, and shopping, though important, had to take second place. The so-called Wars of the Roses had not ended on the field of Bosworth; pretenders to the throne seemingly sprang up everywhere, aristocrats plotted, subjects rose in rebellion: Henry could easily have become a footnote in history – and he knew it. So, at first, he travelled around England incessantly, showing himself to his subjects, moving against traitors and plotters, and anticipating invasions and uprisings.

This was a variation on a pattern long established by English kings. Since the early Middle Ages the royal year had been made up of a series of stays of varying lengths at royal houses and at the residences of the king's subjects. In the winter the court stayed in the Thames valley close to Westminster, then travelled extensively across the country during the summer months. Clearly this pattern was dictated by weather and the condition of the roads, which made it impossible to travel long distances in winter. But other powerful factors were at work too.

First amongst these was quelling disturbance and disloyalty, coupled with the need for the king to observe his subjects and be observed by them, to dispense justice, grant favours and show pleasure or displeasure. Then there were the great religious feasts; Henry needed to stage these in places that could cope with the full weight of liturgy and secular display that accompanied them. There were also administrative functions that the king needed to perform, and these often needed to be undertaken in particular locations. Finally, there was pleasure. Almost all the king's country seats were located in or near royal forests where he could hunt deer. Hunting was the principal recreation of the monarchy and aristocracy and, in the saddle, Henry not only enjoyed himself but created a bond with his companions.

Compiling the king's annual movements was a complex task involving careful and long consultation between the king and senior courtiers. Each year in early spring he would agree the route for the summer progress. Although this was often varied later, once the principles were agreed messages were sent out to the sheriffs of counties and mayors of towns announcing the sovereign's intentions. Aristocrats, abbots and bishops were also alerted to the likelihood of a royal visit so that preparations could be made.[5]

In the first few years after 1485, as Henry established himself and beat off his rivals, his itinerary was frequently interrupted by events outside his control, but by 1490 it had settled into a pattern that it was to retain into the early 1500s. Until fire destroyed the royal chapel at Sheen in 1497, Henry always celebrated Easter there. The progress could not start until this was done, but afterwards the court would set off, at some time in late March, April or May, for its annual perambulation. Some years the progress might be broken in midsummer to enjoy hunting at Windsor or to attend to business at Westminster or the Tower, but the longer progresses did not return until October or even November. Although they started from Sheen, Windsor or Greenwich, depending in which direction they were going, they almost always ended at Windsor, and the court's arrival there marked the start of the winter season. Christmas was generally spent at Greenwich or at Westminster close to the royal abbey and the magnificent entertaining facilities that the king's principal house had to offer.

Between 1485 and 1500 Henry probably moved location around a thousand times. Easily his most favoured place was Westminster and his average length of stay there was longer than anywhere else. Although there were lots of short stays in the winter, he could be in residence for a month before he had to move on to allow the palace to be cleaned. Next in order of preference was Sheen, where he would stay on average for around ten days, rarely for longer. Third was Greenwich and fourth was Windsor. These residences formed the spine of his existence.[6]

Outside London the monarchy owned perhaps as many as eighteen other residences, the largest and most splendid of which, like Woodstock in Oxfordshire or Kenilworth in Warwickshire, Henry would visit fairly regularly, perhaps ten times in fifteen years, staying for a total of 100–120 nights in each. Other royal houses, like Nottingham or Pontefract, might be visited only a handful of times for a few nights. Most of the summer progress was made up of visits to the houses of courtiers, bishops and abbots. Trips to Lincoln, Exeter, Worcester, Rochester, Reading and Dartford, for instance, saw prelates and monks turned out of their lodgings to make way for the king. Courtiers like Sir Thomas Lovell and Giles Daubeney likewise relinquished their houses for the royal party.

HARD TIMES

For the first fifteen years of his reign, Henry VII's hold on the throne often seemed tenuous: he was surrounded by rival claimants, endured sporadic rebellions and was haunted by the betrayal of apparent allies. So vexatious and exhausting was all this that the blind court poet and royal biographer Bernard André composed a poem describing Henry's first twelve years as king as the Labours of Hercules. The magnificent and outwardly confident royal court was, in fact, presided over by a monarch who was insecure, deeply suspicious and watchful.[7]

From the moment Henry left Bosworth Field his obsession with personal security was obvious. Within weeks he had created his own personal bodyguard – the Yeomen of the Guard. There had been royal guards before: Richard III had relied on a body of foot archers called Yeomen of the Crown as well as the traditional sergeants-at-arms. However, Henry's yeomen were modelled on the example of the French court, where he had seen the impressive display made by a permanent royal bodyguard stationed in the king's residences. So while the new yeomen were unquestionably armed and ready to defend their sovereign, they were also ornaments to his magnificence. Because this elite band, initially of around a hundred, operated within the boundaries of the royal residences, they were placed under the control of the king's Lord Chamberlain, the man responsible for the security of the household. At night the yeomen, under their captain, slept on the floor of the outer rooms on pallets (straw-filled mattresses); as a result, in due course the first room in a royal residence became known as the guard chamber, or the watching chamber, after the yeomen who watched over the king's safety. By day, dressed in their green-and-white livery (the Tudor colours), embroidered with a large Tudor rose back and front, they lined the galleries and chambers as the king moved about.[8]

So right from the start of the reign domestic security was a concern, but in 1493 Henry VII reached something of a watershed when two of his highest-ranking courtiers, Sir William Stanley, his Lord Chamberlain, and Lord Fitzwalter, his Lord Steward, were found to be implicated in a Yorkist plot. Stanley, the king's step-uncle, who had handed him victory at Bosworth, was the biggest shock and, though spared hanging, drawing and quartering, he was beheaded on Tower Hill. This was a terrible development, the more so because, as Chamberlain, Stanley was in charge of the king's safety.[9]

As Stanley was thrown into the Tower of London, so orders were given for a massive reconstruction of the Norman White Tower there. Originally its top floor was an echoing, double-height great hall designed by the early medieval kings for the most impressive entertaining. That had long ceased by the time Henry VII came to the throne and the room was mainly used for the storage of valuables and military hardware. In 1493, struck by the fickleness of his household and determined to arm himself against all eventualities, Henry ordered that the hall be divided horizontally, creating a huge new space for the storage of weapons. This massive extension of the Tower's capacity as an arsenal was supervised by John de Vere, Earl of Oxford, one of the king's closest companions, who had been in the thick of Bosworth at Henry's side.[10]

It is very noticeable that Henry increasingly fell back on servants whom he knew he could trust, in particular those who, like Oxford, had been his companions in exile. In around 1495, this preference was institutionalized when the king created a new section in the royal household called the Privy or Secret Chamber. The term is confusing as it can be used to describe both a room and this new section or department at court – a group of servants (grooms) under their chief, the Groom of the Stool. To help ease the confusion, I am capitalizing the household department but keeping the room in lower case.[11] By creating the Privy Chamber, the king's personal wellbeing was removed from the ambitious and potentially treacherous upper classes who traditionally ran the household, and placed in the hands of grooms who were socially insignificant gentlemen who could be completely trusted.[12]

When in 1471 Edward IV had returned to the throne, he had commissioned some new regulations to control expenditure and ensure order in his household. To inform the new rules, research was done to understand how etiquette had worked in the households of Edward II and Edward III and a close look was taken at protocol in other courts.[13] The document that survives from this process is known as the *Black Book* and divides the household into two parts: the *Domus Regie Magnificencie* (House of Magnificence), which was the upstairs world of the court that impressed by its magnificence, and the *Domus Providencie* (House of Provision), which was the downstairs machinery that supported it. The upstairs world was governed by the Lord Chamberlain and the downstairs by the Lord Steward. A third great household officer, the Master of the

Horse, who looked after the stables, made up the triumvirate that ran the royal household.

Until the creation of the Privy Chamber, the Lord Chamberlain presided over the two upstairs zones of the royal houses that together made up the *Domus Regie Magnificencie*: the Hall and the Chamber – meaning the public great hall and audience or presence chamber – and the less public inner chambers and bedchamber. The Privy Chamber created a third zone, one outside the jurisdiction of the Lord Chamberlain. In a very small number of large houses like Westminster and Windsor there was already a room called the privy chamber and, in these places, the door of that room was henceforth barred to everyone but its new staff. Elsewhere, existing rooms were re-designated as privy chambers, or new ones were built.

Of the dozen or so privy chambers in Henry VII's houses we know little; it would be fascinating, for instance, to know something about the privy tower Henry built at Westminster with a bedroom on the top floor, but other than a single ambiguous drawing we know nothing. However, remarkably, we know a good deal about the new privy chamber block he constructed at Windsor Castle between 1498 and 1501. The building survives to this day and is now occupied by the Royal Library, where the privileged visitor can still see the spaces occupied by Henry VII. These have now been altered but, when first built, they were exceptionally elegant in both plan and elevation. Probably designed by Robert Janyns, the master mason at Windsor, the building was an essay in both stylistic innovation and in smooth functionality.

Its external elevation was striking. To maintain security its lower parts had only the smallest windows and stoutest doors, so the elaborately faceted bay windows on the upper floors were balanced on massive plain buttresses below. Crowned roses and fleurs-de-lis were carved beneath the window sills and the string course below the crenellations was studded with royal heraldic beasts.

On the principal floor the tower contained two rooms: the first is likely to have been the king's privy closet – a sort of multipurpose living room managed by his Privy Chamber staff; the second room was the

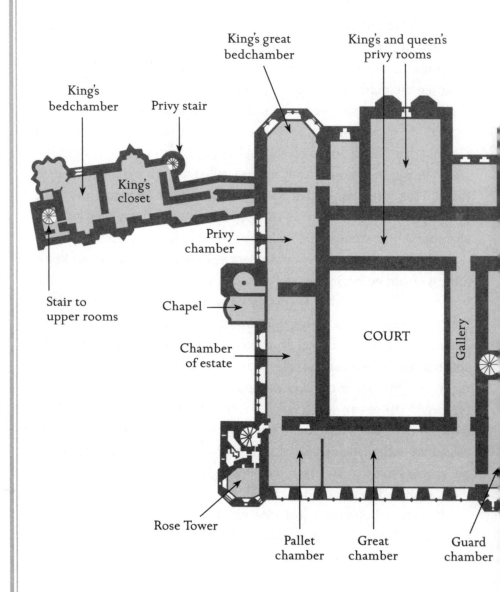

King's great
bedchamber

King's and queen's
privy rooms

King's
bedchamber

Privy stair

King's
closet

Privy
chamber

Stair to
upper rooms

Chapel

Chamber
of estate

COURT

Gallery

Rose Tower

Pallet
chamber

Great
chamber

Guard
chamber

The first floor of the royal lodgings at Windsor in 1509, showing Henry VII's tower adjoining the privy and old state bedchambers.

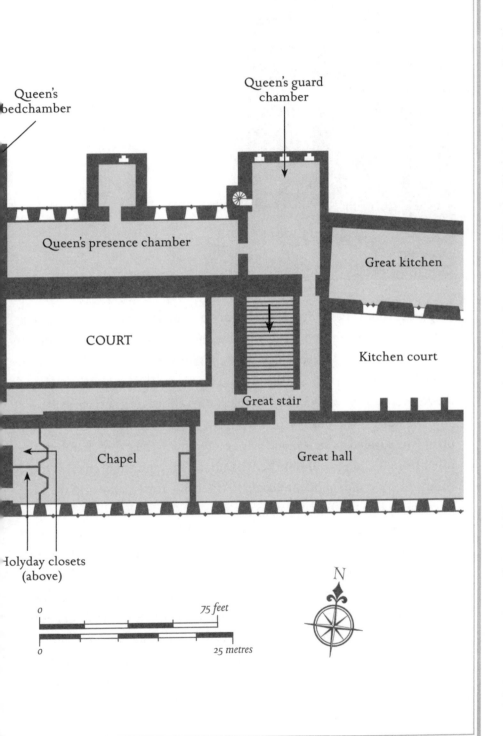

Queen's
bedchamber

Queen's guard
chamber

Queen's presence chamber

Great kitchen

COURT

Great stair

Kitchen court

Chapel

Great hall

Holyday closets
(above)

0   75 feet

0   25 metres

N

Henry VII's privy tower at Windsor Castle. The ground floor was severe and plain, but above, on the first floor, were the lavishly carved windows of Henry VII's private study (*right*) and bedroom (*left*). The small two-light window left of that was his garderobe. Above were two more rooms, probably containing his library.

king's bedroom. From the bedchamber a stair led up to the top floor. Here were two rooms with big windows and fine views. We don't know what they were used for: perhaps they contained further closets and, very likely, the king's library. On the ground floor was the king's Wardrobe of the Robes, conveniently linked to the rooms above by a service stair.

The new tower was reached from the royal lodgings by a link made up of two parallel galleries: one was entered from the privy chamber; the other from the king's old state bedchamber. This cunningly enabled these rooms to have independent access to the privy tower, allowing the king to come and go unobserved if he wished.

The privy closet had a large bay window with tremendous views towards Eton; another faced south with a view of the inner ward. There was a fine fireplace with a four-centred arch, above which was a bold carved frieze of quatrefoils containing portcullises, Tudor roses and fleurs-de-lis; a niche in its centre was reserved for a statue – perhaps of the Virgin Mary, to whom Henry was particularly devoted. The ceiling had a deeply moulded timber fret with more quatrefoils and roses at the intersections (see page 44). Hung with tapestries, and with its woodwork and stonework painted and gilded, this would have been a jewel-like chamber for the king.

Next door, the bedchamber had a smaller fireplace, square-headed with a similarly rich frieze and cornice; presumably the room had another lavish ceiling, though we have no record of it. However, there was only a south-facing window, leaving much more wall space. On the east wall opposite the fireplace stood the king's bed. Its timber frame would have been invisible as its entire structure was richly hung with textiles and probably embroidered with a large crowned Tudor rose on the head and under the canopy. The textiles of the bed would have matched those that hung on the walls.[14] In the west wall were two doors, one leading to a chamber with thick walls, a narrow door and two bow windows looking northwards – this was clearly a room for safekeeping objects of value, probably gold and silver as well as papers. The other door led to the king's private garderobe and a privy stair leading up to the second floor and down to the outer court.

In January 1506 Philip of Burgundy, king of Castile and heir to the Hapsburg throne, was shipwrecked off the Dorset coast. Henry must have seen this as a gift from God, as Philip was the jailer of exiled Edmund de la Pole, Earl of Suffolk, the most credible and dangerous claimant to the English throne. Philip was now, in effect, Henry's prisoner, though in the language of international diplomacy nobody articulated this very obvious point. Henry decided to receive Philip at Windsor. The location must have been chosen specifically with security in mind: even if unspoken, it would have underlined the point that Philip, though a guest, was not free to leave even if he wished. Because of the exceptional nature of the occasion there are incredibly detailed reports of the etiquette observed during the visit.[15]

Housing two kings in a single building was a headache for everyone at court, not least because there had been no notice and no time to prepare or plan. Henry VII decided to set himself up in the queen's lodgings, so when Philip arrived Henry presented his own lodgings, including his new privy tower, to his guest.

From the gushing descriptions of the festivities, it is clear that the king's lodgings comprised a great chamber, a second chamber and the chamber of estate or dining chamber. In the first room waited knights

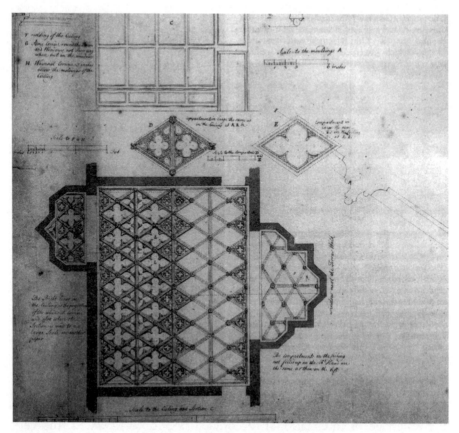

An eighteenth-century drawing showing the beautiful ceiling of Henry VII's privy closet at Windsor Castle, put up in around 1500 and now lost.

and esquires; in the second barons and baronets; and, in the chamber of estate, replete with both a canopy of state and a symbolic state bed, were arrayed the bishops and earls. The fourth chamber was the privy chamber, hung most sumptuously with cloth of gold bordered with crimson velvet.

In the two suites of lodgings the two courts established themselves. On the first night the kings dined in their own rooms, apart, but later they took the chance to meet privately in one of Henry's secret chambers. These movements round the castle were highly choreographed, as Philip was well aware that he was not only a guest but Henry's captive – an impression probably reinforced by Henry's generous disposition of a troop of his own Yeomen of the Guard in the chamber of estate. Over the next few days the kings continued to live under the same roof, going to chapel together, hunting and attending their own council meetings. On 7 February the two of them stood in the bay window in the king's new tower and watched a horse being baited in the inner ward. The entertainments continued for many days, until Henry received word that the Earl of Suffolk had been handed over to his agents in Calais, at which point Philip was, at last, free to go.

Throughout the visit Henry had been extraordinarily proud of Windsor, but the culmination of Philip's stay was not staged there, but at another house on the Thames, as we shall see.

SHEEN

In his long years of penniless exile, Henry had come to realize the supreme importance of cash. Cash bought magnificence and gave aristocrats and kings alike independence and power, two commodities of which Henry had been very short in his youth. In 1485 not only did he inherit all the hereditary lands of the English Crown, but he also came into his father's extensive possessions in Yorkshire and all the personal lands and property of the Yorkist kings. A monarch who had been born to money might have sold or granted away much of this to his followers, but Henry VII held on to virtually everything. Eventually land was to make up 40 per cent of his income; the rest, carefully managed, came, as usual, from prerogative rights, customs, taxation and the profits of the judicial system.[16] What is notable about Henry's reign is that, instead of leaving financial administration to the Exchequer, as was traditional, within two years of coming to the throne he combined control of his private income with the income of the Crown and started to run the nation's finances under personal supervision from his household; to be precise, from his own chamber.

So three quarters of the Crown's revenue came to be managed by John Heron, the king's Treasurer of the Chamber. Heron employed two clerks, who were stationed at the Palace of Westminster, one amidst the great chests of gold coin in the Jewel House and the other in the office of the Exchequer of Receipt near Westminster Hall. Heron himself operated from his own house in the precincts of Westminster Abbey, where more cash was kept. As royal revenues built up, Heron ordered that surpluses be transferred from Westminster to the king's private coffers in the Tower of London. In this way, Henry and Heron managed the royal finances, shifting money physically between the deposit account in the Tower and the current account at Westminster. The king's active and regular involvement with managing his finances is significant because, although some officials presented their accounts to Heron's clerks, some had their accounts signed off by the king himself first. One of these was the Clerk of the King's Works.[17]

The Clerk of Works was the head of the Office of the King's Works, the maintenance arm of the royal household established by Richard II in 1378. It not only repaired buildings but often undertook extensions and adaptations, although for really big projects special arrangements were established for the purpose. Its headquarters, like those of all other administrative departments, was in the Palace of Westminster, where the clerk had his office and store yard. The Office of Works received revenues from the Exchequer at first but, by 1497, its activities were being financed directly from the Chamber.

The Office of Works received very little from the Exchequer in the first twelve years of the reign; but all that changed in the mid-1490s. Through careful management, royal income had risen from £17,000 a year in 1489, reaching about £105,000 in 1505. If lack of cash had been the only thing that had held the king back from building, there was now no reason to stint. While he never became a builder on the scale of his son, expenditure on domestic construction totalled around £28,000 between 1494 and his death in 1509. Meanwhile, he spent another £40,000 on pious building works, often associated with his houses. This £70,000 or so on building was dwarfed by some £250,000 spent on jewels and plate over the same period.[18]

With his coffers swelling, Henry had not only embarked upon work at Windsor but had also ordered improvements at Sheen. While Henry V's stone tower there must have been in robust condition, the rest of the manor may not have been. The timber-framed great hall, chapel and the king's and queen's lodgings erected by Henry V had partly used materials from the old royal manor of Byfleet. It is likely, therefore, that the money Henry VII laid out on his buildings there during the mid-1490s was spent on these principal domestic buildings.[19]

It was at Sheen that the court was staying in December 1497 when a fire broke out in the king's lodgings. It burned for three hours, destroying valuable furniture and textiles before it was brought under control. Raking through the ashes, servants desperately searched for the king's jewels and were rewarded richly when they found them. But the principal casualty was the chapel, part of the manor detached from the stone tower, suggesting that the fire was in the largely timber-framed buildings of the main residence and not in the riverside stone lodgings. At any rate, a lesson of the Windsor Castle blaze of 1992, which burned for twelve hours, was that a fire lasting three hours would have done little to dent the massive stone donjon. Nevertheless, it convinced Henry to do away with the old manor and commission a brand-new residence.[20]

The new manor of Sheen was to differ from the old one in a crucial respect. While in old Sheen the stone tower containing the privy lodgings was a separate private residence which lay on its own moated island at a little distance from the main manor, in the new scheme the tower was to be fully integrated with the rest of the house. It was, of course, far too small to contain the hall and chapel, the two key rooms necessary if the whole household were to use the manor. Therefore the major part of Henry VII's work was to build these anew.

The king did not hold back. His new great hall was a very large stone building raised up on a buttery or beer cellar and approached by a wide ceremonial stair. As was traditional, it contained a hearthstone in the middle of the floor where fires could, theoretically, be lit and smoke could drift its way up and, hopefully, find its way out through a decorative louvre in the roof. The hall was not given an openwork ceiling like Westminster great hall or the one at Eltham, where Edward IV had constructed a magnificent hammerbeam roof. Instead, the ceiling was

Anthonis van den Wyngaerde 1558, sketch of the inner court at Sheen showing the great hall to the right, chapel to the left.

suspended from the roof trusses, boarded over and decorated with ribs and bosses, a bit like the ceiling of the king's closet at Windsor but on a much larger scale. This was a novel construction that seems to have been developed by the king's carpenter, Thomas Banks. Unfortunately, as it was untried and untested, it started to fail soon after it was completed and remedial repairs had to be executed in 1507.

Great rooms such as this were always lit by clerestory windows – that is to say, windows with sills 20 feet or so above the floor, leaving the lower walls blank to allow for hanging tapestries. Above these hangings, between the windows, were corbels which bore life-sized statues of kings of England, armed and crowned. Here King Arthur, William Rufus, Edward III and Henry V were juxtaposed, less plausibly, with Brutus, the legendary descendant of Aeneas and first king of Britain, and the Saxon warrior Hengist. Above the door that led out of the hall was a statue of Henry VII himself. His regal company had been carefully chosen: these were England's greatest warrior kings and the display showed Henry as king by both might and right.

The hall formed the west side of an inner court approached by a gatehouse upon which stood two carved stone heralds blowing their trumpets. Facing the hall across the courtyard was the chapel, which formed the east side of the inner court. This was rather an unusual arrangement, as many fifteenth-century great houses followed the example of Windsor, where the hall and chapel were in a single range. At Sheen the idea was to create a splendid forecourt to announce the royal lodgings, and hall and chapel enclosed the court to the east and west with towering masonry façades. Between them was a large fountain crowned with Henry's red dragons and lions amongst rose bushes; from the red roses fresh water poured into a basin below.

Like the hall, the chapel was raised up on an undercroft, this one used as a wine cellar. Lit by clerestory windows, the area beneath them was hung with tapestry of a suitably devotional nature, but in the chancel the walls were hung with cloth of gold. The upper wall spaces, between the windows, were painted with murals showing saintly Welsh and English kings, including Cadwallader, Edmund and, of course, Edward the Confessor. The chapel thus showed the piety of the monarchy just as the hall proclaimed its power.

The altar was sheathed in gold, encrusted with precious stones and contained sacred relics. The ceiling of the chapel was boarded and decorated in a lozenge pattern, each lozenge containing, alternately, a red rose or a portcullis. Household chapels had closets at first-floor level from which their owners could watch the service. The new chapel at Sheen was unusual in that closets were provided not at the west end, as was usual, but on either side looking down directly on to the altar. This can only have been the king's choice – an express desire to be as close to the altar as possible to see the Elevation of the Host and derive maximum benefit from it.

On the south side of the court, hall and chapel were connected by a gallery, from which sprang a covered bridge, 27 feet long and 18 feet wide, which vaulted over the moat, providing access to the lodgings of the royal family. We have no plan of the rooms inside the great stone tower, but we know that it was three storeys high. The lowest storey contained service

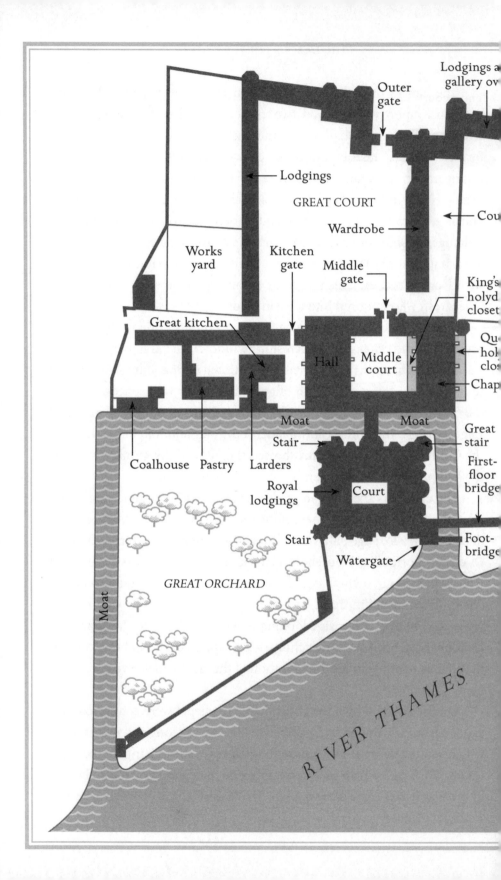

Outer gate

Lodgings a
gallery ov

Lodgings

GREAT COURT

Cou

Wardrobe

Works
yard

Kitchen
gate

Middle
gate

King's
holyd
closet

Great kitchen

Hall

Middle
court

Qu
hol
clos

Chap

Moat

Moat

Great
stair

Stair

Coalhouse   Pastry   Larders

Royal
lodgings

Court

First-
floor
bridge

Stair

Watergate

Foot-
bridge

GREAT ORCHARD

Moat

RIVER THAMES

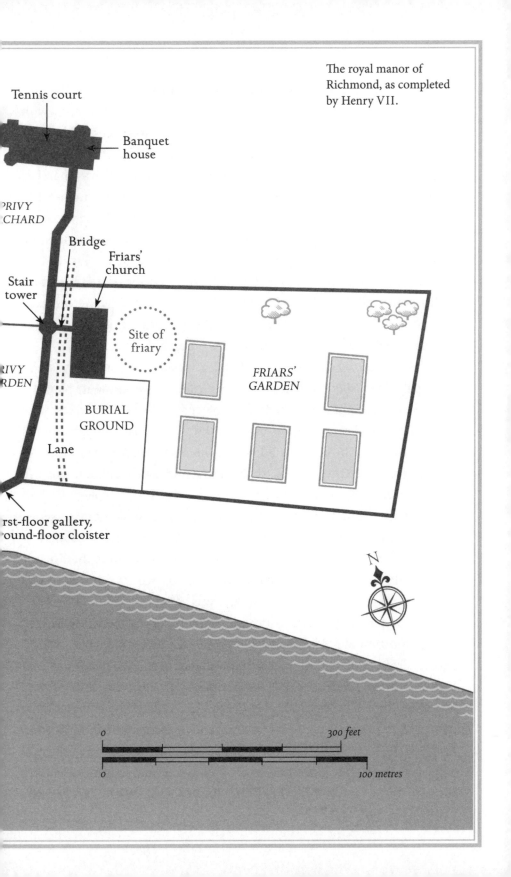

Tennis court

Banquet
house

The royal manor of
Richmond, as completed
by Henry VII.

PRIVY
CHARD

Bridge

Friars'
church

Stair
tower

Site of
friary

RIVY
RDEN

BURIAL
GROUND

FRIARS'
GARDEN

Lane

rst-floor gallery,
ound-floor cloister

N

0   300 *feet*

0   100 *metres*

rooms, including the royal wardrobes and a private kitchen. The two floors above contained the lodgings of the king and queen, each with twelve rooms. These cannot have been cavernous spaces such as at Windsor and Westminster – the rooms were clearly much smaller, but here, for the first time, Henry set up a house with the new Privy Chamber arrangements. There was a watching chamber for the guard, and next to this was the council chamber. Beyond the watching chamber was the chamber of estate for audiences and then the privy chamber, a dressing room and the king's bedroom, beyond which was a closet. Just off the privy chamber was the king's own private WC and a stair that led down to his wardrobe and privy kitchen. The king's lodgings were linked vertically to the queen's by a processional stair encased in a great tower with attached prospect or viewing rooms on each floor.[21]

The completed house, like all great residences of its age, was principally furnished with textiles. Furniture, as we know it, played a minor part and the wooden frames of chairs, beds and tables were essentially vehicles for the display of silks. A cupboard bought by the king in August 1501 cost 26s 8d while, the same month, two pieces of cloth of gold cost him £190 16s 3d; that December a delivery of forms and stools cost him 12s, while over £73 was spent on a purple-coloured cloth of gold at 40s a yard. Hand-woven silk, whether as damask, satin, sarsenet, velvet or carpet, was extremely expensive and took a long time to weave – no wonder the king issued orders that nobody should wipe their hands on the wall hangings or put dishes of food on his bed.[22]

Most expensive and prestigious was cloth of gold, a generic description for silks, woven to a variety of patterns, that contained a very high proportion of gold thread. The walls of the king's innermost rooms and, as already noted, the chancel of the chapel were hung with this. Next in value came tapestries also shot through with large amounts of gold and silver thread. While cloth of gold (and silver) could be bought off the peg, tapestry, as we have seen, was normally commissioned. Thus from 1497, as the new buildings rose, Henry commissioned a number of expensive large-scale tapestries for the hall, chapel and lodgings at Sheen; some of these simply bore his arms, badges and initials, but big sets

View of the royal manor of Richmond by Wenceslaus Hollar, done in 1638. Hollar shows the royal lodgings in the stone tower from the other side of the Thames. On the left-hand side the great hall can be seen peeping out from behind the stone tower and, to its left, is the pointed roof of the great kitchen.

telling biblical or classical stories decorated the principal chambers. In 1499 he ordered a complete set of vestments and altar cloths for the chapel. The copes (liturgical cloaks) were embroidered with portcullises and the altar frontal had the royal arms, two roses and two portcullises.[23] Thus, whilst externally the stonework was clean-cut, cold and hard, on the inside the new buildings were sheathed in richly coloured textiles, softening and warming everything with a rich glow.

THE QUEEN'S HOUSEHOLD

The royal household was not a monolithic organization; it was, in fact, made up of a number of households, one for each member of the royal family. The king's, on which I have concentrated so far, was the largest, but the queen had her own independently run household and residences, as did Lady Margaret Beaufort, Henry VII's mother, and the royal children – we will look at the homes of the children in Chapter IV.

The queen's household was the most important after the king's. As royal consort, her first duty was, of course, to provide an heir, by which was meant a healthy son. But being mother of the heir involved much more than obstetrics. The queen was expected to create a court of magnificence and grace, of piety and feminine virtue, of learning and culture. A dazzling queen's household was an inextricable aspect of good sovereignty. The queen's role was to support the king in creating the environment needed to rule. This involved specific tasks, as we shall see, as well as contributing to a general aura of splendour.[24]

Keeping such a household was expensive and the monarch was expected to settle on his queen the resources to uphold her magnificence and dignity. Traditionally the queen was assigned an annual income of just under £6,700 a year; this would be drawn from land given her for life (her jointure lands) and specific income streams, such as customs revenues. Thus, in practice, income fluctuated and Elizabeth of York's mother and Edward IV's queen, Elizabeth Woodville, regularly received only around £4,500 a year. The queen's jointure was managed by an all-male council who, as well as dealing with her estates and revenues, advised on matters of patronage and politics. They had rooms in Westminster Palace, near the Exchequer, where the administrators worked, records were stored and her council itself met.[25]

In 1485 Henry VII was not generous to his nineteen-year-old queen. She was assigned only some of her mother's lands and a pension that together made up less than half her mother's income and, even after ten years of marriage, a yearly income over £4,000 was exceptional. Elizabeth was unusually dependent on the king for financial support, and in 1496 he had to pay off £2,000 of her debts. The king himself paid for items for the queen out of his chamber accounts and the queen directly obtained household items from the Great Wardrobe.[26]

Central to the jointure were her jointure houses – the houses that the queen was granted for her personal use during her lifetime and which she was expected to maintain and, if she wished, alter and embellish herself. The problem here is that there is no record of any specific house being formally granted to Elizabeth; it seems as if, just as with her finances, Henry retained ultimate control. Greenwich, which had been the traditional country house of the queen, was firmly held by the king, though Elizabeth used it independently. For three weeks before her coronation she lived there, attending to hair, make-up and wardrobe before travelling by barge to London, and it was there that she gave birth to her second and third sons, Henry and Edmund. As far as a town house is concerned, it seems that Elizabeth used Baynard's Castle, to which we have already been introduced. In around 1496, Henry rebuilt it and, judging by the excavations that took place on the site in the 1970s, he did a thorough job of creating a substantially new building. Like Greenwich, it was of brick and showed to the river a façade animated by

Baynard's Castle, as sketched by Anthonis van den Wyngaerde in 1544. The brick range with its fashionable bay windows is set between two stout towers with battlements and machicolations, both crowned with pointy turrets. Thus, the house of the queen was a mixture of ancient and modern, chivalry and luxury.

a series of great bay windows. At either end were massive towers with machicolations and turrets, making the house look, from the river, like an exotic little castle. Perhaps this was the intention: the queen's castle, where she could be wooed by her ardent royal knight. At any rate, by the end of her life Elizabeth was paying for the repairs there, which strongly suggests that, by then, it was hers.[27]

After Elizabeth's death in 1503, the house was not much used; in fact, in 1508 it was handed over to a visiting foreign delegation for lodgings. But the precedent had been set and, soon after they were married, Henry VIII granted Baynard's Castle to Katharine of Aragon. It now became the official London residence of the Tudor queens consort and successively it was granted to Anne of Cleves, Catherine Howard and Katherine Parr.[28]

While Elizabeth had her own residences, she also used her lodgings in the king's houses. From the early Middle Ages royal houses were divided into two wards, courts or sides, one for the king and one for the queen. At Windsor Castle and Westminster the chambers on the queen's side were as large as the king's, but there were fewer of them (see plans on pages 17 and 26–7). At Richmond they were one above the other and at Greenwich they stood facing across a courtyard. We don't know a lot about Elizabeth of York's rooms in these residences but, as we shall see, we do know about the rooms occupied by Henry VIII's queens.

Elizabeth had her own annual itinerary, which was very carefully coordinated with the king's. We have details of her movements for the last year of her life and we can see that in spring, autumn and winter she shuttled up and down the Thames between Richmond and Greenwich, stopping off at Westminster, Baynard's Castle or the Tower on the way through. Sometimes she and Henry were together; she spent Easter 1502 at Richmond with him. At other times, such as in December 1502, when Henry was at the Tower of London deep in his annual cash audit, the queen, perhaps bored by Henry's penny-counting, made her way to Mortlake and then to Hampton Court, as a guest of Henry's close companion Giles, Lord Daubeney; both of these were more comfortable locations for a heavily pregnant queen. In the summer of 1502 the queen accompanied Henry on a long progress into south Wales. Sometimes they stayed at the same place, but often, no house being large enough, the queen stayed at a nearby residence.[29]

Elizabeth's inner household comprised four ladies, sixteen gentlewomen and three chamberers. The ladies were the queen's personal attendants, but the gentlewomen were essentially ornamental – the queen's official entourage who moved with her round the precincts of the royal houses, looking beautiful and magnificent in rich clothes and jewels. At court festivals they were the objects of male chivalry and symbols of chastity and virtue. The Spanish ambassador, Roderigo de Puebla, visited the queen at an unexpected moment in July 1488 and found Elizabeth 'with two and twenty companions of angelical appearance, and all we saw there seemed very magnificent, and in splendid style'.[30]

The queen's lodgings had a particular role to play in court life. The king's lodgings were increasingly circumscribed by rules and regulations and, after the creation of the Privy Chamber, his innermost rooms were effectively off limits. The queen's lodgings were not constricted in the same way and so it was possible to invite ambassadors and other visitors into them to enjoy a more informal time. In September 1497 the splendidly titled Raimondo de'Raimondi de Soncino, the Milanese ambassador, had just such an audience in the queen's chambers at Woodstock after a more formal reception before the king and the whole court.[31]

Given that the king and queen had separate itineraries and, when they were together in a single house, they were located in separate wings, it seems amazing that they ever slept in the same bed. But they did, and Henry VII and Elizabeth had eight children in fourteen years of marriage. Sleeping together, though, required planning and forethought. First it had to be decided in whose bed they would sleep, then the appropriate bedroom would be prepared, the bed would be made and what was known as the 'all night' – wine, ale and bread ceremoniously placed on a buffet in the bedroom – served. At this point someone would be sent to bring the queen to the king or the king to the queen. One or other would then process, accompanied by attendants, to the other's bedchamber. Only then would the staff, who slept every night at the foot of the bed, be ordered to leave and wait outside the door.[32]

Pregnancy and childbirth was a hazardous business, and one that would kill Elizabeth in 1503; but, like all other parts of royal life, it came with a prescribed etiquette. Between four and six weeks before a royal birth, the queen would take to her chamber, which meant withdrawing from the court into the inner rooms of her lodgings. This was done with some ceremony: after attending Mass she would be led to her great chamber, where she would be served wine and spices before taking leave of the court. Her bedchamber was hung with additional tapestries and the floor layered with carpets, while there was normally a new bed with rich hangings and thick curtains. Once the door closed, the queen would inhabit an exclusively feminine world until forty days after the birth, when her re-emergence was marked by her 'churching', or purification. This ceremony required another state bed to be erected in her great chamber; on this the queen would lie fully dressed in her finest outfit, curtains closed. When the court had assembled in the room, two duchesses would draw back the curtains, raise the queen and accompany her to the household chapel, where, during Mass, various thank-offerings were made.[33]

DYNASTY

Nobody knows how Henry VI died in the Tower of London. It was said, at the time, that he just slipped away; later Richard of Gloucester (the future Richard III) was named as his murderer – but it was probably no coincidence that Henry died the very day – 21 May 1471 – that Edward IV entered London to claim the throne. The king's body was embalmed, removed from the Tower and put on open show at St Paul's Cathedral before being taken to the royal friary at Blackfriars for the funeral. The obsequies over, the body was taken by river to Chertsey Abbey for burial. King Henry had spent his last weeks in the Tower in prayer and meditation and soon this, together with the blood that dripped from his coffin at St Paul's and Blackfriars, suggested to people that he had been martyred. In fact, before a year was out, pilgrims were making their way to Chertsey and, within a decade, miracles were reported as taking place there in his name.

This turn of events cannot have been wholly agreeable to either Edward IV or Richard III and, in 1484, King Richard decided to move Henry's body from Chertsey to Windsor Castle. Windsor was, like most castles, divided into two wards or areas: the upper ward was where the royal lodgings were and where King Henry VII was to build his new privy block in 1498–1501; the lower ward was where Edward III had founded the College of St George in 1348 as the headquarters of the Order of the Garter. In 1473 Edward IV had decided to rebuild the old medieval chapel of St George as a splendid new headquarters for the Order and as a mausoleum for himself and his family. It was to this half-built chapel,

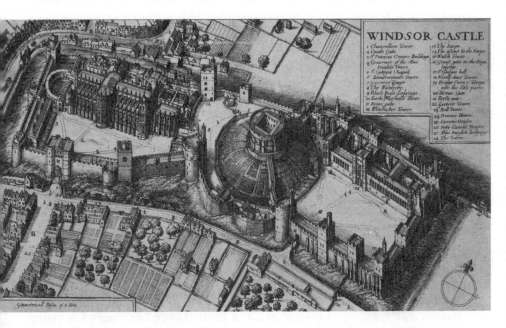

Wenceslaus Hollar, bird's-eye view of Windsor Castle, published in 1672. Hollar brilliantly shows the configuration of Windsor, with St George's Chapel dominating the lower ward (to the left), the old Norman keep in the middle and, in the upper ward, the royal lodgings.

opposite Edward IV's own tomb, that Richard III brought the embalmed body of Henry VI.

By 1484 Richard knew that Henry Tudor was preparing to return from exile to challenge him for the throne and that his claim was partly based on the fact that he was the nephew of King Henry VI. So the relocation of the body to Windsor was both to secure it, preventing it from becoming a focus for Henry's supporters, and, perhaps, as a gesture of reconciliation – the proper and fitting internment of a royal saint in a royal chapel. The tomb that Richard III planned to build was, in the end, built by his rival Henry VII. At this chantry, during the early years of Henry's reign, miracles were reported with increasing frequency. So it should come as no surprise that Henry decided, quite early in his reign, that he himself was to be buried at Windsor near Henry VI and that the chapel there, started as the dynastic mausoleum of the Yorkists, would be completed and appropriated by the Tudors as theirs.[34]

For medieval kings, no less than for the pharaohs of ancient Egypt, preparation for death was an integral part of life. Death was important not only because it marked the passage from life to purgatory and then, hopefully, heaven, but because it was the point in which past, present and future met. Burial in ancestral vaults conferred legitimacy on your heirs. Thus Henry's burial next to his saintly relative was, in part, to help secure his dynasty into the future.

In 1487 Henry had called parliament and, as they sat, he staged the magnificent coronation of his wife, Elizabeth of York. The following spring he decided to move the whole court to Windsor. A programme had been established that would present the king and queen in utmost splendour. Easter Day was one of the four great occasions of the year when the king wore his purple robes. There was an elaborate ecclesiastical procession, not simply within the royal chapel, but round the cloisters of the upper ward accompanied by antiphons, prayers, genuflections and psalms. After Easter the king made a brief trip to Southampton for a naval inspection. While he was away the castle was prepared for St George's Day and the Garter Feast, which was held on the following Sunday, exploiting every opportunity for lavish display. Many aristocrats and prelates were present, as were a large number of ambassadors. New knights were installed, followed by Solemn Mass. On Garter Day there was a magnificent procession to St George's Chapel in the lower ward and, after the chapter meeting, a procession and High Mass, the party marched up to the upper ward again for dinner in St George's Hall. This was the culmination of the celebrations. The king sat on the high table with the Bishop of Winchester, prelate of the Order, at his right hand. Below him, seated at three long tables and arranged in rank order, were the knights and officers of the Order, ambassadors and the nobility of the realm. In the afternoon, in another long-winding procession, the party returned to St George's Chapel for another meeting and evensong. That night the king dined in his great chamber, again with the bishop at his table; the rest of the knights dined at a side table.

This great visit to Windsor demonstrated to Henry VII its extraordinary suitability for staging awe-inspiring court events. The royal lodgings were grand and capacious, the topography of the castle lent itself to showy processions, and the whole place was secure and controllable. This helped further convince the king that Windsor should be his dynastic seat and future place of burial. In 1493 he commissioned Sir John Shaw, one of the two Masters of the Royal Mint in the Tower of London and a major purveyor of jewels for his person, to take financial control of a major new project at the castle. This was to demolish the old lady chapel at the east end of St George's Chapel and rebuild it as his burial place and, at the same time, start work on a magnificent tomb to go in it. In all, around £5,000 was spent on this project up to 1498.[35]

In 1497 two things happened that radically changed the king's plans. First, the monks of Westminster Abbey pointed out that Henry VI had never wanted to be buried at Windsor but had always intended to be interred behind Edward the Confessor's tomb at Westminster. This was clearly embarrassing. To resolve the matter, in early 1498 Henry asked his council to consider the evidence and, after the testimony of various witnesses had been heard, it was declared that Westminster was indeed the intended final resting place of Henry VI. At this, Henry VII dramatically changed tack. Building at Windsor was abandoned and a design was commissioned for a new burial chapel for both Henry VI and himself at Westminster. Windsor thus never became the dynastic seat of the Tudors.

Second, as we have seen, in that same year the fire at Sheen prompted Henry to rebuild that house much more splendidly and to adorn its hall and chapel with evidence of his lineage, might and piety. But, although he was determined to stress his legitimacy to the Crown through his descent from Edward III and kinship to Henry VI, he was also fiercely proud of his own patrimony, in particular his title, Richmond, which had been given to his father, Edmund Tudor, by Henry VI and which, on his birth, Henry had inherited; throughout his exile he was known as Earl of Richmond rather than Henry Tudor. As the new buildings at Sheen rose, he decided to rename them Richmond and thus make it his family seat. In March 1501, the king's chamber accounts, which until then had used the name Sheen consistently, suddenly dropped it and called the king's house there Richmond. Sheen was never mentioned again in an official document. In the Tudor-obsessed twenty-first century it may come as a surprise that the new family seat was not named Tudor and the town beside it Tudor-upon-Thames, but Henry never saw himself as a Tudor; his family name was Richmond, and his new manor was to be named after it.[36]

By this date completing Richmond had become a matter of urgency. In 1489 Henry had signed a treaty with the Spanish kingdoms that would see his eldest son, Prince Arthur, married to Katharine of Aragon. This was the culminating ambition of his reign and his proudest achievement: the marriage of his heir to the daughter of the king of one of Europe's greatest powers. Bringing the two children to the altar had been a slow process as, when it was first suggested, both were infants; but it was a project sustained by a proxy betrothal in 1497, then proxy marriages in 1499 and 1500. It was finally agreed that Katharine would come to England to be married in 1501 but, in fact, minutely detailed plans had existed for the wedding long before and in June 1500 these had even been published as a book, complete with a woodcut image of the pair getting married. The fact was that Henry was determined that this would be the greatest celebration England had ever seen, one that would place his dynasty at the pinnacle of European majesty.[37]

While the wedding would take place at St Paul's and the wedding feast at Westminster, the really important celebration would be at the king's most modern and beautiful country seat – Richmond. And Richmond was not finished. Bringing it to completion in time was a close-run thing: an organ was installed in the chapel in April 1501, the glaziers only finished in the hall and chapel in June, and the painters were still hard at work in August.[38] Yet on 14 November, as Arthur and Katharine, hand in hand, left St Paul's Cathedral man and wife, their arrival at Richmond was prefigured in a special pageant. Before them was an artificial mountain encrusted with jewels and laid with red roses from which fountains of wine poured. This was the rich-mount of England, the visible manifestation of Henry's title, with his new house, sparkling, magnificent, towering and pouring forth liberality.[39]

Richmond was, everyone conceded, a remarkable sight. An approving verdict was passed by one of Henry's grooms of the chamber, an observer of the marriage feasts of 1501. He thought the house 'the lantern spectacle and the beauteous exemplar of all proper lodgings', the 'only chamber and closet elect, the bright and shining star of building, the mirror and pattern of all places of delight, commodity and pleasure' and 'this earthly and second paradise of our region England'.[40]

He was not alone in his praises, for in 1506, with the Earl of Suffolk moving safely into his hands, it was here that Henry gave his royal 'guest', Philip of Burgundy, his final send-off. He was escorted across country from Windsor Castle, hunting and hawking as he went. When he arrived at Richmond, Henry descended the stairs from his lodgings and greeted the king by the waterside. Philip, we learn from an eyewitness, 'admired the house without and greatly praised the beautiful and sumptuous edifice, saying to them that were there near to him, that if it should be his good fortune to return to Brussels that that Beau Regard should be a pattern unto him'.[41]

·III·

GOD AND MAMMON

Personal Priests

THE DAY HENRY VII WON HIS CROWN, 22 August, was the feast of the Coronation of the Virgin Mary. At a distance of five centuries this might seem coincidental, but at the time it was regarded, not least by the victors, as fulfilment of God's will for Henry and for England. Henry himself felt this strongly: when in November 1485 he sat, for the first time, before the assembled House of Commons, he declared that the throne was his not only by inheritance but by the judgement of God given in battle.

Amongst the deluge of business to which he attended during his first weeks as king was a charter granted to the Observant Friars for a convent at Greenwich. The Observants were a reformed branch of the monastic Franciscan Order, committed to a life of poverty, prayer and evangelism. They were the religious fundamentalists of their day. They had been introduced into England by Edward IV, who gave land to create a friary in the village of Greenwich. Edward himself laid the foundation stone, but he died before he could finance their new buildings. Henry VII's charter of December 1485 re-established them as a convent of at least twelve brethren and a warden on a new plot of land right next to the royal manor house in Greenwich. Building started straight away but took nearly a decade to complete, the church not being consecrated until 1493.[1]

The Observants were highly favoured by the royal and ducal families of northern Europe. There was perhaps a feeling that the more extreme the practice of their faith, the more effective their prayers would be for their patrons. Henry had had close contact with them in exile in Brittany and, on coming to the throne, appointed a French Observant from Greenwich as his personal confessor. A steady trickle of friars of various orders from all over Europe made their way to his court, and when he visited any town he was sure to seek out the Observants and give alms there.[2]

Henry may have felt that his trust in the friars' prayers had been well placed. As he looked back from the vantage point of 1501, God's favour had clearly shone on him, for almost everything he had touched had turned to gold: he had won the throne against all odds; married a queen whom he loved and who had given him many children, including three sons; vanquished rival claimants; filled his coffers; built an incredible dynastic seat at Richmond; and married his eldest son to a Spanish princess at a ceremony of unbelievable magnificence.

But in the following eighteen months Henry's life collapsed in tragedy. First, in April 1502, the fifteen-year-old Arthur, Prince of Wales, who was holding court at Ludlow Castle with his wife Katharine, suddenly died. The catastrophic news was conveyed to Henry by his confessor while he was at Richmond, and he and Elizabeth of York were inconsolable. To ease the pain of loss they decided to have another child, and a girl, Katherine, was born in February 1503. She died after just three days. Nine days later Henry's thirty-seven-year-old queen was also dead. With both his wife and heir in the grave, Henry was thrown into a terrible crisis of faith. What was it he had done to cause God to turn against him so viciously?

Before the tragedies of 1502/3 struck, the king's confessor, Stephen Barron, the Provincial, or head, of the Observants in England, probably suggested to Henry that a second friary at Richmond might be a suitable mark of gratitude to God for his good fortune. In December 1501, with Arthur and Katharine's wedding hangovers barely cleared, a huge delivery of stone was made to Richmond for this new project. But the building, originally planned as a thank-offering, instead became an offer of reconciliation to a God whom Henry now thought had abandoned him. Unlike the Greenwich friary, which had taken nearly twenty years to complete, the new friary was driven onwards by the grieving king's own workmen, and money was no object. The roof of the church was being painted in December 1503 and worship took place there before the Pope had granted a licence for it. The final bills were not settled until 1509, when it was revealed that the whole cost had been some £1,500.[3]

The friars' churches at Greenwich and Richmond were simple rectangles without aisles and with steep roofs lit by tall windows on each side. At Greenwich there was a slender tower with a small spire between nave and chancel, presumably for a bell. Although the fundamentalist theology of the Observants meant that they spurned decoration and richness in architecture, we know that Henry VII paid for an elaborate east window in the Greenwich friary, depicting himself in his robes of state surrounded by his family and his arms and badges. The church at Richmond was carved and painted inside and the king seems to have supplied a painted tabernacle and an altarpiece that may be the one that survives in the Royal Collection today (see plate section). As the friaries were largely funded from the royal purse, the friars were also given the richest vestments and vessels for the altar, as well as a steady stream of royal alms. To make all this magnificence possible, Henry was required to obtain a special dispensation from the Pope.

The royal friaries had few domestic buildings, in keeping with the friars' oath of poverty and their mission to work in the surrounding community. At Greenwich a passage between the nave and presbytery under the bell tower led out to a cloister where there was a chapter house, dormitory and refectory. At Richmond there was a dormitory and refectory but probably no cloister.[4]

From the fourteenth century, English royal residences had been increasingly structured around the need of monarchs to safeguard their souls, secure God's support for their military exploits and publicly demonstrate their piety. As with so much else, the blueprint for this had been drawn by Edward III at Windsor Castle and Westminster Palace, where, as I have already described, there were colleges of secular priests.[5] The liturgy employed in the new colleges followed the model set by Salisbury Cathedral known as the *Use of Sarum*. Edward III and all his successors were concerned that the *Sarum* rites were faithfully and fully

Anthonis van den Wyngaerde, a view of the Richmond Friary in 1558 in a state of dereliction. In the foreground can be seen the gallery that linked the friars' church with the king's private closet in the stone tower. Next to the church is the stair tower providing access to the royal pew and against this is the single-storey gallery that linked the friary and the royal chapel. The royal gardens are shown and in the far right corner is the royal tennis court. On the top right is a sketch of the royal lodgings.

performed with the greatest magnificence; this included the correct use of vestments, liturgical equipment, music and choreography. While all these elements were important, not all of them had much impact on the buildings; the part of the *Sarum* rite that did was the specification for processions.

The instructions in the rite set out the way in which a cloister should be used for processions on specific days and feasts. Edward III's two new colleges were the first in which ecclesiastical cloisters, rather than communication cloisters for the joining of buildings, were made an integral part of a royal domestic dwelling. At Westminster and Windsor canons processed round the cloisters and the precincts of the palace at appointed times of the week and year. But more importantly – at least from the reign of King Henry VI, and almost certainly earlier – monarchs themselves participated in these processions, moving, with a singing choir and followed by the rest of the court, round the precincts of their houses. On Wednesdays and Fridays there were processions for the health of the king and queen and the peace of the realm. Then there were processions on feast days, most notably the six great feasts of the year – Christmas, Epiphany, Easter, Whitsun, All Saints and, on 13 October, the Feast of St Edward the Confessor – when the monarch wore his crown and walked in procession 'preceded and followed by his lords according to their degrees . . . with a baron . . . carrying a sword before the king, and a duke or an earl carrying the king's cap and the king's chamberlain following behind to hold up the hem of the royal mantle'.[6]

Henry VII diligently participated in all these processions, some of which were extremely elaborate. At the feast of Corpus Christi, the Blessed Sacrament was carried beneath a heavily embroidered canopy held by six knights, while four Esquires of the Body – personal servants to the king – held tall candlesticks with lit tapers around it. On Palm Sunday the royal procession would move through the whole building and into the great hall, where a cross was erected; in front of this the king would lay his palm before re-entering the chapel.[7]

The annual royal itinerary was dominated by the need for the court to be staying in an appropriate place to celebrate these feasts with the full rites. This was not always straightforward. For instance, the king's preference was to celebrate the feast of St Edward the Confessor at Westminster. But on 13 October he was often still on progress and so it was necessary to organize things so he was at a suitable location. In 1492 he had to celebrate the feast in Calais, making the most of its patriotic overtones, while in 1497 he was in Exeter Cathedral and three times in the 1500s he celebrated the feast at Reading Abbey, the great royal foundation where King Henry I was buried.

From 1489 Henry celebrated almost every Easter at Sheen, only relocating it to Greenwich in 1498 because the chapel at Sheen had burned down. In 1502 he returned to what was now Richmond for Easter, where it was observed every year but two until his death. In the first part of his reign Christmas was generally spent at Westminster, where the very important feast of the Epiphany – Twelfth Night, the coming of the three kings – could be marked with real impact. However, the moment Richmond was completed Henry also moved the Christmas feasts there, where he spent five out of eight of his last Christmases.

So, after Richmond was completed in 1502, we can see that Henry moved all the most important church and court feasts of the year to his new residence, confirming its status as his special dynastic seat. In fact, if we look more broadly at the king's itinerary after the manor was finished, we can see that it became easily his most favoured house. He made more than fifty-seven visits there, staying for a total of at least 840 days. Many of the stays were quite long – the average, in fact, was a fortnight. Westminster, which had been such a favoured location before 1502, was now visited only briefly as the king travelled between Richmond and Greenwich; he spent only 201 days there after 1500.

How much did the friaries at Greenwich and Richmond contribute to this pattern of life and what part did they play in the daily round of court religion? As well as the friaries, each house was provided with other locations in which the king could attend Mass. At Richmond, in addition to the friary, close by was the charterhouse founded by Henry V. Henry VII favoured this almost as much as the Observant Friars, and its prior, John Ingleby, was the man in charge of the transformation of Sheen into Richmond. Before the construction of the friary Henry regularly attended services there.[8] However, his daily devotions were undertaken in a small but richly decorated chapel next to his privy chamber known as the secret or privy closet. In here he would normally hear Mass each morning, and sometimes some of the liturgical offices of the day. In here the Clerk of the King's Closet was in charge, looking after its contents and arranging the rota of chaplains who served the king.

Then there was the Chapel Royal, which was under the control of a dean – a priest appointed directly by the king to be in charge of his domestic chapel. It was the dean's responsibility to oversee services in the royal chapel and to take a slightly reduced number of staff on progress with the king in summer. Under the dean were the gentlemen and children of the chapel, the choir, and their musical director. The king observed Mass from a raised gallery at the west end of the chapel known as the great closet or holyday closet, because it was on Sundays and holy days that he attended the household chapel. There was a small altar in here and the king could observe this as well as, or instead of, the public liturgy below.[9]

Every morning Henry would inform the staff of his privy chamber exactly where he wanted to perform his devotions. It is clear that the friars played their part in the king's life – they had a particular role to preach before him in Lent; they also served as Henry VII's and, later, Katharine of Aragon's confessors. Katharine, we know, also often heard Mass in the Greenwich friary rather than in the royal chapel.[10] However, as far as we can tell, the daily round of religious observance at Greenwich and Richmond was generally in the privy and holyday closets; friaries were used for major court feasts and events – times when the household chapel was too small or too modest for a great event.

The friaries were also important because it was extremely rare for baptisms to be conducted in household chapels. Henry VII's second and third sons, Henry and Edmund, were christened at Greenwich, while in the next reign Henry VIII's first son, the short-lived Prince Henry, was baptized at the Richmond friary and his daughters, Mary and Elizabeth, were christened at Greenwich.[11] When Henry VIII came to the throne the great feasts of the year were often celebrated in the friars' church rather than the Chapel Royal. The Treaty of London was signed at the Greenwich friary in 1519, when the two papal legates, Cardinals Wolsey and Campeggio, 'celebrated high mass in state', and famously, on Easter Day 1532, Henry VIII was first denounced from the pulpit there for his thoughts of divorce. The following Sunday a royal chaplain put the other side of the story to the congregation.[12]

Crucially, both friary churches were connected to the royal houses. At Greenwich there was probably a short straight link to the west door, but at Richmond, after Prince Arthur's death, a second phase of works began, creating an elaborate setting for the manor and friary. The space between the two was laid out with two large, broadly square, compartments, the north one an orchard – or ornamental pleasure ground – and the south one a garden. Round these ran two-storey timber-framed galleries; the ground floor of these was open, like a cloister, and paved in stone; the upper floor was enclosed, glazed and matted. The long, winding south gallery allowed the king to leave his private study next to his bedchamber in the stone tower and walk, at first-floor level, to the friars' church (see plan pages 50–51 and illustration page 69). At the point where the gallery met the church there was a stair tower, which meant Henry could either watch from his own exclusive pew in the church, rather like a box at the theatre, or descend to the nave to participate in the services.

Modern Homes

Despite the fact that one of Henry VII's very first acts was to establish the Observants at Greenwich, it took him a long time to consider building there himself. This must have been, in part, because the house he inherited in 1485 had been in regular use by successive queens of England since it was originally built by Humphrey, Duke of Gloucester in the 1430s.

The Duke of Gloucester was the youngest brother of King Henry V and sometime Protector of the realm during the minority of his nephew Henry VI. He was granted the manor of Greenwich in 1427 and laid out a hunting park there; ten years later he began a house which was completed around 1439. It was a special kind of residence known as a *pleasaunce*. This was just what it sounded like – a pleasure ground, a building reserved for private delectation. A *pleasaunce* was normally a detached house set in a garden, unfortified and laid out for luxury and convenience rather than to impress by scale and might. A fifteen-minute stroll from the mighty Kenilworth Castle in Warwickshire into the farmland to its west will still lead the curious visitor to earthworks remaining from a *pleasaunce* built there by Henry V in 1417. Set by a great lake amidst gardens, this was much like the house built by Duke Humphrey at Greenwich.[13]

In the fifteenth century Greenwich Park was relatively small, only 200 acres, so was more of an ornamental landscape than a hunting ground. It covered steeply rising land south of the Thames, on top of which, on the site of today's Royal Observatory, was a tall but compact stone castle, with spectacular views of London in the distance. Here Humphrey could dine with his close companions. On the lower ground, at the water's edge, was the *pleasaunce*, with two courtyards and a great garden, little garden and orchard to its south. There was also a fine chapel with stained glass, a gallery overlooking the garden, a hall, kitchens, gatehouse and dovecot. Thus Greenwich was, like Sheen, a two-part residence – a castellated stone tower and a large house for more public receptions.[14]

The *pleasaunce* was, unusually for the time, built in brick. In retrospect, this is where the building's importance lay, for between 1430 and 1460 brick effected an architectural revolution in England. After the Romans it had largely disappeared from use until around 1300, when it started to be used as a convenient (and concealed) material in some parts of the country. By the time Henry V built his new manor at Sheen, bricks were used for the core of the building but the finished show faces were all of stone; likewise Henry VII faced his new great hall and chapel at Richmond with stone while brick was reserved for the construction of the outer courts and service areas. This was the last royal building to be so coy about the outward display of brick.[15]

In fact from the 1430s aristocrats and prelates had used the material extensively. The hard-bitten soldier, and model for Shakespeare's Falstaff, Sir John Fastolf built a fine residence of brick at Castor (Caister) in Norfolk in the 1430s. He was followed by a much more substantial figure, Ralph, Lord Cromwell, Lord Treasurer from 1433–43, who started a gigantic brick tower at Tattershall in Lincolnshire in 1434. These buildings were relatively remote from the epicentre of court life, but the Greenwich *pleasaunce* – or Placentia, the Latinized name by which it was sometimes known – was at the heart of things. After Humphrey died it was given by Henry VI to his queen, Margaret of Anjou, and, in the following reign, it became the property of Elizabeth Woodville, Edward IV's queen. As the country house of the queens of England, every English aristocrat and courtier and every visiting foreign dignitary came here, and all would have seen that the building was unexpectedly of brick, not stone. This was a trend-setting moment – a house that was to change the way people thought a royal residence should look.

The old *pleasaunce* was not built as the residence of a king and Henry VII decided to rebuild it as a major royal house on the same site and on the same alignment, that is to say parallel with the river. It too was of brick, hundreds of thousands of which were made in the park nearby.[16] The method was simple and fast. Clay was dug out of the ground and kneaded to get it to an appropriate consistency. It was then thrown into a wooden mould and the brick-shaped lump put out to dry on the grass. Once the green bricks were solid enough to lift without being squashed, they were carefully piled up into a massive heap called a clamp. In the centre of this was a pile of wood delivered to the site in huge bundles. This was lit, and then the clamp left to burn. Restricted oxygen supply in the middle meant that the fire burned for a long time at a high temperature, firing the bricks over a period of several days. When the clamp eventually cooled, the bricks were unstacked, put on carts and trundled to the king's new buildings. Moving brick was expensive, so it was dug and fired as close to the construction site as possible. Firing could take place only in the summer, so work was generally in abeyance from October to April. Decorative effects could be achieved on the bricks by dipping their ends into sand and then placing the sandy ends close to the central fire. Under intense heat the sand vitrified, giving the exposed face a shiny, dark-coloured end. These vitrified headers could be built into the walls in patterns, normally large interlinked diamonds. The lively effect was known as diaper work and it covered the walls of Henry's new building.[17]

The new manor of Greenwich (the Tudors did not call it Placentia) was, like its predecessor, a courtyard house with its principal façade towards the river. Apart from a wall built round the whole of the park, it had no protection – no moat or any other defensive feature. In fact, the house was a very urban building, long and low, with a five-storey tower capped with lead-covered onion domes at one end. Its designer, Robert Vertue, was a mason who had trained at Westminster Abbey and worked on churches in Canterbury and Bath. The evidence does not suggest that

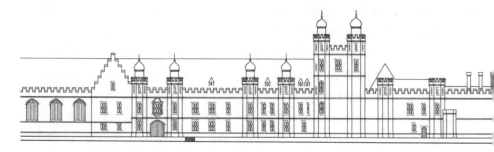

My reconstruction of the riverfront of Henry VII's new house at Greenwich. On the left is the chapel and to the right of the gatehouse is the presence chamber. Next to the tower are the privy chamber and the king's privy closet. To the right of the tower was the king's privy or private kitchen.

he had built in brick before but, for a decade in the 1490s, he worked in the City of London, possibly for a series of rich merchants, and perhaps this was where he gained experience of brickwork. There were several phases of work at Greenwich and plans were changed as they progressed; in early 1503, just before her death, the queen made various suggestions that were captured on a plan – rare evidence of royal participation in the process of design.[18]

Looking closely at Henry VII's house, it becomes obvious that it was not only its brickwork that was novel. The whole composition of the place was nothing like any previous royal residence and we now need to look closely at this to understand what was going on.

HENRY VII AT HOME

Henry VII did not invent a new way of royal life; the pattern of his year, marked by the regular beat of Church festivals, was indistinguishable from what had happened at the court of Edward IV or Henry VI. The details, though, were changing. Gradually, since the time of Richard II, reign by reign, household regulations increased the formality of court life, elevating the sovereign above everyone else through dozens of small marks of respect. None of the usurpers of the fifteenth century, Henry IV, Edward IV or Richard III, saw it as being in their interest to abandon this escalation of royal dignity: in fact, while energetically denigrating their predecessors, they adopted their court rules and elaborated them to boost their own position. In this elevation of majesty Henry VII played a very important part. The creation of the Privy Chamber and the rapid construction of new privy chambers at Windsor, Richmond and Greenwich in the years immediately afterwards meant that the detailed instructions for the personal service of the king had to be completely rewritten.[19]

Under Edward IV the king's chamber was staffed by Yeomen of the Crown – yeomen ushers, grooms and pages – all of whom were menial servants. Then there were carvers, cupbearers, sewers and surveyors, who were of greater rank and who served at the royal table. The king's personal servants were the Knights and Esquires of the Body, and these were significant figures at court. Key to the new arrangements invented by Henry VII was the appointment of one of the gentlemen ushers as the king's Groom of the Stool. With a page and a couple of other hand-picked ushers, he alone had responsibility for the king in his privy chamber. None of the other classes of chamber servants was allowed in, no matter how grand they were.

For most of Henry VII's reign the Groom of the Stool was Hugh Denys, a gentleman of middling rank who became the king's most trusted right-hand man. It was he who distributed the king's alms, paid rewards, bought personal items and provided the king with cash when he needed it. His title, though, was taken from his principal – and most intimate – role, which was attending the king on his close stool or WC. This stool was a wooden box with a hole in the top. Outside it was covered in silk-fringed black velvet and the seat, round the hole, was padded by a cushion. Inside was a pewter bowl that could be emptied out.[20] This was much more comfortable than the old-fashioned fixed garderobe or privy, which was a shaft built into the thickness of the wall with an upholstered wooden seat on the top. It was not for nothing that the euphemism for this type of lavatory was a 'draught'. The Groom of the Stool alone entered the small room off the king's bedchamber in which the close stool was kept and attended the king at his stool, bringing the cloth to wipe the royal bottom.

At night the Groom of the Stool slept in the king's bedroom at the foot of his bed. In the morning he received the king's orders – for instance where the king would hear Mass, when he wanted to dine and what his plans for the day were. Meanwhile the page and another gentleman might be making the fire and clearing the candles from the previous night. Piers Barbour, the king's barber, would then enter the room and shave him, after which the yeomen of the Wardrobe of the Robes would bring clothes from the wardrobe, always sited below the bedchamber, to the privy chamber door. The king would then be dressed by the Groom of the Stool.

The groom would help the Clerk of the Closet set the privy closet for Mass and attend with the king; on Sundays and feast days he would help arrange the procession to the household chapel; he would also supervise the king's eating, checking that everything was appropriately done and that music was provided if wanted. If Henry were to attend his council, the groom would guard the door or ask a junior member of the council to do it for him. If the king was indoors all day, the groom would stand at the door of the privy chamber keeping people who were unauthorized out. The yeomen ushers would be at the doors of the outer chambers controlling access and, in case of doubt, consulting the Lord Chamberlain.[21]

As night drew near the king's bed was made. Monarchs were paranoid about their beds being booby-trapped or poisoned, so a careful ritual was carried out to check the bedding – the straw mattress that lay beneath the luxurious feather-filled mattresses was stabbed several times with a dagger to make sure that there was nothing untoward in it. Once prepared, the bed was guarded by a page until the king was ready. At the bedhead was placed the king's sword – just in case.

When the king was ready for bed the gentlemen served him with the 'all night'. They then helped the king wash and undress, a process that began with bringing in torches and candles to light the shuttered chamber. A page would set a pallet bed on the floor at the foot of the royal bed for the Groom of the Stool. Meanwhile, the yeomen ushers outside the door were charged to stay awake to look out for fire or treason, animals on the loose, loud noises – anything, in short, that could disturb or endanger the king or his property.

Despite all this intimacy with the king's person, the groom and his assistants were emphatically servants: they were not allowed near the king's chair, to stand under his cloth of estate, lean on his bed or even stand on his carpets. They were to keep their distance at the far end of the room, watching and waiting to do their duty. All this was new, because although the king had always had a band of body servants, now that their duties were tied to a specific room in his houses and they were not under the jurisdiction of the Lord Chamberlain, in practical terms Henry VII lived a more private and exclusive existence than his predecessors.

What remained the same was the fact that all the important days at court were days of estate, the major feast days of the Church. On these the king dined in estate in his presence chamber at a trestle table covered with a heavy linen cloth and groaning with silver and gold vessels. His chair would be placed beneath a cloth of estate – a canopy suspended

The *Domus Regie Magnificencie*. A seventeenth-century copy of a lost original drawing probably of Henry VII's reign. It shows the king at his table beneath a throne canopy being served dinner. Far to his right is a bishop and to his left two aristocrats or members of his family.

from the ceiling and displaying the king's coat of arms or badges on the upper suspended part and on its backcloth. Seated at the right-hand end of the table, at a respectful distance that made conversation impossible, would be a bishop; at the left end, equally remote, would sit two aristocrats with royal blood. If the queen was dining too, she would be under a separate canopy (hung slightly lower) in another part of the room, accompanied by a couple of high-ranking female aristocrats.

A day of estate revolved around the king's and queen's attendance at Mass – either in the king's own chapel or in one of the friars' churches – and the processions that accompanied it. The king would wear specific-coloured robes, depending on the day, and on Epiphany his crown, sceptre and orb would be brought from the jewel house. Occasionally, if the event demanded it, the crown would be brought out on another day of estate to emphasize its importance. So when the future Henry VIII was made Duke of York on All Saints' Day 1491, the king, queen and Lady Margaret Beaufort all processed crowned.[22]

On a day of estate, after evensong, the king, queen, bishops and lords would assemble for a 'void', or 'remove' – in other words a meal that was removed from the formality of the presence chamber and was taken in the great chamber with all the participants standing. In here a great tiered buffet would be assembled on which would be plate for display as well as the dishes and vessels needed. Wine and sweetmeats would be served, rather like a modern drinks party. On Twelfth Night, with the court bursting with guests, the void was sometimes held in the great hall.

Gifts were given at court not on Christmas Day or Boxing Day but on New Year's Day. Under Henry VI and Edward IV the king would rise early and, with the queen, start opening presents in bed. Ushers brought in gifts one by one and the king gave cash rewards for every present given. Henry VII brought a bit more dignity to the ceremony, receiving his gifts sitting on the end of his bed. Later, Henry VIII would abandon his bedchamber altogether and receive gifts standing by the buffet in the presence chamber. A page would stand guard over the gift-laden buffet to prevent pilfering.

When not engaged in business, or out hunting, there were plenty of amusements. Henry VII enjoyed reading and liked to play cards, dice and chess. He would listen to his musicians playing stringed instruments and sackbuts – a type of trombone – or organs set up in various parts of his houses, and occasionally bagpipes. Sometimes visiting singers would perform a ballad or poets read out rhymes. More boisterously, he laughed at fools and dwarfs, watched acrobats and once gave the colossal sum of £12 to a little girl who danced before him. On May Day a huge maypole was set up at Westminster, and at Christmas and New Year he smiled at the Lord of Misrule and watched plays in the great hall presented by troops of players.[23]

This was the life that Henry VII led in his new manor of Greenwich. But, as with every one of his houses except Windsor, nothing now remains above ground and no plan survives of the buildings. Luckily this is not the end of the story, because in 1970–71 important excavations were made beneath the lawn of the Royal Naval College, the building which, many centuries later, replaced the royal house. Brick foundations and floors gave us some crucial dimensions that could be added to drawings and paintings to reconstruct the basic outlines of the house, but we still did not have the layout of the rooms inside. This was only deduced by looking at the volumes of repair books that survived from Henry VIII's reign. Using these, it was possible to place within the outer shape of the walls the internal room divisions of the palace.

The largest room, the great hall, lay in a range behind the main riverside block, entered from an inner courtyard from which a staircase led up to the king's watching chamber. A door from here led to a gallery or anteroom on the riverfront. Here you could turn right and be in the holyday closet looking down on to the chapel below, or turn left to enter the presence chamber, which would have been under the control of the Lord Chamberlain.[24] Beyond was the privy chamber and between the two lay a short gallery off which was, on one side, a staircase and, on the other, the privy closet – the king's private chapel. This short gallery was crucial in the smooth operation of the king's everyday life. The staircase connected with the wardrobe on the ground floor and allowed the wardrobe staff to bring clothes up to the privy chamber door and wait in

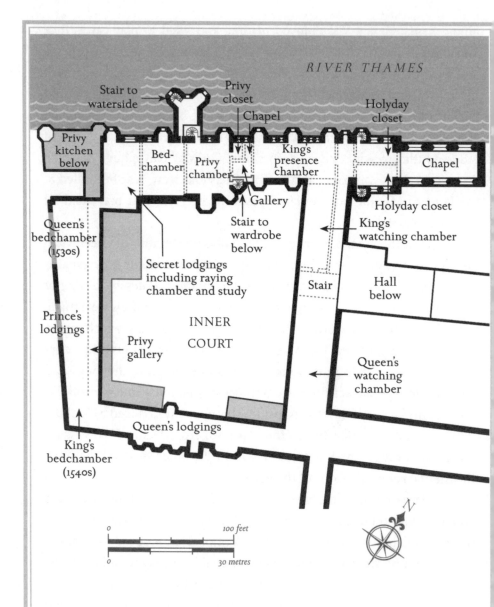

Reconstructed first-floor plan of the king's manor at Greenwich. Unfortunately the documents are not full enough to provide detailed information on the configuration of the queen's rooms or on the layout of the outer court.

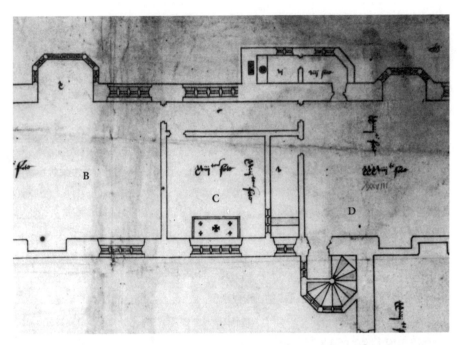

Detail of a plan drawn for Henry VIII in the 1540s. It shows close up the arrangements between the presence chamber B and the privy chamber D. The closet C has an altar under a window and the royal kneeling place next door has a reading desk for the king's missal. The kneeling place can be entered only from the king's privy chamber, while the closet or chapel is entered from a gallery outside.

the gallery, in privacy, before passing the robes in to the groom. The privy closet had two parts: the chapel itself, which was entered off the gallery, and the king's kneeling place – as it was known – which was entered from the privy chamber. The kneeling place had a lattice window that allowed the king, on his knees, to see the altar and the Elevation of the Host (see plate section). This cunning arrangement, probably first installed at Windsor Castle, meant that the king could enter his closet directly from the privy chamber and his chaplain, who had no right of access to the privy chamber, could enter the closet from the gallery.

Beyond the privy chamber was the king's bedchamber and beyond this a study. Above these, in a massive brick tower, were floors containing studies, libraries and other private rooms. The concept of the privy tower was at the heart of the houses of the rich and powerful. A place secure but also with commanding views. The great tower at Greenwich was not the only one that Robert Vertue built for the king, for, at exactly the same time, he was building another at the Tower of London.

TREASURE HOUSE

Arx Palatina meant castle palace, and this was how the Tower of London was sometimes described, because, while it was the principal fortress of the realm, it was also a royal residence. On its south side, on the riverfront, was a watergate with a landing stage that allowed monarchs direct access to the great hall, great chamber and bedchamber of the royal residence. Henry VII used these rooms from time to time in the first fifteen years of his reign, making around fourteen visits. His stays were generally short, although a few were longer than a week. The Tower was not a particularly comfortable place, as the lodgings were in extremely old towers and there were few private spaces. The main reason Henry visited was to inspect the offices that were based there. Apart from the Royal Armoury, what he was most interested in was the Mint and the Treasury.

In the summer of 1501 the king instructed Robert Vertue to start work on an extension to the royal lodgings. This was to be a tower built over a new archway approached by an ingenious gallery from the presence chamber. This was not simply a new privy chamber – it was for another use altogether.

It has already been described how Henry essentially merged national and personal finances, bringing them under personal control of his own chamber. Before paper money, this involved carrying huge quantities of gold and silver coin around the country in heavily armoured carts. It also presupposed a system of deposit treasuries, where huge sums of hard cash could be held long term. The most important deposit was at the Tower of London, where coin was kept in the 'king's coffers' – great chests bound in iron stored, as we saw at the start of this book, in the basement of the White Tower. By 1500 the royal gold deposit was swelling nicely and the king's interest in auditing it had become intense. He decided that his main yearly cash audit should be on 1 January and so began to stay at the Tower in December to supervise the auditors. This is why, in 1501, he commissioned an extension to his Tower lodgings – not to live in, but as a sort of national counting house for the royal treasure. In July 1507 this room, which had only one door, was fitted out with shelves and cupboards for Henry's account books and ledgers. Soon after, he commissioned a new jewel house to be built for the safekeeping of his treasure; this was constructed near the great hall, close to his own lodgings in the residential inner sanctum of the fortress, a purpose-built stronghouse for the royal wealth.[25]

We do not know exactly how much gold lay in the Jewel House by Henry's death in 1509, but it was a lot. He was a rich man and, as he lay dying in his bedchamber at Richmond, he had reason to be confident that his wealth had bought him a place in heaven. As well as the two friaries at his two main houses, he had invested in a lady chapel, almshouses and a hospital in Westminster, a college in Cambridge, a lady chapel at Windsor, and his will allowed for every friary and parish church in England to be given a silver-gilt pyx – a small container for holding the Host. This was a man who had secured his place on earth and was determined to secure his place in heaven.

He was also determined to secure his financial legacy. One of his very last acts was to order the construction of three double doors at the stair foot of the Jewel House in the Tower of London. This was to keep safe cash for his son and heir, but also to protect one of his most treasured possessions. For there, amongst the iron-bound chests, in a specially made case, was a crown described as the one 'which it pleased God to give us with the victory of our enemy at our first field'. This was the precious circlet he had won at Bosworth.[26]

IV

FATHER AND SON

End of an Era

O N THE NIGHT OF SATURDAY, 21 April 1509, clinging to a jewelled crucifix, Henry VII died. He was in his bedchamber at Richmond, a room in the heart of his privy lodgings. As his lungs were consumed by tuberculosis and his throat closed up by a suppurating peritonsillar abscess, the doors of his privy chamber remained firmly shut. Access was now controlled by Richard Weston, who seems to have superseded the long-serving Hugh Denys as Groom of the Stool in the last months of Henry's life. Fourteen people had been admitted, amongst them the king's doctors, confessor, closest friends and, of course, Prince Henry. Remarkably, the deathbed scene was captured in a drawing by Garter King of Arms Thomas Wriothesley, who was soon to be a key figure in organizing court ceremonial, including the king's funeral. His drawing can't be taken as a literal depiction of the scene – Wriothesley was not in the room when Henry died – but he knew the king's inner rooms well and the large bed with its carved posts and plump pillows can be taken as a fair representation of how it really was.

It was at this point that the Privy Chamber worked its magic. Only fourteen people knew of the king's death and that was how it was to remain for two whole days. The iron curtain of security that had protected Henry in life was now to secure his legacy in death. To the court at Richmond, assembling for the annual Garter Day ceremonies, everything proceeded as if the king were still alive. People in the know came and went into the privy lodgings, ceremonies were performed in the dead king's name, and the young Henry was still addressed as prince. The old king's councillors had to smooth the path for the accession of the Prince

Sir Thomas Wriothesley's drawing of the scene in the Richmond bedchamber at Henry VII's death. He is surrounded by his closest courtiers, whose arms appear on the same page. Henry is shown wearing his crown, something he certainly did not do on his deathbed.

of Wales and only when they were sure that they had done this was the king's death announced to the court and country. The Great Wardrobe, which had, no doubt, been on high alert for some weeks, immediately supplied hundreds of yards of black cloth and the royal lodgings at Richmond were hung floor to ceiling with the stuff. The king's body was at first laid in his privy closet, but later was moved to lie in state in the Chapel Royal. While this took place, and the elaborate arrangements for the funeral were put in hand, Henry VIII, as he now was, mounted his horse and rode to the Tower of London, the traditional place from which a new monarch would survey his kingdom.[1]

ROYAL CHILDHOOD

Before starting to look at how Henry VIII built on his father's legacy, metaphorically and literally in terms of architecture, I want to take a few steps back to consider how and where he had been brought up. Royal children did not live with their parents. The court's peripatetic existence was dangerous for babies, so the children were set up with their wet nurses in subsidiary houses near London where their parents could easily

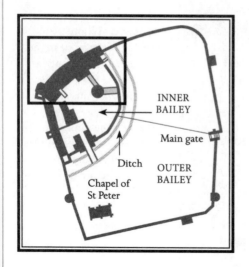

First-floor plan of the royal lodgings at Ludlow Castle in the north range of the inner ward. These are the rooms that Prince Arthur lived and died in – not large or luxurious, but probably comfortable and warm.

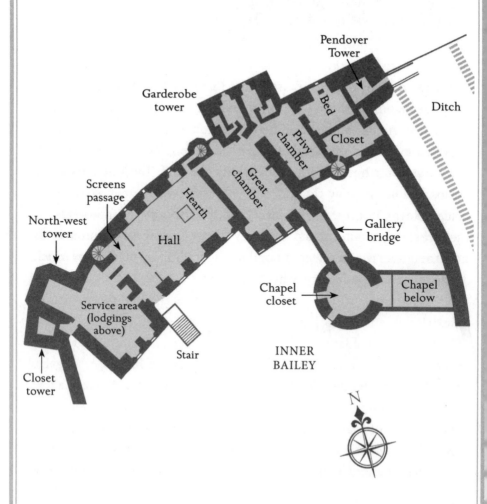

visit them. At a very young age they were granted their own households, at which point they were assigned their own lodgings within the major royal houses and given other houses of their own. Henry VII was following the precedent set by Edward IV when he sent Prince Arthur to Ludlow Castle aged only six. In 1493 Ludlow was a very long way away from Westminster. It was a walled town with seven gates and a population of around 2,000 that had grown rich on wool. It is still dominated by its massive castle, started in the eleventh century, which became the headquarters of Welsh government, such as it was, and therefore a seat of the Prince of Wales. Despite serial modernizations over the centuries, it was rather old-fashioned: the royal rooms were at the upper end of the hall in a three-storey tower. There were two two-room lodgings, one above the other, both served by small closets and garderobes. The first-floor outer chamber had a gallery that linked it to the royal pew in the unusual circular castle chapel. The inside could be made very comfortable with oak panelling and tapestries, and you can still see the remains of the fine fireplaces.[2]

While Arthur was given quasi-vice regal responsibilities in an ancient castle, his younger brother, Henry, was confined to the royal nursery. This was established under one of the queen's ladies, Elizabeth Denton, who, as well as caring for Henry, at various times also looked after his older sister Margaret, his younger sisters Elizabeth and Mary, and his baby brother Edmund. The children occasionally moved around the Thames valley with their parents, but most of the time they were looked after in the royal nursery house at Eltham.

The histories of the royal residences at Eltham and Greenwich are inextricably entwined. Just 4 miles from each other as the crow flies, Eltham was the older of the two and had been developed as a luxurious royal retreat from the time of Edward III. Successive monarchs had added lodgings for courtiers, a dancing chamber, bathrooms and gardens. So, by the reign of Henry VI, Eltham was a large, luxurious and modern house set in fine parkland. Its special attraction was its position on a rise high above the Thames, which meant that the views towards London were breathtaking, as they still are today. From the inner court you could see the spire of St Paul's Cathedral, sitting like a mother hen with the 110 spires and towers of her little chicks, the City parish churches, round about. Between 1436 and 1451 Henry VI spent a lot of time at Eltham and often celebrated Christmas there. The house, which was big by any standards, was divided, like the Palace of Westminster, into three zones: the great palace for public festivities, the privy palace for the king's residence and the prince's palace for the heir to the throne.

Eltham was Edward IV's most important country residence and, after 1475, his coffers full from the French pension he had won that year, he began to rebuild much of the house. His queen, Elizabeth Woodville, gave birth to a baby girl there in 1479 and Edward moved his treasured library to the house in the following year. For Edward and Elizabeth, Eltham and Greenwich worked symbiotically: they could stay together at either house or take their households to their separate residences for recreation or business.[3]

The house in which the future Henry VIII was brought up, then, was one that had been largely rebuilt a decade before. It was, in fact, one of the most modern and innovative buildings of its age and provided an architectural blueprint for many features that are normally associated with the Tudors. At the heart of the house was the new great hall. This was a deliberate anachronism. Great halls were, by the late fifteenth century, not the feasting halls of old, but all-purpose arenas for any activity that was too large, boisterous or public to be staged in the royal lodgings. It could be bedecked with tapestry to create a large antechamber through which visiting ambassadors would be led; it could be fitted up with a stage for a play; or it could be laid out for a Sunday-morning service for the household. Edward had taken as his model Westminster Hall with its angel-encrusted hammerbeam ceiling – a reference that would have been obvious to everyone and which proclaimed the status of his new structure.

Much more interesting architecturally were the rooms built on the west front, which, it seems, were for the queen. Here there was a long brick range with a series of five-sided bay windows and chimneybreasts, at the end of which was a gallery. This long, narrow room ran out from

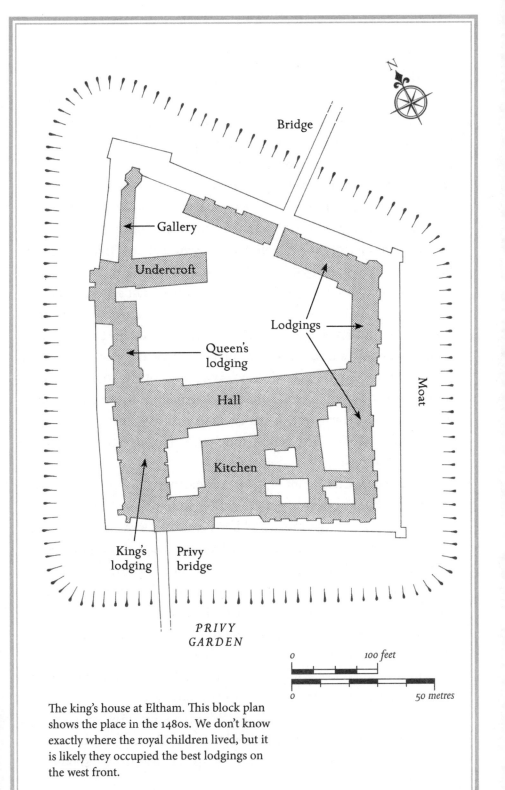

N

Bridge

Gallery

Undercroft

Lodgings

Queen's
lodging

Hall

Moat

Kitchen

King's
lodging

Privy
bridge

PRIVY
GARDEN

0   100 feet

0   50 metres

The king's house at Eltham. This block plan
shows the place in the 1480s. We don't know
exactly where the royal children lived, but it
is likely they occupied the best lodgings on
the west front.

the end of the queen's lodgings and may have terminated in a little closet or perhaps a banqueting house. The whole thing was designed to take advantage of the tremendous views of London. This was one of the first times this sort of bay window had been used, and Richmond and Greenwich, as well as many courtier houses, followed this fashion. A long gallery not designed to take you anywhere but simply for perambulation was also an innovation that was soon to be widely copied.

To the south of the queen's lodgings, at the end of the great hall, were the king's lodgings and then, ranged round the courtyard, were guest suites and rooms for other members of the royal family. Where in all this Henry and his sisters lived we do not know. However, each of them had their own servants and attendants and so Eltham, not a small residence, would have been full and busy as a royal nursery. We get a glimpse of life there in the autumn of 1499 when Desiderius Erasmus, the great humanist scholar and, in his day, a celebrity intellectual, paid a visit to Eltham in the company of Sir Thomas More. Henry, Margaret and Mary were lined up in the royal lodgings surrounded by attendants; More presented the eight-year-old prince with a paper, embarrassing Erasmus, who had come empty-handed. The prince, the Dutch scholar noted, already had 'something of royalty in his demeanour'.[4]

Aged eleven Henry not only lost his brother, thus becoming heir to the throne, but also lost his mother. He had hardly known Arthur, his elder brother by five years; he had been educated away from home and they had only met on great state occasions and his grief was probably not that great. His mother, though, had always been nearby and this was a much greater loss for the lad. But these changes signalled no immediate alteration in his life and he remained at Eltham for two years with an intensified programme of education; then, in 1504 aged fourteen, he was created Prince of Wales and arrived at Court. From this moment on he became the king's close companion, most of the time following him from house to house and accompanying him on progress.

There is no evidence that the royal houses were adapted in any way to allow the prince and his household to attend the king. Perhaps Henry occupied the now vacant queen's lodgings; or perhaps we should take seriously the dispatch of the Spanish ambassador Gutierre Gómez de Fuensalida, who claimed that 'He was never permitted to go out of the palace, except for exercise through a private door leading to the park . . . He took his meals alone, and spent most of his day in his own room, which had no entrance than through the king's bedchamber'. If this is true, Henry was confined to his father's privy chamber. Given Henry VII's paranoia about security, this seems entirely possible and is perhaps lent further credence by a survey of the palace over a century later. In this there may be an echo of Henry VII's cosseting of his son, for in the rooms beyond the king's bedchamber, in the innermost royal sanctum, were rooms known as the Duke of York's chamber and the schoolroom.[5]

THE FUN KING

Henry VIII was seventeen when he became king, old enough to be in his majority but not so old that he had grown out of the passions of his youth. Niccolò Machiavelli described him as '*ricco, feroce et cupido di gloria*' – rich, fierce and lusting for glory.[6] The teenage Henry was all of these: tall, muscular and full of testosterone, with an imagination captured by chivalric romances and the heroic deeds of knights. One of his first knightly deeds was to marry Katharine of Aragon, who had been marooned at the English court since the death of Prince Arthur. As she had been his late brother's wife, Henry had to get a papal dispensation for the wedding, which took place only a couple of months after he became king. Henry had money too. His father had left the royal finances in a good state and, in his last years, had deluged money into projects aimed at saving his soul: King's College Chapel in Cambridge and his own lady chapel at Westminster. Henry VIII had little interest in these and instead lusted after military glory, diverting royal spending towards war and its trappings.

Culturally, the early Tudor court was shaped by chivalry. Henry VII's first-born son was christened Arthur in the ancient English capital of Winchester. There, in the great hall of the royal castle, was the round table that was believed to be the very one belonging to the mythical

English king; Henry VIII was to show it with great pride to the Emperor Charles V as the board of his distant ancestor. Henry VIII was brought up on French chronicles that told the story of Edward III's and Henry V's spectacular victories over France in the Hundred Years' War and was immersed in Sir Thomas Malory's *Le Morte d'Arthur*. Henry VII had encouraged his young son's participation in the ceremonies of the Order of the Garter, Europe's oldest chivalric club, and he was to grow up particularly devoted to the Order, attending thirty-seven of the forty St George's Day feasts in his reign.[7] It is no coincidence that the very first significant work of architecture commissioned by the king in 1513 was a great new gatehouse for Windsor Castle, the headquarters of the Order. The big bold towers cloaked in the architectural language of the thirteenth century exude teenage machismo, while the central gateway is adorned with the new king's arms.

The gatehouse at Windsor, however, was a one-off for Henry VIII. The things that projected the chivalric image of his court more than anything

Henry VIII's first major architectural commission was a vast and powerful gatehouse for Windsor, his premier castle. It was refaced in the nineteenth century but still expresses the young king's militaristic mindset.

else were not grand buildings but war in France and tournaments at home. For over sixty years up to 1530 tournaments were the most important organized entertainment at court. The term tournament was a catch-all for various feats of arms, as they were called. These could be one-to-one foot combat, jousting or running at the ring. The latter two involved heavily armoured mounted knights with timber lances; the difference was the target. In a joust you charged at an opponent and tried to break your lance on his armour, whereas if you were running at the ring you would try to spear a suspended ring and carry it off. This was the hard action, but what surrounded it was pure fantasy. The tournament was the most active expression of the courtly code of chivalry – behaviour based on service to king, country and, especially, a mistress; it was a code that embodied glorious deeds of bravery in the quest of honour and the hand of the lady. The rules were set out by the heralds who proclaimed the challenges, kept the scores and named the winners. Knights would disguise themselves and make elaborate speeches before entering the lists, sometimes wearing the veil of their lady or, on winning, being given her ring. There was a strong undertone of male desire, challenges being floridly issued and prizes gravely awarded in the queen's rooms.

The celebrations for the marriage of Arthur and Katharine of Aragon in 1501 had encapsulated all this. Henry VII had arranged a tournament that took place in front of Westminster Hall in the outer ward of the palace. A grandstand was erected and divided into two parts, one for the king and his knights and another for the queen and her ladies. At one end was a tree of chivalry – a cut-out, richly decorated with flowers and fruit – upon which the challengers hung shields painted with their coats of arms. Knights entered on decorated carts called pageant cars, one like a mountain, another like a pavilion on a lake. The feats of arms continued for eight days, watched by the court, the Lord Mayor of London, the City aldermen and hundreds of ordinary Londoners.

Henry VIII elevated jousting to a different plane because, unlike his father, he jousted himself. At first he only ran at the ring, but in 1510, disguised as an anonymous knight, he took to the lists in person. Between then and his retirement from active tilting in 1527, thirty-nine tournaments were held at court. Henry had a dazzling career in the tiltyard and it was not just flattery that caused people to hail him as one of the great jousters of his age; he was genuinely brilliant at it.[8]

Tournaments were not a cheap hobby: that at Westminster in 1511 cost Henry £4,000, more than twice the cost of a 900-ton warship, and in 1515 just the textiles for the king's outfit cost more than £970.[9] At first the Tudors did not invest in any permanent infrastructure for the events; the grandstands and lists were demountable and were cleared away afterwards. But amongst Henry VIII's first architectural commissions was a series of buildings at Greenwich dedicated to his love of the tilt.

First, only months after his accession, he commissioned new stables, one for his coursers – the horses he used for jousting and hunting – and a second for a stud in Greenwich Park. Both stables were accompanied by a new barn to store hay. The coursers' stable was to the west of the manor and probably looked very much like the surviving stables at Hampton Court, but far larger. Henry's Hampton Court stables, which can still be seen on the Green just outside the main gates, cost only £130 in 1537; the Greenwich stables cost well over £600 and became the headquarters of the king's interest in horses. By 1526 he owned 119 horses, many of which were stabled at Greenwich.[10]

Close to the stables the king commissioned his great armoury mill. This was a highly novel venture. Up to this point the top-quality armour worn by man and horse, both in the tiltyard and on the field of battle, had had to be imported. Now Henry wanted a native workshop making armour to rival the great pieces worn by European princes, so in 1511 he invited Milanese armourers to work in England. But it was the start of construction of his mill in 1515 and the employment of eleven Dutch and German armourers that marked the origin of the Greenwich Armouries, a royal armour factory that supplied the Tudor court.[11]

The armoury was no work of architecture. It was a grouping of functional timber-framed buildings housing the various workshops needed by the armourers. One contained a horse mill, which, by a series of cogs and drives, connected to bellows and polishers that were needed to finish the steel. A list of equipment bought for the armoury reveals

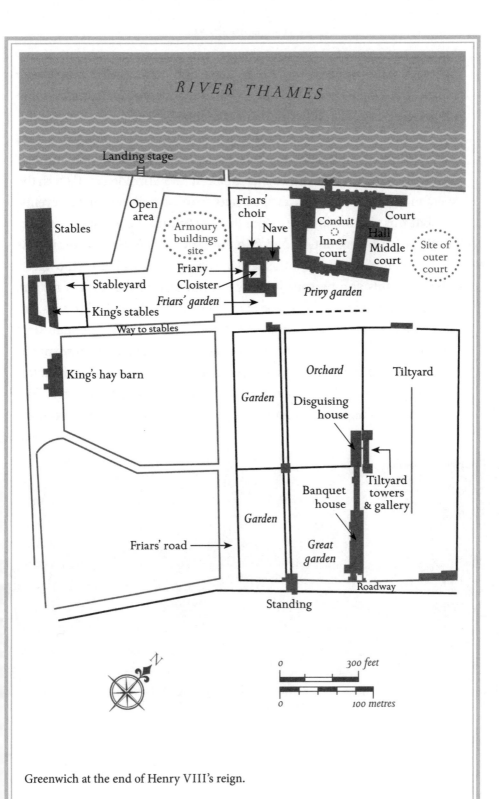

Greenwich at the end of Henry VIII's reign.

furnaces, water troughs, and a large collection of hammers, chisels and punches. So while Henry VII's life at Richmond was accompanied by the pious bells of his religious foundations, Henry VIII at Greenwich would have heard the industrial clash of hammer on steel. No doubt this was a source of intense pleasure and interest to the king. His stable and his armour workshop were immediately adjacent to the residence at which he spent most time and he was able to inspect work at both during his stays.[12]

But this was the infrastructure that lay behind the tournament, and the third great work at Greenwich in the early years of Henry's reign was a permanent tiltyard. As an expert in the sport, the king took a great interest in this and personally drew out the plan of the tiltyard for his meeting with Francis I of France at the Field of Cloth of Gold in 1520. At Greenwich an area approximately 650 feet long and 250 feet wide was laid out, and, in 1516–18, on its western edge were built permanent grandstands in the form of two towers and a linking gallery. These were designed by Henry Redman and built in brick with stone dressings. The towers were octagonal and four storeys high, each floor with a prospect

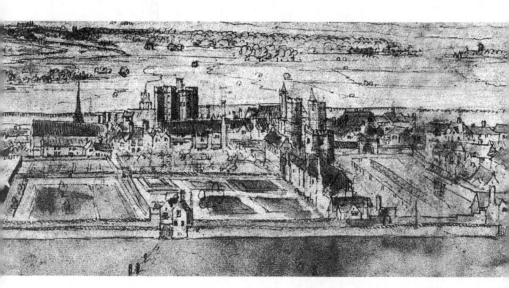

Anthonis van den Wyngaerde's view of Greenwich from the little castle on the hill (now the Royal Observatory), done in 1558. On the right can be seen the tiltyard towers and gallery; in the middle the royal lodgings centred on the great riverside tower containing the king's innermost rooms; and on the left the friary with its spire.

chamber affording views not only over the tiltyard but over the river, up the hill and over the park. The towers were battlemented and had banqueting chambers on their roofs approached by stair towers capped with tall lead-covered pinnacles.[13] Linking them was a gallery with windows overlooking the lists; in the long gaps between tournaments the king's magnificent jousting armour was displayed in here.

Historians have struggled to describe these buildings and the style in which they were constructed. But the essential fact is that chivalry was associated with castles: that was where knights of old lived, from where they rode out on their quests and where their ladies awaited their return. Henry's towers were fantastical castles from which the ladies of the court would watch the exploits of the knights below. In 1525 the romantic atmosphere of Greenwich was further enhanced when the little castle on top of the hill was remodelled with extra battlements and pinnacles to further emphasize the character of Henry VIII's new Camelot.

One of the first times the new towers were used was for the royal jousts held before the Emperor Charles V in 1522. Charles and Katharine of Aragon, surrounded by aristocrats, stood in the gallery and crowded into the towers. The king and the Earl of Devonshire, with ten others, entered the tiltyard mounted on armoured horses and sporting tabards made of cloth of gold with silver letters. Their helms were crested with huge coloured plumes. The challengers entered next, led by the Duke of Suffolk and Marquess of Dorset, all dressed in red velvet. After riding against each other individually, shattering their lances against each other's armour, they all entered the tiltyard at the same time and flew at each other as fast as they could, breaking more lances.[14]

Horsemanship, so important for the tournament, was also fundamental for hunting. This was the sport of kings and had a greater impact than anything else on the royal houses. Hunting required specialized equipment and types of building, but most of all it needed land. This could be enclosed with fences and ditches to keep the game in, in which case it was called a park; or it could be a large unfenced area where deer were protected by law rather than by a physical boundary: this was a royal forest. Royal forests were not necessarily densely wooded, but they had to be well stocked with game. Royal houses away from the Thames valley were all strategically located to take advantage of parks or forests and one of the main reasons for visiting them was the hunting.

The animal that the Tudor kings most desired to hunt was the red deer – then usually called the hart, today the stag. There were essentially two types of stag-hunting, the first of which was the chase. This was the most energetic and skilful of all hunts. A stag would be identified the night before the hunt and in the morning it would be flushed out by the king's dogs – normally bloodhounds. The chase would start and, as the stag ran, more dogs would be brought to bear while the king and his companions gave chase. Stags run fast and far, so the chase often covered many miles and took many hours. In August 1528 Henry chased one stag for ten hours before bringing it to bay.[15] Cornered, the exhausted animal would then turn on the dogs. This was the dangerous bit. The king now had to turn matador and, with his sword, first disable the stag and then kill it with a single stab through its spine into its heart. This was a sport of the forest, as almost every park was far too small for a proper chase.

The other way of hunting was more static. It involved driving the deer towards the huntsmen, who were armed with longbows or, more usually, crossbows. The deer would be chased by dogs but guided towards their death by beaters, nets, sheets of canvas called toils, or, in some parks, by hedges. Hundreds of deer could be killed in one go like this – on one particularly bloodthirsty occasion in 1541 the king and his companions killed 200 deer in a day's hunting in Hatfield chase.[16] This type of hunt was much more likely to take place in one of the enclosed parks surrounding a royal house, and the killing ground, sometimes called the tryst, would be in front of the house. This allowed non-participants to watch the skill of the archers. Sometimes the deer were deliberately driven into a small lake where the killing would be spectacular with the waters turning red. This was not only sport for the king: the queen and several other ladies, including Anne Boleyn, also shot. Once, out hunting at Waltham, Henry accidentally shot a tame buck and had to compensate its lady owner 7s 6d.[17]

'How a Kennell ought to be situate and trimmed for hounds', from an Elizabethan manual for hunting, *The Noble Art of Venerie*, 1575. Henry VIII's kennels at Deptford would have been very similar to this.

For hunting, the king owned a large number of dogs of various types, including mastiffs, bloodhounds, beagles and greyhounds. These were kept separate from the dogs that lived in his houses with him (including his own pet dogs, Ball and Cut). There were several packs of hunting dogs, each under the control of a keeper assisted by various yeomen. Several were designated as privy packs and were for the king's sole use, the most important of these being the privy bloodhounds, of which George Boleyn, Anne's brother, was appointed master in 1528. The headquarters for all the dogs were the large kennels a mile from Greenwich at Deptford, where a 230-foot-long fence prevented them escaping. They were fed with biscuits known as chippings and the beagles, at least, with meat that cost Henry 5s a month. Other houses had kennels too, but when the court went on progress the packs were generally transported in a special dog cart with a canvas cover.[18]

Amongst the various forms of hunting, one other was particularly favoured – hawking. Like stag hunting, this was a sport only for royalty and super-rich aristocrats. Henry was less keen on this in his youth, but in the late 1520s it, too, became an obsession. Hawks were used to catch other birds and would be brought into the field either hooded or unhooded. A hooded bird would be handed to the king, who would wait until the dogs had disturbed the ground birds; at that point the hood would be removed and the hawk would fly to its prey. An unhooded bird would be released into the sky from where it would become a 200mph projectile, killing its prey by impact as much as by using its beak or talons.[19]

Hawking took place during the winter, as the birds moult in the summer months, and the chase took place in the summer, the deer rut in the autumn. Both Henry VII and Elizabeth of York had hunted and bought the very best crossbows, hawks and dogs. In 1498 alone Henry acquired at least thirty-one birds of prey for hunting, as well as two new dogs. Even quite late in his life he would hunt every day, though in his last years his prowess may have been failing as, in July 1507, he accidentally killed a farmyard cockerel with his crossbow.[20]

In his early years as king, the combination of Greenwich and Eltham together formed Henry VIII's most regular hawking ground. The Royal Mews had originally been at Charing Cross, but Henry's most important hawk mews was set up at Greenwich in 1533 on the second floor of the royal lodgings and was nicknamed 'the Cage'. The windows had no glass, but instead had double timber lattices. Hawks were normally taken from the nest and, in August 1531, one of the grooms of the king's chamber was rewarded for waiting out to take birds for the king. Stolen away from a nest, the birds were young and required training, the most important part of which was accepting the proximity of man. As a result, masters would tame their birds by being continually with them for days or even weeks. One way of doing this was to sleep with them and Henry had a bedchamber in the Cage at Greenwich that allowed him to do this. Katharine of Aragon had a bedroom separated from the Cage by only one room, so it seems as if she, too, trained her own birds. The hawks were fed on raw chicken at the cost of a penny a day per hawk; eight hawks were being fed in this way in 1532. Bridges and trackways were made in the parks around Greenwich to allow the king's horses to take the birds out.

Greenwich was not suitable for the chase, however, and it was the summer progress that took the king – normally accompanied by

Katharine – to the royal stag-hunting grounds.[21] The oldest and largest of these was Woodstock in Oxfordshire. Here Henry VII had spent over £4,000 rebuilding the house. He put up a new gatehouse, a new roof for the great hall, bay windows, and a jewel house that allowed him to bring his cash when he visited. The park round the house was, unusually, enclosed by a stone wall; parks were usually fenced with timber paling on top of an earth bank. The circumference of the park wall was 7 miles, so the area inside was small; however, Woodstock was sited within the royal forest of Wychwood, which stretched for 25 miles one way and 20 miles the other. This whole huge landscape was under forest law, restricting what people could do and, in particular, banning anyone other than the royal family and their guests from any sort of hunting. In the western part of the forest was another royal house, Langley, 9 miles in a straight line from Woodstock. Henry VII improved this too and it meant that he could leave his main household at Woodstock and ride westwards hunting, then stay in more privacy and comfort at Langley. Henry VIII used Langley a little less and instead acquired a house to the south, Ewelme, in which he stayed quite often. This pattern of main residence and satellites was fundamental to the royal geography of England, particularly in the 1530s when Henry became much more interested in building.[22]

WOLSEY

The simple fact is that for the first twenty years of his reign Henry VIII was not that much interested in architecture. He was keen to appear magnificent, but the fine details of one building or another were of less interest. This does not mean nothing was built, because it was, only that Henry relied on others to take the decisions, and foremost amongst those was Thomas Wolsey.[23]

Henry VIII and Wolsey are one of the great partnerships of English history. Wolsey, brilliant, calculating, hugely energetic, charming but ruthlessly ambitious, managed the bureaucracy of government while Henry devoted himself to jousting, hunting, shooting, swimming, wrestling, dancing, music, poetry and, when allowed, war.

Wolsey had been one of Henry VII's chaplains; indeed, he may have been one of the fourteen people who stood round the dying king's bed. Soon he was Royal Almoner, in charge of the new king's almsgiving, a position that put him in the royal council. Over the next few years, step by step, he moved ever closer to becoming the king's chief minister, an ambition that he had achieved by 1516. Along the way came big ecclesiastical posts, culminating in his appointment as Archbishop of York and cardinal. His position in government and in the Church brought two things, inextricably linked: money and status. The two went together – a cardinal archbishop who was also Lord Chancellor was expected to maintain great state, with a large household and fine residences. This required huge resources: Wolsey's income in 1515 was probably over £5,000 a year, more than almost every peer; by the mid-1520s he was grossing an annual £9,500, making him by far and away the king's richest subject.[24]

Money and status lay behind Wolsey's building projects. He was, quite simply, the greatest builder of his age, creating a chain of houses in the Thames valley that outclassed all but the king's own. He started relatively modestly, building a house in the City on the banks of the River Fleet at Bridewell, but, as we shall see, he abandoned this in 1514 when he became Archbishop of York, an appointment that came with a very large town house in Westminster called York Place. Just four months later, Wolsey bought a country property. He had had his eye on the house of one of Henry VII's most important friends and councillors, Giles, Lord Daubeney, at Hampton Court. This he leased in 1515. The stage was set for two of the most important building projects of Henry VIII's reign.

Wolsey's career had been founded on efficiency, as much as anything else, and he directed his energetic organizational skills to his two main building projects, setting up a yard in Battersea on the Thames from which both could be serviced. At first this was run by Robert Cromwell – whose cousin Thomas was later to become one of the most powerful figures in Henry VIII's administration – but soon responsibility for building operations was handed over to Thomas Stubbs, a priest who had managed the greatest private building project of the reign so far, the Duke of

Buckingham's house, Thornbury Castle, outside Bristol. In modern terms, Stubbs was the project manager, not the designer, and Wolsey recruited the best architects for his houses too. John Lebons, a royal master mason, was appointed designer of Hampton Court; he had worked for Henry VII on his tomb in Westminster Abbey and probably on other royal works too. At York Place the architect was Henry Redman, whom we have already met designing the tiltyard towers at Greenwich. He had also been involved at both Eton College and King's College Chapel.

The brief for the two designers was very specific. Hampton Court was intended to be a place for recreation and entertainment, the house where Wolsey could invite the king and the royal family and welcome foreign ambassadors. As such, it needed substantial accommodation. In the end there were three main suites of rooms, as well as thirty-four guest suites. York Place, meanwhile, was very definitely a town house, the place from which Wolsey conducted his business. There were some guest rooms here, but far fewer and, crucially, there was only one set of lodgings, those for the cardinal himself. During the legal term Wolsey based himself at York Place, riding each day in pomp to Westminster Palace where he exercised his duties as Lord Chancellor. His house was alive with activity, with a continuous stream of envoys, ambassadors and messengers coming and going.[25]

It is sometimes said that the king was jealous of the cardinal's riches and status, that he envied his houses and furnishings, and that Wolsey, like Icarus, flew too close to the sun. This is to profoundly misunderstand the relationship between the two men. There was no architectural rivalry, not least because Henry was only mildly interested in building at this point in his life. Henry wanted, and expected, his chief minister to have the status that was due to him as both Lord Chancellor and cardinal archbishop and, after 1527, as permanent papal legate. Wolsey's status was a source of pride for Henry; it gave the king a minister who was on equal terms with the super-ministers of France and Spain with whom he was negotiating.[26]

Wolsey's diplomatic masterpiece was an extraordinary treaty pulled off in 1518 to bring universal and everlasting peace to Europe. It was a complicated deal involving a series of sub-treaties and a meeting between the kings of France and England to commit publicly to peace as an example for the whole continent. Wolsey brought about this meeting at the Field of Cloth of Gold in 1520. The 'field' was a tiltyard in northern France, outside Guînes, and the whole focus of the event was a meeting of the knights and kings of the two courts to demonstrate their honour and nobility. It was a chivalric field day at which both courts had to emerge with equal honour and magnificence.

This event is important architecturally because Wolsey masterminded a temporary palace as a setting for the meeting. The king was determined that this should be as large and magnificent as possible, and it seems that the initial idea envisaged something quite a lot bigger than Greenwich or Eltham. In the end the plans were reduced at least twice and something smaller (but not much) was agreed upon. The chief designer was William Vertue, who had become Henry VIII's master mason in 1510. His bread-and-butter work had been designing the brilliant fan vaulting at Windsor, Westminster and King's College Chapel, Cambridge, so the plan for the temporary palace that he drew, and which was signed by the king and retained by Wolsey, was a big departure. Wolsey, whom I suppose we would call a micro-manager today, kept close control of the work as it progressed and all variations were personally approved by him.[27]

The finished structure is famously shown on a painting now in the Royal Collection (see plate section). It was a courtyard house with balancing lodgings for the king and queen and a large chapel at the rear. In the front part were lodgings for the king's sister Mary, Duchess of Suffolk, and for Wolsey himself. This was a sure sign of Henry's confidence in his minister's status as papal legate and architect of the whole event. The painting shows the entrance front with a tantalizing glimpse of the inner court. It illustrates the way the structure was raised up on a brick basement and that the upper walls of canvas had very large glass windows. The whole thing had a strong air of fantasy: it was part castle, part renaissance palace, but most of all it was designed to impress. And this it did. Inside, the walls were hung with the cream of the royal tapestry collection, the ceilings were tented with the finest silks, and anywhere

where it would fit were panes of cloth of gold. In all, fifty-two loads of priceless textiles were delivered.[28]

So between 1515 and 1520 Wolsey not only demonstrated his brilliance at diplomacy and administration, but he showed Henry that he had great architectural taste and could manage building projects. We now need to turn to the king's houses and see the impact that Wolsey had on them.

HAND-ME-DOWNS

In 1512 an event of profound importance in the history of English royal building occurred. The privy palace at the Palace of Westminster was very badly damaged in a fire. In actuality, as we have seen, after the completion of Richmond, Westminster had been used less by Henry VII, and Henry VIII had been there only half a dozen times at the start of his reign. Yet it was still the official seat of the sovereign, and the privy palace, along with Windsor, offered the most extensive accommodation available to the king.

Much more important was the fact that for two centuries the king's principal residence had been integrated with the functions, institutions and administration of the state in a single building. When parliament was summoned it was generally called to the king's residence at Westminster and while the Commons assembled in Westminster Hall to be ticked off against the election returns, the Lords gathered together in the king's old presence chamber – the Painted Chamber. Henry VII had instituted a parliamentary procession from the palace to Westminster Abbey, with the aristocrats and bishops proceeding in order of precedence to celebrate Mass. This innovation gave, for the first time, a public display to the meeting of parliament, which otherwise would have been held behind closed doors in the heart of the palace.

After Mass the king and his lords would process back to the presence chamber through a huge throng of spectators. While they had been at worship the Lord Steward would have brought the Commons to the bar (or barrier) in the presence chamber, where they would listen to speeches by the Lord Chancellor and the king. The two houses then dispersed to discuss matters, the Lords next door to the watching chamber, known as the White Chamber, and the Commons into Westminster Abbey, where they would meet in the monks' refectory. So parliament itself met in the king's own palace before 1512 and near it were assembled most of the crucial offices of state – the Exchequer, the Chancery, the main law courts and many lesser departments such as the Office of Works.[29]

After the fire, then, although in one sense the loss of the privy palace did not interrupt the king's itinerary – Henry certainly made no attempt to repair it – there was a problem, as the crucial architectural interface between monarch, government and central administration had been broken. For a period, when the king wished to be near Westminster, and especially when parliament was meeting, he stayed over the river with the Archbishop of Canterbury at Lambeth, but in 1515 an opportunity was presented to rectify the problem.

In 1510 Wolsey had taken the lease on the Rectory House of St Bride's, Fleet Street, near the northern end of modern Blackfriars Bridge. It was in a useful location, just outside the walls of the City of London, not far from the Great Wardrobe and Baynard's Castle and just over the River Fleet from the Dominican friary of London, the Blackfriars. Here Wolsey started to build himself a house called Bridewell. As far as we can tell, the residence was a single courtyard with a long gallery, like the one at Eltham, jutting out from the main buildings and, in this case, running down to the river. Wolsey put Thomas Larke, his confessor and brother of his mistress, in charge of the work but, before the house got very far, Wolsey became Archbishop of York and so acquired York Place and Hampton Court. His new house was now surplus to requirements and he suggested to Henry that it might suit his. Bridewell thus became Henry VIII's first domestic building project.

In 1978, in advance of a big office redevelopment, part of the site of Bridewell was excavated and, ten years later, using an amazing eighteenth-century survey in the Museum of London, I was able to reconstruct the sequence in which the house was built, as well as some of its internal arrangements. What became clear is that Henry VIII revised Wolsey's original plans and embarked on a larger house with a second courtyard and more extensive kitchens. Work cracked on and, in the end, the king spent £20,000 on this new residence. In 1522 the house was lent to the retinue of the Emperor Charles V when he was Henry's guest in London and was himself staying just on the other side of the Fleet River in the Blackfriars. At this point the two buildings were linked by a very long, spindly gallery that vaulted over the Fleet and the City wall and joined on to the guest suite in Blackfriars. This, of course, meant that the friary and the house could be used together.

Bridewell was the perfect replacement for Westminster. It was situated on the river, so the king could easily reach it by barge; it was quite large and much more modern than Westminster; and, like Richmond and Greenwich, it was connected directly to a friary. Moreover, this was the largest and most important friary in England, with more than a century of close associations with the court. The friary may have been useful to the king for his personal devotions, but it was much more important as a substitute for Westminster Abbey for state ceremonial. It was to Bridewell, then, that Henry summoned parliament in 1523 and 1529. On both occasions the Lords assembled in the king's new house and processed across the bridge to Blackfriars, where they and the Commons held their deliberations.

So in the 1520s Bridewell was the new official royal seat. But it was no more favoured a residence than Westminster had been. Despite all Bridewell's possibilities for ceremonial and political use, Greenwich remained the king's favourite residence near London.[30]

At more or less the same time as Bridewell was rising on the banks of the Thames, the king acquired a new country house. This was in Essex, a house called New Hall which he bought for £1,000 from Sir Thomas Boleyn, father of his future second wife. As at Bridewell, plans were laid immediately for its expansion and, also as at Bridewell, work was put in the hands of one of Wolsey's building administrators, William Bolton, who was in charge of the cardinal's works at Hampton Court. The king spent at least £17,000 rebuilding this house and more furnishing it. One of the clerks of the Great Wardrobe was sent to Flanders and returned with 108 tapestries, all measured to fit specific rooms. Henry thought his

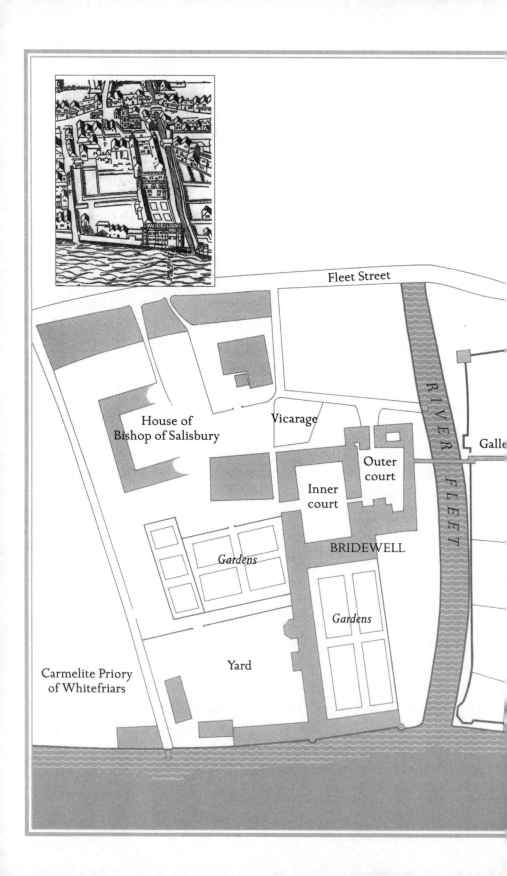

Fleet Street

House of
Bishop of Salisbury

Vicarage

RIVER FLEET

Galle

Outer
court

Inner
court

BRIDEWELL

Gardens

Gardens

Carmelite Priory
of Whitefriars

Yard

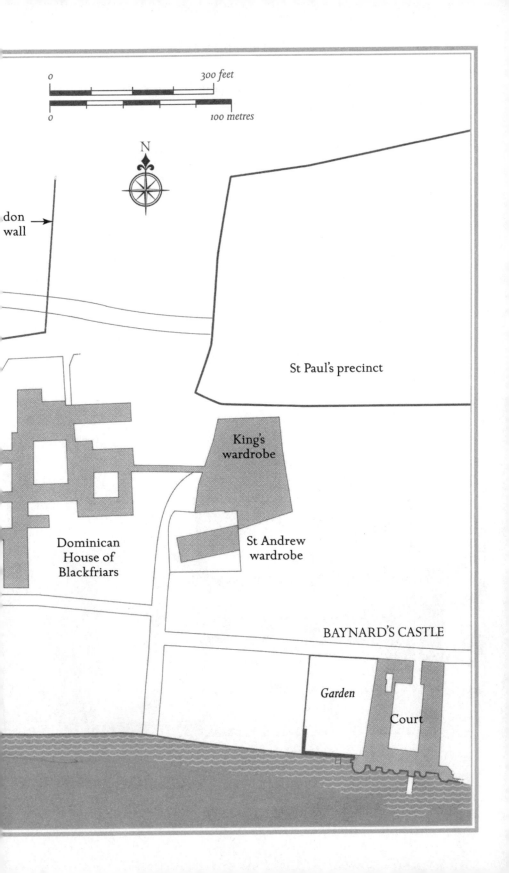

0   300 feet

0   100 metres

N

don
wall

St Paul's precinct

King's
wardrobe

Dominican
House of
Blackfriars

St Andrew
wardrobe

BAYNARD'S CASTLE

Garden

Court

new house so beautiful that he announced that its name would be changed to Beaulieu – beautiful place.

Sir Francis Bryan was made the Master of the Hunt for Beaulieu. One of the king's closest friends, he was a member of the Privy Chamber and the Master of the Toils, the man in charge of the king's hunting equipment. This appointment signalled the purpose of the new acquisition: it was an eastern version of Woodstock. Beaulieu lay on the northern edge of the great royal forest of Essex, the rump of which we know today as Epping Forest, and the king wanted to turn it into a major royal seat where guests could be entertained and he could hunt with his

New Hall, Essex, shown in a print of 1786. The house was renamed Beaulieu, meaning 'beautiful place', by Henry VIII. This view of the gatehouse range shows the very tall first-floor windows, a feature the house shared with Wolsey's Hampton Court and Bridewell.

friends. In 1523 he created Beaulieu an 'honour' – that is to say, the administrative centre of a large number of royal estates – a badge of considerable status.[31]

So in a period of fifteen years Cardinal Wolsey had set the young king up. He had a new house in central London, a big, beautiful new hunting seat in the country, a stunning pavilion in France, while in the meantime Greenwich had been converted into a pleasure dome for a teenage king. The story of royal building at the court of Henry VIII could have been over. But in fact it hadn't really started.

· V ·

NEW PASSIONS

Married Love

ALTHOUGH BY 1525 KATHARINE OF ARAGON had been the king's wife and close companion for sixteen years, and had given him a daughter, the Princess Mary, whom he adored, she had failed in the most important duty of an English consort: to give him a male heir. Worse, six years older than Henry, by this time she had lost her looks, put on weight and become withdrawn from court; her solace was now in her daughter and her religion. The king was still young and handsome, and he knew that he could sire a son: as the result of an affair with Elizabeth Blount he already had a boy, Henry Fitzroy, now a healthy six-year-old. During 1525 the king fell for Anne Boleyn, one of Katharine's ladies. Unlike his previous two mistresses, who had quickly shared his bed, Anne resisted; she would sleep with him only in a marriage bed – and so began a terrible personal tragedy.[1]

Henry wanted a son, but he wanted Anne more, and together they engineered the arguments for divorce, step by step. In June 1527 Henry finally confronted Katharine and told her that, as she had been his brother's wife, their marriage had been illegal and that she should choose the house to which she would like to retire from court. That summer, staying at Beaulieu, the former home of Anne's father, Henry assembled his closest friends for hunting, revelry and serious talk about divorce. Now that the king's passion for Anne was public knowledge, this presented the ultimate dilemma of etiquette. He and Katharine were still married and continued to live their lives constrained by the tightly drawn lines of court protocol. Henry wanted to break free, but Katharine wanted to reinforce all the traditions and norms that kept them together. Anne, on the other hand, was one of the queen's ladies with her own fixed position in a rigid hierarchy; she wanted to circumvent this to spend as much time as possible with the king.[2]

It was an unusual situation. There had been mistresses before, both in Henry's reign and in previous ones; but the divorce of a queen and her replacement by the king's mistress had no precedent in England and, in a world where every situation was managed in terms of precedent, this was extremely problematic. Architecturally, Katharine held all the cards. It was relatively easy for her to exclude Anne and to hold Henry to his duties as husband, which is why he informed her that he wanted to avoid living under the same roof as her. But soon Anne acquired her own base inside the royal houses. As early as May 1527, when Bishop Fox visited Henry at Greenwich the king received him in Anne Boleyn's lodgings. By March 1528 she had her own rooms below the king's at Windsor Castle and, two months later, supposedly because of an outbreak of smallpox, she removed herself from her lodging near the queen at Greenwich and was set up in the tiltyard gallery where she was visited by the king.[3] This was all very unsatisfactory, so Henry asked Wolsey to arrange for a separate residence for Anne near to Bridewell. We don't know what Wolsey suggested, but it is possible that he offered her Durham House, which he had acquired in 1523 upon adding the bishopric of Durham to his quiver of ecclesiastical appointments. At any rate, Anne did not like Wolsey's suggestion, preferring to make her own arrangements by taking the house of another courtier. Again, we don't know whose this was, but the king found it embarrassing and told her that it was not right that he should visit his lady lodged in the 'house of a servant'. Nevertheless, Anne was set up in an establishment of her own choosing near Bridewell. For a few days in November 1528 Henry went down into Surrey and stayed at the home of his close friend and Master of the Horse, Nicholas Carew; Katharine was ordered back to Greenwich and Anne went down to Surrey, staying only 5 miles away from the king.[4]

Marital Homes

The elaborate choreography needed for Henry and Anne to be together meant that they longed for a place of their own. In 1529 it became clear that this was going to be York Place, which Henry took over from Wolsey that year. Renamed Whitehall, it became not only the largest royal palace in England but one of the largest in Europe. It extended from what is now Trafalgar Square in the north to Downing Street in the south and covered both sides of the modern road called Whitehall. Its most important residential parts were destroyed in 1698 in a massive fire, thanks to the carelessness of a maid drying linen, so anyone looking for the Tudor palace today will be disappointed, as there is nothing to see from the street. Yet behind the Portland stone façades of government offices, and under the tarmac of the streets, much of the palace survives – or survived. For over the last seventy years most of it has been excavated.

The first excavations started in 1938 when the government began the massive new office block in Whitehall that we now know as the Ministry of Defence. Building this involved the demolition of the large Georgian mansions that had risen over the remains of the Tudor and Stuart palace. At the time nobody was sure how much would survive beneath them, but a trial trench astonished everyone: only a few feet below the ground were the well-preserved remains of England's greatest palace. Permission was given to record these before they were destroyed, and this was done at great speed by a small but brilliant group of Inspectors of Ancient Monuments from the then Office of Works. Then the bombs started to drop. Work stopped, and the inspectors were dispersed for war duties.

In 1951 it was decided to resume construction of the offices, but this time the pressure to build quickly was intense. The inspectors were allowed in, but only on condition that they did not hinder the main work, which was digging out everything to a depth of 25 feet. The Chancellor of the Exchequer, Sir Stafford Cripps, intervened at one point, buying the archaeologists a bit more time, but soon every scrap of the palace had been removed and replaced with massive concrete bomb-proof basements.

Photograph taken in 1939 from the roof of the old War Office showing the excavation of Whitehall Palace. The area shown covers the great hall and parts of the queen's lodgings. Under a temporary roof on the right is the vaulted wine cellar built by Wolsey.

A hiatus followed. Nobody attempted to write up the digs, and the papers, photographs and finds were put in store. Then, in 1961, Harold Macmillan decided to remodel and restore 10 Downing Street and the Treasury buildings. These were, in fact, built in the midst of the west side of the Tudor palace and again there was an opportunity to have a look at the surviving remains. But there was little enthusiasm for what was seen as the irritating interests of the Inspectors of Ancient Monuments and records were only made against official opposition.[5]

Thanks to the determination of a small number of archaeologists from the Ministry of Works, as it now was, a record was compiled of the findings at Whitehall made between 1938 and 1962. It was, however, a long time before anyone tried to make much sense of them. In 1988, when I had myself become an Inspector of Ancient Monuments, I was asked to help Michael Green, the excavator of the west side of Whitehall, to write up his findings. Between us we managed to fit together the jigsaw of standing remains and buried foundations to reconstruct the history of one half of the palace.

As work on this project was finishing, I began to look at the 1930s and 1950s excavations. Two of the original excavators were still alive and both gave me their papers, photographs and some memories, but really I was on my own. Making sense of the material was truly the archaeology of archaeology. Assembling all the material, I decided to give every wall, window, door opening and floor a unique number and then, from the excavators' notes, plans and photographs, worked out its date. This allowed me to draw a huge phased plan, over 9 feet long, showing every wall coloured up to represent some phase between the earliest buildings on site, dating from 1240, and the eighteenth-century houses. The final stage was drawing each phase on huge sheets of tracing paper, allowing the plan of the palace to be shown at several key points in time. As a result, since 1999 when I finally published my work, we have been able to understand how Henry VIII transformed York Place into Whitehall Palace – and it is a remarkable story.[6]

On 22 October 1529 Wolsey surrendered all his property to the king. He had failed to achieve a divorce for Henry, and he paid a terrible price. Accused of illegally using papal powers in England, he was forced to forfeit his goods and was banished to Yorkshire. Two days later Henry and Anne Boleyn, accompanied by her mother and Henry Norris, Henry's Groom of the Stool, arrived by barge at the York Place landing stage. The king had obviously been to the house many times before as Wolsey's guest, but as it had only one suite of lodgings he had stayed the night there only a couple of times.[7] This meant that he had not fully appreciated the size and splendour of what Wolsey had built and now he was taken aback at its magnificence. He decided to use the house immediately: parliament had been summoned to meet at Blackfriars on 3 November and he now liked York Place much more than his new house at Bridewell. The Great Wardrobe was set to work and the house was set up for the king, who arrived there on 2 November to stay for the parliamentary session.

The house was still full of Wolsey's goods and during the prorogation of parliament, while the king was at Windsor, a detailed inventory was made of all the cardinal's belongings. The king was soon back and spent much of November there, while the lawyers worked to find a way of transferring the freehold to the Crown. York Place was not Wolsey's personal property – it was a tied house that came with the archbishopric of York – so he was forced to assign the house to the king before a judge. The legalities over, Henry and Anne moved to Greenwich, where there was one big topic of conversation: their new house.

Unquestionably one of the most important reasons for their enthusiasm for York Place was that, at this stage, it still had only one set of lodgings – for the king. The fact that there was no queen's lodging made it easy for Henry to stay at the house without Katharine. Anne, meanwhile, was given a cosy panelled apartment directly under the king's rooms while plans were made for the house's renovation.

The plan that Henry and Anne cooked up in December 1529 was astonishingly ambitious. The old archbishop's residence was to remain at the heart of the new building; some of the rooms, and a wonderful long gallery, were virtually new, built by Wolsey, but the house was too small for a king. The idea was for a huge new palace that would contain vastly enlarged lodgings, including a fine suite of new rooms for Henry on the south front, with a long gallery that would be carried by a gatehouse over King Street; there would also be new kitchens. On the other side of the road would be a recreation centre and extensive gardens. Next to this would be a new hunting park that could be easily reached from the king's rooms. Set on the other side of the park would be a satellite house, the future residence of the son and heir that Anne would bear the king. This was all worked out by Henry and Anne and drawn on huge sheets of paper and parchment by James Nedeham, the king's master carpenter.

But there was a problem. York Place, quite unlike Greenwich or Richmond, was in the middle of a town. The archbishop's house, which Wolsey had extended, was bounded to the east by the river, to the west by a road, King Street, and to the north and south by people's houses, taverns and shops. It was not a very promising site for a massive new palace. As usual, Wolsey had the answer – not in person, for he was now in disgrace – but in his legacy. While he owned York Place he had extended it to the south by buying, one by one, the neighbouring private properties. This is what the king now proceeded to do – but on a massive scale. Transactions were in the hands of a rising star at court, Thomas Cromwell, who had made his reputation as Cardinal Wolsey's property lawyer, concluding the complex negotiations associated with the cardinal's two colleges at Ipswich and Oxford, and probably at York Place and his domestic residences too. It was both as a smooth administrator and an amusing, intelligent and cultivated courtier that Cromwell came to Henry's notice. As the king attempted to transfer his fallen minister's assets to himself, who better to unravel the legalities than the man who had ravelled them in the first place? From this point Cromwell became key to the king's architectural ambitions, masterminding at first the legal work of exchange and acquisition and later the financial aspects. Henry ordered Cromwell to have surveyors measure up and value every property along King Street; there were only around twenty-five owners, but some properties had dozens of houses or cottages on them. This was valuable land and the tenanted houses brought their owners a sizable rent; nobody was keen to give away their profits and so houses were valued on the basis of ten times their annual rental yield. Aristocratic owners haggled with Cromwell, securing even better deals. In the end it cost the king £1,129 to buy everyone out.[8]

Henry was in a hurry and did not wait for the boring legalities to be completed. The royal workmen were demolishing people's houses before many owners had actually signed up. This was the start of sixteen years of more or less continuous building. The project was a monster that greedily devoured everything before it. It ate money: over £13,000 in the first eighteen months (a colossal sum, bearing in mind the whole of Beaulieu cost £17,000). It also swallowed up other buildings – the privy palace at Westminster was demolished and its materials carted up the road; the medieval royal manor of Kennington was also crunched up and ferried to York Place, while a new long gallery at Esher Place, another of Wolsey's houses, was dismantled and brought to site.

Section of an Elizabethan map of London dating from the 1560s showing Whitehall in its Tudor prime. At bottom left are Westminster Abbey and Westminster Palace. At the top is Charing Cross, today's Trafalgar Square. The two gates can be seen straddling King Street. On the right of King Street was the residential part of the palace. On the left was the recreation area and beyond that the park.

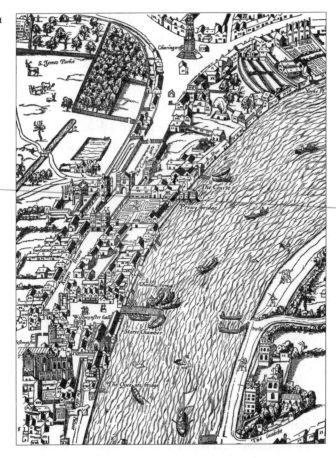

As well as the physical changes, Henry decided that the new royal home must be renamed. 'York Place' was indelibly associated with Wolsey, but the remodelled house was to be something different – indeed it was to become the foremost residence of the realm, the king's palace. So it was proclaimed that it should now be known as the Palace of Westminster. This was probably as confusing then as it is today, there already being a Palace of Westminster, so, in fact, it very quickly acquired a nickname – Whitehall.[9]

Work was never going to be quick. The whole of the Whitehall site was low-lying and wet, and the ground had to be carefully prepared. The riverside walls were masterpieces of engineering. Long, iron-shod oak piles were rammed into the foreshore to make a solid foundation.

On top of these were laid thick elm planks which formed the base for tightly packed chalk foundations. On these were built footings with broken and re-used bricks, and then the fair-faced walls rose above that.

Like Greenwich, Whitehall was a brick palace, but parts of the upper floors were timber-framed and this unquestionably made the work quicker. Soon, though, there was reason for the king to push the project on even faster. In August 1531 Henry brutally and decisively sent Katharine away. Up to that point the structures of the royal itinerary and of court etiquette had preserved her position as royal consort despite the fact that the king was spending all his time with Anne. It was also now widely known that Henry intended to marry his mistress.[10] Whitehall swarmed with workmen, over 900 of them labouring under six clerks, and work continued through lunchtimes and breaktimes into the night.

ROYAL WEDDING

At first Henry had believed in Wolsey's ability to get his marriage to Katharine annulled by the Pope, but as it became clear that this was not going to be agreed he had a religious conversion: he suddenly became aware that the Pope's jurisdiction extended only to his own diocese in Rome and that, in England, the king's own writ was supreme. He, Henry, could therefore define doctrine in his own country and, in the case of his divorce, instruct the Archbishop of Canterbury to investigate the issue and decide what to do. This was not only a matter of conscience; it was also the magic bullet for which the king had been searching and, in January 1531, he demanded that he be recognized as the Supreme Head and Sole Protector of the English Church.

In October 1532 Henry and Anne went to France together to meet King Francis I. During that visit they probably slept together and, back in London, by 17 December when Henry made a visit of inspection to Whitehall, he knew that Anne was pregnant. The royal lovers were at Greenwich for most of January but, early in the morning on the 24th,

Henry slipped into a specially prepared, and newly matted, barge with Anne and made for Whitehall.[11] They disembarked on the landing stage and walked through the near-completed galleries to the gatehouse, where, climbing the spiral staircase, they entered a room that was destined be the king's private study containing all his most treasured possessions. They were accompanied by Roland Lee, one of the king's chaplains; Henry's two closet companions, Henry Norris and Thomas Heneage; as well as a lady-in-waiting for Anne. In this room, overlooking the new palace, the deed was done: Henry and Anne were finally man and wife.

Anne's pregnancy and her coronation, which was set for June 1533, had significant architectural implications. First, at Whitehall, the choice of which for the royal marriage was deliberate and symbolic. It was a new start for the king and for the country: a new queen, a male heir and a modern, up-to-date palace replacing the ancient Palace of Westminster.[12] The builders had more or less finished the king's rooms but, as we have seen, there had intentionally been no rooms for the queen. Now that Katharine was gone, they were directed to make a queen's side; this may always have been the intention, but we know that in early 1533 it became the urgent priority. Then there were implications at the Tower of London, which was to play a crucial part in the coronation ceremonies. There Anne would spend the night before processing through the City to Westminster Abbey. A survey of the fortress put in hand in 1532 listed a huge backlog of general repairs and recommended a variety of improvements to the king's, and especially the queen's, lodgings. They were certainly needed: although, as we have seen, Henry VII had improved the royal lodgings at the Tower as a base for his obsessive accountancy, Henry VIII had hardly stayed at the place, and not at all since 1520. The paymaster of the works at the Tower called the lodgings 'wonderous foul'. Huge numbers of workmen were mobilized to modernize the king's rooms and build a whole new wing for the queen. The queen's watching chamber, the only one to be retained from the old arrangement, was entered from the king's watching chamber, and beyond it was her presence chamber. Then came a long gallery leading to her

Plan and bird's-eye view of the Tower of London done in 1597. In the middle is the White Tower and in front of it the Jewel House and the queen's lodgings built in 1532.

privy chamber and dining chamber, and beyond that four more rooms, presumably including her bedchamber.[13]

It was unusual to place a gallery between the presence chamber and the queen's more private rooms – normally galleries were private spaces accessed only from the privy lodgings. At the Tower, however, the requirements were different, as the coronation involved complex public ceremonial and the gallery created a very large space in the queen's rooms in which this could take place. The door at the end of the gallery led to the private feminine world of the queen, where she would prepare herself for the coronation.

Just as Henry obsessively inspected works at Whitehall, so he made trips upriver from Greenwich to check progress at the Tower. Work there was under the control of Thomas Cromwell, for whom, as he climbed the ladder at court, a crucial rung was his appointment as Master of the Jewel House in April 1533. This gave him not only access to the king's coffers, but a base in the Tower of London too. We have seen that in his dying days Henry VII had built a new Jewel House at the Tower near the great hall – it was in this building that Cromwell first set up shop.

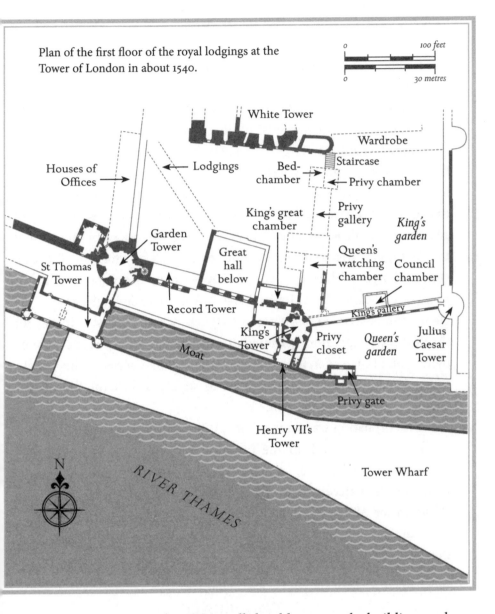

Plan of the first floor of the royal lodgings at the Tower of London in about 1540.

White Tower

Wardrobe

Houses of Offices — Lodgings — Bed-chamber — Staircase — Privy chamber

King's great chamber — Privy gallery — King's garden

Garden Tower

Great hall below

St Thomas' Tower

Record Tower

Queen's watching chamber — Council chamber

King's gallery

King's Tower — Privy closet — Queen's garden — Julius Caesar Tower

Moat

Privy gate

Henry VII's Tower

Tower Wharf

N

RIVER THAMES

0   100 feet
0   30 metres

It was thus obvious that Cromwell should manage the building work at the Tower for Anne's coronation. In December 1532 he welcomed Henry, Anne, an assorted group of courtiers, plus the French ambassador to the Tower. He had reorganized the contents of the Jewel House and showed the party the plate there; perhaps he also took out the regalia for Anne to see. But the real purpose of the visit was for the king to present Anne with plate for her household: £1,188 worth of gold and silver plate, chandeliers, bowls and goblets were identified and made over to the future queen. Cromwell then led them through the royal lodgings to view the progress made so far.[14]

Thanks to the efforts of some 400 workmen toiling round the clock, work was, of course, completed in time, and Anne arrived at the Tower on 29 May 1533 amidst a huge flotilla of barges. These vessels were nothing like a modern barge; they were highly decorated rowing boats up to 70 feet long with covered cabins ornamented with painted and gilded carvings. The queen and her ladies sat in one barge and a second carried additional female attendants. The king's barge was full of his Yeomen of the Guard and was followed by other barges full of courtiers. Together with the barges of the City Guilds and Aldermen, the total fleet was over 300 vessels. Landing at Tower Wharf, Anne was lovingly greeted by Henry and proceeded to their new lodgings, where they were to stay for the next forty-eight hours. Though the two bedchambers were separated by the long range of new rooms, the king still had access to his queen-to-be; James Nedeham was ordered to supply a lock for the queen's chamber 'that serveth the king's key'.[15]

The coronation was set for 1 June, Whitsunday, and the night before, the formal procession from the Tower to Westminster over, Anne stayed in the king's bedchamber at Whitehall. The workmen must have done their job; the palace was ready, and the day after she was crowned in Westminster Abbey, Whitehall played host to a magnificent coronation tournament in the new tiltyard, with a feast and a ball held afterwards in the queen's new lodgings.[16]

WHITEHALL

So what was Whitehall like in the summer of 1533? To the citizen of London there had been a huge transformation. Travelling from the City of London to Whitehall in Wolsey's time, people would have passed a long, high brick wall in which there was a gatehouse that led to a large inner court. On the other side of this was Wolsey's great hall, completed just before his fall. In 1533 this gatehouse was still there, forming the main entrance to the palace, but another much larger and more imposing gatehouse also now spanned the road. You couldn't get from the City to Westminster without going through this, and beyond it were now two very high walls that enclosed the palace on either side. The king had essentially canalized the public thoroughfare, with the result that thousands of people a day with their carts, horses and litters passed through the centre of the palace 'Between the Walls' (as it was called).

Gatehouses were very familiar to Londoners. The City of London was still surrounded by a wall and it was impossible to get in unless through a gatehouse; the many precincts of the City, and all its great houses, were entered through gatehouses. So in one sense the new Whitehall gatehouse was simply another of these, but it did two things, both, I think, novel. The first is that it was decorated with roundels made of terracotta containing the busts of Roman emperors. Roundels decorated the arch of Constantine in Rome, the most famous gateway in classical civilization, and there is a sense in which the Whitehall gate was a triumphal arch proclaiming the entrance to the new royal precinct.

Secondly, the new gate was not just a symbol of the sort of palace Henry wanted to build and the sort of king he wanted to be; it was also an integral part of his own private lodgings. In its upper floor it contained Henry's private study (where he had married) and, on the first floor, carried a gallery across the road linking his private rooms with the whole recreation centre on the west side. We will look at the recreation centre later in this chapter, but for the moment we shall visit Henry and Anne in the residential part of the palace.

Entering the outer court from King Street, through what was known as the court gate, visitors could see in front of them the great hall. It was garishly decorated in large black and white squares, like a chessboard, and its porch, as was usual, led into the lower end of the hall. It was 40 feet wide and 75 feet long, comfortably large enough to park nine London double-decker buses. Like the great hall at Eltham, it had a hammerbeam roof in homage to Westminster's great hall, in the centre of which was a vent or louvre to let smoke out if a fire were lit in the stone hearth in the middle of the room. In practice this never happened, but a great hall was a very traditional building and a central hearth was expected and required for show if nothing else. At the far end of the room was a dais lit by a tall bay window, and opposite this was a large archway leading to a staircase.

At the top of the stairs was a gallery lit by windows overlooking a little cloister. Most people would turn right and enter the watching chamber. This had been built by Wolsey in 1515 and was raised up over an elegant vaulted wine cellar. When the excavations took place in the 1930s the wine cellar was saved, but it was in the way of the new offices so it was put on steel rollers and jacks, then moved sideways and down to sit in one of the basements of the Ministry of Defence, where it can be visited by those patient enough to clear the complex security arrangements. The room above was, of course, long gone by then, but we know that Henry, at least initially, kept its rich panelling, its ceiling decorated in geometrical patterns by gilded timber battens and the brass door locks engraved with Wolsey's arms.

The next room was the presence chamber, the oldest room at Whitehall, originally part of the medieval palace of the archbishops. In this room, swathed with tapestry, was a dais covered by a canopy on which sat a chair of estate, or throne. The king had his coat of arms carved on the fireplace in here, expunging the arms of Wolsey. This room, like the hall and the watching chamber, was open to all at court. But the door from the presence chamber led to a gallery, off which was the king's privy closet and, beyond that, the zone occupied by the Privy Chamber.

This is where the real novelty begins. The privy chamber, which had started life under Henry VII as a single room with a bedchamber and study, expanded at Whitehall to become an entire palace within a palace – a suite of rooms more extensive than the outer rooms themselves. The Whitehall privy chamber led not to the king's bedroom but to a withdrawing chamber and then beyond that to a study, dressing room, dining room, bedroom, bathroom, library and on to a long gallery. At the end of that was the gatehouse in which Henry and Anne had married, with its secret upper study or Jewel House, as it became known. To understand why this was so novel, and why it was so important, we need to take a few steps back and look more closely at how the household of Henry VII morphed into the new household of Henry VIII.[17]

The fact is that at first it didn't. In 1509 the young Henry exerted himself by sacking (and executing) a couple of his father's ministers, by plunging into sport at court and lusting for war with France, but looking closely at his household and government, it was not much different from that of his father. Then, in around 1517, things began to change. This is perhaps not very surprising, as Henry VII had managed his household by keeping it at a distance. His withdrawal into the privy chamber made him a cold and distant monarch. This was not the younger Henry's way. For eight years he had rubbed shoulders with his courtiers in the lists and in the saddle; his kingship was forged in the rough-and-tumble of companionship.

While Henry VII's Groom of the Stool, the chief of his Privy Chamber, had been Hugh Denys, a self-effacing administrator, Henry VIII chose William Compton, his best friend and boon jousting companion. Compton's intimacies with the king extended far beyond holding the royal lavatory paper. He organized trysts with mistresses, conveyed sensitive messages to other courtiers and arrested the Duke of Buckingham at the king's behest. At first he was the only favourite in the Privy Chamber, but the jousts of 1515, and particularly 1517, brought a group of younger courtiers to the fore. They were all under twenty, from noble or knightly backgrounds, and became Henry's best friends.

The king was thus at the centre of a high-spirited gang of young men obsessed with sport and out to have fun, often at other people's expense. In the view of older courtiers, who were used to the monarch being treated with deep respect, it was all rather undignified and completely unstructured. However, in 1518, the king's mates – 'the Minions', as they had been nicknamed – were formally brought into the structure of the household. In imitation of the household of the king of France, who had a similar band of minions, Henry VIII created them Gentlemen of the Privy Chamber. This title distinguished them from the grooms of Henry VII's time, who were responsible for sweeping the floors and lighting the fires. The gentlemen now had full access to the king's private rooms, where they lived in close proximity to their sovereign.

The purpose of the Privy Chamber, as originally conceived, had now

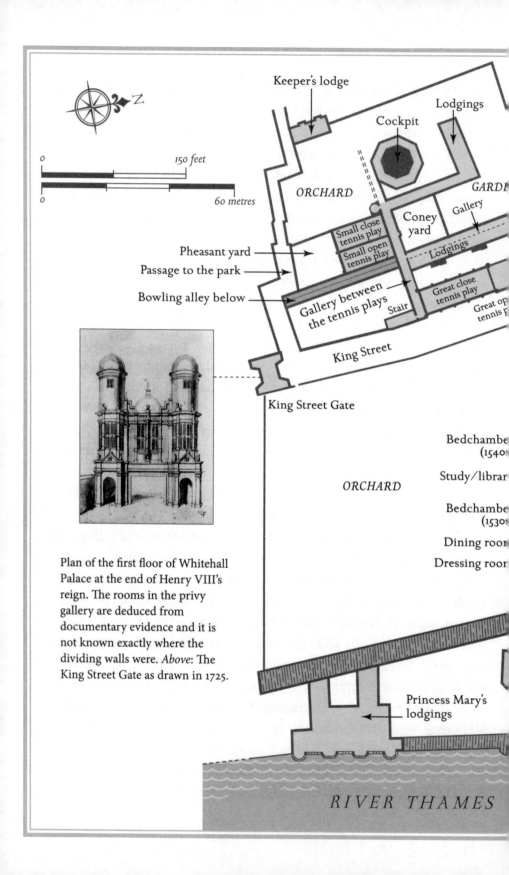

Keeper's lodge

Lodgings

Cockpit

N

0   150 feet

0   60 metres

ORCHARD

GARDI

Coney
yard

Gallery

Small close
tennis play

Pheasant yard

Small open
tennis play

Lodgings

Passage to the park

Bowling alley below

Gallery between
the tennis plays

Great close
tennis play

Stair

Great op
tennis p

King Street

King Street Gate

Bedchambe
(1540)

Study/librar

ORCHARD

Bedchambe
(1530)

Dining roor

Dressing roor

Plan of the first floor of Whitehall
Palace at the end of Henry VIII's
reign. The rooms in the privy
gallery are deduced from
documentary evidence and it is
not known exactly where the
dividing walls were. *Above*: The
King Street Gate as drawn in 1725.

Princess Mary's
lodgings

RIVER THAMES

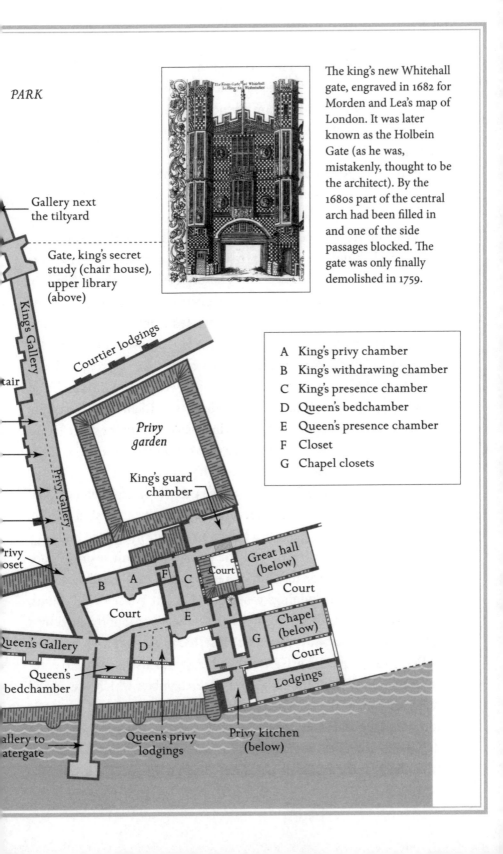

PARK

Gallery next the tiltyard

Gate, king's secret study (chair house), upper library (above)

The king's new Whitehall gate, engraved in 1682 for Morden and Lea's map of London. It was later known as the Holbein Gate (as he was, mistakenly, thought to be the architect). By the 1680s part of the central arch had been filled in and one of the side passages blocked. The gate was only finally demolished in 1759.

King's Gallery

tair

Courtier lodgings

Privy Gallery

Privy garden

King's guard chamber

A King's privy chamber
B King's withdrawing chamber
C King's presence chamber
D Queen's bedchamber
E Queen's presence chamber
F Closet
G Chapel closets

'rivy oset

Great hall (below)

B A F C Court

Court

Court E

Queen's Gallery

D

Chapel (below)

G

Court

Queen's bedchamber

Lodgings

allery to atergate

Queen's privy lodgings

Privy kitchen (below)

been completely subverted. It was no longer a device to guarantee the king's security and privacy, but had become the way in which the king's friends were institutionally bound to him round the clock. We do not need to follow the struggles of first Wolsey, then Thomas Cromwell to try to control and subdue the Privy Chamber during the 1530s, but only to note that over the years between 1518, when the Minions officially became the Gentlemen, and 1532, the Privy Chamber matured into a powerful and structured department of the household filled with the king's closest friends.[18]

This institutional maturity was accompanied by an architectural one. All Henry VII's buildings erected physical as well as institutional barriers between himself and his court. This can be seen in detail at Windsor, where the rooms survive, but it is also plain at Richmond, where the king's rooms were in a moated tower separated from the great hall and chapel, and at Greenwich, where there was also a tower containing the king's privy lodgings. Wolsey, fifteen years older than the young Henry VIII, perpetuated these arrangements at Bridewell, where the king's and queen's lodgings were on top of each other, as at Richmond, and were constrained by a tight courtyard plan. These early Tudor houses reflected the arrangements at the ancient Palace of Westminster, where the king's private life was conducted in a separate privy palace.

Whitehall was different. Instead of the privy lodgings being stacked up in a tower or divided from the rest of the house by a physical barrier, they were laid out in a long line in a gallery in a single integrated building; the public zone flowed directly into the private with only a single door separating them. This was the start of a new sort of royal residence.

In 1533 the queen's lodgings were carved out of Wolsey's old rooms, but they were no less magnificent for that. They were approached by a spiral staircase, 11 feet wide, which was inserted to get people up from the great hall into the queen's presence chamber. It was also possible to enter the queen's rooms from the king's presence chamber, which was useful on state occasions. The queen's presence chamber, which had a big bay window looking out over the river, was Wolsey's old privy chamber. Anne's privy chamber beyond was in Wolsey's bedchamber and her bedchamber was the cardinal's old closet. Beyond this was the loveliest of the cardinal's galleries, around 170 feet long and looking out over the Thames. Its ceiling was decorated with gilded wooden battens in a geometrical pattern, and below this was a richly carved and moulded frieze from which hung, when Wolsey handed it over to the king, panels of cloth of gold.[19] We do not have the detailed accounts that go with the conversion of these rooms for Anne, but we can be certain that every badge and escutcheon of Wolsey's was erased and that the rooms were covered instead in the initials and heraldic devices of the new queen.

Intersecting the queen's side, between her privy lodgings and her long gallery, was a short gallery linking her rooms with the king's – the corridor they used when they wished to sleep with each other. At this crucial nexus of the palace, where the two sets of royal lodgings met, was the entry to the watergate. This was essentially the royal front door. Very rarely would the king arrive on horse through the court gate; for most of the time he moved by barge along the river – the M25 of the Tudor age. The watergate was a large, covered timber landing stage approached by a gallery. This had to be built quite far out into the river, as the Thames was much wider and more sluggish at Westminster than it is now. To ensure that barges could moor at low tide, steps led down from the covered part of the gate on to the water. Because it was roofed and hidden from view, the watergate allowed the royal family to come and go in complete privacy and to enter their privy lodgings without traversing the public rooms of the palace.

Arriving by barge and entering the palace in the 1530s, you might easily imagine that you were at one of the king's country manors. For Whitehall, unlike Westminster, was set in a matrix of gardens and parks. The land to the south of the privy gallery was laid out in 1532 as an orchard – then a type of Tudor ornamental garden which, confusingly, had no trees in it. Later known as the great garden, it was depicted by an anonymous court painter (see plate section). This remarkable painting, in which the garden is an incidental glimpse rather than the main event, shows a large area divided up into compartments by low brick walls topped by painted rails. Intersecting the rails at various points were tall posts, each bearing a heraldic beast; the rails and posts were painted green and white, the Tudor heraldic colours. The compartments were

planted with hedges and low flowers. The whole effect was enjoyable from the ground but designed to have most impact from the windows of the royal rooms. A stair from the king's privy lodgings led down to the garden; at some date this was painted with the story of Adam and Eve, perhaps a reference to the fact that it descended to the royal Garden of Eden.[20]

A second set of stairs – the Park Stairs – on the west side of the gatehouse led down from the royal lodgings and allowed the king to access his new park. Securing the freehold of the land immediately around York Place was the smallest (though the most complex) part of the land transactions that went into the making of Whitehall. The really ambitious acquisitions created a series of hunting grounds to the north and west. Sixty acres were bought from Abingdon Abbey, another 60 acres from

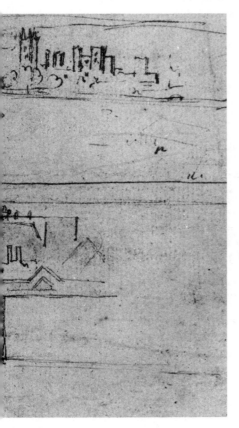

Sketch by Anthonis van den Wyngaerde of around 1544 showing Whitehall from the river. The artist found the perspective baffling and so various elements are in the wrong place. However, in the foreground can be seen the large covered watergate that led into the heart of the privy lodgings. Directly above this is the court gate, the main entrance into the palace from King Street. On the left is the great garden with a fountain in its middle. The gatehouse can be seen spanning the road and on the other side is the cockpit and the great close tennis play (for which see page 144). In the distance, on the right can be seen St James's across the park.

Burton Lazar Hospital, 94 acres from the Mercers' Company, and from Westminster Abbey came the huge manor of Hyde (620 acres) plus the smaller ones of Neate and Ebury. Together these meant that virtually all the land from modern Ebury Bridge in the west to Oxford Street in the north and St Martin's Lane in the east now belonged to the Crown.[21]

The immediate parkland – what today we call St James's Park – was walled. In 1532 more than 12,000 loads of rubble were carted from the old privy palace at Westminster and rammed into 1.7 miles of foundation trench. Millions of bricks were fired and supplied to the bricklayers who slowly encircled the park with an 11-foot-high wall. A section of this survives, nearly to its original height, on the ground floor of 10 Downing Street. In an area used for staff refreshment, large chiller cabinets are pushed up against an expanse of bare red brickwork. Most people who

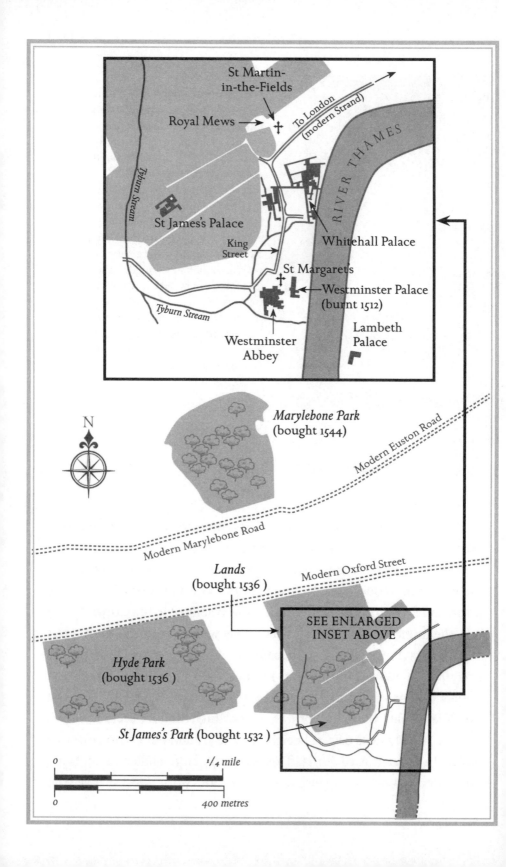

eat their sandwiches in here, glued to their iPhones, don't realize that they are looking at the security wall built by Henry VIII to enclose Whitehall Palace's home park.

The park was full of watercourses and these were diverted and dammed, creating a pond and a number of new culverts. A moat was dug between the park and the palace, and a bridge built over it so the king could ride out from the Park Stairs. Although there was a lodge in the park, the stables were at the Charing Cross mews, on the site of what is now the National Gallery in Trafalgar Square, where, since the thirteenth century, kings had kept their birds of prey. In 1515 Henry VIII had added to the complex, erecting new stables at a cost of £200; although the king had no base in Westminster at this time, he still needed horses when he came by barge from Greenwich, and Charing Cross was a convenient base. With the construction of Whitehall and its parks, the Royal Mews was suddenly at the centre of Henry's geography. Then, in the summer of 1534, disaster struck and a massive fire destroyed everything: hay, horses and all. Temporary arrangements were made which were not superseded until 1547.[22]

At this point the area of London now known as St James's was still open countryside. As a consequence, it had been regarded as a good location for Westminster's leper hospital, founded in the mid-thirteenth century. The hospital, its chapel and the lodgings attached to it were always, to a greater or lesser extent, in the orbit of Westminster Palace. Several royal clerks had rented the residential parts and, in the fifteenth century, several bishops and royal ministers lived there. By the reign of Henry VIII there was not only a comfortable mansion attached to it, but the hospital church had become a fashionable place to worship for the richer residents of Westminster. It was also well endowed, owning 160 acres of land in its immediate environs. So when Henry VIII bought the

Henry VIII's Westminster and Whitehall was not just a centre of residence, government and business; it was a centre of recreation set, by the end of his reign, in a series a large hunting parks. Today's royal parks – Regent's Park, Hyde Park, Green Park and St James's Park – were all bought by the king in the 1530s and 1540s as a setting for Westminster.

hospital and land and annexed them to Whitehall, he also acquired another house.

Most large royal manors had subsidiary houses to which the king could withdraw with a small number of companions: as we have seen, Woodstock had Langley, and we also know that Greenwich had a satellite manor at Wanstead and Richmond had one at Hanworth – so, was St James's intended to be the royal satellite to Whitehall? Or was it perhaps intended for Anne herself, as a new London residence for the queen to replace the riverside Baynard's Castle? Or was it intended to become a nursery house for the heir that Anne was to bear the king, as Eltham had been to the royal manor of Greenwich? As we shall see, St James's did, indeed, become the official nursery house for the royal family and the home of successive Princes of Wales, and there is no reason to imagine that this was anything other than the original intention.

It was to be a handsome thing, with two brick-built courtyards, one on the south with sets of royal lodgings joining in a tall, slender tower overlooking the park. This was to be approached by an outer court through a great gatehouse, the one that you can still see today at the bottom of St James's Street (see page 254). It was small compared to Whitehall and even compared to Bridewell, but it was designed to be subsidiary to Whitehall and its relatively modest size would have suited the smaller household of a royal child.

PARKSIDE

As Henry and Anne laid out Whitehall they designed a large recreation centre known as the Parkside, so called because it was on the other side of King Street next to what is now St James's Park.[23]

The Parkside remained in use as Whitehall's sport, recreation and entertainment centre right up to the Civil War, but, at the Restoration in 1660, it was slowly converted into luxury residences for courtiers and the mistresses of Charles II. It was still a courtier housing estate when Whitehall burned down in 1698. While the whole of the east side of the palace was destroyed, together with all the offices of state that it contained, the Parkside was unscathed and it was decided, on a temporary basis, to relocate the government offices from the east side into it. Today, over 300 years later, the Cabinet Office and the Prime Minister's office are still on the Parkside and, remarkably, you can still see, in number 70 Whitehall, remains of Henry VIII's original recreation zone. These fragments, together with the excavations that took place in 1962, enable us to get a very clear idea of what Henry built in his leisure centre in the early 1530s.

Perhaps slightly surprisingly, Henry VII had taken up tennis in 1494 at the age of thirty-seven and quite quickly commissioned courts – or, to give them their sixteenth-century name, 'tennis plays' – at, amongst other places, Woodstock, Windsor, Westminster and Richmond. In 1506, when he was entertaining Philip of Burgundy (the king of Castile) at Windsor, Henry VII took him to the gallery overlooking the tennis court there, where were 'laid two cushions of cloth of gold for the two kings . . . where played my Lord Marquis [of Dorset], the Lord Howard, and two other knights together and, after the King of Castile had seen them play a while, he made parley with the Lord Marquis of Dorset, the King looking on them, but the King of Castile played with the racquet and gave the Lord Marquis fifteen'. The tennis court at Windsor was set in view of Henry's new privy tower, but at Richmond it formed part of a whole recreation zone in the corner of the gardens. In 1501 this was described as 'houses of pleasure to disport in at chess, tables, dice, cards, bills, bowling alleys butts for archers and goodly tennis plays; as well as to use the said plays and disports as to behold them so disporting'.[24]

Henry VII's Richmond was the model for the Parkside at Whitehall, a collection of sporting facilities like a miniature Olympic park. The largest area was (of course) given over to a tiltyard, first used after the coronation of Anne Boleyn when the king and queen were able to watch from their new gatehouse. To the west of the gatehouse was the tiltyard gallery, a continuation of the privy gallery, at the far end of which were the Park Stairs, already mentioned – the king's back door into the park. The tiltyard gallery was not only a platform for viewing jousting, but also the backdrop to it, with towers at its end to contribute to the chivalric atmosphere. It was thoughtfully provided with its own garderobe for spectators taken short.

Next to the gallery was the first of four tennis courts. Two types of tennis were played in the early sixteenth century, requiring either a small or a large court; the courts could be indoor (close) or outdoor (open). The court next to the tiltyard gallery was a great open court, but south of that was the great close court. This, together with its exactly contemporary pair at Hampton Court, was one of the most extraordinary buildings of its age. Seeing it from the outside, a passing Londoner would have been convinced that he was looking at some great chapel or hall, for the court was more than 50 feet high and 90 feet long, with 20-foot-high windows separated by tall buttresses crowned with stone beasts holding gilded vanes. On each corner was a turret, the top part of which was decorated with a chessboard effect in flint and chalk.

At the south end of the court was a gallery at first-floor level and from this, through windows protected by red-painted wire mesh, you could watch the game below. This gallery, known as the gallery between

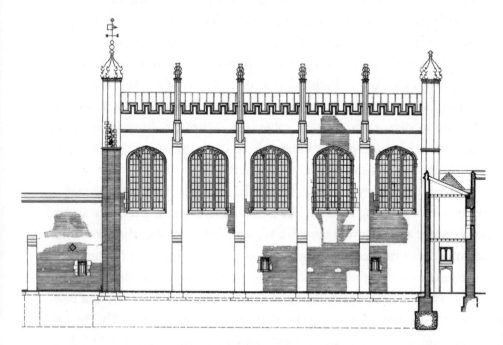

North elevation of the great close tennis play at Whitehall Palace. The gallery between the tennis plays can be seen in section to the right. The shaded areas are surviving patches of Tudor brickwork still visible in the Cabinet Office. Drawing by H. J. M. Green.

the tennis plays, also had windows that allowed spectators to look down into two more courts – the small open tennis play and the small close tennis play. This was the key to sport at court: these were not solitary games undertaken to promote good health or individual sporting prowess; they were intensely competitive activities on which large bets were laid and so it was vital that there were good facilities for the spectators. The gallery between the tennis plays could be reached from the tiltyard gallery by means of another long communication gallery and would be thronged with spectators when the king himself played. One ambassador wrote that 'it was the prettiest thing in the world to see him play; his fair skin glowing through a shirt of finest texture'. In 1533 Henry challenged the Emperor Charles V to a game at his new court at Bridewell; after eleven games they diplomatically called it a draw. Courtiers might not be so generous with their sovereign. Anne Boleyn's brother beat the king four times in a row in April 1530, Henry paying him 10s a game for the privilege. After a vigorous game the king could don his velvet tennis coat, a sort of Tudor tracksuit, and, when he hurt his foot playing, he wore a matching black velvet slipper.[25]

There was a tennis mania at court in the 1530s. Almost every royal house had a tennis court and, in 1528, one Anthony Annesley was appointed as the Keeper of the Plays. At Hampton Court, Greenwich and Whitehall the keeper had a special house in which were, as well as living accommodation, stores for nets, balls and other equipment. The king's own racquets were kept in his lodgings; in 1547 seven were found in a closet next to his privy chamber at Greenwich. Another role of the keeper was to rent the plays out to courtiers – the day rate could be as much as 2s 6d. There was no shortage of takers as most male courtiers liked to take up a racquet.

Another sport popular at court was bowling and the Parkside had a long covered bowling alley next to the small open tennis play. Tudor bowling was unlike any type played in England today. The bowling alleys, which were very long (one at Hampton Court was over 230 feet), had sloped sides which were used to curve the balls as close as possible to a jack. The balls were wooden and when the Whitehall alley was excavated in the 1960s one of them was found beneath the floor. At Hampton Court there was a special turning shop where these balls, shaped like a fat flat cheese, were made. At the far end of the alley was a recess where the royal servants would wait, out of danger, to collect and return the balls. High wooden boards were provided for the spectators to lean on while they watched and betted.

Successfully playing tennis, or bowls, with the king relied on judging his mood. Sir Nicholas Carew, one of Henry's oldest friends, allegedly fatally fell out with him during a game of bowls. Apparently Henry 'gave this knight opprobrious language, betwixt jest and earnest; to which the other returned an answer rather true than discreet'. The king, 'being no good fellow in repartees, was so highly offended thereat that Sir Nicholas fell from the top of his favour to the bottom of his displeasure'. Only months later he ended up on a scaffold on Tower Hill.[26]

The third large sporting building at Whitehall was the cockpit. If the great close tennis play was majestic, this was fantastic. James Nedeham, who was probably its architect, created a building for which not only was there no precedent, but which came straight from the realms of fantasy. Its structure was two octagonal brick enclosures one inside the other. The larger, outside octagon was lower and from within it sprang the smaller interior octagon, which sported a conical roof with a glazed lantern crowned by an openwork imperial crown. At each of the eight corners on the upper level was a stone pier on which stood a beast holding a gilded iron vane; on each corner of the lantern there were gilded vanes too, and on top of the crown was a giant vane described as a 'cockpin'. Like the gatehouse and the tennis court there was a flint chequerboard frieze below the crenellations.

A Spanish doctor who visited Whitehall in 1539 attended a cockfight in the building. He was particularly interested in the habits of the cocks and so didn't mention the lavish ceiling with gold and blue decorations, but he did explain how it was set up for a fight:

> Round about the circumference of the enclosure there were innumerable
> coops, belonging to many princes and lords of the kingdom. In the

centre of this colosseum stood a sort of short, upright, truncated column about a span and a half from the ground . . . very heavy bets were made on the mettle and valour of the cocks . . . they are placed two at a time on the column in full view of the great number of spectators. The Jewels and valuables which are bet on them are placed in the middle. These are taken by whoever's cock wins.[27]

The coops for the cocks were cunningly built into the tiered seating. At Greenwich, where there was a less elaborate cockpit, the king's birds were kept in a special cage underneath his seat during matches. In between times they were kept in a coop with six boxes. In 1533 these prizefighters drove Anne Boleyn mad by their early-morning crowing and were relocated further away from her bedroom. She still enjoyed watching the cockfights, however, and a special viewing place was created for her in an upper gallery.

The cockpit seems to have been set in an elaborate garden decorated with posts topped with beasts. Nearby was the pheasant yard – a square, cobbled yard covered with a layer of sand in which ornamental pheasants and other 'outlandish fowles' were kept both for the table and as ornaments. The pheasants were apparently bred by a French priest who had his breeding coops at Eltham.[28]

A New Palace

By 1536 the original conception of palace, park and satellite house at Whitehall was more or less completed. That year parliament was called for the first time at Whitehall. Once they had assembled, they descended from the royal lodgings into the outer court, where a hundred or so fine horses waited. Mounted, the peers rode out of the court gate into King Street and passed under the new gate, watched by the queen who was standing in a window above. The cavalcade rode down King Street and through the gatehouse into Westminster Palace. Westminster was now just the rump of the old medieval residence. The historic privy palace, home to Henry's predecessors for hundreds of years, had been demolished and what remained were the ancient ceremonial outer rooms. It was outside these that the parliamentary procession dismounted and gathered in the presence chamber before making their traditional procession to the abbey on foot. At that session of parliament they passed an Act officially renaming York Place the Palace of Westminster and transferring to it all the powers and dignities held by the old palace. Henceforth the whole area from Charing Cross to Westminster Abbey was the palace precinct.

When parliament met three years later, this royal dignity was reinforced and the ceremonial was completely centred on Whitehall. The lords assembled in the king's lodgings there and this time rode in magnificent procession directly to the Abbey. The route was lined by Yeomen of the King's Guard and thousands of spectators were held back by barriers. After Mass and hearing the speech in the presence chamber of the old palace, they rode back to Whitehall for a feast in the king's lodgings. Thus Henry VIII created a new official seat for the English Crown, one that was to remain at the heart of the national story till it was destroyed by fire in 1698. He also instituted the procession that precedes the State Opening of Parliament, one that Queen Elizabeth II undertakes to this day.[29]

◆VI◆
TOWN AND COUNTRY

A House in the Country

THOMAS WOLSEY HAD BEEN the greatest builder of his age. As well as York Place and Hampton Court, there was a vast country house near Rickmansworth in Hertfordshire called the Manor of the More, two smaller ones at Tyttenhanger (Hertfordshire) and Esher (Surrey), as well as various residences associated with his many ecclesiastical appointments. Funded by the vast wealth that these brought, his houses had many purposes, one of the most important of which was allowing him to be close to the king at all times. Tudor power was gained and sustained by proximity to the monarch and, as Henry moved round the country, his ministers had to lodge nearby. It was for this reason that Hampton Court was begun. Its first significant owner had been Giles, Lord Daubeney, Henry VII's Lord Chamberlain, who bought the house to be close to the king at Richmond. It was probably for exactly the same reason that, in 1514, Wolsey acquired a ninety-nine-year lease on it from Daubeney's son.

Hampton Court has always been better understood than Whitehall, mainly because so much of the Tudor buildings actually survives. As a result, it has been available for investigation. During the 1980s, the Tudor buildings were drawn and dated brick by brick by Daphne Ford, meaning that we now know the sequence in which every part of what survives was built. This was an extraordinary achievement, particularly when you consider that during Henry VIII's time at least 26 million bricks were used. Daphne's is a study that has never, as far as I know, been replicated on such a scale. I went to work at Hampton Court in 1989 just as this mammoth exercise was drawing to a close and I realized that it would be possible to fill in the gaps left by Daphne's pioneering work through analysing the original building accounts. These survived because Henry VIII's builders opened an 'extraordinary account' covering just the construction work at Hampton Court. Often such accounts survive only in the enrolled version – that is to say, a summary, with summary descriptions of the work and the bare totals. But at Hampton Court we have the 'Particular Books'. These were the original unsummarized accounts or particulars made up from the actual bills submitted by the workmen. There are 6,500 pages of them, written in cramped sixteenth-century secretary hand, and covering work from 1529 to 1538. They were kept by two clerks who sat beneath the king's paymaster, Henry Williams. In a decade they paid out £46,000, well over twice the amount spent on building Bridewell in the previous decade.

These accounts are a really remarkable archive which nobody had tried to make detailed sense of. So I set out to try to meld together the evidence of Daphne's brick typology with the results of various archaeological excavations and the Particular Books. By 1998 I was able to publish my preliminary findings, which went on to be refined over the next few years.[1]

As I was undertaking this analysis, in collaboration with Daphne, we were also busy restoring the later buildings added by Christopher Wren. As service trenches were dug, we were able to get down into the dirt and uncover Tudor foundations that had been hidden for three centuries. This gave me a unique opportunity to check archaeologically the hypotheses that I was putting forward. As a result, we now have a pretty good picture of what Henry VIII was building at Hampton Court. But before we look at this, it is necessary to take one step back and consider what it was that the king inherited from his cardinal.

In 1514 Hampton Court was a brick-built courtyard surrounded by a moat on the banks of the River Thames. It was not a large house and for Wolsey it simply provided the raw materials for an enormous expansion. The plan was to rebuild most of the existing courtyard and add to it a really big new court containing lodgings for guests. The new courtyard – the present Base Court – survives, although the great gatehouse through

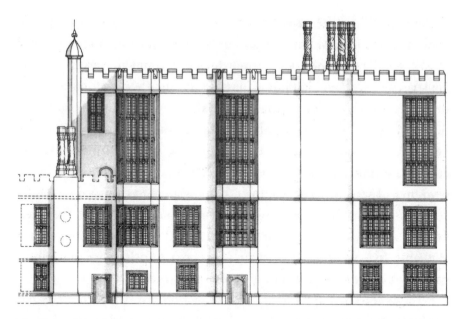

Reconstruction of the east side of Wolsey's inner court (now Clock Court) at Hampton Court as it would have appeared in 1529. The tall top floor contained the queen's rooms, the middle floor the king's and the ground floor a suite for Wolsey. Drawing by Daphne Ford.

which people enter was viciously cut down by the Georgians. The second courtyard is now unrecognizable, having been altered so many times since Wolsey's day. But on its east side, embedded in later buildings, are Wolsey's original lodgings. Of course they were magnificent, but only one surviving fireplace now gives an inkling of just how splendid they were.

The royal lodgings built to entertain the royal family were spread over three floors and served by a very large stair tower with a prospect room at its top offering amazing views across the Thames and beyond. The queen's lodgings seem to have been on the upper floor in rooms with enormously tall bay windows. She had only three rooms, but on the middle floor below was the king's suite and here there seem to have been four rooms. On the ground floor was another prestigious suite of rooms that could be used by Wolsey, Princess Mary or a high-ranking guest.

From the king's rooms a short linking passage led to the cardinal's long gallery. This was a remarkable room to which we will have cause to return, but for now we should note that it was of the Eltham/Bridewell type in that it ran out into the gardens. When I was working on the restoration of Hampton Court after a fire there in 1986, I was able to take a close look at this. Various pipe trenches had to be laid for new lavatories and I asked that Daphne and I might have time to dig the trenches ourselves. What turned up immediately below the later floors were the massive foundations of Wolsey's gallery, from which we were able to work out that it must have been 200 feet long and, inside, have had a width of around 15 feet. It was raised up on an arcade below that looked out on to a garden. So whatever the weather, you could either walk along the cloister looking at the northern gardens, or stroll in the gallery above looking out at gardens on both sides.[2]

Sadly, we cannot ask great historical figures such as Wolsey about their likes and dislikes. Yet, looking at how much Wolsey used Hampton Court for entertaining both the king and foreign dignitaries, we can perhaps begin to guess what an affection he had for his country house. This, perhaps, made the events of 1528 particularly hard to bear. With his relationship with the king rapidly deteriorating, Wolsey received a letter in September from the Treasurer of the Household, Sir William Fitzwilliam. It ordered the cardinal out of Hampton Court so that the king could entertain the papal legate there for four days. Henry had never taken such steps before, but from this point onwards he began to use the house as his own and, as we have seen, by March 1529 Anne Boleyn had her own lodging there.[3]

ARCHITECT ROYAL

The smooth royal takeover of Hampton Court was accompanied, like that at Whitehall, with the drawing up of plans for expansion. The architectural team was a new one. Henry Redman, who had designed most of Wolsey's buildings and had worked for the king at Greenwich, died in 1528. He had been a great figure and Henry openly expressed his regret at his death. He was replaced by his deputy, another mason, John Moulton, who was to be assisted by Christopher Dickinson. Some people have been shy about calling men like these architects, insisting that they

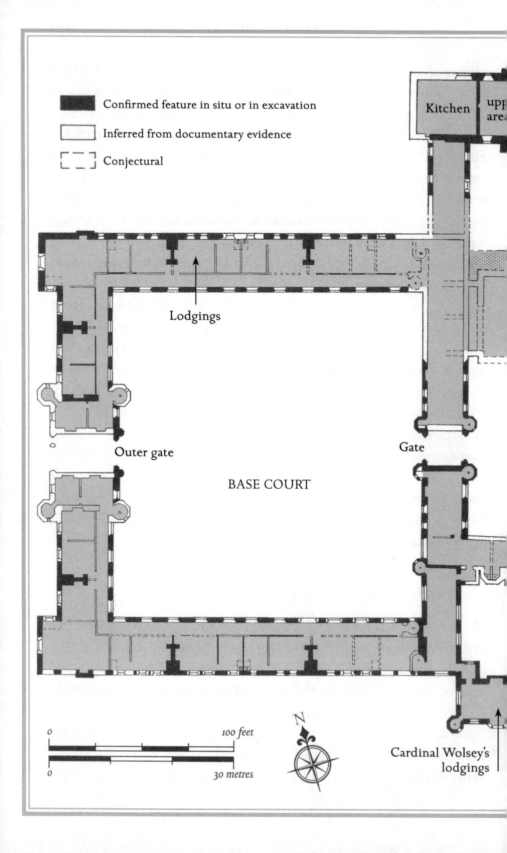

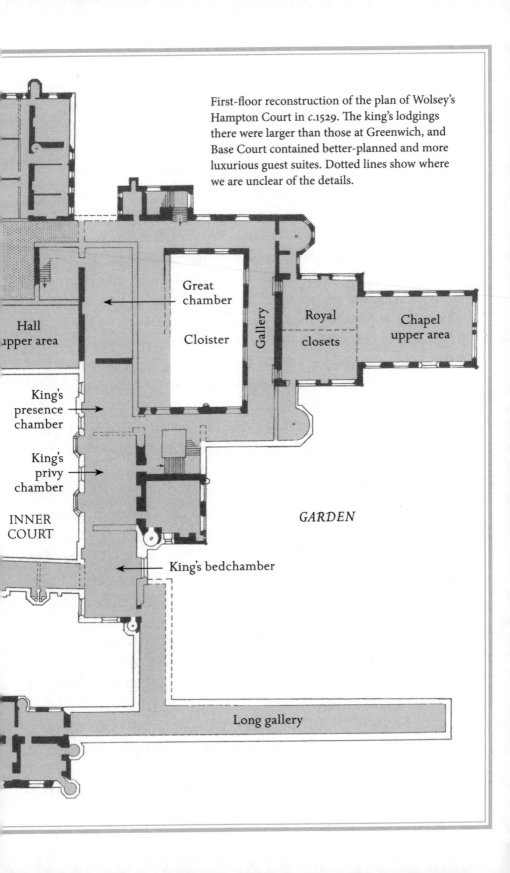

First-floor reconstruction of the plan of Wolsey's Hampton Court in *c.*1529. The king's lodgings there were larger than those at Greenwich, and Base Court contained better-planned and more luxurious guest suites. Dotted lines show where we are unclear of the details.

Great chamber

Cloister

Gallery

Royal closets

Chapel upper area

Hall upper area

King's presence chamber

King's privy chamber

INNER COURT

GARDEN

King's bedchamber

Long gallery

were master craftsmen, but we know that they drew plans and elevations, made models and were admired for their skill in engineering and construction. So I shall call them architects. Just as Henry and Anne worked with James Nedeham on the design of Whitehall, so they worked with Moulton and Dickinson at Hampton Court.[4]

Henry VIII's introduction to architecture had not been through palace-building but through his fascination with warfare. In 1509, his head filled with the chivalric exploits of his forebears, the young Henry lusted after war. More mature heads round his council table wanted him to renew the peace treaties made by his father. But in 1513 Henry won the arguments and set out at the head of an army bent on conquering Normandy. It besieged Thérouanne and, having beaten off the French king's relieving force, the town was taken and the nearby city of Tournai surrendered. Meanwhile, back in England, King James IV of Scotland invaded and the Earl of Surrey massacred the Scottish king and most of his nobles at the Battle of Flodden.

These victories inflated Henry's already swollen ego, convincing him that he was a military hero and master strategist. In reality, he was neither, but his first-hand engagement in war gave him practical experience of the latest military hardware and the science of fortification. We have already seen that he established an armoury at Greenwich, where he fancied himself as an armour designer, and at the same time he began to acquire a reputation as an expert in military engineering; his first architectural commission was, of course, a brutal gateway into Windsor Castle. In 1525 at Greenwich he designed a siege engine, but 'the carpenters were so dull, that they understood not his intent and wrought all things contrary'. We don't know when the king first put pen to parchment, but after the visit he made to the English stronghold in Calais in 1532 one Mr Anmer was instructed to draw up plans for the fortification of the town based on Henry's designs. Some of the king's requirements for Calais were very detailed, such as the angle of the splays in one of the bulwarks. This is merely the first of dozens of references to Henry's participation in the design of forts and castles.[5]

There is no question that from 1529 Henry was actively engaged in designing his own houses, at first with Anne Boleyn and later on his own account. In the inventory of the king's possessions drawn up after his death we have lots of evidence for his involvement in the drawing of plans: the closet at Greenwich contained a number of plans in a case made of yellow cloth and another in a tin case. In the closet next to his bedchamber were two designs for bridges, a pair of scissors, a pair of compasses, two rulers and a steel drawing pen. A similar cache of drawing instruments was in his private wardrobe at Hampton Court, together with twelve plans and maps of various forts.

Plans, normally drawn on large sheets of paper or parchment (and called plats), were frequently ferried from one place to another for Henry to examine, comment upon and approve. Sometimes a mock-up would be erected for him to inspect before he decided on a design. Generally when a plan was agreed he would sign the drawing to signify his consent for work to start. This, however, was no guarantee that he would not change his mind. Rooms were frequently completed only to be visited by the king and then immediately changed.[6]

Ceaseless experimentation and indecision were accompanied by gnawing impatience. Once plans were agreed the king wanted immediate results. Workmen frequently toiled all night by candlelight and then lit braziers to dry out paint and plaster in anticipation of a royal visit. Works on the Whitehall gatehouse continued under a vast canvas tent so that the weather did not slow the masons down. In the middle of the night barrels of beer, loaves of bread and rounds of cheese were issued to men manning the pumps to keep the foundations at Whitehall dry. Henry was a hands-on patron who would directly quiz his workmen on site. In May 1545 he inspected the site of his new house of Nonsuch and discovered that work was not nearly as far advanced as he had hoped. He found that one senior craftsman had been persistently absent and, when challenged, had said he would not deal with the royal architects and only answered directly to the Privy Council. Henry, extremely annoyed, wrote to the council 'marvelling in case these words are true that you have not made us aware of this' and warning them that 'he is a fellow that much glories in himself and his doings.'[7]

All this meant that the king had very close relationships with his architects. For most of the first part of his reign, the administrative head of the Office of Works was Henry Smith, a clerk who had risen up to be in charge of Henry VII's works at Windsor and then was promoted to oversee operations everywhere. This was a perfectly sensible arrangement while Henry VIII had limited interest in architecture, but in the early 1530s, when almost every day he was involved in architectural decisions of some sort, it was a less good choice, as Smith lacked the expert knowledge the king sought. In October 1532 there was an orderly transition and Smith's successor, another efficient administrator who had been in post only four years, handed over to James Nedeham, the man who had conceived the plan for Whitehall with Henry and Anne and who was, just then, very much in favour. It was a decisive moment, as it meant control of the Office of Works passed from an administrator to an architect.[8]

This was marked by a very visible alteration in status. The royal architects, together with a select band of other officials, were issued with a uniform or livery. In 1519 William Vertue and Henry Redman were given liveries equivalent to those of the Esquires of the Household – a fur-trimmed gown and doublet. But in 1533, as a reflection of the increased status of the officers of the King's Works and the interest that the king had in building, the key architects and administrators were issued with fine red coats embroidered with the king's initials, 'HR'. As they donned their new outfits, the Office of Works was relocated. It had long been based in the Palace of Westminster but, as part of the huge series of land transactions executed in the early 1530s, the land to the north of York Place was brought into royal control. This included some lands from Westminster Abbey and a number of ecclesiastical properties, but also an area of land known as Scotland. This whole area, eventually to be known as Scotland Yard, was taken over by the Office of Works as a vast building yard and the location of their workshops, counting houses and drawing offices. With the massive increase in the volume of building, Scotland Yard was soon bustling with hundreds of workmen, suppliers, craftsmen and administrators supervised by the king's red-coated architects.[9]

The way the Office of Works was organized did not mean that Nedeham now automatically designed everything. We know that he designed a great deal; he took on specific projects and was called in when his expertise was needed – he designed the great hall roof at Hampton Court, for example. The design work – and during the 1530s and 1540s there was a huge amount of it – was, in fact, shared with other architects. Two have already been mentioned: the king's master mason, John Moulton, and the mason from Windsor Castle, Christopher Dickinson; two others were also important – the master carpenters John Russell and William Clement. These men all lived in and around Westminster, their families intermarried, in old age they witnessed each other's wills, they dined at each other's tables and they all owed their success to the king's favour. They also relied on the legal and financial support of Thomas Cromwell, who was appointed Henry VIII's chief minister in 1534. Nedeham, in particular, worked closely with Cromwell throughout the 1530s on realizing royal architectural aspirations. [10]

But this is running ahead. In the autumn of 1528 the king sat down with Moulton and Dickinson and devised two major projects for Hampton Court, each a direct consequence of the change in ownership from cardinal to king. The first was a massive extension of the kitchens. Wolsey had used the kitchens built by Lord Daubeney, although these must have been barely large enough for the ambitious scale of his entertaining; now they were certainly too small for the combined households of the king and queen. The second project was to extend the king's privy lodgings, including a new gallery.

DREAM KITCHENS

Although all the houses we have looked at so far had kitchens, we have not properly considered how these were designed and operated and it is to this which we now must turn. We have seen that from the Middle Ages the household indoors was divided into the Lord Chamberlain's department, sometimes known as the *Domus Regie Magnificencie,* responsible for the public-facing life of the court in the royal lodgings, and the Lord Steward's department, *Domus Providencie*, responsible for what the Victorians would have called life below stairs.

The Lord Steward (whose title was aggrandized in 1540 to Lord Great Master) presided over an extremely complex and costly operation and, as a result, the post was always held by a high-ranking courtier. Also as a result, the steward himself had little to do with the day-to-day running of the department; this was in the hands of the Cofferer, the chief financial officer. He was assisted by a deputy, the Treasurer, the Comptroller beneath him, and a number of clerks. Together they made up the Board of the Greencloth, so called because they met in an office with a large table covered with green baize. This powerful board even had its own coat of arms: a white stave crossed with a key, symbolizing their power of access and discipline. The background shield was, of course, green.[11]

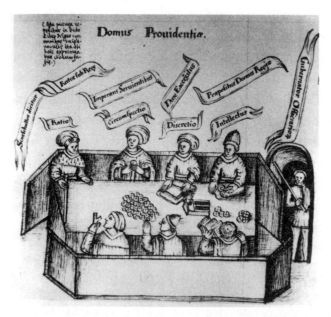

The Board of the Greencloth meeting, shown in a seventeenth-century copy of a lost original drawing probably of Henry VII's reign. The Lord Steward and Treasurer sit at the board with their white staves of office, while around them are the clerks of the Greencloth. Above are the virtues of their office, including reason, circumspection and intelligence. On the table are check rolls, counters and a till. When I was working at Hampton Court we found one of these lead counters under the floorboards of the Tudor Greencloth office.

The Greencloth procured all the consumables needed by the court, including firewood and candles, but their central focus was feeding people. Generally there were two meals a day, one at midday and the other at 4pm, but timing was flexible as there were few clocks and the blowing of trumpets announced that food was about to be served. The 600 members of the king's household who were entitled to eat at court were on a list known as the Bouche of Court (literally, the mouth of court) which specified how much food they were entitled to and where they were allowed to eat it. In addition, there were the 230 or so domestic servants who worked in the king's kitchens who also required feeding. Controlling all this had been a headache since the fourteenth century, as people wanted to take the food away, cafeteria-style, and eat in their own rooms. Requiring them to dine in set locations was a key part of controlling cost and waste.

The Yeomen of the Guard, and most of the lower servants above stairs, ate in the great hall at long, narrow trestle tables, sitting on benches. Henry VIII's great hall at Hampton Court could sit around 300 people in this way and so there were normally two sittings when the court was here. Next door in the watching chamber, hosted by the Lord Chamberlain, were the more senior members of the court, including the captain of the guard and the king's body servants not on duty. The Lord Steward presided in the council chamber or the presence chamber with any lords above the rank of baron at court at that time. A visiting ambassador might be invited to join the party. In 1498 Henry VII was surprised to hear that the Spanish ambassador was coming to court and asked what his business was. A quick-witted courtier answered 'To eat,' playing on the ambassador's reputation for freeloading. The king laughed.[12]

If the queen were staying with the king at one of the large houses in the Thames valley, her household also had to be fed on the same timetable. This was normally around another 120 people, for the queen was attended by about forty-five women in her privy chamber and inner rooms and fifty-one men in her outer chambers. In addition were her officers (Lord Chamberlain, Master of the Horse, Secretary, etc.) and her chapel, another twenty or so men. The more junior men on the queen's side would eat in the hall with the king's servants, but her upper servants and ladies would eat in her watching chamber and presence chamber.[13]

Those eating in the watching chambers, council or presence chambers were served by gentlemen, grooms, pages and other serving men, while in the hall everything was supervised by the Marshal of the Hall, whose charges both served and later ate in the room. When most of the household had been fed, the domestic servants would eat in their own offices, store rooms and kitchens.

So twice a day a hugely complex, tightly choreographed production was performed and it was essential that the layout of the kitchens made it work as smoothly as possible. During Edward IV's reign the way high-status kitchens were organized had changed. For hundreds of years kitchens had normally been built on an axis with the great hall, separated from it only by a narrow passage known as the screens passage. With the growing formality and ceremony of royal dining, this plan became increasingly impractical and when King Edward built his new hall at Eltham the kitchen was constructed to one side of it with a large area set aside for marshalling the serving men and organizing the presentation and destination of dishes. This new way of designing high-status kitchens had already been introduced to Hampton Court by Lord Daubeney and so when Henry VIII came to extend them in 1529–31 he followed the latest arrangement.[14]

The plan of the king's new kitchens was conceived like a factory production line and anticipated the industrial planning of early factories like Josiah Wedgwood's Etruria by 250 years. They clustered in a network of courtyards ranged along almost the entire length of the north side – a distance of 400 feet (kitchens were always on the sunless side of houses, reserving the warmer south front for the royal lodgings). The complex had its own gatehouse through which the colossal quantities of consumables entered the house. Above the gatehouse was the office of the Greencloth, ideally placed to monitor goods coming in by cart and packhorse. Those who worked in the Lord Steward's department had rooms next to or above the places in which they worked, as while the court was in residence the kitchens were in operation round the clock.

In the first, or western, court were stored the least perishable items, such as spices, charcoal, candles and linen. In the eastern court were the confectory, where sweetmeats were made, and the pastry, responsible for shaping the pastry coffins that encased Tudor pies. Pastry-making took place within the cooler workhouses in the main complex, but bread was baked in the hot, detached bakehouse in the outer court. This was normally the case, as bakehouses had a tendency to burn down, as indeed the one at Hampton Court did in 1606. The outer offices had their own landing stage on the river so that grain and flour could be sent in and out. The bakehouses produced both the fine bread eaten by the upper courtiers called 'manchet' as well as the coarser wholemeal bread called 'cheat' eaten by everyone else. Each day when the court was in residence the bakehouse would produce around 1,000 loaves of cheat and 700 of the smaller white manchets. Also in the outer court was the poultry and scalding house. Here great vats of boiling water were used to blanch everything from chickens to swans, plovers to larks. The blanched birds were easier to pluck; they were then gutted before being passed through to the larders ready to cook.

In the main kitchens, round a narrow court close to the great kitchen, were the larders. This court was entered by a single door that could be securely locked to prevent unauthorized access. From these larders ready-butchered meat, poultry, fresh fish or rehydrated dried fish could be brought straight into the great kitchen; doors from the pastry and the boiling house (where food was heated in a 75-gallon built-in cauldron) also led directly to the kitchen. Because food was served according to rank, the great kitchen was divided into two parts – the hall kitchen and the lords' kitchen. The first provided food for the household dining on trestles in the hall, while the lords' kitchen supplied the watching chamber and the council chamber. Both spaces were vast, 40 feet high, and contained huge, arched fireplaces for boiling and roasting meat. Food was checked out as it passed from kitchen staff to the waiting chamber staff who would serve at table.

Meat was the backbone of the diet at court. In Queen Elizabeth's reign it was calculated that each year the royal kitchens cooked, amongst

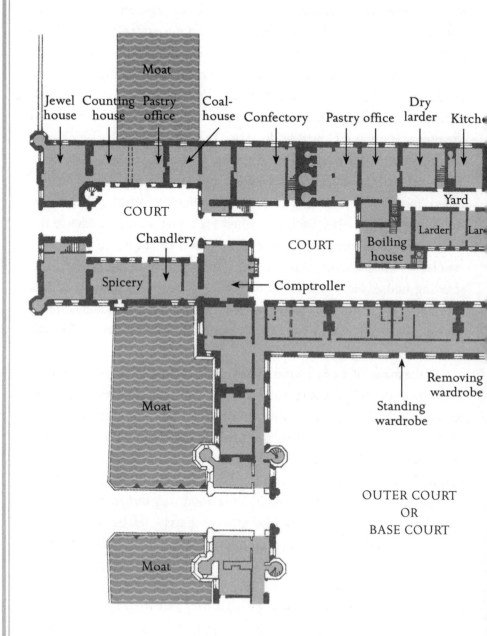

Ground floor of the kitchens at Hampton Court, as extended by Henry VIII in 1529–31. Offices, working-houses, larders and kitchens were carefully arranged to facilitate the most efficient operation possible. Other residences had kitchens laid out similarly, making it easy for staff to adapt themselves to working at any royal house.

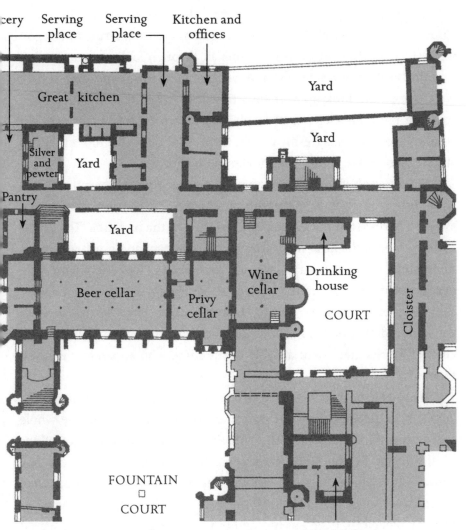

PRIVY ORCHARD

N

cery · Serving place · Serving place · Kitchen and offices

Great kitchen

Yard

Yard

Silver and pewter

Yard

Pantry

Yard

Beer cellar

Privy cellar

Wine cellar

Drinking house

COURT

Cloister

FOUNTAIN
COURT

Privy kitchen

other things, 1,240 oxen, 8,200 sheep, 2,330 deer, 760 calves, 1,870 pigs and 53 wild boar. But every aspect of life at court was conditioned by religion and meat was forbidden on Wednesdays, Fridays and Saturdays, and generally on Fridays there was only a single meal. There were various other so-called 'ember days' of fasting, as well as the long haul of Lent and Advent. Added together, on almost half the days of a year there was some sort of dietary abstinence. During Lent 1509 Katharine of Aragon wrote to her father in despair, feeling ill through lack of meat, telling him that at Richmond 'they would not give meat to anyone, even if they were dying, and look upon them who eat it as heretics'. This degree of stricture required a constant supply of fish, which was either brought from the coast or was freshly caught from fish ponds like those that can still be seen on the south front of Hampton Court.[15]

Most royal houses, in fact, supplied a proportion of their own food: fresh fish from ponds, pheasants and other birds from ornamental aviaries, herbs from the gardens and fruit from the orchards. The eating of deer killed at the hunt was particularly important and much was made of feasting on particularly large or fast beasts. On one memorable occasion Francis I of France, keen to show Henry that the French were Europe's greatest hunters, sent to Hampton Court large pasties, three of venison and two of boar. They came accompanied by a French royal chef who presented them at table to the king, who apparently enjoyed them.[16]

Wine and beer were stored in Hampton Court's three cellars. The largest was the long, low, dark great cellar, which occupied the whole space beneath the great hall. This contained some of the 600,000 gallons of ale drunk by the court each year. This was one of the very few commodities stored between visits by the court and so the doors were locked with two keys, one held by the Keeper of the Cellar and the other by the Greencloth. Beer was brought out under tight control and served through the buttery at the west end of the great hall. The wine cellar, architecturally more pretentious, stored both wine for upper members of the household and, in a separate section, the wine for the royal table.

In all royal houses the king's food was cooked entirely separately from the kitchens I have just described. This was inevitable, not only because what the royal family ate had to be of the highest quality, nor just because it had to be securely made to guard against poisoning, but because they refused to be bound by the very rigid timetable imposed by the great kitchens. In 1530 a new privy kitchen was built at Hampton Court beneath the king's dining chamber, but at all houses there were separate kitchens for the king and queen, normally sited immediately below their inner lodgings. In due course the royal children had their own kitchens too.

Henry, of course, had his own cook and the ingredients he used were specially selected and supplied for the sovereign's mouth. His longest-serving cook was a Frenchman (of course) called Piero le Doux, who was issued with a fur-trimmed gown and a velvet doublet. The royal diet comprised huge quantities of meat and fish, with stolid, sweet puddings made for the king by one of the very few women who worked at court. The king was always being given gifts of food by well-wishers; each person was dutifully rewarded, often with a sum greater than the gift was worth. Henry's Privy Purse accounts record gifts of grapes, peaches, apples, artichokes, radishes, pears, pomegranates, figs, oranges, lemons, all sorts of fish and, occasionally, cooked foods such as cake and marmalade. We don't know whether he ate the fruit, but even if he did his diet was very deficient in vegetables. His bread was fine and white and everything was washed down with quantities of wine and ale. This was all a recipe for chronic constipation, from which the king suffered, compounded inevitably by dreadful haemorrhoids. After 1536, when a riding accident triggered a leg ulcer leading to a painful septic infection of his thigh bone, Henry took much less exercise and quickly put on weight. From a trim 35-inch waist in 1515, he expanded to a 49-inch waist in 1540 and, in due course, developed type 2 diabetes.[17]

Despite the fact that Henry's privy kitchen was slowly killing him, there was a strong awareness of the connection between diet and health. In 1535, when Princess Mary was suffering from a menstrual disorder, it was reported that she 'was much desirous to have her meat immediately after she was ready in the morning or else she should be in danger of returning to her infirmity' – such refinements in dietary regime were possible only for the royal family with their own kitchens.[18]

So far we have been considering the everyday role of the kitchens, but the year was punctuated both by the regular cycle of religious feast days and the less predictable round of feasts to celebrate great events. These could, of course, be very large, feeding 1,500 people or more. Normally the largest residences, Hampton Court or Whitehall, could cope with such events, but at Greenwich in 1533 special working houses had to be constructed for the cook at Twelfth Night and frequently special ranges were built for the 'boiling of brawnes' – the preparation of whole sides of wild boar – that took place at Christmas.

LAP OF LUXURY

During 1529–31 the king cannot have been much concerned by the huge construction works on the north side of his new house. As long as the kitchens could sustain the great feasts he had in mind for Hampton Court, Henry must have been happy for work to continue. His focus was on his own rooms and those of Anne. The smaller privy rooms at Hampton Court had been built by Wolsey on the south front and were disconnected from the king's lodgings on the principal floor. Henry's first decision was to get Christopher Dickinson to design a tower containing privy lodgings for himself, neatly squeezed in between the old bedchamber and the long gallery.[19]

The tower was on three levels. On the ground there was an office for Sir Brian Tuke, Treasurer of the Chamber, who was responsible for paying the wages of Privy Chamber staff. Next to him was a safe – a room without a window and with hugely thick walls; this is where, when the court was on the move, large quantities of cash were deposited for the use of the household. A second store for valuables was in the outer kitchen court. Here plate for the tables in the outer rooms was kept, as well as cash for paying domestic suppliers.

Also on the ground floor of the tower was the king's Wardrobe of the Robes, where his clothes were stored. Above, on the first floor, entered

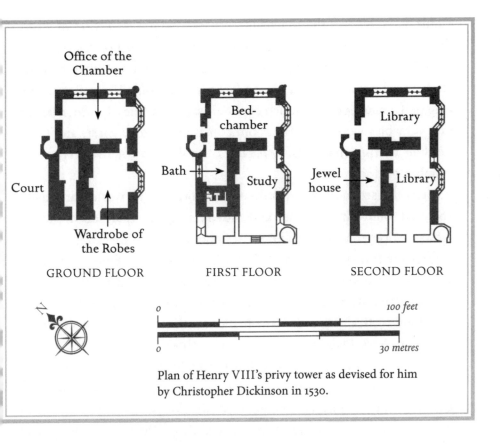

Plan of Henry VIII's privy tower as devised for him by Christopher Dickinson in 1530.

from the state lodgings, was Henry's new bedchamber with an ensuite bathroom. The baths were circular and wooden and were made by a cooper. They were filled by a great tap with hot water from a boiler in the next room; water came from a cistern on the floor above. Incredibly, parts of this survived until the 1950s when it was decided to demolish it to make way for a lift shaft; as a consequence we don't know exactly how it worked. Yet we do know that the ceiling of the bathroom was white and decorated with gilded timber battens.

Next to the bedroom was the king's study, a room in which he took special interest. The room was panelled up to head height and above this the Italian Toto del Nunziata painted four large panels: two of the four evangelists, one pietà and one of Christ washing the apostles' feet. Some idea of the effect of this room can still be gained from a room at Hampton

Court assembled in the nineteenth century from a collection of Tudor fragments. It is brilliantly done and, because it incorporates paintings from Henry VIII's time, it gives a convincing evocation of what the king's study may have looked like in 1530 (see plate section). The wall panelling originally incorporated hidden cupboards, or aumbries, in which papers and valuables were kept. The room contained various chests and boxes holding writing materials, two tables, stools, tills (or drawers) and a number of clocks.

On the second floor was the king's library. This was a particularly splendid room with a painted and gilded ceiling, many windows and fine views. Wolsey had had a library in another part of the house and the fittings for this were dismantled and installed in the king's new room. Cases for the books had glazed doors with curtains hung in front of them for protection from light. The books were laid horizontally on the shelves, not stood vertically as today. The first ones started to arrive in November 1530 from York Place and from Reading Abbey. Off the library was the king's secret jewel house. This didn't contain cash, but housed all the valuables that needed to be locked away when he was not at Hampton Court. In 1547, for instance, it contained two globes, hawk hoods, a mirror, hawking gloves and various plans and drawings. The man in charge of all this luxury and splendour was the Groom of the Stool, who in 1529 was Henry Norris, who was assigned a room next to the jewel house.

As we have seen, it was Edward IV's work at Eltham that started the fashion for a long gallery at the end of the privy lodgings and Wolsey imitated this in all his houses, with the gallery at Hampton Court raised up on a brick cloister below. The upper parts of the gallery were of timber and were fortunately sturdily built because Henry VIII decided to add another storey to it. The roof came off Wolsey's gallery and the carpenters assembled a new wooden frame on top of the existing walls. To us it seems extraordinary that Tudor carpenters could put up buildings so quickly and confidently. Their techniques were very like the steel-framed construction of today. Pieces could be prefabricated off site and then moved into position when needed – for Whitehall the royal carpenters dismantled the gallery at Esher Place built by Wolsey and moved it to York Place where it was re-erected.

Unlike Wolsey's buildings at Hampton Court, which were all of brick, large parts of Henry's Hampton Court were timber-framed; this was undoubtedly for speed of construction, but was also, as in the case of his new gallery, for structural reasons.[20]

So what was a long gallery actually for? The short answer is recreation. It was a way of creating a large flexible space for a whole range of private pleasures while maintaining a sense of intimacy of scale. The galleries were very long, but they were narrow and relatively low and so still seemed intimate, unlike the great echoing state rooms. Their length was broken up with furniture – tables, cupboards and stools – and with musical instruments. The walls were generally panelled (although Wolsey's gallery in Whitehall was hung with tapestry). The Hampton Court double-decker galleries had windows on both sides and the panelling was adorned with paintings hung from red ribbons and often provided with a curtain to protect them. The windows were key to this type of gallery, as they were designed to give views over the gardens, or over the river or parkland. The Hampton Court galleries were no exception, looking out on both sides on to gardens.

The sequence of building work at Hampton Court in 1529–30 was, like that at York Place, driven by the timetable of divorce. At neither house, while he was still married to Katharine of Aragon, did Henry build new queen's lodgings. It might be imagined that he held back out of respect, waiting until he was officially divorced from a woman he claimed never legally to have married. The reality was more calculating. Katharine had her own itinerary and until July 1533 was able to stay in the royal houses; by not having queen's lodgings at York Place or Hampton Court Henry was removing the possibility that he and Katharine could stay in the same place together. In the autumn of 1528 the king stayed at Hampton Court without the queen for a week before moving off to Bridewell. Once Hampton Court was vacated, the queen and her household moved in. This separation of households meant that Anne could move about with the king and, indeed, she had lodgings at Hampton Court as early as June 1529, and in July 1532 the nearby royal house of Hanworth was fitted up for her at considerable expense.

East front of Hampton Court in the seventeenth century showing the queen's lodgings as they appeared by the end of Henry's reign. From right to left the structures are: Charles II's tennis court and gallery with the great hall behind it; the queen's privy gallery with the great tennis court behind it; the tall bay window to the queen's bedchamber; in the middle the queen's privy lodgings; and to the left the king's privy lodgings.

As at York Place, the plan at Hampton Court must have always been to build a queen's side; in fact the very month Anne was crowned, the royal bricklayers began to measure out the foundations for her new lodgings. Presumably the plan had been long agreed, and the royal lovers had probably collaborated on the design with Christopher Dickinson and William Clement. The idea was to make a new courtyard on the east side of the house facing the park. This would incorporate the new double-decker gallery as its south side and be matched by a new gallery two storeys high on the north. The whole thing would be harmonized by matching the arches on which Wolsey's gallery had been built, giving the new court its name – Cloister Court.

Everything was done at high speed and within an astonishing ten months the carcass was up. The rooms were built in a fairly standard sequence but had some refinements of note. The queen's presence chamber had an adjacent room for her ladies and two discreet garderobes attached. Next to the queen's bedchamber was a jewel chamber, which presumably acted as a closet and dressing room. But most importantly, it looks as if the king built himself a second bedchamber at the end of the

long gallery that more or less intercommunicated with the queen's bedchamber. Henry's bedchamber was particularly richly decorated, with a frieze of gilded *putti* and blue-painted window sills inlaid with his motto in gilt letters.[21]

This was a very significant change in the way royal houses were arranged. As described earlier, for a century or more the king would leave his own lodgings and be escorted to the queen's side if he wished to sleep with his wife. It was often quite a journey, because at Windsor and Westminster their bedrooms were in separate ranges and at Richmond they were on different floors. Henry had probably stopped sleeping with Katharine of Aragon when their marriage was put under legal scrutiny in May 1527, and his extra-marital affairs were arranged by his Groom of the Stool in discreet locations apart from the royal rooms. When he contemplated building new residences with Anne, the sleeping arrangements were to be very different. At Whitehall the king's and queen's bedchambers were not together, but at Hampton Court, for the first time, the royal bedrooms were close to each other and the nightshirted parade to the queen's bedchamber came to an end. This arrangement was unquestionably to service the king's lust for his new wife and, as we shall see, it was replicated in all his new houses and had important consequences in the future.

Next to the king's new bedchamber, at the end of the gallery, was a staircase, 20 feet square, descending to the gardens. This, of course, enabled

Henry and Anne to go down privately but, much more importantly, it also acted as a new, and alternative, entrance to the house. For, as the double-decker gallery rose on the south front, elaborate gardens were laid out leading down to the Thames. At the bottom of these, at the river's edge, a very large new watergate with a covered landing stage was built. The various drawings of Hampton Court from the south seem to suggest that the watergate may have been linked to the royal lodgings by a series of covered galleries that would have allowed the royal family to disembark and walk in the dry to the privy stair on the south front.[22]

In 1992, when I was supervising the restoration of the William and Mary gardens on the south front at Hampton Court, we had a chance to test the theory that there was a gallery linking the house and the river. Our archaeologists dug up two small banqueting houses that had been built against the garden wall – both with their original floors, so we could step on the very tiles on which Tudor courtiers had walked. Frustratingly, later work to the gardens had destroyed any evidence of a gallery, so we can't prove there was one, but it is hard to imagine the king walking across his gardens in the driving rain.[23]

DOWN TO BUSINESS

What is striking about Henry VIII's adaptation of Hampton Court in the early 1530s is how different it was in nature to his conversion of York Place. Instead of laying out his lodgings in a long range off a gallery, at Hampton Court the king maintained the medieval arrangement of putting his privy lodgings in a tower. This was due to the differences in function of the two houses, in particular the role that Whitehall was to play in the governance of the realm.

It has been emphasized so far that the business of government bored the young Henry. This is true – up to a point. For Henry was still king and was interested in foreign affairs and in the general peace and welfare of his realm. He was also interested in the huge patronage exercised by the Crown. Wolsey had taken on a huge amount of administration, but he was not the only one involved in advising the king, for there was also

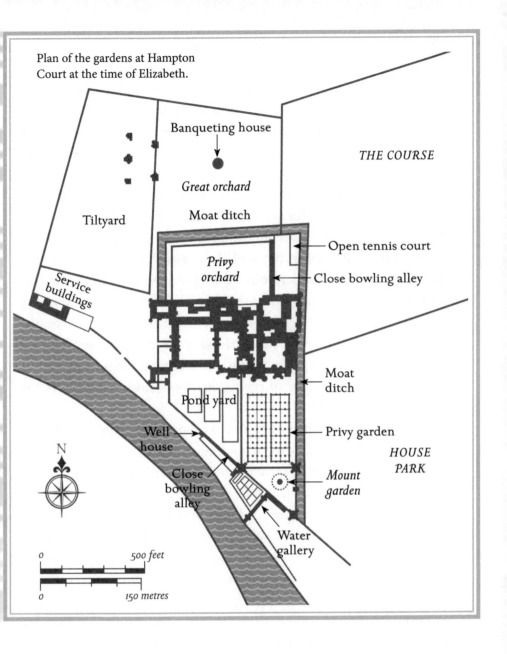

Plan of the gardens at Hampton Court at the time of Elizabeth.

Banqueting house

THE COURSE

Great orchard

Moat ditch

Tiltyard

Privy orchard

Open tennis court

Close bowling alley

Service buildings

Moat ditch

Pond yard

Privy garden

Well house

N

HOUSE PARK

Close bowling alley

Mount garden

Water gallery

0   500 feet

0   150 metres

the Royal Council. In the age of modern government it is difficult to comprehend how amorphous the Tudor Royal Council was and how informal its proceedings. Under Henry VII its functions had effectively been divided in two. Its judicial responsibilities were undertaken at regular meetings in the legal term time in a room in the old Westminster Palace called the Star Chamber. In modern terms, this was like the Supreme Court and ruled on the judgements of all other courts. Henry would attend Star Chamber a few times a year in a purely ceremonial role, but otherwise it ran without royal involvement. The council's job of advising the king on policy was undertaken in the royal manors themselves, wherever the king might be staying, or occasionally in Wolsey's houses.

While Wolsey was chief minister he chaired the meetings of the Star Chamber, processing on his mule daily in term time to the old Palace of Westminster from York Place. In contrast, the king's Privy Council was assembled by Henry when he needed it. There was an official list of councillors, but this was enormous: more than seventy people, including almost everyone who might come to court with an official position. In practice, the king called together the people he needed when he wanted either advice or something done. He also assembled councillors on important state occasions – when he was receiving foreign envoys, for instance, as a large number of prestigious councillors were part of the ornament of majesty.[24]

These meetings tended to happen in the winter months when the king's court was shuttling between his houses in the Thames valley. When he was on progress only the most important business could turn Henry's head from pleasure. In 1522 the Spanish ambassador complained that the king was on progress 'accompanied only by a few persons, but making great cheer and taking his pleasure. War and business are not discussed in his court'. The informality of the summer progress is reflected in the fact that it was only the large houses in and around London that had council chambers.[25]

We have details of some of these. At Richmond the council chamber was situated near the watching chamber at the top of the stairs that led into the royal lodgings; it seems as if it had an internal glazed window borrowing light from the watching chamber. At the Tower Henry VII had built a council chamber in the middle of a long gallery and at Bridewell, presumably specified by Wolsey, there was one off the long gallery approached from the king's presence chamber. The Richmond watching chamber and the galleries at the Tower and Bridewell presumably provided a comfortable area for people to await their summons to the council table. Wolsey had a council chamber off his gallery at York Place too; in this room he frequently chaired meetings of the council without the king being present. Yet at Hampton Court there was none. This is because, for Wolsey, Hampton Court had been a private residence, not part of the architectural mechanics of his rule. So in October 1528, the month after he had turned Wolsey out, while Henry was staying at Hampton Court he went daily by river to Richmond where the council was meeting and where he stayed late every evening discussing his divorce. This was clearly unsatisfactory and, when in March 1529 the king summoned his council to Hampton Court, the building of a new council chamber was far advanced. Like the other council chambers, it was off a gallery where people could wait to be called and beneath it were offices for the clerks.[26]

Other than the council chamber there was, at first, no permanent infrastructure for rule in the king's houses. First Wolsey, then after 1534 Thomas Cromwell, managed the administration of the king's affairs from rooms at court and, after they had become established, from their own houses. Wolsey was granted the use of Eltham, which he altered to his own convenience, and later he was allowed to use Richmond. Cromwell, at the peak of his influence, was granted St James's so that he could operate close to the king at Whitehall, but he also had rooms at Greenwich – the Spanish ambassador described Cromwell's chamber there as being one 'to which the king can go by certain galleries without being perceived'.[27] After Cromwell's fall and execution in 1540, Henry seems to have resolved not to rely again on a single all-powerful minister and instead created two posts of Secretary of State, one of whom would stay with the Privy Council while the other would follow the king around the country. It was from this date that proper records began to be kept.

In 1543 Sir William Paget was appointed one of the two Secretaries of State, rapidly becoming the most important and powerful of Henry's ministers, speaking for the king, controlling vast patronage and becoming the linchpin of royal diplomacy. In 1545, while Paget was away at the court of the Emperor Charles V, the lodgings in the privy gallery at Whitehall were re-organized and he heard that his rooms had been relocated to the old court gatehouse. Furious, he wrote to William Petre, his co-Secretary, explaining:

> the chamber over the gate will scant receive my bed and a table to write at for myself . . . I have no place neither for my clerks, nor such others as must serve his majesty, as the Latin Secretary, the French Secretary, the Clerks of the Council, the Clerks of the signet to write in; and his majesty's affairs be not written in every place, but where they may be kept secret and where I may resort to see the doing of the same . . . And his service, at this present, is greater, than it hath been of many years before, and requires many hands . . . If I had no more, but my chamber keepers, and three or four of my own men, the two little rooms were big enough; but you know what a number we have always, both of necessary ministers and also of suiters to be dispatched in them.[28]

Whitehall was a residence but, as Paget pointed out, it was also the centre of the national administration and was teeming with people on all sorts of business. There was no separate office for that business: it was conducted in the private rooms allocated to the various officials. At court you worked where you lived and you lived in close proximity to the king.

To Have and to Hold

KLEPTOMANIA

H ENRY VIII BROKE WITH ROME TO satisfy his conscience and open the way for his marriage to Anne Boleyn. What nobody knew at the time was how far-reaching the consequences of this would be. Within six weeks of Henry's assuming his supreme headship, he appointed Thomas Cromwell as his deputy in all spiritual affairs. Cromwell's first job was to undertake a Domesday Book-like survey of all Church assets. This incredible task, the twenty-two volume *Valor Ecclesiasticus* (Value of the Church), was completed at great speed and two beautifully illuminated volumes, a sort of executive summary, were put into the king's hands in the summer of 1535. This was initially a basis for Church taxation, but soon it became a shopping list for the king as he began suppressing monastic houses and appropriating their wealth himself.[1]

To deal with the huge flows of land and cash that came from the Church, Thomas Cromwell established the Court of Augmentations. This new administrative organ received some £1,304,859 during Henry's reign, a colossal sum for the time. In 1537 a headquarters for the new court was erected at the old Palace of Westminster. The handsome brick building, three storeys high, was arguably the first government office to be purpose-built in England. It was followed by other courts, or offices, amongst the remains of the old palace. The Augmentations soon became the nation's treasury, supplanting other sources of royal revenue and expenditure, especially the Chamber, which had been paying for the king's buildings previously. Expenditure shot up, and amongst those who were now flush with cash were the king's architects and builders.[2]

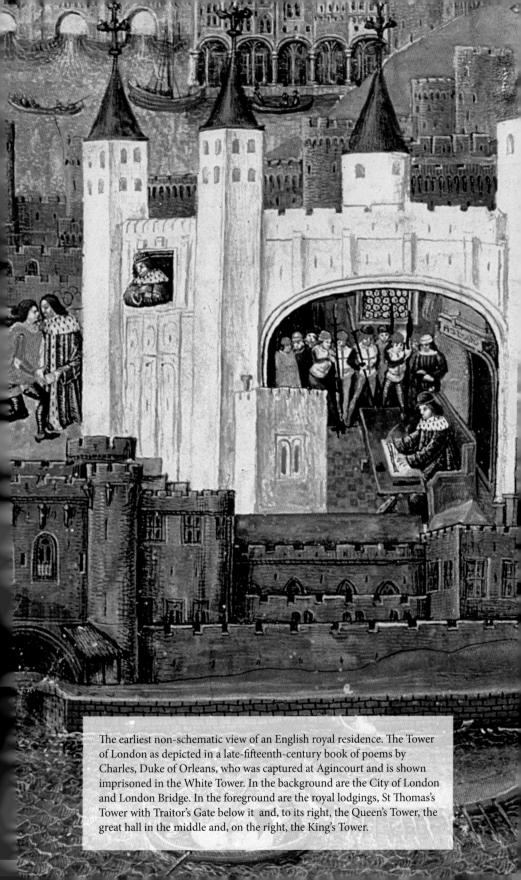

The earliest non-schematic view of an English royal residence. The Tower of London as depicted in a late-fifteenth-century book of poems by Charles, Duke of Orleans, who was captured at Agincourt and is shown imprisoned in the White Tower. In the background are the City of London and London Bridge. In the foreground are the royal lodgings, St Thomas's Tower with Traitor's Gate below it and, to its right, the Queen's Tower, the great hall in the middle and, on the right, the King's Tower.

Above: The Talbot Shrewsbury Book was compiled as a gift to Margaret of Anjou, on her betrothal to King Henry VI of England, from the 1st Earl of Shrewsbury, who escorted her to England for her marriage and coronation in 1445. This illumination from it shows Henry VI seated beneath a throne canopy in an interior of great magnificence giving the sword of the Constable of France to the Earl of Shrewsbury.

Below: Miniature painting from the early fifteenth-century Book of Hours *Les Très Riches Heures du duc de Berry*, showing the month of October. The Louvre is as it was when the future Henry VII visited it. The painting is extremely accurate and shows the royal lodgings behind a high external wall. The lodgings formed a square with a large courtyard in the middle. In this was built the donjon, or keep: a circular tower whose conical roof can be seen above the roofs of the royal rooms.

ABOVE: The royal manor of Richmond (formerly Sheen) in *c.*1640, from a painting attributed to Wenceslaus Hollar. The main block of royal lodgings is in the foreground and to the left of it can just be seen the corner of the great hall. The hall and lodgings are all of stone, but the chimneys and the kitchens to the left of the picture are built of brick.

ABOVE: *The Family of Henry VII with St George and the Dragon.* This extremely interesting painting may once have been an altarpiece at Richmond. It shows the king and queen and their children, many of whom did not survive infancy; it therefore may have been to encourage the friars to pray for their souls. The background contains fantastic buildings, one of which has a marked similarity to the later cockpit at Whitehall Palace.

ABOVE: Henry VIII at prayer in his privy closet. This miniature, done in the late 1530s, shows the king, beneath a richly embroidered canopy, kneeling at a desk with an open book on it. To his left you can see the lattice window between the kneeling place and the chapel.

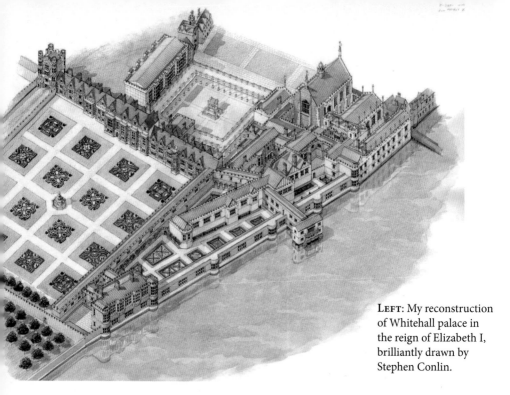

LEFT: My reconstruction of Whitehall palace in the reign of Elizabeth I, brilliantly drawn by Stephen Conlin.

BELOW: Detail from the famous painting, by an anonymous hand, of Henry VIII and Francis I of France meeting at the Field of Cloth of Gold outside Guînes in 1520. Here the temporary palace can be seen, a confection of traditional and renaissance motifs and designs constructed of brick and canvas. In front is a remarkable fountain and around it are tents containing kitchens and other service quarters.

ABOVE: Two details from a painting known as *The Family of Henry VIII* in the Royal Collection. The unknown painter set the picture at Whitehall Palace and included two very detailed and accurate views looking out of the palace into the gardens. On the left can be seen one wing of the palace covered in black-and-white painted grotesque-work. In the right view the transept of Westminster Abbey can be seen in the distance, and on the other side of the wall, one of the turrets of the great close tennis court is glimpsed. Both views show the gardens with low brick walls supporting green-and-white striped rails. Dotted amongst these are posts bearing heraldic beasts.

LEFT: Could this be James Nedeham or one of the king's architects? This unidentified man, painted by Hans Holbein the Younger in *c.*1534, is a senior court official wearing the court livery assigned to Nedeham and the other master craftsmen: a red coat with black cotton lining emblazoned with the letters HR.

LEFT: The so-called Wolsey Closet at Hampton Court Palace. This room was assembled in the nineteenth century from a variety of Tudor fragments and some specially made-up pieces. However, it gives some impression of what a small royal closet may have looked like in the late 1530s and contains paintings commissioned for Henry VIII's court.

BELOW: Hans Holbein's mural in the Whitehall privy chamber, done in 1536–7. Incredibly lifelike and powerful, this painting was sited above the throne canopy occupying the whole of the upper part of the south wall. It became the defining image of Henry VIII and the dominating presence in the palace until its destruction in 1698. Charles II commissioned this copy from Remigius van Leemput in May 1669 at a cost of £150.

ABOVE: A lock with no handles. This is a royal lock from Beddington Place in Surrey, a house acquired by the king in 1539. It has two keyholes with separate bolts; they can be operated at the same time by the insertion of a pin. Such locks were positioned on the doors of the secret lodgings. The king's locksmith would carry them to far-flung residences and install them where security was deemed to be poor.

ABOVE: The east front of Hampton Court, painted for Charles II by Hendrick Danckerts in c.1666. On the right you can see the long gallery built for Jane Seymour, ending in the very tall window of the queen's bedchamber. A balcony fronts the queen's drawing room and to its left is the doorway from the inner court to the park. To the left of this are the queen's and king's secret lodgings.

RIGHT: A record by Sir Thomas Wriothesley, Garter King of Arms, of arms and heraldic beasts, including those of Henry VIII and Francis I of France. Such records were made for royal painters, glaziers and carvers so that they could get the complexities of Tudor heraldry exactly right.

ABOVE: A tapestry from Henry VIII's great set of the story of David, *c.*1526–8. This one shows David seeing Bathsheba washing and inviting her into his palace. It is typical of tapestries in the early part of Henry's reign, with figures crowded together in shallow perspective. It measures 4.52 x 7.14 metres and is now in the Musée National de la Renaissance, Écouen, France.

ABOVE: A tapestry from Henry VIII's great set of St Paul, *c.*1540–45. Here Paul defends himself before Agrippa. This is in a completely different style, with big dramatic and dynamic figures in deep perspective. Such tapestries transformed the appearance of royal interiors in the late 1530s and 1540s. The tapestry measures 3.7 x 7 metres and is now in the Detroit Institute of Arts, USA.

We don't actually know how much Henry spent on building during his reign: if all the recorded expenditure is added up, it comes to around £250,000, but it must have been at least twice that as financial records are not full enough to give us a total for work at houses like Greenwich, where there was a great deal of building. Added to whatever figure we take as a total for bricks and mortar is the cost of furnishings and plate; all in all, the amount spent on his domestic residences can hardly have been less than £1 million. Most of this was spent after 1530, much of it after 1536 when the Court of Augmentations came into being.

We need to put this figure into perspective. The average income of a noble family was around £900 a year and only four families were worth more than £2,000; the average for a bishop was around £1,000. These were the richest men in England. To take up a knighthood you needed to earn at least £40 a year, but most gentry earned less than that. In all, over 90 per cent of the population earned less than £20 a year.[3] A million pounds on buildings, in this context, looks like uncontrolled megalomania and in 1534, even before the king's extravagance peaked, Thomas Cromwell wrote, 'what a great charge it is to your highness to continue his buildings in so many places at once. How proud and false the workmen are; if only his grace would spare [building] for one year, how profitable it would be for him'. There was no hope. With the unparalleled resources of the Church, Henry's architects devoured cash on more and more houses.[4]

Calculating exactly how many houses the king had is surprisingly difficult. The official history of the Office of the King's Works suggests that there were in total around sixty-four at his death, but these were only the ones on which the king's own architects and administrators worked. So, for instance, there were houses like Hitchin in Hertfordshire, which was part of Queen Katharine's jointure and so didn't appear in the king's financial records; but Henry often stayed there and the house had suites of lodgings for both the king and the queen. Looking at approximate numbers, though, the story is clear. In 1509 there were around twenty royal houses and a small number of royal castles that were still set up for royal use, including the Tower of London, Dover and Leeds (in Kent). In the first twenty years of Henry's reign were added around another twenty, and between 1529 and his death in 1547 there were at least another twenty-five. So, all in all, Edward VI inherited perhaps seventy domestic residences.[5]

It is perhaps not surprising, given these facts, that in August 1540 Charles de Marillac, the French ambassador, delivered an excoriating analysis of Henry's greed. He said the king was consumed by three vices, which he called plagues, the first of which was covetousness: 'he is so covetous', he wrote, 'that all the riches in the world would not satisfy him. Hence the ruin of the abbeys, spoil of all churches that had anything to take ... hence the accusation of so many rich men, who, whether condemned or acquitted, are always plucked ... Everything is good prize, and he does not reflect that to make himself rich he has impoverished his people, and does not gain in goods what he loses in renown ...'[6] It was true. Almost all the houses that Henry acquired after 1529 were at the expense of someone else. Although he did purchase a small number, most came to him through forfeit, a supposed swap, or he just took them from the Church.

Early in his reign Henry bought a small number of new residences, like Beaulieu and the handsome hunting lodge at Ampthill in Bedfordshire, but many more houses he took from courtiers who fell from favour. Of course, from Wolsey he gained the greatest prizes, but before that, in 1521, came the Duke of Buckingham's best houses after the duke was executed for treason. Later, and in the same manner, came the residences of Henry Courtenay, Marquess of Exeter, and Sir Nicholas Carew, both of whom were victims of Thomas Cromwell's ruthless political manoeuvring. Exchange was also a good mechanism for the king, whose landholdings tended to be very dispersed across England. It made good sense for him to swap outlying lands in remote places for houses and their parks where he wanted them. The deals struck were always to Henry's advantage. Thirteen new houses came into his hands in this way between 1526 and 1540, most spectacularly the colossal residences of the Archbishop of Canterbury at Otford and Knole in Kent.

Otford was one of the largest houses in England, and Knole, though less up to date, was a very handsome house in a beautiful setting. In the summer of 1537 Henry suggested to Archbishop Cranmer that he might like to exchange Otford for a fairly motley group of former monastic and church lands in Kent. Cranmer, fearing that the king would also ask for Knole, talked Knole down, telling Henry that it was far too small for the royal court. This was a mistake. Henry, flexing his mighty muscles, told Cranmer that he would rather have Knole than Otford, 'for it stands on better soil. This house [Otford] stands low and is rheumatic . . . and as for Knole it stands on a sound, perfect, handsome ground. And if I should make my abode here, as I do surely mind to do now and then, I myself will lie at Knole and most of my household shall lie at Otford'. Thus, on a royal whim, Cranmer lost both houses in return for lands with a fraction of the value of his mansions.[7]

Quite different circumstances surrounded the acquisition of houses formerly owned by monasteries.[8] Two Acts of Parliament, in 1536 and 1539, opened the way to the ending of nearly a thousand years of English monasticism. They also gave the king a headache. The abbot's lodgings and guest houses of many monasteries had been regularly used by the royal family on progresses and they formed a key part of the royal geography of England. At some, like Rochester Priory, a suite of rooms had been kept at the ready for royal visits since the fourteenth century, and at Guildford Friary Henry VIII had actually built his own lodgings with a garden. In many cases, therefore, the king had little choice but to take on dissolved monasteries as royal residences. So, for instance, he had stayed at St Augustine's Priory, Canterbury, nine times before the Dissolution and after it became a royal house he used it four times more. But it was not an automatic choice simply to appropriate monasteries he regularly used. Each case was carefully considered. Abingdon Abbey had been a favourite stopping-off point on the way to Woodstock; in 1538 Sir Richard Rich was sent to inspect it and he reported 'that the most part of the houses of office thereof be in much ruin and decay except the church . . . and as concerning the abbots lodging, I think it is not like for a habitation of the king's majesty, unless his Highness will expend great treasure'. This was not the only problem with the abbey, for he continued, 'as I and others can judge, no ground thereabout on the northeast side [is suitable] to be conveniently imparked for the king's disport and pleasure' – unless, that is, he took in all the land round the town, which would wipe out the townspeople's fields.

Instead of taking Abingdon, Henry's advisors suggested he take Reading Abbey, another monastery used as a staging post west and only a day's ride from Windsor Castle. In 1518 the king had stayed there and it was said at the time that the abbot had 'made to the [king's] grace and all his servants good cheer'.[9] In September 1538 Thomas Cromwell was being reassured by his agents that the whole place was being preserved until the king decided whether to take it or not, which he did.

In the end, eleven former monasteries were turned into royal houses and most were chosen on the basis of their location, but Ashridge in Hertfordshire was acquired as a nursery house, York principally for the use of the Council of the North, and Syon nunnery was to be turned into a munitions factory.

Unlike houses swapped or exchanged, which often needed little work, converting abbeys into houses required ingenuity and cash. It was James Nedeham who specialized in this and at Rochester, Canterbury and Dartford he created three large new royal houses out of the monastic structures. These were particularly singled out as they lay on key royal routes to the south coast and to Dover, and were used both by the king and by royal guests travelling to and from London from the continent. The conversions were big projects. At Dartford nearly 2 million bricks were fired and hundreds of bargeloads of stone were brought from Barking Abbey; the total cost of the works was £6,600.

Dartford was, in fact, the most architecturally pretentious of the new ex-monastic houses. In the great court Nedeham designed a magnificent broad stair leading up to the royal lodgings. On either side of the bottom step stood a gilded dragon and a gilded lion holding gilded metal standards with the royal arms. At the stair top a gallery led in one direction to a suite for the queen and in the other to the king's rooms. As in most of the monastic conversions, the royal lodgings were built on top of the monastic cloisters with the added refinement of bay windows supported on pillars.

The King's Progress

Almost all the houses acquired by the king in the 1530s and 1540s were in the Home Counties and the south of England. Other than Hull, York and Newcastle, there wasn't a royal manor further north than Collyweston in Northamptonshire, and that was further north than most of the regularly used houses. This pattern requires some explanation and to do that we need to look backwards into the early Middle Ages.

In the thirteenth century the royal household had numbered only about 100 people and it was possible for it to move relatively quickly between houses that were spread out in a band across the Midlands and the south-west. Over the following century the size of the royal household steadily increased, reaching about 500 people by 1300, and, as it got larger, it became less mobile and travelled shorter distances. At the same time, Westminster became the national capital and the headquarters for the monarchy and, as a consequence, houses further away from Westminster, or that were difficult to reach, were abandoned and those closer to the capital were made larger. The result was that, by the reign of Henry VII, there were a relatively small number of royal manors of a good size clustered in the Home Counties and visited by the court – still of perhaps 500 people – during its summer progresses.[10]

The progress was a formal event that required considerable planning.[11] Each year the king's ministers would sit down and devise a route that combined excellent hunting with visits to people and places that the king needed to see. It was a skilful job, because as well as being alive to the prevailing political context, the compilers had to know the conditions of the roads, the distances between houses and the king's likes and dislikes. The route, known as the gests (pronounced guests), was then shown to the king for his approval. Once resolved, the Office of Works would be informed and James Nedeham would ride the route to inspect the houses that the king intended to visit. Before 1530 Henry

Royal residences at the end of Henry VIII's reign. The map makes the point that the king's itinerary was narrowly focused on the Home Counties and the south-east. The importance of the Thames as a travel artery can also be seen.

Grafton ◆

◆ Ampthill

Dunstable ◆

◆ Woodstock

Hunsdo

Ashridge ◆

Hertford ◆　◆

St Albans ◆　◆ Hatfield

◆ Langley

◆ Tyttenhangar

The More ◆

Enfield ◆

Ewelme ◆

Westminster & St James

Haverin

Bridewell

◆

Chelsea

Wanste

Parlaunt

◆

Hackney

Ditton

◆

Mortlake

Tower

Windsor ◆

Syon ◆

Suffolk Place

Reading ◆

Hanworth

Greenwio

Hampton Court

Richmond

Oatlands

Bedding

Chobham ◆

Esher　Nonsuch

Otford

◆ Woking

◆ West Horsley

Knol

Guildford ◆

Penshur

Oatlands House

Petworth
◆

Nonsuch

Halnaker
◆

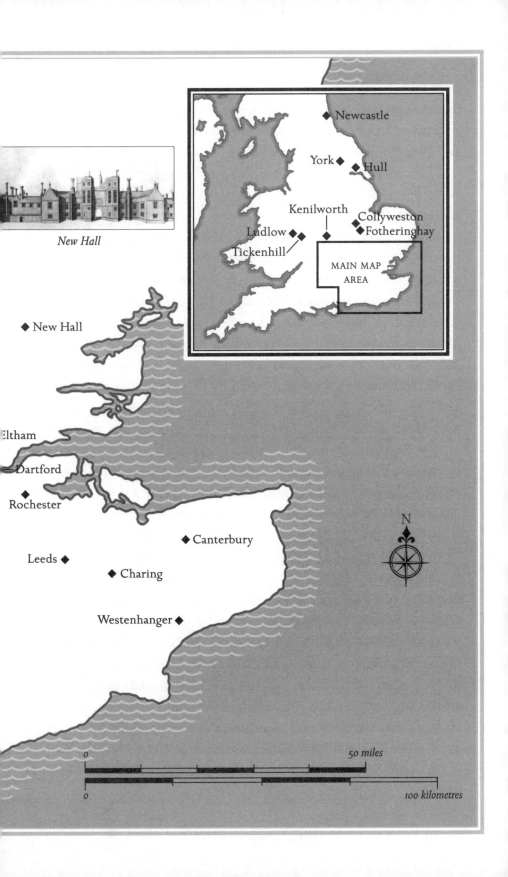

New Hall

◆ Newcastle

York ◆   ◆ Hull

Kenilworth

Ludlow ◆ ◆   ◆ Collyweston
Tickenhill   ◆ Fotheringhay

MAIN MAP
AREA

◆ New Hall

Eltham

Dartford

◆
Rochester

◆ Canterbury

Leeds ◆

◆ Charing

Westenhanger ◆

N

0   50 miles

0   100 kilometres

often stayed with courtiers, but later in the reign he had so many houses that over 90 per cent of the time he would stay in his own buildings. A long list of repairs and improvements would be drawn up by Nedeham and these would be put in hand before the progress began.

The court on progress was perhaps only half the size of the wintertime court, but it still numbered 600–800 people. It is hard to find a modern equivalent of the Tudor progress. A rock band on tour, or a movie on location, is probably the closest equivalent that now exists – a self-contained mass of people moving, with its own infrastructure, from place to place.[12] In the sixteenth century simply moving so many around the countryside was a huge task. The king and his family had the royal stables containing perhaps 300 horses, while aristocrats, churchmen and ministers following the progress would have their own. Most people rode, but the very young or infirm might be carried in a horse litter, a lightly built curtained cabin attached by two long poles to a couple of gently ambling horses. Ladies, if they rode, would mount a palfrey, the most expensive and highly bred horse with a smooth, ambling gait.[13]

The vast Lord Steward's department did not have its own transport, so towns and villages through which the court passed were required to supply horses and carts at a fixed rate – generally 2d a mile (the commercial rate was around 12d); this was very unpopular, particularly at harvest time when they were needed by their owners. In the late 1520s when the court moved through west Kent, sixteen villages were required to supply 26 carts for summer progresses within the county. This was a fraction of the number needed; in 1589, 169 carts were needed to move Queen Elizabeth's household: the Wardrobe of the Beds required ten, the jewel coffers thirteen and the chapel ten. Then there were the carts for the kitchen departments; most, such as the boiling house, the pastry and the scalding house, needed only one, but the Cofferer needed four. The great officers were entitled to a single cart, but the Lord Chamberlain, Master of the Horse, Secretary, etc., were allocated three additional carts each. Various other household departments also had carts, such as the Yeomen of the Guard, who had one to transport their uniforms, and the Master of the King's Hounds, who had carts for the dogs.

The richest aristocrats moved their own furniture, bedding and tapestries on progress in their own or hired carts, so, in all, the total number of carts on progress might be 300–350. Henry VIII's court on the move must have been an impressive sight as it wended through the lanes and byways of England, but progress was very slow by modern standards: it would average only 12 miles a day, though on some more often travelled routes it might manage as many as 18 miles. As it went, it attracted its share of vagabonds and beggars, so security and discipline were tight and undesirables were ruthlessly ejected.[14]

As well as transport, careful provision had to be made for the supply of the royal kitchens and the royal Clerk of the Market had to ride ahead of the progress to ensure that there was enough bread, beer and meat for the court. This, like cart-taking, was unpopular, because the Royal Purveyors (responsible for acquiring food for the court) were entitled to buy goods at something known as the King's Price. Inevitably this was cheaper than the price everyone else had to pay, so the arrival of the court did not mean profits for local producers. In the 1520s the fixed price the court paid for poultry, for instance, was 5s per swan, 2s for a peacock, 7d for a hen and 6d for a dozen larks. This discount did not apply to courtiers or churchmen who put the king up, however, so the honour of a royal visit was accompanied by a hefty bill. When the court arrived at Wolfhall in Wiltshire to visit Sir Edward Seymour in 1539, he had to convert a barn on his estate for his household servants. On the first night he gave supper for 70, but this was a mere prelude to the dinner for 800 the following night and the 1,500 guests on the next two nights.[15]

Also in the advance guard were the Gentleman Harbingers. They had an extremely important role, because few houses at progress time could accommodate the whole court and people had to be put up in subsidiary royal houses, in the houses of the gentry or even in inns. The harbingers would allocate everyone in the household a set number of rooms and stables for their horses. A chit or billet was issued to each person allocated space and this would be presented at court or in peripheral accommodation nearby. A harbinger was in a powerful position as courtiers vied with each other for the best places to stay.

Although Wolsey tried to crack down on courtiers bribing the harbingers for the most comfortable beds, he was not free from it himself. On one occasion in 1520 we know that he offered 20s if the harbingers could put him in the best lodgings in Canterbury, Sandwich and Dover.[16]

When the Emperor Charles V came to England in 1522 the harbingers calculated that there would be space for 105 people in Sittingbourne in three inns. The capacity of a local town to take large numbers of people was a really important factor. When the king's surveyors were considering whether to keep the house at Writtle, in Essex, which the Duke of Buckingham had forfeit at his attainder, they advised that the king should take it as Writtle had lots of good lodgings and only a mile away was Chelmsford, where hundreds of people could stay. Henry did take the house, but never used it himself – instead it ended up as a sort of bed and breakfast for senior figures when the court was nearby at Beaulieu.[17]

The progress of 1526 was one of the king's most expansive, crossing seven counties starting at Windsor at the beginning of June and ending at Greenwich on 18 October. In July, when Henry entered Sussex, he was met by a delegation led by the aristocrats and courtiers of the county, who escorted him to Petworth, a house belonging to the Duke of Northumberland (later to be acquired by the king). The duke was away, but his household presented Henry with six oxen and four sheep.

All summer long Henry hunted with landowners and aristocrats. The chase was the bond that united them: the men of the shires were flattered to hunt with their king and Henry happy to have energetic companions to enjoy new hunting grounds. Hunting, like jousting, broke down the formality of royal life and gave crucial access to the king's person.

As the reign went on, the king was more and more often able to stay in his own houses but, even so, as he ventured outside the Home Counties, more complex arrangements had to be made. In 1541, in response to continued discontent and rebellion in the north, and triggered by a plot hatched in Wakefield, Henry decided to make a great progress north to quell discontent by a show of power and magnificence. According to the Spanish ambassador, he was to take 5,000 horses with him; this was an

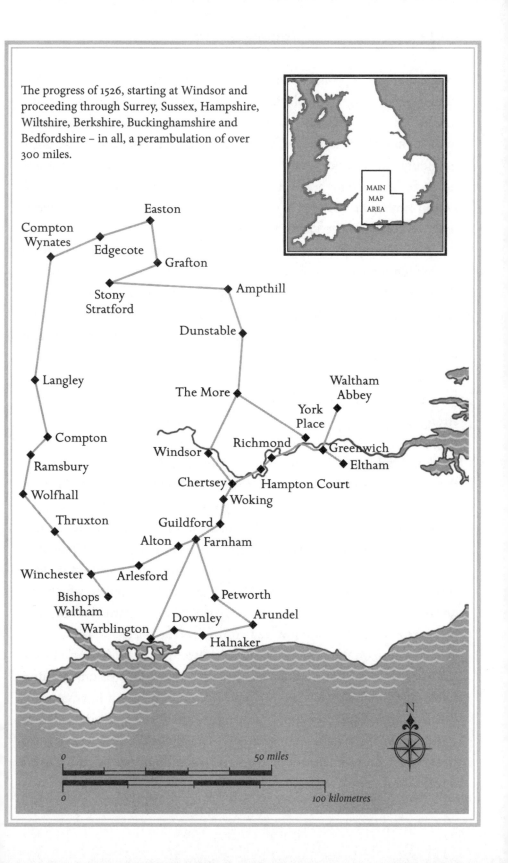

The progress of 1526, starting at Windsor and proceeding through Surrey, Sussex, Hampshire, Wiltshire, Berkshire, Buckinghamshire and Bedfordshire – in all, a perambulation of over 300 miles.

MAIN MAP AREA

Easton

Compton Wynates

Edgecote

Grafton

Stony Stratford

Ampthill

Dunstable

Langley

The More

Waltham Abbey

York Place

Compton

Windsor

Richmond

Greenwich

Ramsbury

Chertsey

Hampton Court

Eltham

Wolfhall

Woking

Thruxton

Guildford

Alton

Farnham

Winchester

Arlesford

Bishops Waltham

Petworth

Warblington

Downley

Arundel

Halnaker

0   50 miles

0   100 kilometres

N

exaggeration, but probably not by much. In July the vast royal train was lumbering through Lincolnshire, far to the north of the king's usual haunts. An official from the Court of Augmentations had been sent ahead with a budget of well over £800 to prepare residences in advance, including two fine new ones at Hull and York. In some places there was nowhere large enough to take the whole royal party and Henry and Queen Catherine Howard were accommodated in extremely luxurious tents – a sort of Tudor glamping.[18]

As the progress continued, its route embraced a number of royal castles. Other than the Tower of London, Windsor and Kenilworth, there were few castles that had suitable accommodation for the court. The Crown still held a huge number – perhaps as many as fifty-five – but most were simply retained to prevent other people owning them and were left to decay gently. The most important castle in the north was the mighty Pontefract, a fortress so powerful that during the Civil War in the next century it took three sieges to capture it. In Henry's day its strength had been recognized by northern rebels, who had made it a target, so the king's arrival there was not only utilizing a large royal residence but symbolized his control. Henry and Catherine moved into the king's and queen's lodgings, massive stone towers linked to the great hall and outer rooms. The royal lodgings had been built in the early fifteenth century and were similar to those to which Henry VII had come at the Tower of London. There was a substantial great hall with a tower at each end. Both towers were square and consisted of four storeys above a basement. On the king's side, his bedchamber, which was on the first floor of the tower, was approached by a guard chamber and presence chamber. Above it were two rooms. The queen's tower had five levels: a room on the principal floor, with two rooms above it and below it a room that was known in the seventeenth century as the nursery, and underneath that a cellar. Seventy pounds had to be spent in advance of the royal arrival and every stick of furniture and scrap of textile had to be imported, as there were no permanent furnishings there. For nearly two weeks the court remained in medieval splendour before moving off towards York.[19]

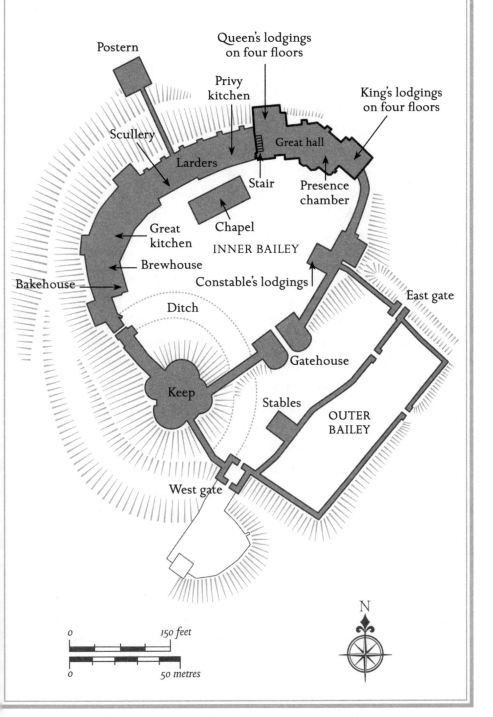

Pontefract Castle in the reign of Henry VIII. The fortress was a spectacular place but could only be made suitable as a royal residence in 1541 by importing all the furnishings and overhauling the royal lodgings.

Postern

Queen's lodgings on four floors

Privy kitchen

King's lodgings on four floors

Scullery

Larders

Great hall

Stair

Presence chamber

Great kitchen

Chapel

INNER BAILEY

Brewhouse

Bakehouse

Constable's lodgings

East gate

Ditch

Gatehouse

Keep

Stables

OUTER BAILEY

West gate

N

0   150 feet

0   50 metres

KEEPERS

Although the Office of Works did take responsibility for maintaining castles, especially in the face of the arrival of the king, most were under the control of a constable or keeper, who often had delegated responsibility for repair and maintenance funded by the surrounding forestry and lands. As we shall see in the case of Windsor, an active, or high-profile, constable could have a significant impact on the place.

Everything at the Tudor court had a keeper. Whether it was a pack of hounds, a clock, a park, a tennis court, a fishpond or a fool, someone was given a title and a wage to look after it. Amongst the most prestigious keeperships were those of the royal houses and parks, as with these positions came considerable benefits and responsibilities.

To start with the benefits: keeperships came with a salary ranging from 2d a day for a small house like Wanstead, 16d a day for a large country house like Beaulieu and 1s 8d for Whitehall; normally the cash came with various perks such as free firewood and leave to hunt in the park. The keeper was assigned fine lodgings in the house where he could stay during a royal visit, and was often also given a large lodge in the immediate vicinity as a personal residence. Along with these material boons came the prestige and access that the keepership gave to the king's person, especially when he came to stay.[20]

On the other side were the responsibilities – which were significant. The keeper had to liaise with the Office of Works on repairs and make sure the house was clean and ready for the court when it came. The accounts of the Marquess of Exeter, who was keeper of the house of Birling in Kent, show that in 1527 his servants were scrubbing out the stables in anticipation of a royal visit and ordering in 'horse bread'.[21]

The keeper was in charge of the security of the house and any contents, and this meant he had charge of the keys. On arrival of the court these would be given up to the Cofferer and the keys to the king's rooms to the Groom of the Stool. Often, particularly at the smaller houses, the king would travel with his locksmith, who would change the locks on the doors of the king's and queen's privy lodgings. To these there were two keys, master keys, held by members of the royal family and the Groom of the Stool, which opened every door, and by-keys that opened only a single specific door.

When I was restoring King William III's apartments at Hampton Court in 1990 I had the chance to examine very closely the locks that were put on the doors in 1700. The system was exactly the same as Henry VIII's. We found that keys would open some doors and not others, and that the king's own bedroom door had no handle on the outside and could be entered only with a master key, which was held by the Groom of the Stool. By Elizabeth I's reign the groom wore the key on an orange silk ribbon hanging round his neck. When Catherine Howard was arrested and confined to her privy lodgings in 1541, she was specifically allowed to retain her master keys so she could move from room to room, showing that the most important Tudor doors also only had keys and no handles (see plate section).[22]

Security was important for the king's flesh and blood, but also because of his possessions. Henry's houses contained colossal quantities of textiles and furniture. The inventory taken on his death lists 2,770 pieces of tapestry, 638 carpets, 687 cushions, 97 bedsteads and 30 cloths of estate. These were objects of incredible value; between 1509 and 1521 the king spent approximately £50,000 on cloth and furs, both for dress and for furnishings; this is roughly the same amount that he spent on armour and munitions for the army and navy. Displaying, securing and maintaining household objects was one of the major tasks that fell to the keepers.

Furnishings were managed centrally by the Lord Chamberlain and the Wardrobe of the Beds, which had a central store at the Tower of London built in 1532 near the White Tower. This was 101 feet long and only 24 feet wide – more like a gallery than a warehouse; much of its content was textiles, which were kept rolled up and were frequently fumigated and aired.[23] If the Tower was the deposit account, the current account was a series of standing wardrobes at the king's most frequently used houses under the care of keepers. These were stores that contained the furnishings permanently assigned to each house, but which were taken down and carefully packed away when the court was not in residence. Generally these standing wardrobes were in the outer courts, where there was space for carts to come and go delivering large objects. They were fitted with cupboards and storage racks, some of which were gigantic: at Greenwich one cupboard was 55 feet long to take the largest tapestries. Also stored in the wardrobes were long ladders used by the wardrobe staff to erect and take down tapestries, beds and throne canopies. At any one time Henry kept four or five houses more or less fully furnished; these were known as the standing houses. At first these were Richmond, Greenwich, Eltham, Windsor and Westminster, but later they included Hampton Court and his favoured houses of the 1540s.

The remainder of the royal houses were more like stage sets that had to be dressed for the impending pageant of the royal court. The Wardrobe of the Beds had up to six staff who travelled from house to house in advance of the court to set rooms up before the king arrived. When the house was dormant, the objects carefully rolled up, covered in dustsheets and packed in cases, the keys to the Wardrobe of the Beds were handed to the keeper of the house; at the big houses a designated wardrobe keeper served under him, keeping an eye on everything. At the king's death in 1547 there were fourteen standing Wardrobes of the Beds. In addition to these, Henry's queens and children had wardrobes for their household stuff. These were smaller, but they too contained large quantities of rich furnishings.

Many of the smaller houses would keep some basic furnishings in store, but there would be none of the valuable textiles that were necessary for a court visit – for instance, the very valuable canopies of state were rarely left at remote and infrequently visited houses. This is where the Removing (or Travelling) Wardrobe came in. On progress the wardrobe would load its carts with the textiles and other furnishings needed to set up a less frequently visited house. The Removing Wardrobe varied in size and in its contents, drawing appropriate items from the Tower or from the other standing wardrobes when needed.[24]

Decisions as to what would go where were not made by the wardrobe staff: they were factotums, not interior decorators. The ultimate decision on how the rooms would be prepared was the king's, but under him the Lord Chamberlain and, crucially, the gentlemen ushers would order the rooms for him. In around 1558 one of Henry VIII's gentlemen ushers, John Norris, recorded his former duties in setting up a house for the king and queen. After viewing the rooms available, the gentleman usher was to 'warn the groom of the wardrobe . . . to bring in arras [tapestry] to hang the chambers aforesaid and to bring also a cloth of estate with a chair and cushions and then the yeoman of the chamber shall hang the said chamber'. Once done, the work would be inspected by the gentleman usher and passed for service. Cardinal Wolsey's gentleman usher recorded his memory of setting up Hampton Court in 1527:

> Our pains were not small or light, but travelling daily from chamber to chamber . . . the yeomen and grooms of the wardrobes were busied in hanging of the chambers with costly hangings and furnishing the same with beds of silk and other furniture apt for the same in every degree . . . the carpenters, the joiners, the masons and painters and all other artificers necessary to glorify the house and feasts were set to work. There was carriage and re-carriage of plate, stuff, and other rich implements so that there was nothing lacking.

In 1540 it took nine grooms and ushers to set up the same rooms for Henry VIII. Small and valuable items were always locked up when the king was away and all the large houses had a privy or secret jewel house close to the king's inner lodgings where his personal knick-knacks were kept – the keys to this would be secured by the keeper of the house.[25]

In use, a royal house was bursting with people and the textiles were incredibly vulnerable. One of the jobs of the ushers, grooms and pages was to 'give attendance at all times from the morning unto time for the watch to be charged for the king's chambers: that is to say for rich arras, rich beds, carpets, cushions, counterpanes, forms, stools, tables and all other things . . . Wherefore it hath been seen often in times past that there has been cut, stolen and borne away diverse of the said stuff'. Special guard was also to be posted to prevent people wiping their greasy hands on tapestries or other textiles.[26]

The other important repositories of textiles were the Wardrobes of the Robes, one at each house for each member of the royal family. The king's and queen's were always sited below their privy or bedchambers and were linked to them by a spiral staircase. Originally the king's Wardrobe of the Robes had been part of the Chamber, like the Wardrobe of the Beds, and this continued through most of Henry's reign; however, sometime between 1536 and 1540 the office became part of the Privy Chamber under control of the Groom of the Stool. It is strange that this change had not been made before, given the extreme intimacy that the wardrobe had with the king. Strictly speaking, before 1536 wardrobe officers could not enter the privy lodgings and had to hand in clothes through the door of the privy chamber to the king's body servants. The Groom of the Stool was in charge of the king's underwear and shirts, which he carried around separately from the Wardrobe of the Robes. However, underwear and top wear were united under the control of the Groom of the Stool in the Privy Chamber in the late 1530s. This was all part of the redefinition of the use of the privy chamber. Even in the early 1530s the king was no longer getting dressed in a chamber that was becoming the main public reception room. At Whitehall there was a separate dressing room between his private dining room and his library. At Greenwich there was a raying (i.e. arraying) chamber near his bedchamber and the queen's lodgings, and at Richmond one next his bedchamber.[27]

Because the royal clothes were continually being carried around, the wardrobe had a large selection of chests and coffers, sacks and wicker baskets, all of which travelled from place to place in the Wardrobe of the Robes cart – a substantial wagon with a wooden roof painted with the king's arms, badges and beasts, all with a trim of antique-work – or in their own little boat on the Thames. Within the wardrobes themselves there were large fixed coffers or chests, which were like a modern wardrobe with sturdy locks.[28]

Most of the king's clothes would simply be brushed, but most residences had laundries, normally sited in the outer courts. Here five or six people worked and some of the very few women at court were employed. One laundress was specifically required to wash the queen's linen and to be discreet about it, but the king had laundresses too. One was in charge of his table linen and, in 1542, was issued with 4 tablecloths, 56 breakfast cloths, 28 hand towels and 144 napkins, a quarter of which she had to wash each week. The laundries were characterized by big fireplaces for boiling water and for drying linen indoors. Washing was done in wooden tubs.[29]

By the 1540s the long-standing and well-oiled machinery of the royal household that had developed stage by stage since the Middle Ages had reached a peak of complexity. Never before had there been so many large, richly furnished and well equipped residences. Never before had the mechanisms of royal life been so efficiently run and rigidly policed. Henry was supported by a vast organic life-support system involving thousands of his subjects in specifically designated roles. These people were as much an ornament to his rule as the buildings in which they served. In fact, entourage was just as important an ingredient in royal magnificence as architecture; the sheer size and complexity of his household gave him status rather than in any way detracting from it. To appreciate this fully, I now want to explain in greater detail exactly how Henry's life-support machine actually worked.

·VIII·

ROOM SERVICE

Mid-life Crisis

THERE IS NO QUESTION THAT HENRY VIII and Anne Boleyn were a love match and, although she was feisty and would stand up to him, arguments were resolved with a kiss and a cuddle. This is, of course, why Anne's sudden fall in 1536 is so extraordinary. Historians still argue about how a woman with whom the king was apparently still in love could be beheaded by him, but some basic facts are clear. On 29 January, the day Katharine of Aragon was buried in Peterborough Abbey, Anne miscarried a male foetus. It may have been her second miscarriage, but this one was very public and the king and queen were devastated. She told Henry that it was because she had been traumatized by the fall he had in the tiltyard that had knocked him unconscious for two hours, but the king, already shaken by this accident – which burst an ulcer on his leg and triggered the infection that would eventually make him completely lame – thought that it signified that he would never have a male child.

What happened next was probably Anne's own fault. Nine years younger than her husband, she had entertained various men in her privy chamber. While this might have been (just) all right for a young noblewoman, horsing about with unmarried men was open to serious ambiguity if you were queen. A combination of bad appearances, Anne's vanity, misinterpretation and malice in Anne's enemies turned the young queen's flirtatious games into an accusation of adultery, incest and treason. Archbishop Thomas Cranmer, who knew her better than most, refused to believe it and the queen protested her innocence, but Henry, consumed with a lust for retribution, ordered her to the Tower, where, after a 'trial', she was beheaded together with her supposed lovers. It all happened so quickly. In late January Henry was anticipating becoming father to an heir and on 19 May Anne was dead. More extraordinary still, eleven days later he was remarried – to the young Jane Seymour, with whom he had been conducting a flirtation for several months.

Henry's marriage to Anne Boleyn and its grisly aftermath signalled a process that saw the king, by 1540, living very differently to the way he had done in the 1520s. The houses that he had enjoyed in his twenties and early thirties were no longer the places he favoured. The changes that began around 1530 and continued for the whole of the following decade saw not just a major reorganization and rebuilding of the royal residences but also a reshaping of the royal family's itinerary.

Behind the re-engineering of the itinerary lay some important changes in the way the royal household was organized. From early 1537, Thomas Cromwell was trying to institute reforms that would both save money and ensure the king was properly attended, but it was not until Christmas Eve 1539 that, at Greenwich, the new measures were announced. Some of these were short-lived, such as an attempt to combine the responsibilities of Lord Chamberlain and Lord Steward under a single Master of the Household. But the most important and long-lasting of these reforms didn't save money at all, rather cost it. This was the establishment of a new household guard called the Spears or the Gentlemen Pensioners. Numbering fifty, they took precedence over the Yeomen of the Guard and wore striking high-necked black doublets with fur-trimmed black gowns. On their chests was the gold pensioners' medallion hung on a chunky gold chain. The establishment of this guard was probably in imitation of that employed by the French king Francis I, but was more generally about boosting the magnificence of Henry's entourage. While the pensioners certainly had genuine security responsibilities, their *raison d'être* was as an ornament to the court: the equivalent in flesh and blood of the gold leaf that encrusted the royal interiors.[1]

THE END OF THE HALL

The changes that began to take place in the royal household were not just organizational – they were also architectural and, of these, the most significant was Henry VIII's decision, taken sometime around 1535, that he didn't need great halls in all his houses any more. This was a decisive break with 300 years of tradition: every royal and noble house had, at its heart, a great hall – a cavernous room symbolizing the owner's willingness – in fact his duty – to feed his household and entertain guests on a lavish scale. Thanks to Richard II's remodelling of Westminster Hall from 1393, there was a national architectural prototype too, followed by everyone from merchants in the City, through the aristocracy in their castles, to the king in his royal manors. The assumption that at the heart of any great residence was a hall was reinforced by Edward IV's magnificent hall at Eltham, started in 1475, and Henry VII's hall at Richmond, completed in 1501.

Yet by the reign of Henry VII the social gravity of a great house had long shifted from the great hall to the Chamber and, as we have seen, Henry VII moved it further still, relocating the king's private life out of the Chamber into the Privy Chamber. Despite the huge expense of the Richmond great hall, and the care taken with its decoration, for most of the time it was, in fact, the dining room for the most junior people at court. Despite this, for Henry VII the great hall retained a symbolic function. One of his last architectural commissions was the construction of a new great hall at Woking on the River Wey in Surrey. This house had been the property of his mother, Lady Margaret, and he had obtained it from her in 1503. Various works were commissioned to make it fit for a monarch, culminating in the construction of the new hall. Very little was known about this until a series of excavations, ending in 2015, uncovered the archaeological evidence for it. What is very interesting is that the new hall was apparently detached from the royal lodgings rather than being an integral part of the royal rooms. The Woking great hall was thus purely symbolic of the manor's new status as a royal dwelling rather than being part of the social fabric of the house.

By the mid-1520s it had become the practice for certain members of the household to give up their dining rights in the great hall and receive, instead, board wages – a sum of money paid in lieu of dining at court so that the recipient could organize his own nourishment and eat where he liked. Household servants could elect to take board wages or sometimes, in the name of economy, they would be instructed to take them. Either way, it was increasingly the case that the great hall was half empty and, at mealtimes, junior members of the court were idly loitering round the king's houses.

In 1526, in his reforming household ordinance issued at Eltham, Cardinal Wolsey required the household to attend hall at the five largest royal houses – Beaulieu, Eltham, Greenwich, Richmond and Woodstock – and at Hampton Court. This was not only a matter of domestic economy, it was one of prestige: after all, the whole idea of a great hall was to express the ancient duties and responsibilities of a lord to his household – difficult to do if the hall was half empty.[2]

When the king took over Hampton Court from Wolsey, one of his first projects was the construction of a new great hall. The existing hall was on the ground floor, not raised up on a basement, and was too modest for the house he intended to create. The new hall, which can still be visited today, was the only one Henry built and, like his father's halls at Richmond and Woking, it was a deliberate anachronism. It was covered with an extremely beautiful and elaborate hammerbeam roof, which was not a structural necessity, as the hall was only 40 feet wide, but was, again, an echo of Westminster Hall. The roof was crowned with a soaring louvre encrusted with a menagerie of lions, dragons and greyhounds carrying gilded and painted vanes. This was supposedly to let out smoke from a fire lit on a stone hearth in the centre of the room. Such a fire was never lit – at least, when the paint on the ceiling was microscopically analysed in the 1920s no trace of any soot could be found.[3]

When it was completed, this marvellous room was used as court

Hampton Court seen from the north by Anthonis van den Wyngaerde, c.1558. The great hall completed in 1535 was the only hall built by Henry VIII and the last royal hall in England. It is also the first mansard roof in England. In the foreground are the royal kitchens; on the far right the bulk of the great gatehouse; on the far left the great close tennis court.

cafeteria. In normal circumstances it was laid out with trestles, benches and stools. We don't know how many were used at Hampton Court, but at Whitehall in 1542 there were 38 tables, 25 pairs of trestles, 64 benches and 73 joined stools, enough to seat a large number of people. The lower ranks ate off trenchers – square wooden boards with a dip in the centre for their food. These had a short life and were regularly replaced: in 1532 the Marshal of the Hall purchased 336 replacements which were delivered to the pantry responsible for issuing them.[4] In this, the hall's normal mundane function, the walls would be left bare plaster, but round the room was a heavy carved timber cornice called, by the Tudors, a jewel piece; from this could be hung tapestries when the hall moved into its alternative use as a grand reception room. When the hall at Hampton Court was prepared for the extremely lavish entertainment of the Admiral of France in 1546, it was hung with the largest and greatest set of tapestries Henry owned. Telling the story of Abraham, these ten weighty pieces

laced with gold thread were paid for by the king in 1544 and were almost certainly made for this hall, where, astonishingly, they can still be seen today. Hanging the Hampton Court hall with the single most valuable tapestry commission of his entire reign emphasizes the fact that it was intended to be a spectacular ceremonial space and, for the most important guests, as a special mark of respect the king would come out of his lodgings and stand in the hall to greet them.[5]

Soon after completing the new hall at Hampton Court, Henry decided that there would be great halls only at houses that performed ceremonial functions – this essentially meant Whitehall, Windsor and Greenwich besides Hampton Court. The consequence of this was that newly acquired houses that had great halls had them demolished or converted, and those being built from scratch completely omitted them. So, for example, when the king acquired from Wolsey the Manor of the More in Hertfordshire – a house described by contemporaries as just as splendid as Hampton Court, though not as large – it had a great hall, which, in 1535, Henry divided horizontally, creating a new upper chamber that served as the communal anteroom to the king's and queen's lodgings. At Dartford, where James Nedeham converted the priory into a large royal residence, there was a

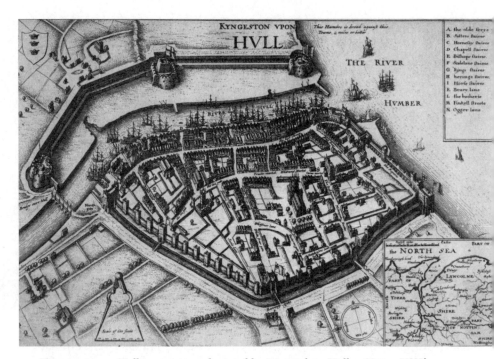

Kingston upon Hull in *c.*1640, as depicted by Wenceslaus Hollar. Henry VIII's fortifications encircle the town and within, centre left, can be seen the exaggerated tower and gatehouse of Hull Manor.

spectacular processional stair that led to an anteroom off which were the king's and queen's watching chambers. There was no great hall.[6]

This change signified a much more private way of life in the lesser houses outside the Thames valley. The king could travel with far fewer attendants and servants, and a single outer dining room could be set aside for this inner circle, while the king could be fed from his privy kitchen. A remarkable illustration of this new way of life is the house that the king planned for himself in Hull. Kingston upon Hull was chosen, in 1539, as one of the twenty-five sites in England that Henry would fortify against attack by the papal powers of Europe who wanted to use military force to bring England back into harmony with Rome. During two visits to the city in 1541, Henry devised a scheme of fortification encircling the town with walls and towers.

Henry stayed at Hull Manor, a town-centre house which he had

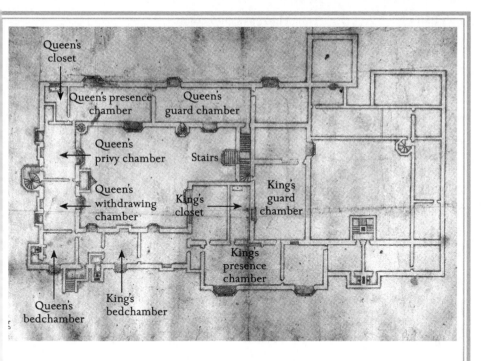

Plan of the first floor at Hull Manor, drawn by John Rogers. The queen's guard chamber was originally the great hall and the kitchen was to its right. In the new scheme the royal lodgings were approached by a ceremonial stair that led to the king's and queen's guard chambers.

originally granted to a favoured courtier, Sir William Sydney, but which he had re-acquired, by exchange, in 1538. It was a brick-built courtyard house of the sort popular in the 1530s. It had a great hall and a suite of lodgings for Sydney. At first the king's architect, John Rogers, assumed that Henry would want to keep the bones of the old house, adding a suite of rooms for the queen. He was wrong. After his visit in 1541 the king instructed Rogers to do away with the great hall and build a processional staircase up to the royal lodgings. These were to be arranged round the inner courtyard so that they met at a corner with conjoined bedrooms.

The house, sadly, is long gone, but Rogers' plan for it, drawn in ink on a large sheet of vellum, can be seen in the British Library – a precious and rare survival. The queen's watching chamber was originally the great hall and the square kitchen at its end would have served the whole household. Henry's new house could accommodate only the king, queen and their closest body servants and attendants. They would be fed from the manor's kitchen, while everyone else had to get board and lodging in the many taverns and inns in the city, or be billeted with wealthy merchants in their houses.[7]

The concept of the king having smaller houses of retreat was not new: even King Edward III, who loved Windsor so much, in his old age spent most of his time in smaller houses with just a few attendants. Henry VII, we have seen, did the same, but what was new about Henry VIII's arrangements was that the majority of the king's houses in the countryside were now retreat houses, deliberately set up to inhibit the numbers of attendants and provide the maximum amount of comfort and privacy for himself.

How Private Became Public

The king's changing preferences affected the state rooms of royal houses too. The only room that did not change function throughout the whole Tudor period was the watching (or guard) chamber – the room in which the Yeomen of the Guard stood securing access to the king's rooms beyond. Dressed during the day in their green-and-white uniforms, holding tall halberds, the yeomen slept in the guard chamber at night, using a small garderobe attached to the room when necessary. Though watching chambers were used during big court ceremonials, their everyday function remained as the dining room for the senior officers of the household, the Yeomen of the Guard setting up and clearing away tables and benches when required. There was normally a pages' chamber attached to the room; this was the HQ of the pages, whose role it was to secure and tidy the room and assist on ceremonial occasions.[8]

Next to the watching chamber was the presence chamber, sometimes known as the chamber of estate. Its principal furnishing was a large textile canopy with a backcloth embroidered with the king's arms and badges. This was generally known as a cloth of estate and had long

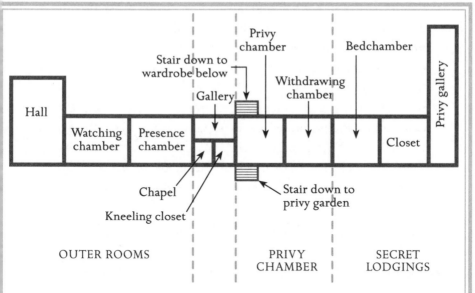

Typical layout of a large royal house at the end of Henry VIII's reign. Once established in the 1530s, the sequence of rooms remained the standard plan in royal houses throughout the Tudor period and into the reign of James I.

denoted the superior rank of the person sitting beneath it. At the Tudor court it had become more than that: it was the permanent symbol of sovereignty and even if the king were not beneath it courtiers were required to raise their hats as they passed; it was unacceptable to touch it or to pass beneath it, let alone snatch a quick sit-down on the chair. The chair and its cushion were set on a low dais covered with a valuable carpet. At the start of the reign the presence chamber was Henry's principal ceremonial room, in which ambassadors would be received, occasions of state enacted and in which he would dine in public, watched by the court standing at a respectful distance. During prestigious embassies Henry would throw a feast in here, sitting at the head of a great U-shaped table. When the room was not in use by the king it was used by senior aristocrats as a dining room.[9]

On St George's Day 1515 the new Venetian ambassador Magnifico Piero Pasqualigo received his first audience with Henry VIII at Richmond. His dispatch explains:

they led us to a sort of hall, and though it was before mass, they made
us breakfast, for fear we should faint; after which we were conducted
to the presence, through sundry chambers all hung with the most
beautiful tapestry, figured in gold and silver and in silk, passing down
the ranks of the body-guard . . . We at length reached the king, who
was under a canopy of cloth of gold embroidered at Florence, the most
costly thing I ever witnessed: he was leaning against his gilt throne, on
which there was a large brocade cushion . . . To the right of his majesty
were eight noblemen . . . to the left were a number of prelates . . . Then
there were six men with six gold sceptres, besides ten heralds . . .

After the magnifico had made his speech, the St George's Day Mass
was celebrated and the king then dined in the presence chamber, 'where
he chose us to see the service of the courses, contained in sixteen dishes

Henry VIII dining. This is an Elizabethan depiction of Henry at table, probably in one
of his presence chambers. In the left and right foreground can be seen spectators and
the king is surrounded by noblemen and members of the Privy Chamber. To the right
is a buffet groaning with silver gilt. The king sits alone beneath a canopy of state.

of massive gold with sixteen covers'. The ambassadors were then led to another chamber where they dined.[10]

Other than on exceptional occasions when the rank of a guest demanded it, Henry VII never admitted guests further into the royal lodgings than this. But Henry VIII, young, gregarious and, at first, informal with his friends, started as early as 1517 asking people into his privy chamber to observe him eating. This was, according to the Venetian ambassador who saw him do it, 'contrary to the custom of the kings of England'[11] and was the start of a process that saw the privy chamber, not the presence chamber, assume the role of the principal public room in any royal house. The presence chamber thus became a splendid anteroom to the privy chamber. When in 1544 the Duke of Nájera arrived at Whitehall for his audience with Henry VIII, he entered the presence chamber where, according to his Secretary who made an account of the event, 'were nobles, knights and gentlemen, and here was a canopy made of a rich figured brocade, with a chair of the same material . . . Here the brother of the queen and other noblemen entertained the Duke for a quarter of an hour, until it was announced that he should enter the chamber of the king'.[12]

Without doubt a major step in the change in function of these rooms had been the creation in 1539 of the band of Gentlemen Pensioners, who were required to stand guard in the presence chamber, overseeing access to the privy chamber beyond. Their positioning removed any remaining intimacy from the presence chamber and helped ensure that the privy chamber took its place as the most important room at court.[13] Thus in the thirty years since the privy chamber had been established by Henry VII, it was transformed from being the secret inner preserve of a paranoid king into the glittering public reception room of an extrovert monarch. To fully understand how this happened, we need to go back a few steps.

In 1526, in a book of household regulations issued at Eltham, Cardinal Wolsey formally recognized the fact that there were by then three departments at court: the household under the Lord Steward; the Chamber under the Lord Chamberlain; and the Privy Chamber under the Groom of the Stool. Wolsey's ordinances stated that in the Privy

Chamber there would be seven gentlemen (one of whom would be Groom of the Stool), two gentlemen ushers, four grooms, a barber and a page. The important people were the high-born gentlemen, the companions of the king whose formal duties included dressing and undressing him, serving at his table, arranging his bedtime and sleeping at the foot of his bed on a mattress. Informally, they were also the men who hunted, jousted, played tennis, cards and dice with Henry, and who played music, debated poetry and theology and discussed in detail the king's current building projects. These men occupied incredibly powerful positions in a world where the king's word was an order not to be disobeyed. As a result, there was a built-in imperative for the Privy Chamber to grow, and this it did. In 1526 there were in total fifteen members; by 1539 there were twenty-eight. The following year the Privy Council was established as a fully fledged body of state and its members (some nineteen) were admitted, by right, into the privy lodgings so that they could attend meetings in the council chamber. What had happened is that the highly restricted zone created by Henry VII to provide privacy and security for himself was now populated by an official staff of around fifty.[14]

As a consequence, as use have seen, there developed around the privy chamber a large number of ancillary spaces creating a new maze of rooms and backstairs around the king's bedchamber. This was the secret lodging, a part of the king's houses beyond the privy chamber to which his private life was relocated. It is possible to get a sense of what this meant by looking again at some of the larger residences, starting with Whitehall.[15]

After 1530 Whitehall became the king's single most visited residence. It was not merely a pleasure palace, but the king's place of work. It is notable that he rarely spent any of the great feasts of the year there, preferring to celebrate these at Greenwich or, later, Hampton Court; equally, while parliament was in session, Henry based himself at Whitehall so he could be close by. The business of government took place at Whitehall and the king's principal secretaries had offices there. It was also the place where the most important ceremonial took place – the formal reception of ambassadors, for instance. No wonder that he spent more money at Whitehall than any other residence – at least £40,000 in twenty-seven years. This means that it was not typical, and when we look at its plan we can see that.[16]

Even in the early 1530s there was, beyond the privy chamber, a room called the withdrawing room. We don't know how this was used, but it was necessary to go through it from the privy chamber to reach the privy lodgings and privy gallery. In later reigns the withdrawing room became institutionalized and was the place, in every royal residence, where the monarch withdrew from the public privy chamber. It is possible that Henry VIII was already doing this, especially as all the evidence points to the fact that the Whitehall privy chamber was used for public receptions in the mid-1530s. Key to this is understanding the giant mural he commissioned from Hans Holbein the Younger in 1537 on the south wall of the privy chamber.

Having left his native Germany at a young age and made his name as a painter in Basel, Holbein first came to England in 1526, meeting Sir Thomas More and painting a huge portrait of his family. He went back to Basel but returned on a second visit to London in 1532, when he was deluged by offers of work. He painted, designed metalwork and furniture, and may even have designed architectural features such as fireplaces. But his largest commission was to paint what we know today as the Whitehall Mural. Completed in 1537 it was a huge piece of work, 9 feet high and 12 feet wide, and was painted on the upper part of the south wall of the privy chamber facing people who entered the room.[17]

The mural was completely destroyed in the Whitehall fire of 1698 but fortunately in 1669, when King Charles II had been contemplating rebuilding the palace and destroying the mural, he had had a copy of it painted (see plate section). In the mural, Holbein established the image of Henry VIII that we know so well: the fat, piggy face, the bulky body richly draped, supported by stocky legs apart, one hand clutching his gloves, the other hanging down beside his dagger. In the midst of the rich fabric bursts out an enormous codpiece, symbolic of his supposed (and much doubted) sexual vigour. Like Henry VII's great hall at Richmond, studded with statues of his forebears, this was about dynasty: the protagonists were Henry VIII and Jane Seymour, with Henry VII and

Elizabeth of York behind. The great stone altar that the king's father leans on was inscribed with a legend that opened the debate about whether father or son was the greater, before concluding:

> . . . both indeed are supreme. The former often overcame his enemies and the fires of his country and finally gave peace to its citizens. The son, born indeed for greater tasks, from the altar removed the unworthy, and put worthy men in their place. To unerring virtue, the audacity of the popes has yielded. And so long as Henry the Eighth carries the sceptre in his hand, Religion is renewed, and during his reign the doctrines of God have begun to be held in his honour.

This was the language of dynastic triumphalism, announcing the Tudor legacy of peace and truth. It both established Whitehall as the seat of the Tudors and the privy chamber as its centre. Subsequent history shows that the Stuarts likewise saw Whitehall as symbolic of their rule, commissioning Peter Paul Rubens to paint a ceiling in their principal audience chamber, the banqueting house. The whole *mise en scène* of Henry's privy chamber was tremendously successful. The mural, up high, was lit from the side by a large bay window, ensuring that there were no reflections on the varnished oil paint. A visitor in 1604 said it was 'life-sized and so lifelike that anyone who sees it gets a fright for it seems as if it is alive and that one might see the head and all the limbs moving and functioning naturally'.[18] In Henry's lifetime that presence was corporeal. He sat on a chair of estate directly beneath the mural under a throne canopy made of 'gold tissue raised with purple velvet pearled, paned with crimson velvet embroidered [with] . . . his grace's badges crowned. And in the middle thereof his highnesses arms crowned, held by beasts within a garland'. The walls of the room were hung with the finest tapestry and in one wall were two doors, decorated with pearls and gold thread, which opened to reveal a rock grotto with a fountain decorated with a rock crystal ball, gold busts and cameos.[19]

One strange feature of the room was a result of its conversion from a private to a public purpose. Between the presence chamber and the privy chamber there was, as at every house, a narrow passageway off which was the king's privy closet and chapel. A Frenchman, André Hurault, Sieur de Maisse, came on a diplomatic mission to Queen Elizabeth I in 1597 and was brought in the royal barge to Whitehall. After walking through the watching chamber, he waited in the presence chamber to be called in. The Lord Chamberlain then appeared and 'He led me along a passage somewhat dark, into a chamber they call the Privy Chamber, at the head of which was the Queen seated in a low chair, by herself, and withdrawn from all the Lords and ladies that were present ...' The entrance to Whitehall's most important room was therefore not at all grand and was, by accident, rather theatrical.[20]

Whitehall was the most important of all the royal residences, but it was also the most unusual. It had to perform functions that none of the others did. There was a degree of formality about Whitehall that could not be expunged from the king's life even with his withdrawal into the depths of the privy lodgings. At Hampton Court, though, things were different. This was a pleasure palace, a place for recreation and relaxation, and what happened there was, in fact, more typical of the changes of the late 1530s and 1540s.

The Queen's Side

Henry married his third wife Jane Seymour in the queen's privy closet at Whitehall on 30 May 1536. Jane was an unexpected choice: she had neither the breeding of Henry's first wife nor the magnetism of his second. What she did have was the potential to give Henry a quiet time – and a son. Sir John Russell wrote to Lord Lisle bringing him up to date with things at court: 'the King hath come out of hell into heaven', he said, believing the new queen 'as fair a queen as any in Christendom'.[21]

Although Anne Boleyn's new lodgings at Hampton Court were completed in early 1536, she never saw them. On her last visits to the house she was still staying in the old rooms built by Wolsey for Katharine of Aragon; it was in these rooms on the second floor that, allegedly, William Brereton, a member of the king's Privy Chamber, had an intimate

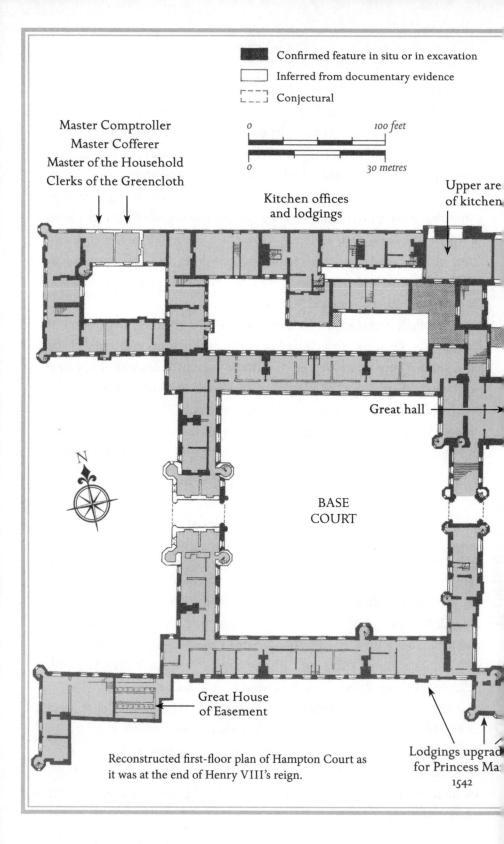

Confirmed feature in situ or in excavation

Inferred from documentary evidence

Conjectural

Master Comptroller
Master Cofferer
Master of the Household
Clerks of the Greencloth

Kitchen offices
and lodgings

Upper are
of kitchen

100 feet

30 metres

Great hall

N

BASE
COURT

Great House
of Easement

Lodgings upgrad
for Princess Ma
1542

Reconstructed first-floor plan of Hampton Court as
it was at the end of Henry VIII's reign.

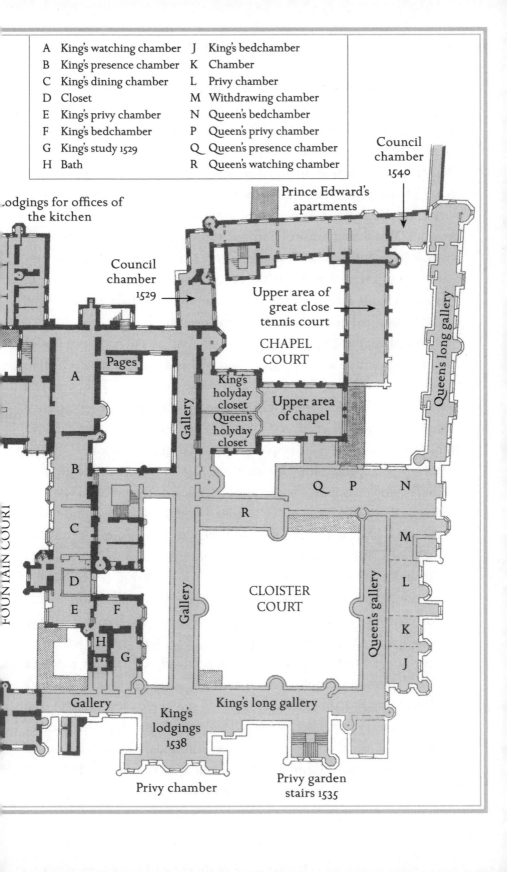

A	King's watching chamber	J	King's bedchamber
B	King's presence chamber	K	Chamber
C	King's dining chamber	L	Privy chamber
D	Closet	M	Withdrawing chamber
E	King's privy chamber	N	Queen's bedchamber
F	King's bedchamber	P	Queen's privy chamber
G	King's study 1529	Q	Queen's presence chamber
H	Bath	R	Queen's watching chamber

Council chamber 1540

Lodgings for offices of the kitchen

Prince Edward's apartments

Council chamber 1529

Upper area of great close tennis court

CHAPEL COURT

Pages

King's holyday closet

Queen's holyday closet

Upper area of chapel

Gallery

A

B

C

D

E

F

H

G

Q P N

R

M

L

K

J

FOUNTAIN COURT

CLOISTER COURT

Gallery

Queen's gallery

Queen's long gallery

Gallery

King's long gallery

King's lodgings 1538

Privy chamber

Privy garden stairs 1535

liaison with her. Anne's sudden fall and death did not slow works at Hampton Court, but it did change the whole tone of the king's building programmes. While Anne was alive architecture was a shared enterprise: the royal couple took delight in poring over plans and visiting building sites; in anticipation of their visits the workmen were thrown into a frenzy of overtime, working by candlelight to complete their tasks. A dozen times Henry and Anne made the trip to Hampton Court to admire the work. This shared sense of purpose was never replicated with his later wives. Work continued at Hampton Court after Anne's fall, but the new royal lodgings went forward with reduced royal engagement. When, in May 1537, Henry and Jane arrived at Hampton Court for the first time together, they had been married for nearly a year.[22]

Jane, of course, knew Hampton Court well, as she had been one of Anne's ladies, and so, in May 1537, she was well aware of the transformation that had been effected. She was able to move into a suite of completely new rooms on the east front, approached by a fine new gallery. Henry, though, was not satisfied and, probably to the astonishment of his architectural team – Christopher Dickinson the bricklayer, William Clement his carpenter, John Moulton the mason – orders were given to remodel completely what they had just completed. The problem was this. Although there were now separate queen's lodgings at Hampton Court on the same level, and conjoined with the king's, they were far smaller than his own. This mattered because the queen's rooms were not simply an appendix to those of the sovereign – they played a crucial and distinctive part in royal life. This now requires some explanation.

In contrast to the penny-pinching attitude that Henry VII had towards his queen, Elizabeth of York, Henry VIII had granted Katharine of Aragon a jointure worth £4,129 a year, nearly double his mother's income.[23] Katharine took over Baynard's Castle, her mother-in-law's London house, and, though the king was to stay there a few times in 1515, this became very much her personal residence. In its presence chamber was a cloth of estate of gold and crimson embroidered with the arms of Spain and the arms of Henry VIII. The matching chair of estate that sat beneath the canopy had a much smaller pair, presumably designed for

Princess Mary. Her inner closet had hangings, paned red and green, embroidered with the arms of England and Spain with borders of roses and pomegranates, while her state bed had a tester (backcloth) embroidered only with the Spanish arms. Visitors were left in no doubt that they were in the presence of double royalty.[24]

This display of royal pedigree was confined to Katharine's own residences. Like Henry's other queens, she sat beneath her own arms in her jointure houses, but in the king's houses beneath a cloth of estate containing only the arms of the king. This was because she was an appendage of the sovereign with duties to fulfil on his behalf, particularly when it came to international diplomacy. After being presented to the sovereign, ambassadors always visited the queen in her lodgings, while other court occasions ended in the queen's rooms with an audience or a dinner hosted by the queen or sometimes jointly with the king. The queen's presence chamber was where the court, by invitation, would assemble informally in the evenings for recreation: in 1519 Henry Courtenay, Earl of Devon, was playing cards and shuffleboard there with his friends. Sometimes, as a mark of special favour, ambassadors were allowed to join these informal events. In 1517 the Spanish envoys were invited after dinner to Katharine's presence chamber, where they had 'amusements of every description', including a gruelling organ recital lasting four hours. The French ambassadors, invited into the queen's rooms after a dinner in 1527, danced with Princess Mary. In 1544 the Duke of Nájera, having finished a half-hour audience with the king, was ushered into Queen Katherine Parr's presence chamber, where musicians assembled and he watched, for several hours, as the queen, her ladies and various professional dancers took to the floor. Katherine sat under her cloth of estate dressed from top to toe in cloth of gold, Princess Mary had a petticoat of gold too and both were lightly sprinkled with diamonds and pearls.[25]

Beyond the presence chamber, where these carefully crafted events took place, the door to the queen's privy chamber was barred to all except the king, the queen's ladies and an extremely select circle of the king's and queen's closest companions. By definition, we have very little information of what took place behind this locked door, but the interrogations of the households of Anne Boleyn and Catherine Howard, when they were under suspicion of adultery, lifts the veil. In particular we get the strong impression that Anne admitted more people into her privy chamber than Katharine of Aragon had ever done. Her own Lord Chamberlain, Sir Edward Bainton, writing to Anne's brother George in June 1533, informed him that 'as for pastime [i.e. entertainment/fun] in the queen's chamber, [there] was never more. If any of you that be now departed have ladies that you thought favoured you, and somewhat would morn at parting of their servants [i.e. admirers], I can no way perceive the same by their dancing and pastime they do use here . . . as ever hath been the custom.'[26] The 'pastime', although dominated by ladies, also included men – musicians, pages and members of the king's Privy Chamber – and it was possible, if the right doors were left open, for them to gain access even to the queen's bedchamber. The cases of Anne and Catherine show how unwise it was for a queen to entertain men in her lodgings privately: in the informal atmosphere free from the rules of etiquette, love, lust and misunderstandings easily developed.[27]

Anne Boleyn not only changed the way the queen's lodgings were used but altered their disposition. They remained a place where high court ceremonial took place and where the court could let its communal hair down a little, but, after the construction of the new queen's lodgings

The east front at Hampton Court in the seventeenth century. On the left can be seen the wall of the privy garden, in the middle the queen's lodgings and on the right the eleven bays of the queen's gallery.

at Hampton Court, the king's and queen's innermost rooms conjoined and the king was able easily, and completely privately, to get from his lodgings to hers. Nobody else now knew which side he was on. As a consequence, from the 1530s, Henry spent as much time on the queen's side as his own. His own rooms, bound by the strictures of etiquette, had been, as I have explained, flooded by people who had right of access, but the queen's were open to no one except by the queen's pleasure and so it was on her side that the king had 'his comfort, pastime, solace and disport'. This explains why Henry kept falling in love with the queen's ladies: Anne Boleyn had been one of Katharine of Aragon's, Jane Seymour had been one of Anne Boleyn's and Katherine Parr served Anne of Cleves. There was lots of gossip about the king and the queen's ladies as, free from the crushing formality of the king's side, looks, glances and gestures could be easily misinterpreted.[28]

The king's increasing withdrawal to the queen's rooms explains the next major building project at Hampton Court: a remarkable campaign that completely remodelled the queen's side for Jane Seymour. To achieve this, not only was work forced ahead at perilous speed, but the king and queen were in residence throughout most of it. Jane and Henry were at Hampton Court at the start of May 1537, for the whole of June and most of September. Life cannot have been very peaceful: there were some 450 workmen on site every day, 700,000 bricks were burned in the park and

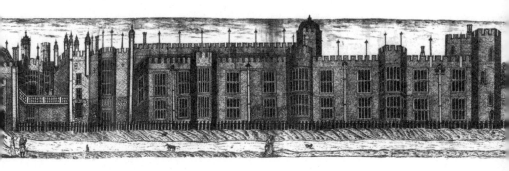

more than twice that number were delivered by barge. The lodgings built for Anne were partially dismantled and reconstituted, while a magnificent privy gallery, 185 feet long, was built for Jane on the east front. At the same time as this took place, Henry's own rooms were remodelled again to provide a new complex of secret lodgings. On the north front a whole new range was built to accommodate the prince that Jane was expected to bear, and off this was a new bowling alley. The whole lot was completed in just five months.

So what was the result? On the east side there was now a courtyard with the king's lodgings on the south side and the queen's on the north. Off the queen's bedchamber was her new long gallery, with big windows and a water-filled moat immediately in front of it. On the east were the king's and queen's joint private lodgings, where Henry dined privately with his queen, received his children and welcomed chosen guests free from the crowds of people who had right of access into his lodgings. Here also was the 'king's bedchamber on the queen's side' – the room in which he seems to have increasingly slept as the pain from his bad leg kept him awake.[29] As we shall see, Hampton Court became the king's favourite out-of-town residence and the key to understanding this is the degree of privacy it afforded him. There, deep in the east-front lodgings, cocooned by the queen's ladies and remote even from his own Groom of the Stool, Henry could do as he liked.

· IX ·
THE NEW LOOK

Tudor Aesthetics

CHANGES AT COURT IN THE 1530S were not only about the way the king and queen lived. They were also about the way things looked, for, in less than a decade, the decoration and furnishing of royal houses was transformed.

In Tudor England everyone occupied a set place in society and in a hierarchy ordained by God, and that place was symbolized by the type and quantity of a person's possessions. Of these, the clothes people wore were the most visible and immediate, so laws known as the Sumptuary Legislation set out what certain types of people were allowed to wear. The Tudors were as expert at recognizing an Italian velvet or a French necklace as people today would be at identifying a Gucci handbag or a Rolex watch,[1] and a sense of what was appropriately expensive for a particular individual extended to all possessions, from plate and furnishings to architecture. The monarch sat at the top of this hierarchy of display, with all the finest possessions; beneath him, in a strictly defined order of precedence, came everyone else from cardinals at the altar to peasants in the fields. There was a sense of outrage when people stepped outside the limits of material display appropriate to their station, whether this be in dress, architecture or even horseflesh.

Kings, at the top of the tree, were thus expected to be magnificent. In a political treatise called *The Governance of England*, written by Sir John Fortescue in around 1470, the principles of this were set out:

> it shall need be that the king have such treasure as he may make new buildings when he will for his pleasure and magnificence; and as he may

buy him rich clothes, rich furs . . . rich stones . . . and other jewels and ornaments convenient to his estate royal. And often times he will buy rich hangings and other apparel for his houses . . . for if a king did not so . . . he lived then not like his estate, but rather in misery and in more subjection than doth a private person.[2]

It was not simply enough that a king should be invested with the power to rule; he had to be visibly supported by the magnificence of power. In his will, King Henry VII set out how he wanted his lady chapel at Westminster Abbey to be completed, directing that it be decorated with his 'arms, badges, cognisants, and other convenient painting', not because 'such work requireth' it but because such lavish decoration 'to a king's work appertaineth'. In other words, the decoration was there because it was appropriate to a king.[3]

Throwing money at architecture was certainly expected, but tastes were not simply conditioned by cost. Expense was one of the things people took into account in aesthetic appreciation, but they were also interested in craftsmanship, which, at the time, was defined as cunning – the skill with which something was made. Then there was also novelty, a much-prized characteristic then, as now. Finally there was placement – the relationship one thing had with another. Contemporaries who wrote about what they saw at the Tudor court judged everything against cost, cunning, novelty and placement; take the example of George Cavendish, who in 1527 described the splendour with which Wolsey entertained the French embassy at Hampton Court, after which they were to move on to Greenwich where they would be guests of the king:

the king was privy of all this worthy feast [at Hampton Court] and intended to far exceed the same . . . but to describe the dishes, the subtleties [desserts], the many strange devices, and order the same, I do both lack wit in my gross old head and cunning in my bowels to declare the wonderful and curious imaginations in the same invented and devised . . . yet did this banquet far exceed the same as fine gold doth silver in weight and value.[4]

While 'wonderful and curious imaginations' were the mainspring of early Tudor architecture, at all times they were tempered by hierarchy. For not only did a person occupy a place in the set order of the universe, in architecture so did the parts of every building. This can also be seen in churches, where the chancel or presbytery was more important than the nave. This was expressed by the activities that went on in it (the celebration of Mass), the status of the people allowed in (the priests), the clothes worn in the space (vestments) and the surrounding architecture – a chancel is generally more elaborately decorated than a nave.

So in a Tudor royal house each room occupied a position in a hierarchy and its decoration was appropriate to that. When Henry VII proposed to marry his daughter Princess Mary to the Prince of Castile in 1508, the way in which Mary's rooms was to be decorated was minutely specified. She was to have four rooms. Her bedchamber was to be hung in cloth of gold with a border embroidered with her badges; there was to be a large bed and chair with hangings matching those on the walls, various carpets and covers, and five golden cushions to complete the room's décor. The second chamber was to be slightly less magnificent, hung with tapestry containing gold thread and furnished with textiles of gold and purple. In the third chamber the tapestry was not to be 'so fine as in the second chamber', while the fourth room was only to have 'good and fine tapestry'. The principle was simple: the more private the room, the more magnificent the furnishings. This went for the external appearance of a royal house too. The outer courts would have a flourish around the gatehouse, but would otherwise be much plainer than the innermost parts where the royal family lived.[5]

So how do we describe the style in which the Tudor kings built? Art historians love to give a name to a style and the Tudors have always fallen in a gap between various art-historical categories. The prevailing architecture of the fifteenth century was Gothic, that is to say a structural system based on the pointed arch; and the particular brand of Gothic at the time is known as Perpendicular, a term used to describe a set of architectural features used from around 1350 into the 1520s. But Henry VII's new tower at Windsor, or the bold brick range on the river at

Greenwich, don't comply with most notions of Perpendicular Gothic. This is because from the 1490s the consensus about architectural style and decoration that had existed for more than a hundred years started to break down. We have already seen that the use of brick had begun to change the way buildings looked and introduced new decorative possibilities. We have also seen that Henry VII, and even more Henry VIII, wanted to revive chivalry both in the tiltyard and on the building site.

Early Tudor royal buildings self-consciously revived features of genuinely defensive buildings from the Middle Ages: Henry VIII's first building was the gatehouse at Windsor Castle, and at Greenwich there were turrets, battlements and pinnacles in the tiltyard, while the Parkside at Whitehall looked like an encampment of glittering tents. But it was not only the overall form of these buildings that expressed chivalric values, it was the detail of the decoration.[6]

CHIVALRIC ARCHITECTURE

Heraldry started as a system for identifying knights on the field of battle and, during the thirteenth century, this became a formal system of visual communication policed by the royal heralds. The shield, with any supporters, the helm, the crest, together with mottos, badges and seals, were increasingly used by knights not only in the field and at the tournament, but every day to express their knightly status. It was Henry III who had set the fashion for using such heraldry in architectural display and by the 1260s anyone who had arms would flaunt them on their buildings. As with almost everything else, Henry VIII took this to ridiculous lengths. His houses were slathered with heraldic devices – and there were plenty to choose from. From 1198 the royal shield had three crawling leopards, which, over the course of time, were transmogrified into lions and then paired with fleurs-de-lis to make the royal arms used by Henry VII. This shield was supported either by the red dragon of Cadwallader (the Welsh king from whom Henry claimed descent), a greyhound (for his mother, Lady Margaret Beaufort) or a lion (for England).

Guilelmus de Saliceto, *De Salute Corporis*, commissioned by Piers de Champagne, one of Henry VIII's Esquires of the Body, to celebrate the king's marriage in December 1509. The royal arms are upheld by the dragon and greyhound. Above a crown is the Tudor rose and two portcullises flank the shield. On the next page of the book are the arms of Katharine of Aragon.

This was the raw material of royal heraldry, but there were many other possibilities: the badge of Beaufort, the portcullis, and Henry VII's own badge, the combined red and white roses – both of which were normally shown crowned. For the first twenty years of Henry VIII's reign Katharine of Aragon's badges – the pomegranate of Granada, the silver arrows of Aragon and the castle of Castile – were used everywhere. Then there was the simple use of initials: HR for Henry, or sometimes an H entwined or juxtaposed with the initial of his queen. Often the royal badges were supplemented by the symbol of the Order of the Garter – a blue garter with the motto *Honi Soit qui Mal y Pense* (Shame on Him who Thinks Evil of It) – which could conveniently encircle a shield. As under Henry VIII one queen superseded another, the heraldic palette changed rapidly – Katharine of Aragon's badges were expunged by those of Anne Boleyn, and all too soon Anne's leopards were being altered by the royal carvers to look like the panthers of Jane Seymour: this particular problem was solved by 'new making of the heads and tails', but more often heraldic stained glass had to be replaced and coats of arms overpainted.[7]

Detail of an engraving of
Henry VIII by Cornelis
Metsys, 1544, showing Henry's
shield encircled by the Garter
crowned.

In the decades after Bosworth these badges and arms were used by
Henry VII as demonstrations of his pedigree, but, as his son's reign
dawned, they were shown as something very different – badges of dynasty.
These were not meant to be complex or subtle – they were straightforward
seals of ownership. Heraldic symbols in the early sixteenth century were
relatively clean and simple, far less complicated than they later became,
and so lent themselves well to architectural display. Heraldry meant
something to the men and women of the Tudor court; there was no need
for a complex process of decoding, because everyone recognized the
meaning of a badge or an emblem immediately, just as today we would be
able to read the marque on the back of a motor car. But like a modern
marque, the use of heraldry was very strictly controlled and the illegal
use of arms was viciously punished. The case of Henry Howard, Earl of
Surrey, who placed 'the old arms of England, the three lions, in the first
quarter of his shield', is sobering. His use of the royal style was used as an
excuse for his arrest and execution in 1546.[8]

The heralds were responsible for checking the correct use of badges
and arms and it was their report that was responsible for damning Surrey.

Their more normal work was issuing to royal painters and carvers books of arms showing how they should be correctly used. Thomas Wriothesley, Garter King of Arms, who was intimately involved in every major ceremony of the first half of Henry's reign, maintained a workshop where a team of painters kept the records needed to ensure that everything was done correctly. During the preparations for the Field of Cloth of Gold, the Governor of Guînes wrote, in a panic, to Wolsey asking that Wriothesley's heralds produce a book showing all the complex heraldry necessary for the meeting of two kings. The book does not survive, but that it was commissioned demonstrates the close working between the heralds and the king's craftsmen. In fact, the king's painter John Browne worked so closely with Wriothesley that their workshops were sited in adjacent houses in Cripplegate.[9]

Henry's VIII's houses were therefore encrusted with dynastic signs and symbols, as indeed were many of its occupants, from the humble Yeomen of the Guard to the Lord Chancellor wearing his heavy gold chain of office. Entering a royal house, the first thing you would see was the royal arms carved, painted and gilded over the entrance gate: visitors to Hampton Court can still see these today. From this point every step further brought more dynastic display, in paint, carved wood and stone, in glass, ceramic, metalwork, textile or leatherwork.

The Antique

While during the whole Tudor period heraldry was never superseded as the primary vehicle for royal display, newer streams of thought and inspiration were becoming available to both patrons and designers from around 1515. The courts of the two Henrys were cosmopolitan places. Most people were bilingual, speaking fluent French; many also spoke Latin and most had travelled abroad to the Low Countries, to France and some as far as Spain or even Italy. There was a strong sense that the English were part of the universal culture of Western Christendom, and the City of London, as a major centre of trade, reinforced international cultural ties. There were thus many arteries through which artistic influences flowed, but, from the mid-1490s, northern Europe began to be increasingly exposed to architectural and decorative fashions from Italy. This was largely due to the fact that the French king, Charles VIII, had invaded Italy and over a period of twenty years his aristocrats, diplomats, merchants and soldiers helped diffuse across Europe the fashions that they saw.[10]

Thus into England from France and northern European countries came an enthusiasm for a form of decoration known as the antique. This term, which first appears in England around 1513, refers to any form of architecture or decoration that drew its inspiration from ancient Rome. In particular it referred to a form of decoration known as grotesque-work, which was invented in the last years of the fifteenth century.

In the Rome of the 1490s a group of daring painters began to explore the maze of underground passages and caverns that made up the buried remains of the *Domus Aurea*, the Golden House of the Emperor Nero. This was a megalomaniac building project that made Henry VIII look like an amateur. It was a vast villa set in landscaped gardens covering 300 acres right in the middle of Rome, and it was described by the ancient Roman historian Suetonius as 'ruinously prodigal'. Until the explorers found their way into its buried rooms, nobody had ever seen the decorated interior of a high-status Roman domestic building, but painters like Pinturicchio, by the light of their burning torches, discovered for the first time the wonderland of painting that had ornamented Nero's house. The decorations they recorded soon became known as grotesques after the 'grottoes' in which they had been found.

Grotesque-work was at first used to decorate architectural elements such as friezes and the strip down the centre of pilasters, but soon it came to decorate panelling, walls and ceilings. Its key feature was the use of Roman masks, vessels, shields, plates, helmets and breastplates. These would most often be linked together by a sort of crazy candelabra into a tottering tower of treasure normally framed by *putti* and swirling foliage. By the early 1500s grotesque-work was all the rage, and within a few years craftsmen and designers began to export it across Europe both in person and by the circulation of prints.

A pattern sheet published by Perino del Vaga in 1532, with a poem explaining that the design, taken from a grotto, was intended for the use of craftsmen.

Printing was hugely important in the transmission of fashions in architecture and interior decoration. For the first time images could be mass-produced and circulated quickly. From the 1460s English carvers were using printed sheets and books as inspiration for their work; most of these were produced in Germany, but some also came from France and Italy. In 1504 Henry VII appointed Richard Pynson to be his official printer and, in 1518, Pynson produced the first English title pages in the grotesque style. Prints became a source of inspiration for the decorators of Henry VIII's houses and everything, from stone carving, through stained glass, to textiles was influenced by them. We should not imagine that this was a sign of some paucity of imagination. It wasn't. The great Holbein himself relied on a print to provide inspiration for the background of the Whitehall Mural.[11]

Enterprising designers and printers collected together numbers of printed designs and issued them in so-called pattern books. In 1538 a

ASSERTIO SEPTEM SA=
cramentorum aduerſus Martin.
Lutherũ,ædita ab ínuíctiſ
ſimo Angliæ et Fran=
ciæ rege, et do.Hy=
berniæ Henri=
co eius no
minis
o=
ctauo.

Title page designed by Holbein in Basel in 1516 and then used by the king's printer Richard Pynson in England in 1518. It was recycled by Pynson in 1521 as the title page (seen here) of Henry VIII's book *Assertio Septem Sacramentorum* (Defence of the Seven Sacraments), which defended the sacramental nature of marriage and the supremacy of the Pope, winning Henry the title of Defender of the Faith.

publisher in Strasbourg prefaced his book of patterns (which were for everything from the walls of a grand palace to the headdress of a merchant's wife) with the words 'I . . . have assembled an anthology of exotic and difficult details that should guide the artists who are burdened with wife and children and those who have not travelled'.[12] Many of the king's craftsmen owned such books, as indeed did Henry himself. On his death a number of patterns are recorded as being in the various studies in his houses and one book survives from his library, now in the British Library, with fine scaled drawings of the orders of ancient architecture.[13]

This book is particularly interesting because, unusually, it is about the structural system of architecture and not purely its decorative motifs – what we would call classical architecture, which was based on four orders (Doric, Ionic, Corinthian and Composite), an order being a component of the colonnade of a Greek or Roman temple. Each order comprises a column with its base and a superstructure, or entablature, made up of various elements including the architrave, frieze and cornice.

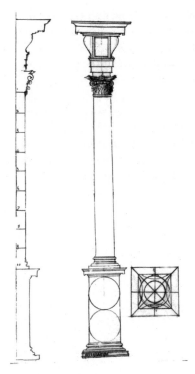

A French treatise on geometry owned by Henry VIII, open at the page that shows the Corinthian order. Although Henry owned this book, and it demonstrates that he had access to information about classical architecture, he never regarded the four orders as anything more than decorative motifs.

This treatise, as well as other painted, drawn and printed sources, shows that there was a good awareness of classical architecture at Henry VIII's court, but there was little or no appetite to imitate it as anything more than decoration. Thus columns, pilasters, friezes and other classical components were important parts of the decoration of royal houses. Much of this, in the first part of the king's reign, was achieved through the use of architectural terracotta, a material that began to be used at around the same time that antique sources became available and seems to have been introduced from northern Germany, where there was a long tradition of firing bricks in decorative shapes.

Both Wolsey's Hampton Court and Suffolk Place, the house of Charles Brandon, Duke of Suffolk, Henry's brother-in-law, were heavily decorated in terracotta. While I was supervising the reconstruction of the seventeenth-century gardens at Hampton Court we found a big pit into which King William III's workmen had hurled parts of Wolsey's long gallery when it was demolished in 1689. It was incredibly exciting to take out of the ground the bases of columns, capitals and other elements of classical architecture. In 2015 I had the chance to don my hard hat and visit the excavations on the site of Suffolk Place in Southwark, where a large block of flats was being built. Here the finds were, if anything, even more spectacular, including big elements of terracotta frieze studded with busts of roman ladies.[14]

Terracotta was popular because it was a quick and easy way of achieving a spectacular effect. The individual elements were made by pressing clay into carved wooden moulds that had the architectural features in negative. The clays were then dried like bricks and fired. Unlike brickmaking, firing architectural terracotta was highly skilled because each terracotta was designed to fit with another so that columns, friezes and window surrounds could be built up. The manufacturers had to allow for exactly the right amount of shrinkage in the kiln and so, as far as we understand it, the work was done by German immigrants who were known as the 'douch'.

There is no royal building on which terracotta survives, so we don't know exactly what Wolsey's gallery at Hampton Court, for instance, looked like. However, it is clear that the terracotta was painted to look like stone – it was basically a way of cheating, of creating the effect of stone quickly and easily. So the pilasters, badges and heads of Roman gods and goddesses would have appeared as stone embellishments to the dark-red Tudor brick walls. The effect would have been very striking, and very modern, because antique-work would have been completely new to most people.

CHANGING ROOMS

These changes are easier for us to understand when we look at the very fragmentary remains of surviving Henrician royal interiors. For here, just as on the outside, royal houses were transformed in the 1530s.

To the modern eye, the single biggest impact on entering one of Henry's houses would be the huge quantity of tapestry. In the early sixteenth century most tapestry was woven in the Low Countries and either bought off the peg from merchants or commissioned for specific locations or particular subjects. Quality varied enormously with the skill of the artist, the expertise of the weavers and the quality of the yarns and threads used. The best was arras and was woven with gold thread (a gold filament wrapped round a silk core). Very few people other than the king owned any of this and so, even for contemporaries, rooms hung with arras would have been arresting. Most tapestry was less glitzy and valuable, and was woven with varying mixtures of silk and wool. Wool tapestry could be bought for 8d per ell (27 inches), while silk cost a great deal more at 3s 4d per ell and arras was a steep 40s.[15]

Tapestry was integrated with the architectural features in a room and was either made for it, or in the case of arras the room could be designed round the tapestry. Normally it was hung from a cornice, what the Tudors called a jewel piece, and reached down almost to the floor. There was a black-painted skirting at the bottom of the plaster to prevent a gleam of lime-washed wall peeping out at the bottom, like a white sock under a pair of trousers. At the start of his reign, Henry VIII hung and bought tapestries in the prevailing style, which was for extremely dense compositions with large numbers of figures crammed into scenes in very shallow perspective. The effect was dense and rich and reinforced the value and impact of textiles.

In 1528 Henry bought one of his largest and most expensive sets of tapestry, telling the story of King David. At a cost of £1,548, it was worth the same as a Tudor warship and with ten pieces covering 420 square yards (a tennis court is 312 square yards), it was vast. The only rooms that could fit such a set were the outer chambers in the largest houses in the Thames valley, such as Greenwich. The tapestries set the biblical story in the sixteenth-century Low Countries and King David's court could have been Henry's. But, by the time the Davids were hung, they were distinctly old-fashioned, as the great tapestry designers, influenced by stylistic innovations from the Italian painter Raphael, began to produce tapestries with deeper perspective and a smaller number of more life-like figures rendered much larger and in dynamic poses. In 1538 Henry acquired such a set that told the story of St Paul in nine scenes. It was another extremely rich weave, laden with gold thread, and was valued at the king's death at over £3,000. The change in style must have been startling to people at court, and it must have influenced the whole feel of the state rooms. These tapestries were less oppressive, more three-dimensional and exciting.

It is worth noting that the outer rooms at court were normally hung with tapestries depicting biblical scenes, and that Henry took great care with the subject matter. In the late 1520s he was obsessed with his lack of a son and the idea that he had been cursed for marrying his brother's wife. This may help explain his choice of the story of David, who was, of course, God's anointed king but who was also childless; his first wife was cursed. Likewise, the story of St Paul had resonance in late 1536 or early 1537 when the set was commissioned. St Paul provided an alternative to St Peter, whom the popes claimed as their predecessor. Paul gave emphasis to rendering to Caesar what was Caesar's and to God what was God's – an idea central to Henry's whole world picture at that time.

While biblical subjects occupied the outer rooms, the inner chambers provided a more varied visual diet. Scenes from classical mythology dominated here, so, for instance, while Whitehall was under construction several sets of tapestries were ordered for the privy lodgings. In 1533 a set telling the story of Dido and Aeneas was made with borders of grotesque-work; it is not certain which room this was for, but each panel was a different size, ensuring that the chamber would be hung wall to wall and floor to ceiling.[16] These rooms, like the great outer chambers, would have been brightened and enlivened by new tapestry styles and integrated with new architectural schemes of antique-work.

The cornices from which tapestries hung were carved and painted with rich colours and above them, below the ceiling, was a broad frieze area which was decorated with antique-work and grotesque-work. The frieze was in harmony with the ceiling – normally decorated with a geometrical pattern of ribs enriched with more antique-work. Friezes were generally not carved from timber but made of a special compound called leather maché. Like terracotta, leather maché was a way of cheating – of producing lengths of frieze, or ceiling components, quickly and cheaply out of moulds. The maché was made from glovemakers' offcuts mixed with brick dust and size. Once the dried pieces were painted and gilded, it was indistinguishable from carved wood. Sometimes cast lead decorations were added – these might be a motto in lead letters, oak leaves at the junctions of ceiling ribs, or additional gilded antique motifs.

As well as moulded work, there was also carved wood and stone done by the best carvers. Stone chimneypieces, window and door surrounds were decorated and painted and, where there was no tapestry, there was panelling, which could be plain, painted and gilded or finely carved and gilded. Windows were filled with stained glass, much of it depicting various heraldic motifs. Most of the king's rooms had timber floorboards that were then plastered and had woven rush matting laid on top. On top of that more loose rushes were spread to protect the matting from wear, but more importantly to provide a fresh green smell throughout the rooms. Occasionally, in the most important rooms, a carpet might be laid on the matting, but generally carpets were for covering tables and

Henry VIII enthroned, as depicted in the 1563 edition of John Foxe's *Acts and Monuments*, otherwise known as the 'Book of Martyrs'. This is an Elizabethan rendering of a mid-Henrician interior. The antique-work frieze, perhaps of leather maché, can be seen above the hangings and the ceiling is decorated with cast-lead ornaments. The floor is painted plaster.

cupboards rather than for walking on. In other grand spaces the plaster floor was not matted but painted in geometrical designs. Essentially, no internal surface was left unadorned – this was the architecture of excess: richness of effect was what was desired.[17]

During the mid-1530s Henry gradually re-did the interiors that had been decorated either by his father or by Wolsey. In the privy chamber at Greenwich, for instance, in 1537 he ordered Richard Ridge, one of the principal carvers of the great hall roof at Hampton Court, to fit up a new cornice and ceiling in the antique fashion. For Anne Boleyn's coronation all the king's rooms at the Tower of London were modernized: medieval fireplaces were taken out and new ones in the antique style were inserted. Compare the drawing of the ceiling in Henry VII's closet in his new tower at Windsor, set up in 1502 (shown on page 44), with the ceiling of St James's Chapel, made in 1540 (below). The closet is entirely in the tradition of the fifteenth century, while the chapel ceiling is based on an Italian pattern book published in 1537.

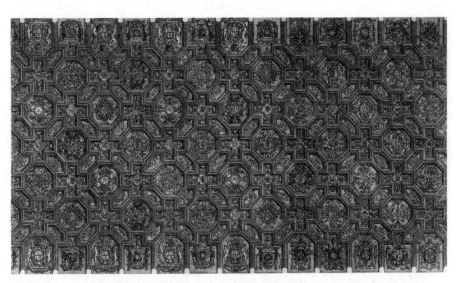

The ceiling of the Chapel Royal in St James's Palace, which is dated 1540 and bears the mottoes and cyphers of Anne of Cleves. The design is identical to one published in 1537 in Venice in Sebastiano Serlio's *Regole generali di Architettura*. The ceiling is made up of wooden battens decorated with gilded cast-lead grotesques. The ground is painted with grotesque and antique designs. This print is taken from Richardson's *Architectural Remains* of 1840.

WORKFORCE

Combining antique-work and heraldry with the existing vocabulary of architectural design required a new set of skills and, as well as native craftsmen, Henry's court attracted craftsmen and designers from all over Europe. As today, immigration was controversial and often unpopular. The craft guilds, based in the City of London, were trade monopolies restricting the practice of a craft to their membership. Foreigners were excluded and, to escape the jurisdiction of the City of London, tended to settle in Southwark and Westminster. There they could ply their trades in relative freedom and there they established workshops and companies of tradesmen. Some foreign craftsmen achieved a status known as 'denization': this was a sort of permanent residency which fell short of full citizenship but crucially meant that they could hold property.

Despite the efforts of native craftsmen to stop them, firms of northern German and Dutch joiners and glaziers captured large contracts in the royal works. A joiner named Harmon West acquired denization in 1541 and established a workshop of joiners who worked for the king at Greenwich, Dartford, Richmond and elsewhere. West's company included six other alien joiners who were not only involved in specialist interior joinery but made furniture. Their tables cost 8s a piece, forms 8d and stools 18d. West also seems to have held the equivalent of a royal warrant for making the king's close stools, providing all the joinery and ironwork ready-made for the upholsterers. All the major royal glazing contracts went to foreign craftsmen: glass was not made in England and the best expertise was perceived to be foreign. This was tested in the courts by English glaziers and the case of the aliens was upheld. The king's blacksmith was also from northern Germany, as was his locksmith.

Many of the royal interior decorators were immigrants. An interior design partnership between two Germans, Robert Schenck, a moulder of leather maché, and Henry Blankston, a painter, was particularly successful. Blankston was widely employed to paint everything from heraldic beasts in the royal gardens to antique terracotta heads and targets for the king's

Design for an interior wall of one of Henry VIII's houses by an unknown hand, *c.*1545. This is of extremely high quality and shows a richly panelled lower wall with a boldly modelled stucco frieze above it. The frieze is similar to those that King Francis I of France was commissioning at Fontainebleau and on which Nicholas Bellin of Modena worked. Such stucco-work was certainly used at Henry's court and this design could have been executed, probably at Whitehall.

shooting practice. Schenck and Blankston collaborated on one of the most lavish rooms ever commissioned by Henry VIII – a room later known as the Paradise Room at the end of the king's long gallery at Hampton Court. This was covered in painted and gilded leather maché. But the Germans did not have a monopoly on royal decoration. A prominent English decorator, Clement Urmenson, was also a moulder of antique-work and, after making his name working for Cardinal Wolsey, won the commission to decorate the privy gallery at Whitehall in 1531.[18]

Although it was mainly northern European craftsmen and designers who infiltrated the royal works in the 1520s and 1530s, there were also some Italians, though very few and they tended to employ French or German assistants. The Italians, however, brought quite a different quality to Henrician design. In the early 1520s Wolsey had employed the sculptor Giovanni de Maiano, who had supplied terracotta roundels containing heads of Roman emperors and other figures from classical antiquity for Hampton Court. Henry VIII later commissioned more of these high-quality sculptures for chimneypieces at St James's, Greenwich, Hanworth and Whitehall. Another Italian, Nicholas Bellin of Modena, seems to have brought the use of moulded stucco-work into fashion at court. This was extensively used at Henry VIII's last great building work at Nonsuch, as we shall see. However, it was most likely first used at Whitehall, probably in imitation of King Francis I of France's long gallery at Fontainebleau.[19]

None of this should obscure the fact that the vast majority of the royal workforce was English. In the surviving financial accounts we have the names of 3,500 men whose individual trades are known and foreigners make up only a small proportion of these. Most had come up through the building trades from youth and sometimes their names can be traced through documents from apprentice to master craftsman. If we take a close look at Hampton Court we can understand who these people were and where they came from because ten years of building there is chronicled by many thousands of pages of detailed accounts.

Building work was constant at Hampton Court for more than a decade – in fact for nearly twenty years if Wolsey's works are included. During that time Hampton, and the villages around, were home to an enormous workforce. At the peak of royal works, in summer 1535, there were 70 masons, 45 carpenters, 81 bricklayers, 21 joiners and 208 labourers in direct employment. It would have been impossible for the Crown to gather so many craftsmen together if it had not been for its powers of impressment. This was a royal prerogative similar to purveyance for the royal table. The Crown had the right to require craftsmen to leave their homes and work on a royal building at set wages for the period for which they were needed. The royal master craftsmen, purveyors and clerks would ride out and hunt down skilled masons and carpenters and require them, on pain of imprisonment, to join the royal works. Victims were paid travelling expenses – normally 6d for 20 miles – but they were then required to stay away from home for a considerable time. As well as being vexatious for the craftsmen, it was infuriating for bishops and aristocrats building cathedrals and houses, as well as for relatively ordinary people who needed work done. In a lawsuit for breach of contract in the City of London in 1532, John Hawkins, a carpenter, defended himself for not erecting houses in Shoreditch because he and his assistants had all been impressed to work on York Place and were held there until after the date in his contract had passed. Craftsmen working at Hampton Court had been impressed from as far afield as Gloucestershire, Somerset and Essex.

Officially, just as there was a king's price for food, so there was one for labour. A law of 1514 set the wages of a mason working for the king at 6d a day, whereas work for a private client might gain 8d. However, it is clear that if the king wanted things done faster he would pay more, including overtime. At 8d a day skilled craftsmen were paid the same as archers in the army or clerks in the king's works; a porter on a gate was paid 5d a day and labourers were paid 4d a day; the king's architects at Hampton Court, William Clement and Christopher Dickinson, were both paid £25 a year by the Crown, but they also ran their own businesses that turned a profit and so earned much more. When James Nedeham died he left his son his manor house in Kent with various lands elsewhere; his wife, Alice, was left a house and land in Chislehurst, plate to the value of £33 6s 8d, and £66 13s 4d in cash, as well as all her jewels and textiles. He also set up a trust fund to educate his four younger sons. The king's service had been very good to him.[20]

Those in the king's direct employ were only part of the vast, complex ecosystem that was the Hampton Court office in the 1530s. Between 1529 and 1539 about 16 million bricks were made by commercial brickmakers in Home Park and a further 10 million were brought to Hampton Court from makers elsewhere. Tiles for the roofs were manufactured in Kingston and Chertsey. Supplying the clay, firewood and labour for these operations was a huge undertaking. But fortunately Hampton Court is sited on a bend in the Thames and, in the sixteenth century, the Thames was tidal up to and beyond the landing stages on the west front. Lime, stone, timber, ironwork, lead and glass could all be brought by flat-bottomed barge. Some materials were prefabricated, such as the complete windows brought downstream from Oxford by William Johnson of Barrington in Gloucestershire. Ready-sawn boards from the Baltic and boxes of French glass packed in straw were brought upstream from the Pool of London; cut oak beams were brought from as far afield as Oxfordshire. When the Thames froze in December 1537 almost 500 men were employed to carry stone from Oxford to its nearest flowing stretch.[21]

All this activity was presided over by the clerks. Their offices were stocked with paper and parchment, ink and account books. Their own working materials were as minutely accounted for as the beams and stones that their books recorded. Using an oversized hourglass, they ensured that the works bell tolled to signal the start of work and its finish. They would receive the craftsmen's bills, check the supplies and measure the work done, just like a modern quantity surveyor. Paperwork would be sent downriver from the various building sites to Scotland Yard, where the accountants would check that the figures reconciled before authorizing payments.[22]

Behind this order and control was the reality of Tudor construction. Whether it was digging in a water-filled ditch on the Thames foreshore by candlelight or balancing on scaffold poles lashed together on the highest pinnacles of the tallest gatehouse, safety was not much in people's minds. A surgeon living in Charing Cross was regularly paid for 'curing and healing' various craftsmen and labourers injured at Whitehall, including one whose leg was crushed in the timber yard. On one occasion a gang of labourers were at work trying to salvage timber from a barge that had sunk while it was unloading at the works jetty. Despite the locks on storeyards and storerooms, materials were lost, pilfered and damaged, and the keeper at Whitehall imprisoned various miscreants in the palace gatehouse before having them sent to the Marshalsea.[23]

Though the Tudor royal workforce would have spectacularly failed a modern health-and-safety inspection, and a building control inspector would have shut down operations, they did achieve some extraordinary feats. So much has been lost that we are robbed of a proper chance to admire their skill, but looking at the perfectly jointed stone waterfronts at Whitehall or the magnificent carved oak ceiling in the great hall at Hampton Court we cannot fail to be impressed with the quality of some of the work. Nor can we fail to admire the sheer energy and organizational ability that mobilized huge workforces and supplied them with materials from across the land and beyond. Theatrical and gaudy the finished effect may have been, but a time-traveller transported back to any one of Henry's many residences could not have failed to be impressed.

◆ X ◆
GRAND FINALE

The Royal Offspring

BEING A ROYAL CHILD IN SIXTEENTH-CENTURY Europe was not entirely a privilege, and in Tudor England it was a tough lot. While Henry VIII's bastard son Henry Fitzroy, born in 1519, enjoyed consistent affection and respect from his father, for twenty years his daughters, Mary and Elizabeth, swung unpredictably in and out of favour. Mary, who was born in 1516, was, at first, adored by the king and cared for in rooms adjacent to the queen's. But before she was two nurseries were set up at Hanworth near Hampton Court and Ditton near Windsor, where, initially, she was put under the care of the king's own former governess, Elizabeth Denton.[1] Henry, nearby at Windsor, would visit his daughter and she would sometimes be brought to the castle. When she was three her household was enlarged to include a chamberlain and treasurer, a chaplain and twenty or so male attendants. At this stage it was very much a nursery, but in 1521 Mary became a pawn in her father's power politics. The plan was to marry her to Katharine of Aragon's twenty-two-year-old nephew, Charles V, King of Spain and Holy Roman Emperor. The marriage was agreed in principle at a meeting in Bruges in 1521 and became part of a formal treaty at a meeting between Charles and Henry in London the following year. In preparation, Mary's nursery was transformed into a fully fledged household by the attentions of the Great Wardrobe. Tapestries were allocated, a bed of state provided and a cloth and chair of estate delivered for her presence chamber.[2]

The arrival of Charles V at Greenwich in May 1522 must have been one of the proudest moments in Katharine of Aragon's life and it marked a high point in the importance and respect afforded to the six-year-old Mary. But Charles was wary, never committing to the marriage, so, although promises were made and treaties signed, there was general scepticism that a wedding would ever take place. Worse still for Katharine, the king's son, Henry Fitzroy, was growing to be strong, handsome and vigorous like his father. In 1525, aged six, the boy was given a coat of arms, made a Knight of the Garter and, at a magnificently staged investiture at Bridewell, was made Duke of Richmond and Somerset. We don't know where Fitzroy had been living before this event, but immediately afterwards he was granted a valuable and prestigious portfolio of lands worth nearly £5,000 a year, as well as his great-grandmother Margaret Beaufort's favourite country residence at Collyweston in Northamptonshire.[3]

To many observers it must have seemed that Henry had settled on Fitzroy as his heir. Katharine, who was now forty, was clearly not going to have more children and as, so far, divorce had not been discussed, the lavish ceremonies of 1525 must have been very suggestive. Yet Mary was not forgotten; she was still a royal princess and a potential diplomatic asset. As Fitzroy was sent to the massive medieval castle of Middleham in Yorkshire to be titular head of a new Council of the North, it was announced that the nine-year-old Mary was to be sent to Ludlow, where she was to be installed as head of the Council of the Marches of Wales. This was effectively a vice-regal appointment, confirming Mary, in all but formal title, as Princess of Wales. Her household comprised almost 350 people and was based, like her long-dead uncle Arthur's, at Ludlow Castle. Although the administration of the Council of the Marches had remained at Ludlow ever since Arthur's death, little had been done to the residence and Mary is unlikely to have spent much, if any, time there. Instead she availed herself of the hospitality of various local abbots and bishops until Tickenhill Manor, perched up on a high bluff west of nearby Bewdley, was ready for her. The £400 or so spent on putting the place to rights enabled the princess to celebrate Christmas there in 1527.[4]

Mary was recalled from Ludlow in 1527 to perform once again in Wolsey's and Henry's contorted diplomacy – this time as a potential bride of either the French king, Francis I, or of his second son, Henry, duc

The timber-framed gatehouse of Tickenhill Manor, dating from the time of Prince Arthur's residence.

d'Orléans. But all too soon the focus was on the king's new love, Anne, and the son that Henry was convinced she would bear. Mary was sent away from court to Beaulieu, where she lived in some comfort and style. Meanwhile, Henry Fitzroy was recalled from the north and came to court. At first Henry gave him the Manor of the More, Wolsey's extremely large and magnificent house in Rickmansworth, but in 1533 he ordered new lodgings for him at Windsor Castle. These were entered from the great chamber, a sort of antechamber to the king's rooms, suggesting that he had a mini royal suite close to Henry's. Windsor became the duke's out-of-town base and here he joined in the Garter festivities and enjoyed archery and music with his father. In 1534 he was also given Baynard's Castle, Katharine of Aragon's former house on the Thames, where he moved with his young wife, Mary Howard.[5]

If on 7 September 1533, instead of giving birth to Elizabeth, Anne Boleyn had produced a son who had lived, history would have been very different, not least for Mary. But, as it was, the court was too small for two princesses and Mary, now declared illegitimate and stripped of her royal titles and livery, was to be utterly humiliated by her father and stepmother. Aged almost eighteen, her household was dissolved, and she was removed from Beaulieu and sent to the Bishop of Ely's house at Hatfield to live with the baby Elizabeth, whose household she joined, effectively, as a lady-in-waiting. Hatfield was not Beaulieu, but it was a very fine house, much liked by Henry VIII, who consistently borrowed it from the bishop; eventually, in 1538, he acquired it himself. There was only one state suite in the house, on the south front overlooking the gardens and approached by a great stair, and this must have been assigned to Elizabeth. Under James Nedeham's instructions, carpenters and bricklayers set up rooms for Mary elsewhere, possibly on the ground floor or in the guest rooms on the north front. Perhaps understandably, given her treatment, Mary was a difficult teenager who gave her governesses at Hatfield a terrible time. She was in turn cajoled and forced to behave, and eventually was denied the privilege of eating in her own room, forced to sit instead in the hall with the household at mealtimes. Mary's miserable exile lasted for over two years, until Anne was executed and Elizabeth, in her turn, was deprived of her titles, as well as the privileges and luxuries due to a princess.[6]

The way Henry used his children was, by modern standards, disgraceful. Between 1516 and 1537 they were moved from place to place to serve his political ends, his favour or displeasure signalled by the status of their accommodation and furnishings. The humiliation of Mary, the affectionate promotion of Henry Fitzroy and the abandonment of Elizabeth were in different ways brutal and calculating. Everything began to change in 1536. After the death of Katharine of Aragon and the execution of Anne Boleyn, Mary was forced to make a humiliating submission to her father and was received back at court; it was probably due to the influence of Jane Seymour that she was then allocated rooms at Hampton Court and Greenwich, where she stayed on the riverfront close to the king. That summer Henry Fitzroy caught severe bronchial pneumonia and died at St James's. For a brief moment Henry, Mary and Elizabeth were together at court; not a normal family by any means, but apparently a happy one.[7]

On 12 October 1537 Henry's longed-for son was born in the queen's bedchamber at Hampton Court. Despite fevered construction work to complete the new queen's lodgings there, Jane gave birth in the

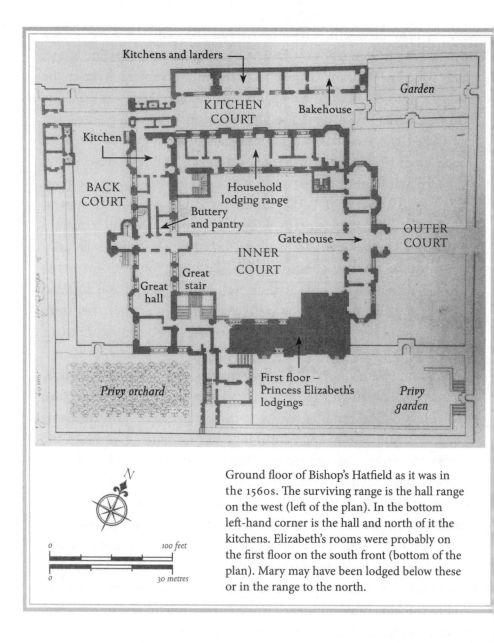

Ground floor of Bishop's Hatfield as it was in the 1560s. The surviving range is the hall range on the west (left of the plan). In the bottom left-hand corner is the hall and north of it the kitchens. Elizabeth's rooms were probably on the first floor on the south front (bottom of the plan). Mary may have been lodged below these or in the range to the north.

second-floor bedchamber that both Queen Anne and Queen Katharine had occupied before her. She never left the bed in which Edward was born, dying there on the 24th. While her body was embalmed, the royal glaziers removed recently installed panes of glass to allow air to circulate. Next door the presence chamber was hung with black cloth, an altar was set up and twenty-four tall tapers set around the room. In the middle was placed the queen's coffin, covered with a great pall and surmounted by a cross. For a week, in this makeshift chapel, Masses were said and dirges sung. Jane's body was then moved to the Chapel Royal and from there to a hearse in the middle court. Her wax effigy was laid on the catafalque and a funeral procession, led by Princess Mary, made its solemn way to Windsor, where she was interred in St George's Chapel.[8]

While his mother was buried and his father grieved, Prince Edward was established in his nursery. The hurried construction works of 1537 had, as a prime objective, the fabrication of a suite of lodgings for a Prince of Wales. These were built on ground to the north, forming a new courtyard. The prince's lodgings were a suite of monarchical rooms in miniature: there was a processional stair rising up to a watching chamber and chamber of presence, and beyond these a honeycomb of smaller rooms, including a bedroom, rocking chamber for his cradle, a bathroom, a privy kitchen and a garderobe. The lodgings neatly linked with the queen's privy gallery, allowing access to the prince's inner rooms directly from the queen's bedchamber – albeit at a distance of 100 yards.[9]

The last time Henry had built so confidently for an heir was in 1532 at St James's. In the end that project was a botched job. Although work had been pushed forward with all speed, things ground to a halt in 1536 with no son and the execution of Anne. By then there seems to have been a completed and usable house, because Henry allowed his chief minister, Thomas Cromwell, to live there. What he lived in was probably the miniature royal residence created for the son that Anne never had. Henry Fitzroy was living at St James's at the time of his death and the house was richly furnished with a large quantity of tapestry, two state beds with four sets of hangings, a golden cloth of estate with a matching chair and cushion. However, the cloth of estate did not bear the royal arms, nor indeed his own: Fitzroy may have been living in the house of the Prince of Wales, but he was a long way from being recognized as heir.[10]

It is worth speculating why Henry started afresh with new lodgings for Edward at Hampton Court. There were a number of reasons, I think.

The gatehouse at St James's from a nineteenth-century drawing. To the right of the gate can be seen the 'East' window of the chapel. Never properly completed, the house was modified over the centuries and is still in use today. Nevertheless, it did ultimately fulfil its original function as the house of the heir to the throne.

St James's, unfinished, was too close to London to be safe; it and Greenwich, the other obvious option, were close to dense, disease-carrying populations, whereas Hampton Court, far to the west, was isolated from infection harboured by the unwashed crowds. Just as important was the fact that Hampton Court was being remodelled to become the king's principal country seat – in fact, his favourite residence outside London. During the 1540s it was the focus of Henry's itinerary and Edward's establishment there meant that he was at the centre of royal geography.[11]

The death of Queen Jane left Henry a widower with three children by three marriages. The tensions between the girls that had been so strong in the 1530s slowly unwound after 1540, and the children increasingly lived together. In 1542 they all spent Christmas at Enfield, north of London. This had formerly been the house of Sir Thomas Lovell, a trusted royal councillor, who had served both King Henrys. Both had been his guest there and, after his death in 1524, the house had passed into the king's hands. Enfield is of particular interest as, on Lovell's death, an inventory was taken that listed all its rooms and it appears that he had maintained a suite of chambers exclusively for royal use. This meant that Enfield was particularly well suited to accommodating multiple households. As early as 1538 a nursery was built in the house, then for a visit in 1541 extensive repairs and improvements were made, including fixing wooden shutters to Prince Edward's rooms (presumably to keep them warm), providing furniture for Mary, fitting out Edward's privy kitchen and building mounting blocks for the king to mount his horse.[12]

Henry's fifth wife, Catherine Howard, went out of her way to continue the conciliation between the children and their father; this seems to have had a positive effect because at New Year 1543, after her execution, they all, for the first time, exchanged New Year's gifts.

In July 1543, Mary and Elizabeth attended their father at his sixth and final marriage, to Katherine Parr, in the queen's rooms at Hampton Court. By now Elizabeth was nine and Mary was twenty-seven, and it was decided that Mary should formally live at court and Elizabeth should join Edward's household. Mary was quickly assigned her own lodgings at many of the lesser houses like Enfield, Woking or Guildford (both in Surrey), Westenhanger and Otford (both in Kent). But far more important was the fact that in 1543 a large new lodging was under construction for her at Whitehall.[13]

At the Tudor court a person's importance was directly related to the size, positioning and magnificence of their lodgings and Princess Mary's ups and downs had been accompanied by architectural promotion and demotion. The king's construction of an extremely prominent and fine house for Mary signified her complete rehabilitation. It was located on the waterfront and was approached by a riverside gallery over 400 feet long. The house itself was set round a courtyard, but had all its main windows overlooking the river, including four large bow windows. Mary inspected work while it was under way and tipped the roofers as the building was topped out. We don't know how the rooms were arranged inside, but there was plenty of space for the princess's ladies and her household. She took a personal interest in its furnishings, buying a clock, coffers, a mirror and various paintings, including a portrait of herself. In

1547, after Henry's death, the furnishings were inventoried together with the king's and were then re-granted to her by Edward VI. It is clear that, as well as lots of tapestry, she had a cloth of estate (seemingly without the royal arms) and matching chair and cushion. In her bedchamber was a magnificent bed of state and her chapel was adorned with an embroidered altar frontal. Here, in comfort and splendour, she was finally able to be herself; with her greyhounds at her feet she enjoyed playing cards, listening to music and laughing at the antics of her fool, Jane.[14]

The last years of Henry's life saw the healing influence of Katherine Parr on his family. She presided over them at Hampton Court, on progress and at Whitehall. Edward and Elizabeth still spent much time isolated in the nursery houses at Ashridge in Hertfordshire and at Hanworth, and Elizabeth often spent time by herself at Hatfield.[15] But just as the king's love for Anne Boleyn had changed everything architecturally, so had the birth of Prince Edward. In the last decade of his reign Henry decided to reorganize the geography of his life completely and embarked on a series of projects that, incredibly, were to put all his architectural achievements so far into the shadows.

THE GRAND PROJECT

In 1538 Hampton Court was finished. It had been Henry's single most important building project to date and had cost in the region of £62,000 for the buildings and as much again for the furnishings. It's always hard to get a sense of value in modern terms, but multiplying by 1,000 gives an idea – so perhaps in today's values the king had spent £120 million on making his perfect country seat.

From this point we see a big change in his itinerary. Before 1540 he celebrated most of the major religious feasts of the year at Greenwich, which had long been the principal out-of-town residence of the Crown, but Greenwich was now small and old-fashioned compared to Hampton Court. Richmond, so beloved of his father, was deemed to be even more out of date and so, in the aftermath of his disastrous and short-lived marriage to Anne of Cleves, he gave the house to her and she lived there happily between 1540 and 1547. This meant that after 1540, the king switched all the major court events to Hampton Court. In 1540/41, and then every year from 1541/42 until his death, Henry spent the crucial court feasts of Christmas and Epiphany there, and in September 1546 Hampton Court hosted the largest and most prestigious diplomatic event for twenty years when the king received a huge French embassy. Also, in 1543 the king made the last of his great progresses to the hunting grounds centred on Woodstock and from then on Hampton Court became the base for an almost incessant round of mini-progresses.[16]

Since the Middle Ages there had been a direct correlation between the size and importance of a great seat and the lands that surrounded it. All the greatest residences, like the Duke of Buckingham's Thornbury Castle near Bristol, were set in massive landholdings – woods, waterways, arable lands, villages, even towns. Wolsey's Hampton Court was not like this; it had its own hunting parks, but Wolsey owned no significant land nearby. In 1536 Henry VIII embarked on a project to set Hampton Court within property suitable to its prestige and, over the following decade, acquired some 40,000 acres of Surrey and Middlesex. This was no random assemblage for, under the expert guidance of Thomas Cromwell, a commission visited, surveyed and assessed lands that might be suitable for royal acquisition. Some land was subsequently bought by the Crown, but former Church property was simply transferred and some private property was exchanged, while a few key estates were forfeit to the Crown by falling courtiers. In 1539 the process had gone so far that Henry passed an Act of Parliament creating an 'honour' of Hampton Court.[17]

An honour was simply a group of landholdings centred on a principal residence; Henry had created honours before at Beaulieu in 1523 and at Hunsdon in Hertfordshire in 1531. In both cases this symbolized the prestige the king wished to give them. Neither Beaulieu nor Hunsdon was to endure as a long-term favourite, but in 1545, after the acquisition of vast new lands north of the palace in Marylebone, an Act of Parliament created Whitehall an honour too. So the Act of 1539 for Hampton Court was unusual, but not unique. Why was it that the king felt that he had to create honours? Being an honour conferred no legal benefits, nor was it

The Honour of Hampton Court, showing the royal houses to the west of London, the approximate area of land purchased by the king and the extent of Hampton Court Chase.

N

MIDDLESEX

London

Whitehall

Windsor

Richmond

Greenwich

River Thames

Hampton Court

Croydon

Oatlands

Nonsuch

Woking

River Mole

River Wey

Guildford

Reigate

SURREY

0   15 miles

0   20 kilometres

Honour of Hampton Court

Royal Park

Hampton Court Chase

•••••• County boundary

the most modern or efficient way to collect income. It was a feudal title, a reference to ancient duties and responsibilities. It was, in fact, part of the chivalric image Henry wanted to create around his houses and estates.[18]

The Hampton Court Honour, though, had a special feature not yet seen, for the Act also created a chase. This was essentially a private forest – a game reserve protected by law and enforced by royal bailiffs; such a thing had not been created in anyone's living memory, and it was huge. The chase covered four whole parishes, some 10,000 acres. Its northern boundary was the River Thames but the whole of the east, south and west side were enclosed by a pale. This was a special type of deer fence, cunningly designed so that deer could leap it from the outside and enter but, because of a deep ditch on the inner face, could not jump out again: in this way the enclosure automatically filled up with deer. The pale and its ditches cost nearly £1,500. In the Middle Ages forests were not fenced and deer stayed in by habit not confinement; the Hampton Court chase was therefore more like a gigantic fenced park under draconian forest law.

The chase extended from Hampton Court westwards south of the Thames and, at its extremity, joined Windsor Forest. This meant theoretically that the king could hunt uninterrupted along the whole south bank of the river from Hampton Court to Windsor Castle. Yet he probably never did so. By the time the chase was completed, Henry was fifty-two and not in good health. His leg was ulcerated and painful and he often had to use a stick, while immobility and overeating had caused his waistline to bulge. When in 1549, as it was being abolished, the purpose of the chase was formally explained, it was said that it had been erected when 'his highness waxed heavy with sickness, age and corpulence of body, and might not travail so readily abroad, but was constrained to seek to have his game and pleasure readily at hand'. The chase was thus not actually for the chase, as Henry was not capable of long hours in the saddle any more; it was for mass slaughter from a standing – a timber platform from which the king and his guests would shoot driven deer with crossbows.[19]

Left: The Tudor royal standing that survives in Waltham Forest. It would originally have been fully plastered externally.

Below: Oatlands, a working sketch by Anthonis van den Wyngaerde of 1558. This shows the outer court where, over the inner gatehouse, the king's and queen's inner lodgings met. He carefully noted the colour of building materials.

One such standing survives, built by Henry not in Hampton Court Chase but in Epping Forest, where the king formed a park in 1541. Today it looks like a charming, if rather tall, cottage, but the large square stair on the back led up not to bedrooms but to a platform with unglazed openings from which the king could shoot. The floor, made of heavy oak planks, sloped in order to drain rain blown in by the wind.

One afternoon in September 1546 Chertsey meads was the scene of a great 'killing of stags'. Startled by the royal hounds, they were chased past the royal hunting party mounted in a standing; each time a fine stag was about to come in range trumpets sounded, alerting the king and his fellow crossbowmen to their prize. The deer that escaped the royal crossbow bolts were chased down by mounted hunters with darts and spears. In panic, many deer attempted to swim the Thames and some crossed the river, escaping into the woods on the other side. A spectator thought 'the most princely sport had been seen.'[20]

Honour and chase were part of an even larger and more ambitious plan for the setting of Hampton Court, because now Henry had moved his centre of gravity there he needed the royal family to do likewise. The first task was to provide a satellite residence for the queen. We have seen that queens were allotted land and property as part of their jointure and that Baynard's Castle in the City was provided as the queen's principal residence. Katharine of Aragon was granted Havering-atte-Bower as her country house in 1509. Anne Boleyn did very well out of Henry. As well as Baynard's Castle and Havering, she was granted Ditton, Hanworth and, further afield, Collyweston in Northamptonshire. Later wives were not so lucky – or didn't last long enough – and the only constant residence was Baynard's Castle, although Katherine Parr also received Hanworth and houses at Chelsea and Mortlake in 1544.

With the focus on Hampton Court, Hanworth was near, but it was relatively small, so in 1538 Henry decided to purchase a house at Oatlands which Katharine of Aragon had sometimes used and which was now in the middle of the chase.[21] As so often, he acquired the house in an underhand way. It had belonged to William Reed, an extremely wealthy goldsmith, but on his death his son and heir was a minor who was put into the guardianship of Thomas Cromwell. Cromwell 'agreed' an exchange, much to the king's favour, which saw the freehold transferred to the Crown. The Office of Works went on to spend £17,000 on it – a very substantial sum. The conversion of the house created two suites of lodgings, a large one for the queen and a smaller one for the king; the suites joined in the inner gatehouse which faced south. The great hall was dismantled and a dining room set up in the outer court for communal eating. There were two spectacular long galleries offering sweeping views over the park and, towering above the king's gallery, there was a prospect tower – a completely glazed octagonal viewing chamber giving a panorama of the house, park and gardens. Either side of the king's and queen's lodgings were privy gardens and in the queen's garden was a long brick ramp that allowed Henry to ride his horse up to first-floor level and dismount directly into the queen's privy gallery.

This was the archetypical house of the 1540s: all the emphasis was on the queen's side, where the king could repose in peace. The king's lodgings were compact and contained a withdrawing room beyond the privy chamber to allow Henry to retreat from public scrutiny. There was no great hall, as the house was used by a household of reduced size so that the king could hunt conveniently and privately. Yet the house was large enough for the king to continue with the business of state and while he was in residence in 1545, for instance, the Privy Council met daily in the council chamber. In November 1546 the Scottish ambassadors were even received there by the council.[22]

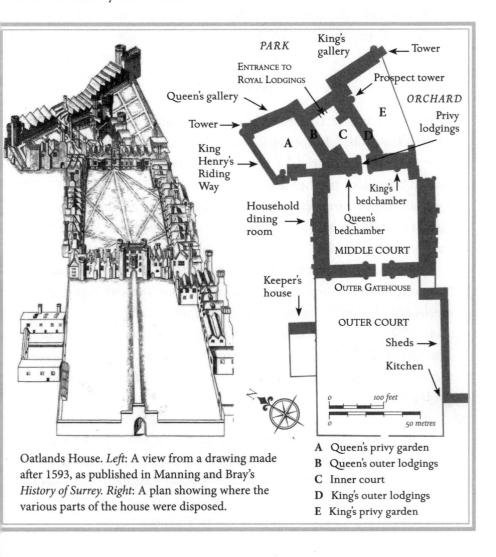

Oatlands House. *Left*: A view from a drawing made after 1593, as published in Manning and Bray's *History of Surrey*. *Right*: A plan showing where the various parts of the house were disposed.

A Queen's privy garden
B Queen's outer lodgings
C Inner court
D King's outer lodgings
E King's privy garden

The remodelled Oatlands was designed by William Clement and Christopher Dickinson, the architects of Hampton Court and the men who knew better than anyone how the king now wanted to live.[23] The use of Oatlands in the few years before Henry's death suggests that it was intended as a retreat where the king could stay with the queen in seclusion and privacy. Yet it was never formally granted to Katherine Parr, although she used it independently and had Mary and the other children to stay with her there. At Henry's death it was one of the standing houses kept at the ready for visits of the court. Furnishings included 408 tapestries, five great state beds, one of which was known as Queen Anne's bed, and three canopies of state, as well as all the other furniture one would expect.[24]

NONSUCH

Henry VIII was at Hampton Court in February and March 1538 and returned again in July; for the first time in a decade he was not planning new works there; indeed he had diverted his architects on to not just Oatlands but also another new project: Nonsuch. No house built by any English monarch arouses such curiosity as Nonsuch. In this, if in nothing else, Henry succeeded: for this building was indeed intended to be *non such* – nothing like it.

It was begun on the thirtieth anniversary of Henry's accession to the throne, a symbolic moment unquestionably, but it was also started three weeks after Edward's household had been fully established at Hampton Court.[25] This is the crucial context behind the construction of Nonsuch. The text on Holbein's charming portrait of the young Edward, given to Henry as a New Year's gift in 1539, publicly articulated the king's ambitions for his son:

Little one emulate your father and be the heir of his virtue; the world contains nothing greater. Heaven and earth could scarcely provide a son whose glory would surpass that of his father. Only equal the deeds of your parent and men can ask for no more. Surpass him and you have outstripped all the kings the world ever revered and none will surpass you.

This little boy, in Henry's mind, was destined to be the greatest king ever and, to ensure that this was the case, his education was paramount. In 1544 the women of his nursery were sent away and the six-year-old was given a grown-up, all-male, household at Hampton Court. In Edward's own words, he was surrounded by 'well-learned men' who sought to bring him up 'learning of tongues, of the scripture, of philosophy, and all liberal sciences'. The boy seems to have genuinely enjoyed his studies and excelled at them, having by the age of nine a good command of Latin and a thoroughgoing knowledge of classical mythology and the Bible.[26]

Henry was quite clear, even in 1538, that Edward would soon outgrow the baby lodgings on the north side of Hampton Court and, while the king and queen used Oatlands, he would need somewhere to stay nearby. The king's surveyors were sent out to identify a suitable place and recommended the village of Cuddington close to Cheam. It had various advantages, the surveyors stated – such as nearby quarries and a good water supply – but crucially it was a large estate with enough good land to create a hunting park covering nearly 2,000 acres. Here, 6 miles from Hampton Court, Henry built his last residence, one he was not to see finished and one that outlasted his death by only 136 years, being completely demolished in 1683.[27]

In the early 1950s nobody was quite sure where Nonsuch had been or what it had looked like. It had become a thing of legend and mystery; even paintings of it were misidentified as being of other royal houses. Curiosity eventually caused John Dent, the librarian at Epsom and Ewell borough, to try to sift fact from fiction and his investigations soon merged with official interest from the Ministry of Works, who were preparing a great history of royal building for publication. In 1959 Dent joined forces with the ministry and, under the direction of Martin Biddle, the site of Nonsuch was excavated. It was an extraordinary dig which revealed the whole layout of the lost mansion.

There were two main courtyards, an outer one with a wide gatehouse and an inner one with a narrow gatehouse; to one side was a third court for the kitchens. This was the basic arrangement at Hampton Court, but Nonsuch was far smaller. It is easy to think of it as a big building, but the

The excavations at Nonsuch in 1959 from the air, looking west. In the foreground are the kitchens; to the right the outer court and to the left the inner court.

excavations demonstrated that it wasn't. While Whitehall covered 23 acres, Oatlands 10 acres and Hampton Court 6 acres, Nonsuch covered only 2. The inner court was smaller than the Base Court at Hampton Court and both courts would have fitted inside the first two courts there. It was a pocket palace where everything was in miniature.

The excavations also revealed its unusual construction. All new royal domestic building since the beginning of the sixteenth century had been of brick with stone embellishments. But while Nonsuch's outer court, with its service rooms and kitchens, was of brick and stone, the inner court was timber-framed. Many buildings, such as the galleries at Hampton Court and Whitehall, had timber frames, but this was on a much larger scale. Not only was the extent of timber-framing larger – it comprised the entire courtyard – but the structural members themselves were of extraordinary dimensions: some of the timbers were 80 feet long, others 55 feet, and to carry them a special vehicle, the king's great wain, had to be designed. Normally the massive oak frame would have been filled with brickwork panels and then the whole thing rendered over with plaster. At Nonsuch, however, a new technique was introduced: the panels were filled with moulded stucco and the frame was covered with strips of carved slate with gilded highlights.

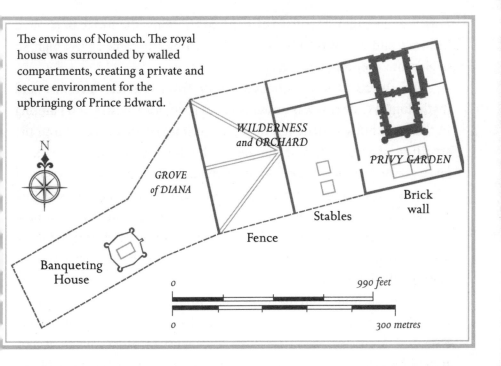

The environs of Nonsuch. The royal house was surrounded by walled compartments, creating a private and secure environment for the upbringing of Prince Edward.

N

WILDERNESS and ORCHARD

GROVE of DIANA

PRIVY GARDEN

Brick wall

Stables

Fence

Banqueting House

0   990 *feet*

0   300 *metres*

A crucial aspect of this technique was speed. Henry VIII's builders and architects had been interested from the 1520s in ways of building things quickly. They had been especially keen to find ways of achieving decorative effects without laborious carving. Thus, as we have seen, the interiors of buildings were covered in leather maché and, throughout the 1520s and early 1530s, there was the widespread use of terracotta painted to look like stone. Stucco was a new development in the same ilk brought to England via France by Nicholas Bellin of Modena. The stucco mixture contained marble dust and set quickly to a hard, creamy, stone-like texture, giving the impression of a stone-clad building. At Nonsuch the stucco was made in panels, with some of the repetitive detail pressed out of moulds, but the figures were moulded in situ. Hundreds of these panels were made by extremely skilled modellers.[28] The timber-framing between the panels was clad with strips of slate, a technique you can still see in Normandy and the Loire today. This was in part practical, as it protected the timber members from rotting, but it was also a decorative treatment. The slate strips were carved and gilded by Bellin's French craftsmen with royal badges, fruit, flowers and a guilloche pattern of interlaced ribbons. The area to be covered in stucco and slate was truly vast – 900 feet long and some 24 feet high, so in all some 21,600 square feet.

The stucco panels contained scenes from classical literature and mythology. While this was not unusual in itself, for tapestry and painting in the royal houses made use of the same sources, its application to the structure of a building was unique. In the inner court there were three levels: at the top, all the way round, were busts of the Roman emperors in roundels – probably of terracotta; below were gods and goddesses; and, on the ground floor, on one side were the liberal arts and virtues (for the queen) and, on the other, the labours and adventures of Hercules (for the king). Just in case people were unable to identify the subjects, many – perhaps all – of the panels were labelled with gilded text cast in lead. The visitor approaching from the outer court would mount seven steps inside the inner gatehouse to enter the inner court. On its opposite side, beyond a central fountain, was a large stucco figure of Henry VIII seated, trampling a lion beneath his feet, and to one side of him was Prince Edward. Father and son were thus flanked by Roman emperors and gods and goddesses.

So what was it like inside? Nonsuch was designed with privacy and

A reconstructed stucco panel from the excavations at Nonsuch showing a seated Roman soldier. Drawing by David Honour.

John Speed's print of
Nonsuch, showing the
large, full-size figures on
the bottom row of stucco
panels. The upper levels
of the inner court are
also visible.

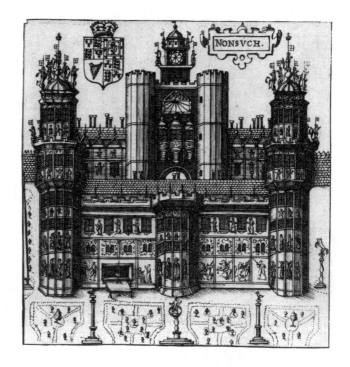

security in mind. Like all Henry's later buildings, the emphasis was on
keeping people away from the privy lodgings. At Nonsuch there were some
nice refinements. The watching chambers on both sides were sited on the
ground floor and were announced by figures of Scipio (the Roman general
and philosopher) and Penthesilea (the queen of the Amazons). Being located
downstairs, the Yeomen of the Guard were kept at the foot of a processional
stair that led up to the presence chamber on the first floor. As normal, there
was a gallery and closet between the presence chamber and privy
chamber. The privy chamber was a good size and served as the principal
audience room, but it led to the really important part of the house: the
privy lodgings on the south front. These took the form of a series of small
rooms, more on the king's side than the queen's, which backed on to the
privy gallery and were joined by a lobby that led to a capacious staircase
giving access to the privy garden below.[29]

For whom were these rooms intended? Nonsuch was a very small
house, with accommodation for the household and for courtiers provided
in the attics. On the single occasion when Henry VIII decided to visit, in

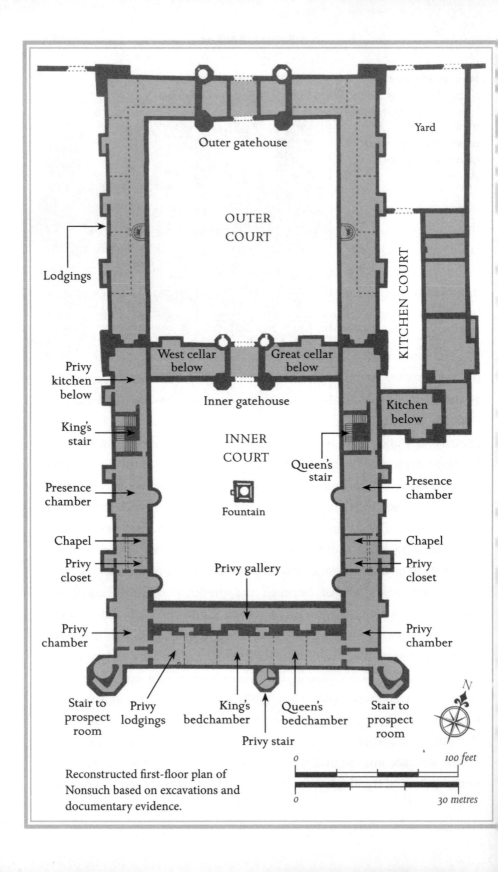

Reconstructed first-floor plan of Nonsuch based on excavations and documentary evidence.

1545, a great encampment of tents and temporary structures had to be provided to accommodate the whole court. There was no household chapel and so the court could not stay there on any great religious feast. There was also no great hall; in the outer court was a dining room for the small number of attendants who accompanied a reduced household. The kitchen court was small and contained three kitchens, one each for the king's and queen's sides and one for the dining room in the outer court. There were no workhouses and barely any space for larders. When Queen Elizabeth I started to use the house regularly in the 1580s and 1590s extra kitchens had to be built.[30] This was a residence designed for a small household – either the king's much reduced riding household or the household of the prince, smaller and in need of security and privacy.

Henry was paranoid about Edward's health and safety, and the fate of his own brother Arthur, who had died aged only fifteen, must have been at the front of his mind. Every year Edward lived he would become stronger and more able to resist illness, so his household was under draconian regulations. Strangers were forbidden to enter the prince's lodgings and those who did gain access were probably personally authorized by either the king or, in the early years, Thomas Cromwell. Edward's servants were not allowed to visit London, the poor begging alms were kept away from his gates, his food and drink was highly regulated and new clothes were washed before they were given him. Nonsuch was about as secure and private as it was possible to get. The inner privy court was entered from the outer court only through a gatehouse, and the outside of the inner court was completely enclosed by a very high brick wall; gates in this could be controlled by locks and the careful issue of master and by-keys.[31]

But over and above this, Nonsuch contained, in its inner courtyard, a three-dimensional educational programme for the prince. Here, ranged round the walls, were the lessons from his schoolbooks rendered life-size, tangible and memorable. Here visitors would be reminded of the education that the prince had received and be in no doubt of his knowledge and wisdom. We do not know who was responsible for choosing the subjects of the stucco panels, but they certainly would not have been left to the whim of the architect or to Nicholas Bellin. Most likely the programme was devised by Edward's tutor John Cheke, the most brilliant classical scholar in England, who would have carefully consulted the king.[32]

So in the 1540s Henry replicated, to the west of London, the arrangements he had in his capital. Whitehall, Baynard's Castle and St James's – home to monarch, consort and heir – were mirrored in the country by Hampton Court, Oatlands and Nonsuch. But Henry died before Nonsuch was completed and before Edward was old enough to start an adult programme of progresses. Immediately on ascending the throne, Edward the boy king used both St James's and Nonsuch, but the patterns of residence intended by his father were never fully realized.[33]

Nonsuch, unfinished, small, and very close to the most splendid and modern country residences, was a bit of a white elephant, or perhaps something a bit smaller – a white hippopotamus. It is not really surprising that Queen Mary I, who disposed of a large number of houses, sold Nonsuch to Henry Fitzalan, the 12th Earl of Arundel. So the building that Henry VIII had conceived as a fitting country residence for his son and heir, as a building to outshine any of his architectural achievements so far, was sold off by his elder daughter as an unwanted liability. By that stage, however, it had been superseded in fashion. The Duke of Somerset, King Edward's guardian, had built himself a great town house on the Strand. Somerset House was infinitely more sophisticated than Nonsuch in architectural terms. Although it probably did have a couple of panels of stucco on its façade, it relied for its effect on the subtle use of classical orders, not rumbustious allegory.[34]

MAKING SENSE OF WHITEHALL

Nonsuch was prodigiously expensive – it cost at least £25,000 – but it was not Henry's only project at the time, nor his largest. During the late 1530s the focus had been on building out of town, but in 1540 the king decided that it was time for Whitehall to catch up and work started on a massive programme of modernization. This was to eclipse Nonsuch in size and cost: the final bill was some £28,676. At the core of this programme were two aims: the first was to make architectural sense of the conglomeration of structures that made up the king's principal residence; the other was to make Whitehall a proper setting for the ceremonies of the Tudor court.

Work at Whitehall was under a separate team of architects from Hampton Court, Nonsuch and Oatlands. The Whitehall scheme was devised by the masons John Moulton and Nicholas Ellis, with the master carpenter John Russell – and it was technically and aesthetically challenging. There were three projects: the riverfront, the road approaches and the gardens. Each was affected by the big problem at Whitehall – lack of space. As an urban palace there was no obvious room for expansion, especially after all the neighbouring properties had been bought. The solution was something that had already been tried on a small scale in the early 1530s – land reclamation. Whitehall was on the Thames, a river much wider then than it is today, with broad tidal mudflats. Moulton and Ellis designed a massive new waterfront wall 512 feet long and reaching up to 100 feet further into the river than the 1530s waterfront. This reclaimed 4,000 square yards of new land from the Thames foreshore.

In 1950 most of the waterfront built in the early 1540s was dug up and the photograph overleaf shows a demolition contractor walking along the top of Moulton's and Ellis's 6-foot-6-inch-wide stone waterfront. During the excavations, as pneumatic drills systematically destroyed the Tudor wall, they eventually exposed its foundations and it was possible to see how it had been constructed. It was built on elm piles about 10 inches square and between 7 and 12 feet long. Each one was tipped with an iron shoe so that, as they were rammed in by massive stones dropped from a timber rig, they would easily push their way into the mud. Thousands of these iron-shod stakes were piled into the foreshore, creating a platform on to which oak boards were nailed with 10-inch spikes. These timber platforms were used as the base for the waterfront wall.

Incredibly, after 400 years, the contractors of 1950 found the wall

Whitehall Palace being excavated in the early 1950s. On the left is an aerial view of Henry VIII's 1540s waterfront in the course of excavation and demolition; and on the right is the largely demolished wall, showing how it sat on oak planks supported by elm piles driven into the foreshore.

plates and piles as solid as Henry VIII's engineers had left them. The late John Harvey, the brilliant historian and archaeologist who worked on the Whitehall digs, sawed off the tip of one of the piles and took it home with him as a paperweight. Many years later, when I visited him in his study to ask him about excavating Whitehall, he gave the pile tip to me and it sits on my desk as I write.

Henry's new waterfront was intended to bear an enormously long gallery punctuated by a series of bow windows looking out over the river. The gallery, like the inner court at Nonsuch, was timber-framed and had been prefabricated at Enfield and Helgrove, then shipped to Whitehall in sixty-one huge loads. We have seen that this gallery led, at its far end, to a new lodging for Princess Mary, but this cannot have been its only function. It was not necessary to build a 411-foot long gallery 11 feet wide just to get the princess to her lodgings in the dry. The project was mainly about architectural coherence: the gallery visually pulled together the disparate structures on the waterfront and gave a consistent modern face to Whitehall.

Works in the 1540s were also concerned with giving a more impressive view of the palace from the street. King Street, the main thoroughfare from the City of London to Westminster, sliced Whitehall in two. There was nothing that Henry could do about this and, at the end of his first phase of work in the 1530s, the street was enclosed by high walls on both sides, bridged by the king's new gatehouse. Extraordinarily, the gate contained the king's most important and private rooms and so Londoners ebbed and flowed about their daily business under his feet. More than this, beneath his study passed the funeral cortèges of the dead who had lived in the north part of the parish of St Margaret up near Charing Cross. Extremely anxious about being infected by 'disease, pestilence, ague or any other contagious sickness', Henry first required people living north of the palace to be buried in St Martin's churchyard and then in 1542 (because his instructions were being ignored), he re-drew the parish boundaries to remove any incentive to move corpses through the middle of the palace.[35]

While this might have relieved one anxiety, it didn't address the issue of magnificence, for the road between the walls with a gateway at one end was neither coherent nor impressive. So a scheme was devised to construct a second gateway at the north end, making the street between the walls into a coherent and defined space. This structure became known as the King Street Gate and was built in the last few years of Henry's reign. It looked very different from the first gateway in that it was capped by hemispherical domes and sported pilasters and pediments over the pedestrian gates on either side.

As we have seen, gateways were architectural bread and butter to Tudor Londoners. But the form had been given new meaning in the early sixteenth century. During royal entries to the City, pageants had been created that included ephemeral gateways of timber and canvas loaded with imagery and text. These gateways were triumphal arches in the ancient Roman sense – an archway through which the glorious victor would process. Although there are descriptions, no image survives of an English arch; however, there is a fine print of one erected by the English merchants in Antwerp in 1549, part of a pageant for the entry of Philip of Spain. This is architecturally sophisticated, much more so than the King

Left: The King Street Gate, Whitehall Palace, completed *c*.1546, as drawn in 1725 by George Vertue. It was encrusted with busts of figures from classical antiquity. *Right*: The English Arch, built at a cost of 4,200 florins in Antwerp for the entry of Philip of Spain in 1549.

Street Gate, but it illustrates the meaning invested in gateways by the time Henry's new gate was being built.[36]

So the King Street Gate was essentially another triumphal arch and the two gateways together formed part of a processional way to Westminster. From now on, when parliament met, the all-important procession from Whitehall to Westminster that signalled its opening would be framed by its progression through great triumphal arches. The king, like a Roman emperor at the head of an ancient triumphal procession, would move from his palace to parliament.

This concern with enriching the setting of the pageantry of monarchy was reflected in the third great work at Whitehall of the mid-1540s – the privy garden. A privy garden was just that – a private garden with access restricted in exactly the same way as it was for the king's chambers. At Whitehall from the early 1530s the Adam and Eve stair led down from the privy lodgings to the privy garden on the south front. But this was increasingly unsatisfactory, as the privy garden was the only garden at Whitehall and controlling access to a garden on to which the lodgings of many courtiers and officials looked was not easy. So the works of the mid-1540s converted the south gardens into the public great garden and relocated the privy garden to the north of the privy gallery.

This also had the effect of tidying up another hotchpotch of buildings that made up the core of Whitehall. A new wall was built round a large rhomboid of old cobbled courtyard to the north of the privy gallery and on the inside face, on all four sides, was erected a timber cloister with pillars 8 feet apart. These were painted blue and gold and decorated with the royal coats of arms and antique-work. In 1544 a visitor saw in the cloister walk 'busts of men and women, children, birds, monsters and other figures both above and below'; perhaps these were of stucco like those at Nonsuch. The cloister had a solid roof and a balustrade, which allowed people to walk round the top. A doorway was cut out of the watching chamber so that courtiers could gain access to the roof and look down on the garden. This might, at first sight, seem strange for a private garden, but the cloister had another use. As we shall see, it could be used for ecclesiastical processions and on these occasions the terrace above the cloister was opened up as a vast viewing gallery to allow the maximum number of people to see the splendour below.[37] (See plan, pages 134–5, and engraving, page 297.)

None of these improvements was put to the test in Henry's reign. In his remaining days no parliament was to meet and no procession wound its way round the privy garden cloister, for the king was gravely ill. Changes in the Whitehall privy lodgings illustrate the physical decline of this once magnificently athletic man. Wheelchairs, called trams, were installed in the privy gallery so that he could be moved from room to room. To allow these to be manoeuvred into his bedroom, it was enlarged; Henry's bed, too, was made bigger to enable his attendants to help him in and out.

In the last year of his life, the attacks of fever caused by Henry's poisoned leg got more frequent. On 23 December 1546, soon after he arrived at Whitehall, he was overcome again by a very high temperature, leaving him extremely weak. The king now faced his mortality and, on Boxing Day, called a group of his closest councillors and asked to see his will. Though he rallied in mid-January, Henry died in his bedchamber at

Whitehall on the 28th, soon after giving Archbishop Cranmer a sign that his trust was in God.

LEGACY: THE ONLY PHOENIX OF HIS TIME?

Thirty years after Henry's death, the Protestant historian and topographer William Harrison lavished praise on the king's architectural patronage:

> Those palaces that were built before the time of Henry the eighth, retain to this day the show and image of the ancient workmanship used in this land: but such as he erected (after his own devise – for he was nothing inferior in this trade to Hadrian the Emperor and Justinian the Lawyer) do represent another manner of pattern, which, as they are supposed to excel all the rest that he found standing in this realm . . . shall be, a perpetual precedent to those that do come after to follow in their works and buildings of importance. Certainly masonry did never better flourish in England than in his time.

Henry was, according to Harrison, 'the only phoenix of his time for fine and curious masonry'. Another Elizabethan fan of the king christened him 'a perfect builder as well of fortresses as of pleasant palaces'.[38]

But there was another view. After Henry passed the Act of Supremacy in November 1534, it was made treasonable to speak badly of the royal family, to deny their titles or to threaten them. Early the following year two priests mounted the pulpit and publicly called the king 'a great tyrant . . . the cruellest, capital heretic puffed with vainglory and pride', his morals were 'more foul and more stinking than a sow, wallowing and defiling herself in a filthy place'. The two admitted their views and suffered the horrific fate of hanging, castration and disembowelling – the punishment doled out to the lower orders who were found guilty of treason.[39] Can these two Middlesex priests have been the only ones to be disgusted by their king and his doings? Certainly not: but they were amongst the very few to be foolish enough to say so openly.

Of course, it is possible to reconcile the two views: the same king who was tyrannical and morally corrupt was the man who built many remarkable residences. But what was the relationship between the two Henrys, architect and tyrant? Architecture communicates primal issues like power, glory, spectacle, memory and identity – all these were reasons for Henry to build. But it also satisfies emotional and psychological needs, and he had these too. Henry VIII's quest for glory, for recognition as a great and powerful ruler, was one of the driving forces behind his architectural megalomania. But building was also a quest for satisfaction, for self-fulfilment and, in striving for this, Henry clearly believed that more was more. More houses, more parks, more tapestries, plate, fortifications, ships, gold . . . in all this materialism the king sought solace. But did he find it?

Henry obviously loved building and his enjoyment of it never slowed. After the execution of Catherine Howard in February 1542 he returned to Whitehall, where he celebrated the coming of Lent with three days of feasting, culminating on Shrove Tuesday with a sort of ladies' day at which he fêted the ladies of the court. Anxious that everything should be perfect, he spent the whole morning going from room to room, making sure that everything was as he wanted it. Henry was proud of his doings and loved showing them off. In 1527, after having, at huge cost, constructed and decorated two great banqueting chambers at Greenwich, he was determined that they should be properly admired and so, according to the chronicler Edward Hall, 'these two houses with cupboards, hangings and all other things the king commanded should stand still for three or four days that all honest persons might see and behold the houses and riches and thither came a great number of people to see and behold the riches and costly devices'. Henry would conduct tours of his houses himself, had he the chance: the French ambassador Jean du Bellay described how, when arriving at a royal house on progress, the king would show him round, describing what he had done and explaining his plans for the future.[40]

In his final phase of building at Whitehall, Henry extended the low, or stone, gallery that overlooked his garden. In the 1530s he had had it

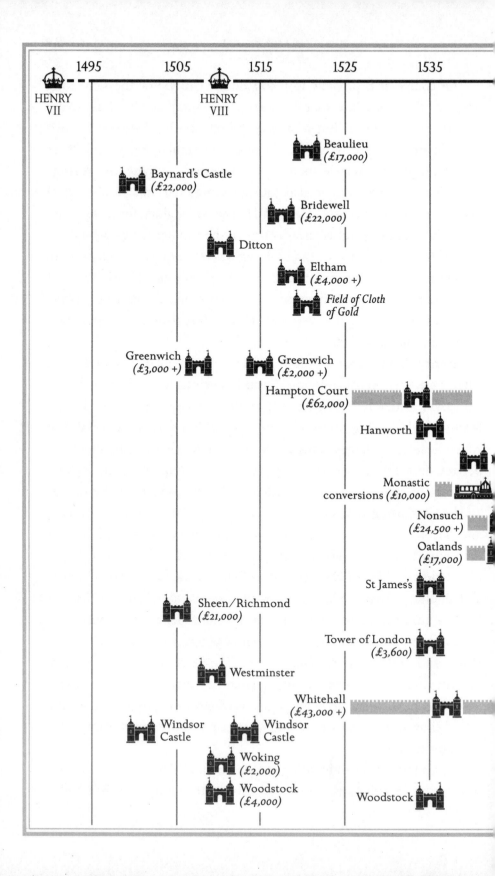

1495   1505   1515   1525   1535

HENRY
VII

HENRY
VIII

Beaulieu
(£17,000)

Baynard's Castle
(£22,000)

Bridewell
(£22,000)

Ditton

Eltham
(£4,000 +)

Field of Cloth
of Gold

Greenwich
(£3,000 +)

Greenwich
(£2,000 +)

Hampton Court
(£62,000)

Hanworth

Monastic
conversions (£10,000)

Nonsuch
(£24,500 +)

Oatlands
(£17,000)

St James's

Sheen/Richmond
(£21,000)

Tower of London
(£3,600)

Westminster

Whitehall
(£43,000 +)

Windsor
Castle

Windsor
Castle

Woking
(£2,000)

Woodstock
(£4,000)

Woodstock

ARD MARY   ELIZABETH
I   I   I

This shows the principal
royal domestic building
works undertaken in the
Tudor period with an
indication of how much
each work cost. Money
spent on small alterations
and maintenance is not
included. Although Tudor
royal building records are
very full, large gaps in the
record mean we will never
know the total amount
spent on royal houses.

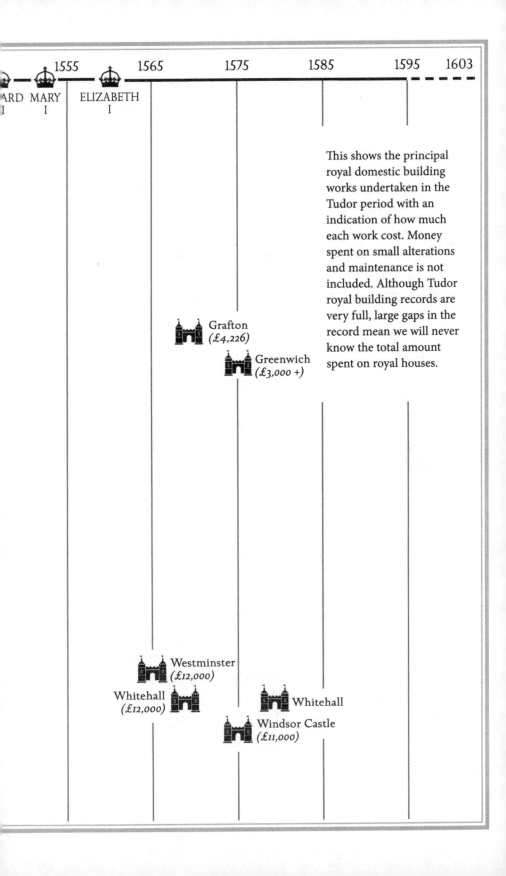

Grafton
(£4,226)

Greenwich
(£3,000 +)

Westminster
(£12,000)

Whitehall
(£12,000)

Whitehall

Windsor Castle
(£11,000)

painted with a great mural showing his coronation procession; in the extension, built in the 1540s, he created a gallery of great English royal houses. Above the dado the stucco-makers were instructed to model three-dimensional images of the king's favourite buildings, including Whitehall itself and Nonsuch, but also Eltham, the queen's house at Havering and the mighty Pontefract Castle. In another room at Whitehall there was a series of watercolours showing Hampton Court in the context of the great French château at Amboise. These suggest that architectural achievements ranked high in Henry's score-card of glory: when in the early 1530s Thomas Cromwell made a list of the things he had achieved for the king, a substantial part of it was about acquiring and building new houses.[41]

We will never know whether Henry VIII ultimately found fulfilment in either building or the commemoration of his achievements in it. But one must wonder whether, by the 1540s, the man who in his youth had delighted in opening the banqueting houses at Greenwich to the public was capable of empathy or emotional engagement at all. The golden youth of the 1500s and 1520s was now a dangerous, bloated tyrant. In the pathetic correspondence from Prince Edward to his father, craving attention and paternal approval, there is no evidence that Henry even bothered to reply to his son; instead, he substituted gifts for affection. Edward wrote to him saying, 'you have treated me so kindly, like a most loving father . . . I also thank you that you have given me great and costly gifts such as chains, rings, jewelled buttons, neck-chains, and breast-pins, and necklaces, garments, and many other things; in which things and gifts is conspicuous your fatherly affection towards me; for if you did not love me, you would not give me these fine gifts of jewellery'.[42] Henry had no love to give, but he had things. This is the tragic epitaph of a king who raped the English Church and terrorized his subjects to fund his lust for scores of houses filled with more possessions than anyone could ever use. In the end, like a fat dragon astride his mountain of gold, there was no self-fulfilment, only the emptiness that comes through gross materialism.

·XI·

King Edward's Godly Court

Politics

Henry's VIII's will was twenty-eight pages long and, unlike that of his father, which was principally concerned with his own salvation, it focused on how to transfer power to his nine-year-old son. Minors had acceded to the throne before, of course, but for most people the accession of Edward V, and his grisly end in the Tower of London at the hands of his uncle, was a warning of how it could go terribly wrong. Henry's will specified a novel arrangement whereby, instead of a regency, the king would be governed by a council 'in all matters concerning both his private affairs and public affairs of the realm'. This body would comprise sixteen councillors who could draw on a wider penumbra of a dozen advisors, all hand-picked by Henry.

Despite these precautions, so carefully set out, it was perhaps inevitable that one man would end up in charge – and so it was to be. Edward Seymour, the king's uncle, quickly established himself as Lord Protector of the Realm. Edward, too young fully to understand Seymour's aggrandizement of himself in terms of influence and wealth, was marginalized and power moved from Whitehall and the Privy Council to Seymour's own residence on the Strand, Somerset Place. However, in October 1549 Seymour's haplessness in the face of popular rebellions caused by economic privation and religious change brought him down. By this time Edward was twelve, precocious and opinionated; he was also now aware that his uncle had sidelined him. The new regime, established under the more nuanced control of John Dudley, Duke of Northumberland, brought power back into the royal houses and increasingly involved the king in decisions. Of course, at that point everyone, including Dudley, expected the king to assume his majority in no more than five years, so it was in everyone's interest to win the king's confidence and affection.[1]

SECURITY

The key to everything was the young king's person, its safety and control. On the death of his father, Edward was immediately removed to the Tower of London, where he was set up in the royal lodgings. Here, in the medieval presence chamber with its great windows overlooking the waterside, the nobility knelt one by one to kiss the boy's hand, murmuring 'God Save your Grace'. Edward remained at the Tower for three weeks while his council settled the protectorship on Seymour, who took the title Duke of Somerset. Meanwhile the dead king lay in Whitehall and was prepared for burial; his body was eventually placed on a carriage and transported slowly to Windsor Castle where he was interred. The way was now open for Edward's coronation and, three days after Henry's funeral, the traditional procession made its way from the Tower to Westminster where the boy king was crowned.[2]

At first Whitehall was thought unsuitable for the boy, too big and insecure, so when he was in London he was lodged at St James's, it being easier to safeguard.[3] This is exactly how Henry VIII had envisaged the use of the house in the early 1530s. Secure St James's may have been from the populace, but not from the court. Thomas Seymour, brother to the Lord Protector and uncle to the king, aggrieved by his lack of status and power, paid a visit to Edward at St James's at nine one morning. John Fowler, one of Edward's Privy Chamber, told how Seymour had come 'into the gallery where I was playing the lute. He said that there was slender company about the king, no-one in the presence chamber and not a dozen in the whole house'; he then went on to say, 'a man might steal away the king now if he came with more men than were in the house'. It was exactly this that he then tried to do. With the complicity of Henry Fitzalan, Earl of Arundel, the Lord Chamberlain, Seymour acquired a pass key to the privy garden and the privy lodgings.

He got all the way to the bedchamber door with a loaded pistol and was foiled only by the barks of the king's dog. Seymour went to the Tower in January 1549 and was beheaded two months later. Fitzalan, supposedly responsible for security at court, was accused of neglecting his duties, of removing 'bolts and locks' and not properly securing the doors of the privy chamber: he was heavily fined. Orders were immediately given to tighten security around the king. More guards were stationed in the watching chamber at St James's and, at Whitehall, door locks were reinforced.[4]

In October 1549, with Somerset's protectorship collapsed, he made a desperate attempt to reassert his authority by seizing the king and taking him from Whitehall to Hampton Court, where he tried to raise forces to 'protect' him. Moving on to Windsor Castle, a place better suited for the 'protection' of his ward, Somerset eventually realized he was not going to win, gave himself up, and he too was sent to the Tower. This was the second time security at court was shown to be ineffective and John Dudley, Duke of Northumberland, who now became Lord Great Master of the Household with complete control and authority over the king, moved to stop up the weaknesses. First, the Yeomen of the Guard who stood in the watching chamber of each residence were increased in number from 100 to 400. Then Henry VIII's splendid band of Gentlemen Pensioners, a mounted fighting force who were meant to be stationed, on foot, in the presence chamber, were found to be a feeble gang of thirty-eight disabled and over-age veterans incapable of securing anything but their pensions. In May 1550 they were replaced, to a man, by the Gentlemen-at-Arms, sixty demobilized mounted troops recently released from service in Boulogne, who were henceforth to guard the privy lodgings on foot. Not content with this, the following year Northumberland created a mounted guard, the gendarmes, 850 men who were retained by members of the Privy Council but paid for out of the royal coffers. These could not only deter a palace coup but would show the populace of London, should it be tempted to support one, that the king was armed and ready to defend himself.[5]

As the king could go nowhere without military protection, the court increasingly felt like a barracks. Far from making the young king feel imprisoned, he loved the show, enthusing about the gendarmes, their uniforms, horses and equipment; in 1551, to his delight, he reviewed the gendarmes mounted on his horses as they paraded past St James's.[6] Edward was a chip off the old block. Exactly like his father at the same age, he was obsessed with military hardware, fortresses and talk of battles and wars. The Office of Works built a fortress at Greenwich for a mock battle, and a floating castle on the Thames, particularly admired by the king. The Greenwich armourers were given a new working house, new stables were built at Richmond and stables elsewhere were repaired. Two ambling nags, horses suitable for a nine-year-old, were bought for the boy. At Whitehall, a new tennis court was built and the tiltyard was overhauled.[7]

The largest architectural work of the reign was the reconstruction of the Royal Mews at Charing Cross at a cost of at least £6,500. The new mews can be seen on Faithorne and Newcourt's map of Westminster of 1658 (overleaf) as a large rectangular courtyard entered by a gatehouse and containing scores of loose boxes, with a central pond or drinking trough. Here there were lodgings for the staff of the Master of the Horse and a smithy for the king's yeoman smith. Edward would have unquestionably been interested in this great work, but the reason behind it was the need of the regime to stable the vast number of horses associated with the king's new mounted guards. In the summer of 1552 Edward himself estimated that to move the court with the Yeomen of the Guard, the gendarmes and Gentlemen-at-Arms in tow would take some 4,000 horses.[8]

Just as the outward appearance of the court took on a militarized aspect, so the inner arrangements tightened Northumberland's grip on the king. The organization of Edward's everyday life was reformed and the men attending him were all to be Northumberland's friends. The post of first gentleman of the Privy Chamber (Groom of the Stool) was abolished and replaced by four Principal Gentlemen, two of whom were always to be present with the king. The new guard was instructed to admit only these four into the king's inner rooms. At night two attendants

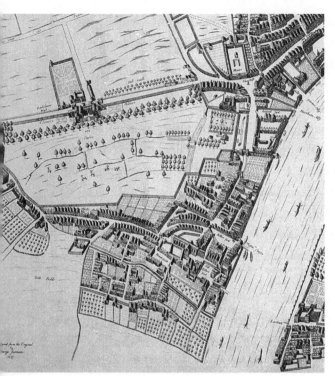

Faithorne and Newcourt's map of the cities of London and Westminster, done in 1658. It brilliantly shows the inner core of the Whitehall estate, with Westminster at the bottom and, in the middle, Whitehall set in its gardens. The park wall completely encloses what is today St James's Park and on its north side is St James's Palace. At Charing Cross the mews is clearly labelled.

were required to stand guard outside the king's bedchamber, as well as the two Principal Gentlemen sleeping inside.

These arrangements created a two-tier Privy Chamber: the wider group of attendants who had access to the privy lodgings and a smaller group of four who had access to what Edward called his 'inner privy chamber', in other words the secret lodgings of Henry's day. Although nobody at the time realized it, this was a decisive moment in the arrangements made for the body service of an English monarch. From this time on, through the reigns of Mary and Elizabeth, as well as the Privy Chamber staff there were separate bedchamber attendants. In fact, when James I came to the throne in 1603 he formally instituted a department in the household called the Bedchamber, giving institutional formality to what had long been everyday practice. But this is rushing ahead. In Edward's reign it was a novel arrangement, and one designed to secure his safety.[9]

We get a rare glimpse of Edward's secret or inner lodgings in July 1551 when he received the Maréchal Saint-André at Hampton Court. In a carefully staged series of privileged glimpses behind the scenes, Edward dined with him in his privy chamber and then, the king recorded, 'The next morning he came to see my arraying [dressing] and saw my bedchamber and went a hunting with hounds and saw me shoot and saw my guard shoot together. He dined with me, heard me play on the lute, ride, came to me in my study, supped with me and so departed to Richmond'.[10]

Governing King and Country

Life in the privy lodgings under Edward was pretty indistinguishable from the days of his father and required no physical alterations. Yet there were differences, and the most important of these was the transfer of power from an individual – the sovereign – to a corporate body – the Privy Council. Soon after Henry's death the council decided to make a visible architectural statement of the new status quo. Although there were council chambers in several of the royal houses, and indeed one at Whitehall, there was no visible place from which the Privy Council governed. It was decided to demolish part of the recently completed south side of the privy garden cloister at Whitehall and erect, against the privy gallery's north side, a new council chamber. This location was carefully chosen with two things in mind. First, the chamber would be accessible from the king's privy lodgings – a crucially important point, as the new council was made up of a mix of Privy Chamber staff and privy councillors, all of whom had access to the privy lodgings. Second, as we shall see, the privy garden was destined to become a public arena for the promulgation of the regime's religious views and the new room would thus be highly visible to Londoners. We do not know upon whose initiative the council chamber was constructed, but Protector Somerset was then building his house upon the Strand and understood the symbolic power of architecture well; it would be entirely in keeping that he ordered it as one of his first acts.[11]

The new building contained two rooms on each floor and a staircase linking them. On the first floor was the council chamber itself, with a big window looking out into the garden and a handsome fireplace. Next door was a room for the clerks. In this room, by the clerks' desks, stood the council chest – a vast bureau laced with drawers and compartments containing letters, account books, contracts and even bags of cash. In charge of this elaborate filing cabinet was the Keeper of the Council Chest, an archivist who produced papers from it on demand. As documents became less current, they were put in labelled bags and boxes and stashed in one of the Whitehall studies. During 1548, as cupboards and drawers bulged in the king's own rooms, a house in the precinct of Westminster Abbey was bought, demolished and replaced with a purpose-built store for the royal papers.

Two other servants were crucial to the working of the council: the keeper of the council chamber and the keeper of the council chamber door. The former saw to it that the room was cleaned and supplied with everything from logs for the fire to ink for the clerks' pens; the latter ensured that only authorized people were admitted. At Whitehall it is likely that people arrived through the cloister in the privy garden and waited in a downstairs room before being ushered upstairs to face the councillors. In other residences, arrangements were more straightforward. At a council meeting at Oatlands in 1551, it was somehow possible to bypass the keeper of the council chamber door, for one Thomas Trowghton was able to stuff papers beneath the closed door to attract the attention of the council at work.[12]

Because in due course Protector Somerset bypassed the council and took most decisions himself, the meeting of the body was initially symbolic; but under the presidency of the council established by the Duke of Northumberland after 1550, it once again became something like the ruling body that Henry VIII had intended. In 1549 Edward started to attend some council meetings himself and in August 1551 he noted that he was now required to attend; by January 1552 he was confident enough to write to the council asking them to consider certain 'weighty matters'.[13]

Since the fire of 1512 that had marked the end of Westminster Palace

Richard Grafton's representation of Edward VI's council chamber, and the council at work, from Edward Hall's *Chronicle*, published in 1548.

as a residence, it had been used by the various legal and administrative courts of state. When parliament assembled in London it had generally assembled in the refectory of Westminster Abbey, but the abbey had been suppressed in 1540 and converted into a cathedral, so where the parliament of 1547 met is unknown. The 1547 parliament passed the legislation that suppressed all chantry chapels, amongst them the king's own royal foundation of St Stephen in Westminster Palace. While some of the buildings of the old college were granted to favoured courtiers, the main building, St Stephen's Chapel, was set aside to be a permanent meeting place for the House of Commons. Money was spent on some minimal alterations and parliament met in the chapel for the first time in November 1548. Now for the first time the Commons and the Lords convened in the same building in chambers of similar layout in close proximity to each other.

The Commons adopted more or less wholesale the arrangement of the old chapel. The speaker sat on the raised altar step, from where he had a good view of the chamber; the 379 MPs sat facing each other where the choir stalls had been. The Office of Works provided an office for the clerk, a committee chamber, a record office and a large communal privy. This was the first permanent infrastructure that the Commons had ever enjoyed. This concern with providing proper basic facilities for the organs of state continued as the regime converted the chapter house at Westminster into a store for the records of the Court of Augmentations.[14]

Edward's reign thus marked a distinct watershed in both the regularization of the administration and the record-keeping of government, but also in the construction of permanent settings for its performance. The House of Commons today meets in a building adjacent to the site where the Edwardian Commons first gathered and the modern Cabinet meets only 50 yards or so from the council chamber built in 1547–8.

Religion I: the Henrician Conversion

The first four Tudor monarchs were all extremely devout. For them, their religion was not merely an ingredient in the formula of successful sovereignty, or a burdensome tradition, it was a real, present and urgent force in everyday life. While, as we have seen, Henry VII expressed this in bricks and mortar, Henry VIII's interest in religion was more intellectual. He had a profound interest in theology and the intellectual prowess not only to debate the issues but to write about them. He would, as Erasmus noted, 'enjoy the discussion of some theological point even over his wine'. It was, in fact, this intense interest in biblical study that first led him to question the validity of his marriage to Katharine and then led him to break with Rome: he believed that God had opened his eyes and shown him the reason for his lack of a legitimate son and that it was he, rather than the Pope, whom God had appointed as guardian and leader of his people in religion.[15]

From Henry's religious epiphany in the early 1530s flowed changes in the Church, but also in the practice of religion at court. The most visible effect of this was the suppression of the friaries at Greenwich and Richmond and the move of all the major religious feasts from Greenwich to Hampton Court. Hampton Court was a new kind of royal residence, one without a conjoined monastery – a major royal house where the Chapel Royal was the sole purveyor of spiritual services to the court. The

The ceiling of the chapel at Hampton Court, built in 1535–6. It is entirely decorative, hung by iron straps from conventional roof trusses above. Although the paintwork dates from a redecoration of 1847, it represents the appearance of the ceiling in Henry's reign. The illusion was that this was the heavenly star-spangled vault full of angels praising God. It thus followed Westminster great hall in providing a heavenly host under which the monarch sat.

The Hampton Court great hall, England's last royal great hall, started by Henry VIII in 1532. This huge space was both the common dining room for the lower orders at court and the splendid anteroom for the reception of the most important guests. It also doubled at various times as theatre and chapel.

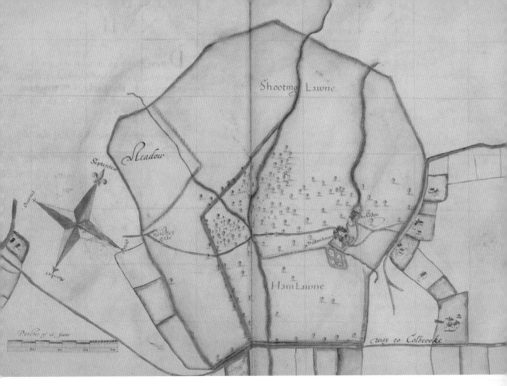

ABOVE: Ditton House was one of the principal homes of Princess Mary when she was a child. It was just across the river from Windsor, so it was easy to visit her parents there. In 1532, as part of the package of humiliation doled out to the teenage 'Princess of Wales', the house was granted to Anne Boleyn. This perspective was done in 1607 as part of John Norden's *Description of the Honour of Windesor*.

ABOVE: Whitehall Palace from the river by an anonymous hand in the 1660s. This is the best view of Princess Mary's waterfront lodgings, built in 1543. On the riverfront, right to left, can be seen the great hall with its decorative louvre, the royal watergate or landing stage, the 400-foot-long riverside gallery and the princess's lodgings. The large square building in the centre of the painting is the Banqueting House built for James I.

ABOVE: Georg Hoefnagel's presentation watercolour of Nonsuch, given to the 12th Earl of Arundel in 1568. The privy garden wall obscures the lower part of the building, but the stucco-covered first-floor privy lodgings can be clearly seen, as can the two great prospect chambers capped with onion domes.

LEFT: Prince Edward painted at Hunsdon. Here the prince stands in the pose invented by Hans Holbein for Henry VIII in the Whitehall privy chamber. It is a fictitious setting, but out of the window can be seen Hunsdon House, the prince's childhood country residence.

ABOVE: Henry VIII and his family at Whitehall Palace. This fictional scene, by an unknown hand, captures some of the lavishness of an Henrician royal interior. All the elements are here: an embroidered canopy of state; the Turkey rug laid on a painted plaster floor; delicately carved and gilded panelling; and a moulded ceiling supported by columns decorated with grotesque-work.

BELOW: *The Somerset House Conference, 1604.* This is an extremely rare painting of the interior of a royal house. Although done just after Elizabeth's death, it shows the Elizabethan council chamber at Somerset Place in use and the large transom and mullioned window that looked out on to the courtyard. The Tudor royal council met in rooms exactly like this.

LEFT: Mary I and Philip of Spain under throne canopies of cloth of gold in a painting by Hans Eworth. Mary sits on an X-frame chair of estate while Philip leans on his. The floor is painted plaster. Beyond the cushion on the sill, St Paul's Cathedral is visible through the open casement.

BELOW: John Norden's presentation copy of his survey of Windsor Forest of 1607 included an aerial view of the castle. This section shows the upper ward where the royal lodgings were. In the centre of the court can be seen Queen Elizabeth's fountain. At the bottom are the two courts of royal lodgings, on the right Queen Elizabeth's gallery and Henry VII's tower.

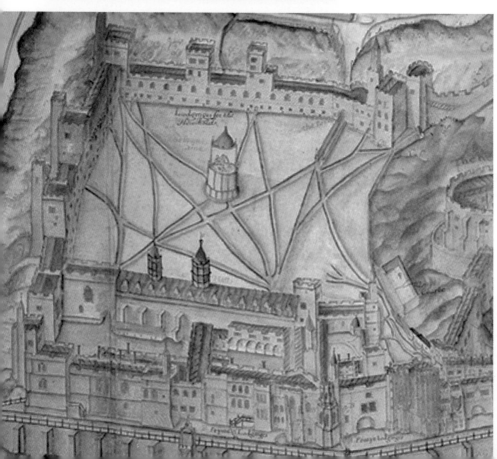

LEFT: Cloth of estate made for Queen Elizabeth's visit to Kimberley, Norfolk, on 22 August 1578. It bore the arms of the queen's hosts, Roger Wodehouse and his wife Mary Corbet.

BELOW: Elizabeth I receiving Dutch emissaries in 1585. This small watercolour is frequently reproduced as one of the only surviving depictions of an Elizabethan royal interior. Despite suggestions that it might not have been painted in England, all the details can be closely corroborated from what we know of such interiors: the matted floor, the tightly fitted tapestry, a birdcage in the window, a canopy with cloth of gold and, most interestingly, the queen's ladies sitting on cushions on the floor.

LEFT: Elizabeth I by Marcus Gheeraerts the Elder, *c.*1580–85. This painting is full of rich detail. Particularly interesting is the glimpse of a privy garden in the background. Here Elizabeth is seen entering through a gate guarded by one of the Yeomen of the Guard.

BELOW: Elizabeth I by an unknown painter. This painting, commissioned by Elizabeth Talbot, Countess of Shrewsbury, is famous for the dress the queen wears, crawling with creatures of land and sea. It also shows, in great detail and with accuracy, the interior of a royal house. The queen stands on a dais covered with a carpet next to a splendidly embroidered throne with cushions.

king was now in complete control of court religion and everything, from words spoken in the pulpit to the vestments on the backs of the choir, was under his authority. This changed the status of the Chapel Royal both in an architectural and a ceremonial sense.[16]

The last part of Wolsey's Hampton Court to be improved by Henry was the chapel. Work started in 1535, the year after the Act of Supremacy was passed. The visual centrepiece was the chapel ceiling, which represented the star-dusted vault of heaven complete with heavenly choirs. Prominently written in gold letters on the ribs dividing each bay was the royal motto, *Dieu et Mon Droit* – literally, God and My Right – which, in the context of the Supremacy, was about Henry's (God-given) right to rule (see plate section). Sitting in the raised first-floor pew, the king was closer to this representation of heaven than even the priests celebrating Mass below.

The royal pew, the holyday closet, was divided into two by a richly painted and decorated timber wall containing stained-glass windows. On one side of this sat the queen and her ladies and on the other the king. Each closet had its own spiral staircase providing access to the floor of the chapel for the times when the king and queen participated in the liturgy. The holyday closets were not open to the lower chapel like a modern theatre box, but were glazed with floor-to-ceiling bay windows. The royal family was thus separated from the service below by a wall of glass which had small opening casements so that they could hear what was going on. Henry was notoriously inattentive during Mass and would be given letters to read and sign while he was in the closet.[17]

As the chapel was completed, Henry also remodelled the court to its south, a cloistered square of about 115 feet. This regularized the courtyard containing the principal royal lodgings, at the same time providing a cloister attached to the chapel for ecclesiastical processions. At the great feasts of the year Henry, the supreme Governor of the Church in England, could join the processions round the cloisters, watched by hundreds of spectators.[18]

Whitehall was, of course, the most important residence and here the changes that accompanied the Supremacy were even more sweeping. We have seen that Henry constructed a huge cloister that enabled him to be seen participating in magnificent ecclesiastical processions by perhaps a thousand or more. But Whitehall became more than another vast ecclesiastical arena. Henry did not only legislate to make it a palace and the centre of an honour; he seized complete control of the town of Westminster. With the abbot's authority gone, a High Steward of Westminster was created as the officer who dispensed patronage and represented the town to the Crown. This post was handed to Sir Anthony Denny, who was keeper of Whitehall Palace. Then Henry declared that Westminster was a city that would return two MPs and legislated to transform Westminster Abbey into a cathedral, appointing, as its bishop, Thomas Thirlby, his own Dean of the Chapel Royal. The city of Westminster, as it had now become, was a thus royal city with its own MPs, the sovereign as lord of the manor, the keeper of the king's palace as High Steward, the royal coronation church and mausoleum as its cathedral, and the head of the king's personal chapel as its bishop.[19]

People at court would certainly have noticed these changes, all of which aggrandized the king and his participation in royal religion. But when we look closely at how liturgy was performed at chapel, we find that it remained extremely traditional. Though Henry had turned away from purgatory and relics, he still believed in, and practised, traditional Catholic rites. So, in 1545, the king's goldsmith supplied the Whitehall chapel with a complete new set of altar ornaments, including an elaborate crucifix with figures of Mary and John, two candlesticks, two basins, a chalice, two cruets, a bell and a holy water pot with sprinkler. The royal vestries were full of copes, including three large sets of choir copes that were worn only by the choir in procession. The sergeant of the vestry at Whitehall had, amongst other books, three ordinals, three Mass books and twenty-four processionals (guides to ecclesiastical processions). One of the processionals survives in the British Library and contains woodcuts showing the order of procession on feast days.[20]

Henry wanted to purify and reform traditional religion, not sweep it away, and so Christian observance remained the pivot upon which life at court turned. What changed was the focus upon the king. The physical

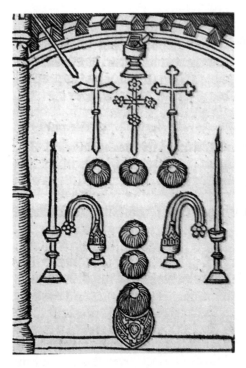

Woodcut from a processional supplied for the Chapel Royal at Whitehall. The priests are represented by their tonsured heads and they can be seen to be carrying two large lit tapers, two thuribles (incense swingers), three crucifixes and a holy water pot and sprinkler.

setting of the Supremacy was designed to emphasize the monarch's position as the head of the Church in England; he was no longer surrounded by cardinals and friars representing papal powers. The splendour of religion at court, which in many ways increased after the Supremacy, upheld Henry's new self-proclaimed status as both secular and religious ruler of his kingdom.

RELIGION II: THE EDWARDIAN REFORMATION

Edward VI believed with all the conviction of an opinionated teenager that traditional religion was misguided and sinful. When Henry died, Edward, influenced by a group of aristocratic evangelicals, quickly drove through deeper reforms than his father had done. A set of injunctions issued in 1547 banned a number of practices. Holy Communion replaced Mass, a wooden table replaced the consecrated altar, and a plain white surplice replaced a cope and alb. Images and candles were banned and so were processions.[21] In the Chapel Royal, altars were dismantled and communion tables installed, the most prominent and easy-to-reach images were removed or painted out. In the Chapel of St George at Windsor we have the details: all the altars were dismantled, wall paintings covered up, a pulpit installed and the organ dismantled. Changes were made to the liturgy and in 1549 the chapel adopted the English Book of Common Prayer. However, the Chapel Royal still remained exempt from the provisions abolishing chantries, and chantry priests remained at Windsor praying for the souls of former monarchs (just in case).[22]

Despite these reforms, the Chapel Royal still needed to be part of the magnificence of court. In July 1551 when the Maréchal Saint-André came to London to present the young king with the Order of St Michael, the culmination of the ceremony took place in the Hampton Court chapel, where canopies had been erected for Edward and the French king *in absentia*. There was a procession into the chapel, where Edward took his seat under his badge and communion was celebrated.[23] Such an occasion could not take place in a whitewashed barn, nor indeed did it. In a dispute with John Hooper, the Bishop of Gloucester elect, over the wearing of vestments, Edward told the bishop that as long as he wore his vestments at court, he could do whatever he liked in his diocese or elsewhere.[24] Thus 'abuses' could be tolerated at court for the sake of a fine show and the proper expression of the dignity and authority of the Church. The same went for music, as Edward's chapel still comprised forty men and 'the children'. They sang newly composed settings for the Edwardian liturgy and 'reformed' versions of the Te Deum and various anthems.[25]

The most significant change that the new regime brought about in a royal residence was the creation of a vast new arena for preaching at Whitehall. This was the initiative of Thomas Cranmer, Henry VIII's reforming archbishop, who was now driving forward religious reform under Edward. Preaching was central to Cranmer's vision of national religious revival and, as the great cloister at Whitehall Palace was no longer being used for processions, it was adapted as an outdoor preaching arena. In March 1548, in the middle of the former garden within the cloister, a pulpit was erected, easily visible from the new royal council chamber on its south side, and 'therin Doctor Latimer preached before the king, where he might be heard of more than foure times so many people as could have stoode in the king's chapel'.[26] A woodcut from the 1563 edition of Foxe's *Acts and Monuments* shows the king and his councillors at the window of the council chamber, listening to this sermon. The conscientious young monarch took notes in a book, in which he also carefully recorded the preacher's name and the time and place of the sermon.[27]

The appropriation of the cloister as a preaching place was a masterstroke. The floor area was at least 55,000 square feet, capable of accommodating perhaps 5,000 people plus a large number more on the terraces around the courtyard. Here in the heart of Whitehall people could see the council chamber from where they were governed and,

Hugh Latimer preaching before Edward VI in the pulpit in the Preaching Place at Whitehall Palace in 1549. This is a woodcut from John Foxe's book *Acts and Monuments*. The woodcut was originally used to illustrate a printed edition of Latimer's sermons and is, as far as we can tell, an accurate depiction of the Preaching Place as used in Edward's and Elizabeth's reigns.

within earshot, the pulpit that proclaimed the reformed religion that they professed.

In Lent 1549 Hugh Latimer, Bishop of Worcester and the most brilliant preacher of his day, used the new pulpit to preach a series of Friday sermons. In the sixth of seven he began to realize the shortcomings of the new arrangements and complained that while he was speaking people were walking round the courtyard and there was 'such huzzing and buzzing in the preacher's ear that it makes him oftentimes to forget his matter'. He then appealed to his congregation, 'Let us consider the king's goodness! This place was prepared for banqueting of the body: and his majesty has made it a place for the comfort of the soul, and to have the word of God preached in it'; the king would like, Latimer went on, all his subjects to come to the new arena, if that were possible. Respect, therefore, he said, the word of God and the presence of the king. Whether his appeal had any impact on a restless audience is not recorded.[28]

People and Places

Edward was a nice-looking boy, not as tall as his father and with the gangly frame of an adolescent. His skin was pale, his eyes grey and his hair auburn. His features were set off by clothes of the richest sort, laced with gold and silver and encrusted with precious stones. He was a bit of a dandy, but for a teenager he was quite serious-minded and his intensive studies, which continued daily throughout his life, gave him an extraordinary grasp of languages, but also of geography, astronomy and, of course, theology.

If Edward felt anywhere was home it was likely to have been Hampton Court, the place of his birth and childhood. As king, it became his most favoured country residence, followed by Oatlands and Greenwich. For the first five years of his reign he was kept close to London, moving between the houses on the Thames by barge and occasionally riding out further afield. It was only in July 1552 that he began his first (and, as it happened, last) summer progress. We have no proof, but it is very likely that the route had been chosen by Edward himself. This is because the eventual destination was Portsmouth, strategically one of the most important sites on the coast, where major works of military engineering were under way. Like his father, Edward was fascinated by fortifications; he had engaged directly in discussions about the fortification of Berwick, ordered a report on the state of those at Guînes, and paid £10 for a plan of Calais and its surrounds for his own use. His personal notes and letters on the subject reveal a solid grasp of the technicalities, not just childish enthusiasm. When the court arrived at Portsmouth Edward was given a comprehensive tour by land and sea, and plunged into discussions about the construction of two new forts at the entrance to the haven. This all came naturally to him: although as a child his nursery houses had never been full of workmen, he must have seen the huge works at Whitehall in the last years of his father's reign, and Henry had shown him maps and plans for coastal forts and castles.[29]

Edward's progress was unusually magnificent; no fewer than seven privy councillors attended him and Northumberland had ordered the entire new force of gendarmes to follow. Only just over a week into the expedition, it was realized that the gendarmes would have to be disbanded because their horses 'were enough to eat up the country; for there was little meadow or hay all the way'. Reduced to 150 guards, the progress must still have been an impressive sight – in just two months it had consumed some £6,875. The tour took in an unusually large number of courtier houses, which perhaps explains why Edward ordered an incredibly lavish travelling bed with a crown of cloth of gold and posts topped with golden cups and a gilded lion – this allowed him to stay in splendour outside his own houses.[30]

In Edward's name, Somerset and Northumberland disposed of a number of the more peripheral royal houses. Ten in all were either taken by Northumberland or granted to members of the ruling inner circle. The one Edward himself seems to have taken interest in was Bridewell. In February 1552, listening to a Lent sermon in the preaching place at Whitehall, the king was struck by Bishop Ridley's plea to do something about the destitute, the disabled and the lepers who disfigured the streets of London. Calling Ridley into his lodgings, 'he made him come into a great gallery, where there were present no more persons than they two, he himself sitting down in one chair and the king in the other, and causing him to be covered, entered into conversation with him.' The result of the fireside chat was an order to the Mayor of London to come up with a plan to deal with poverty and destitution.

Two months later Ridley and the mayor returned to the king with their solution and, on bended knee, explained that their suit was 'for one of your grace's houses, called Bridewell, a thing no doubt unmeet to ask for'. Edward was unable to grant their wish immediately, as he had to consult with his council, but at an audience at Whitehall in April 1553 the king, now weak and ill, granted Bridewell 'to be a workhouse for the poor and idle persons of the city of London'. In this way Henry VIII's first new house, scene of the dramas of his divorce, passed out of royal hands and gave its name colloquially to prisons, police stations and even to Chicago city's main jail.[31]

·XII·
QUEENS REGNANT

A New Sort of Court

IN APRIL 1552 EDWARD SURVIVED A nasty bout of measles. What nobody could have known was that the attack had fatally reduced his resistance to tuberculosis, to which he was also exposed at about that time. By the end of the year he was showing signs of the disease and, from February 1553, his health noticeably began to deteriorate. To everyone's horror, the strong, healthy lad, who was showing enormous promise as king, started to fade away before their eyes. He died in July 1553 after a horrible, harrowing illness. He was only fifteen.

Despite efforts by the Duke of Northumberland to subvert Henry VIII's will and place Lady Jane Grey on the throne, Mary Tudor, at Kenninghall in Norfolk, declared herself queen and, with a show of military force, decisively claimed the crown that was hers by hereditary right. Mary had been part of the national scene for thirty-seven years and was a familiar and popular figure to many Londoners, so, as she entered the City on 3 August 1553, there was genuine joy at her accession. Partly due to the incredible emotional stresses placed on her since Henry VIII's repudiation of her mother, she had not enjoyed good health, but she had a determined character and a highly trained mind. As she entered London, these qualities, enhanced by her love of rich dress, gave the slight woman with reddish hair and poor eyesight a regal air.

Regal, and unique. England had never before crowned a queen as sovereign. In the twelfth century Matilda was recognized by her father, Henry I, as his legitimate heir but the throne was seized by Stephen of Blois as soon as Henry died. Mary was thus destined to become England's first queen regnant. She moved straight to the Tower of London, where, like her half-brother before her, she received the homage of her council and household. There was no wholesale purge of Edward's household staff; only around 10 per cent of his men were replaced by Mary's followers. The exception was, of course, in the Chapel Royal, where the dean and all the royal chaplains lost their jobs, for Mary was determined that both her household and her kingdom would be brought back into unity with Rome.

From the Tower she couldn't go to Whitehall because Edward's body was lying in state waiting for burial, and so, while the funeral took place and Whitehall was prepared for her, Mary moved to Richmond. This choice was probably influenced by the fact that the privy lodgings there were separated from the rest of the house and secured by a moat; her mounted guard were stationed in the outer court and eight pieces of artillery set up with a stockpile of ammunition. Safely incarcerated, the new queen and her councillors, in constant communication with her patron, protector and cousin the Emperor Charles V, decided what to do next.[1]

One of the first problems was her nineteen-year-old half-sister Elizabeth, of whom her Spanish advisors were deeply suspicious. Elizabeth pleaded an audience with Mary and came before her sister in a privy gallery at Richmond. On her knees, with only two attendants present, she dissembled about her religion, offering to take instruction in Roman rites. The following Sunday her resolution was put to the test as it was the Nativity of the Virgin and the Richmond chapel was prepared for a feast abolished by the previous regime. Elizabeth tried to wriggle out of attending and when forced to do so complained of acute stomach ache all the way to the chapel.[2]

Two things were now pressing: arranging the coronation and summoning a parliament. The queen's council felt that these arrangements would be better made in London, so Mary came downriver and set up at St James's. As her brother had demonstrated, of all the London houses, this was the most secure, being at a distance from the population – a proportion of whom harboured murderous intentions towards the new queen they regarded as a heretic. Equally, St James's was a discreet location where the queen could see whom she pleased without too much notice. One evening, the Spanish ambassadors, for instance, were able to come across the park from Whitehall and enter through the garden to see the queen in complete secrecy.[3]

So it was from the seclusion of St James's that the queen set off on 1 October 1553 for the Tower of London and, like her grandfather, father and brother before her, processed from there to Westminster for her coronation. A queen regnant was not only an entirely novel proposition; in Tudor England it was the world turned upside down, as women, even crowned ones, were subservient to men. This is why, immediately after her coronation, it was felt necessary to underline Mary's rights and powers in an Act of Parliament that reassured everyone that she would enjoy 'all regal power . . . in as full, large and ample manner' as any male sovereign before her.[4]

This resolution was soon complicated by the queen's announcement that she intended to marry Emperor Charles V's son, Philip of Spain. Under the marriage contract, Philip was not to be crowned king but was to be called upon to 'aid' the queen in the government of the realm, yet many assumed that, as a man, he would rule his wife and therefore rule England. On 25 July 1554, they were married in Winchester Cathedral. For Mary, the marriage crowned her plans to return England to the Catholic faith and, for Philip's father, it finally enabled the Hapsburgs to straddle France and dominate Europe.

Mary's passion for her new husband, eleven years her junior, was matched in almost equal measure by Philip's reservations about his thirty-eight-year-old English wife. None the less, the two made an effective public show of togetherness as they moved from Winchester, via Windsor and Richmond, to London, where on 18 August they made their triumphal entrance and established themselves at Whitehall. The two weeks following Philip's landing cannot have been easy. Not only was the ceremonial that accompanied the wedding and progress to London gruelling, but the two retinues were continually at each other's throats. One of Philip's household noted that 'The English hate us Spaniards worse than they hate the Devil, and treat us accordingly';[5] the feeling, in fact, was mutual.

All royal houses, as we have seen, had a side for the king and one for the queen and, as sovereign, Mary moved into the king's side. During Edward's reign the queen's chambers had been used for various court feasts, accommodation for the Duke of Somerset, lodgings for high-powered visiting ambassadors and, in November 1551, as the lodging of Mary of Guise, the dowager Queen of Scotland.[6] In August 1554 the queen's side became, for the first time in English history, the lodgings of a king consort. Philip had brought with him a large entourage of courtiers and attendants and, while some of these could be accommodated in his lodgings, most could not. Houses and inns had to be rented and there was a lot of bad feeling amongst those who could not live at court. Tensions were eased when Philip sent away around eighty of his Spanish retinue and then announced that he was happy to have English attendants in his outer rooms, although his Privy Chamber was comprised of Spaniards.[7]

The changes in the queen's household were more radical. Henry VIII had made the privy chamber the theatre of national politics, staffed by the men who administrated and ruled as well as entertained and amused the king. Under Mary it could be no such thing. As a woman, she had to be served by female attendants and the doors of the secret lodgings and bedchamber were barred to all men apart from her husband. Politics moved out from the innermost rooms of the royal houses into the council chamber. Mary's privy chamber thus reverted to its original job, the one invented by her grandfather in the 1490s – it was the place where she lived her private life, insulated from the rest of the court.

During the reign of Edward, Princess Mary had kept her distance from the Chapel Royal. At Christmas 1549 Edward had invited his half-sister to come to court, but Mary declined as she thought, 'They wished me to be at court so that I could not get the mass celebrated for me and that the king might take me with him to hear their sermons.'[8] She was right: Edward wanted his sister to give up the Mass or, alternatively, be excluded from the succession. In the end, in 1553, on the throne and using parliamentary sanction, Mary repealed all the parts of Edward VI's reformation that had been enshrined in statute and rolled back the liturgical and ritual clock to the last year of Henry VIII's reign.

The Henrician Chapel Royal was immediately restored: altars, vestments, crosses, candles and images of saints were all re-introduced. So was the daily round of Roman observance: the daily Matins with Lauds, Lady Mass, Prime and High Mass, followed in the afternoon by Vespers with Compline – in all five or six hours of service every day. Mary was determined that her chapel would set an example for her country. After her marriage, numbers in the Chapel Royal were increased, including a large number of Spanish singing men brought by Philip. Meanwhile, Mary reinstated the Greenwich Observant friary, the monks at the Sheen charterhouse and the nuns at Syon; royal foundations once again ministered to the court.[9]

The joint Anglo-Spanish court was not a comfortable place to be in 1554. A proclamation was issued forbidding anyone to come to court without a paper proving whose service they were in. It was noted that at Hampton Court the 'hall door within the court was continually shut . . . which seemed strange to Englishmen that had not been used thereto'.[10] Yet Philip was apparently a devoted husband. Ruy Gómez de Silva, one of his entourage, wrote on 24 August, 'The King entertains the Queen excellently and well knows how to pass over what is not attractive in her for the sensibility of the flesh. He keeps her so pleased that verily when they were together the other day alone she almost made love to him and he answered in the same fashion.'[11] Mary believed that it was at Hampton Court, during August, that she conceived a child.

The queen's baby was due on 9 May 1555, and on 3 April Mary, Philip and the court retired to Hampton Court for her confinement. Hampton Court was not Mary's first choice: one Spanish observer believed that she would have preferred to enter her confinement at Windsor, but that she felt it to be too far from London.[12] As the expected birth of a Catholic heir drew closer, in order to avoid unrest in the event of the legitimacy of the child being questioned, Princess Elizabeth was summoned to Hampton Court, where she remained effectively under house arrest. The queen meanwhile showed few signs of giving birth and was seen wandering around the privy garden perfectly at ease. By 1 June she was feeling some pains and letters were prepared to announce the forthcoming birth to the crowned heads of Europe. Mary was now confined to her chamber, once a day appearing at a window to watch the procession to Mass. Preparations included the delivery of a sumptuous cradle and the employment of rockers.

Time moved on and by 10 July the queen was up and about conducting business again, giving rise to questions about the genuineness of her condition. By the beginning of August the situation had become intolerable. The house was full to bursting with the ladies of the nobility and their gentlewomen, who were being entertained at royal expense whilst they waited for the birth. The queen, meanwhile, was barely seen, surrounded only by her attendants and physicians. Hampton Court was creaking under the strain, the garderobes were full, the kitchens and moat filthy; the court simply had to move. On 3 August the queen and her closest attendants travelled to Oatlands, diffusing the tension aroused by the imaginary pregnancy and allowing Hampton Court to be cleaned and repaired. Elizabeth, meanwhile, left for Ashridge in Hertfordshire.[13]

Throughout this time Philip attempted to live the life of a king, receiving ambassadors and emissaries and attending Mass accompanied by foreign dignitaries. But life at Hampton Court was unhappy. The Venetian ambassador reported that 'since the residence here of the court, there have been many affrays between the Spaniards and the English, several persons on either side having been wounded and killed'. Philip was forced to issue a proclamation forbidding the Spaniards to draw their swords at court on pain of losing their right hand.[14] His withdrawal to Oatlands and the final public admission that the queen's pregnancy had been a phantom was a prelude to Philip's departure for the Low Countries. His remaining household was ordered from Hampton Court to Whitehall in October 1555, and left London to join him in the Low Countries in December. Philip returned to England only in March 1557, intent on winning English support for his wars. He remained for a little under four months, staying at Whitehall, but going to Hampton Court to hunt with Mary on 10 June.[15]

Less than a month later Mary waved goodbye to her husband at Dover, never to see him again. She did not know it, but it is likely that she had stomach cancer, the cause of her swollen belly. In November 1558 she died, without actively opposing the succession of the sister whom for twenty-five years she had regarded as a heretic and a bastard.

Princess Elizabeth Becomes Queen

By the provisions of Henry VIII's will, Mary had received estates worth £4,000 a year and Elizabeth estates worth £3,000. Mary's were confirmed in 1547; Elizabeth, who was still a minor when her father died, had to wait until 1550 to come into hers. Amongst Elizabeth's lands were a number of royal houses – Hatfield, where her nursery had first been established; Ashridge and Enfield, houses which she had later shared with Edward; and Collyweston, her great-grandmother's house in Northamptonshire. In London she was granted the very large and splendid house formerly belonging to the Bishop of Durham, Durham Place. To the princess now passed responsibility for the repair and maintenance of these places, and in particular Hatfield, Ashridge and Enfield, the houses she favoured. In 1551–2 she spent some £42 at these manors on basic tiling and glazing, suggesting that they were essentially in good repair.[16]

Elizabeth had barely ever used Durham Place and, in 1553, the Duke of Northumberland engineered a swap, whereby Elizabeth would have the Duke of Somerset's former house, Somerset Place, while he would add Durham Place to his personal estate.[17] In this way Elizabeth came into the possession of the most modern and striking town house in London, sited strategically on the Strand. The only problem was that much of it was uninhabitable. Most of the interior fittings installed before Seymour's death had been removed and sold to pay his debts, and the rest of the house was incomplete. To make up for this, the Office of Works was instructed to finish the half-built residence. It is not clear whether Elizabeth had seen the house at this juncture or whether the work was simply commissioned by Northumberland. Either way, the considerable sum of £900 was to be spent on the princess's new home.

The keeper of Somerset Place was Robert Dudley, the fifth son of the Duke of Northumberland. He was exactly Elizabeth's age and it is likely that he had been brought up with Edward VI and thus lived with Henry VIII's children during the 1540s. His father may have appointed him keeper because of his childhood friendship with Elizabeth, and it is likely that his lifelong interest in building and engineering was first exercised at Somerset Place as he supervised works on her behalf.

Building can hardly have started when King Edward, who had been very ill for some months, died and, from his base at Durham Place, Northumberland attempted to install Lady Jane Grey on the throne. Elizabeth, loyal to her sister, was at Hatfield House and, on 29 July, entered London with an escort of 2,000 mounted and armed retainers dressed in striking green-and-white Tudor livery. They came to Somerset Place, where the princess was to remain on and off for about six months.[18]

Dudley had been marched off to the Tower of London with the rest of his family when Mary came to the throne and so, after Elizabeth's arrival in July, responsibility for building works passed directly to her household and this was her first adult experience of commissioning architects. It is likely that she would have expressed her preferences to the craftsman in charge, John Revell, Somerset's master carpenter; over a period of twenty-three weeks he spent about £200 on the wages of craftsmen and labourers.[19]

After her interview with Mary at Richmond and her sister's coronation, Elizabeth left court and London, only to be implicated in the first of many plots against the queen. Wyatt's rebellion, which had been triggered by dismay at the queen's marriage, was the most serious of these, and Elizabeth, outraged, appalled and terrified, was arrested and sent to the Tower of London.

The Yeoman Warders, to this day, enjoy telling the tale of Elizabeth's arrival and incarceration in the Bell Tower. As with so many details of Tower history, the Beefeaters' account is wrong, for Elizabeth, like her mother before her, was taken to the royal lodgings – the very rooms built for Anne Boleyn's coronation. Here she had the run of the place, including the long gallery and the queen's garden, but her attendants and the lieutenant of the Tower tussled over the status that should be accorded to a royal prisoner – should she be served in her privy chamber by the

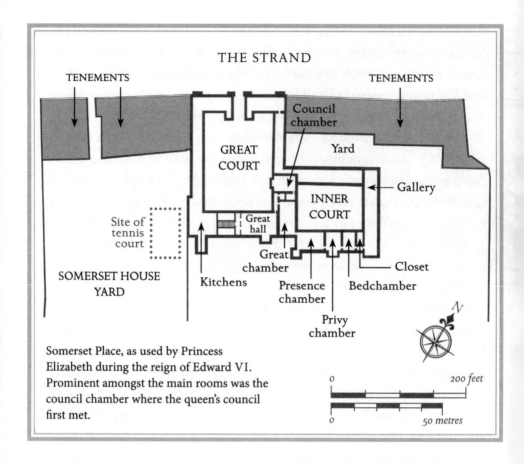

THE STRAND

TENEMENTS   TENEMENTS

Council chamber

GREAT COURT   Yard

Gallery

INNER COURT

Site of tennis court

Great hall

SOMERSET HOUSE YARD

Great chamber

Kitchens   Closet

Presence chamber   Bedchamber

Privy chamber

N

Somerset Place, as used by Princess Elizabeth during the reign of Edward VI. Prominent amongst the main rooms was the council chamber where the queen's council first met.

0   200 feet

0   50 metres

lieutenant's common servants or her own household? Elizabeth managed to retain some sort of princely state and her interrogation by members of the Privy Council was conducted with great skill and apparent honesty. Two months, to the day, after she entered the Tower, Elizabeth was freed and her entourage left London, guarded by ninety armed horsemen, to make its slow and stately way to Woodstock, where she was to remain under house arrest for a year.[20]

Woodstock was one of the Crown's most venerable, important and largest country houses: it was no prison. Both Henry VII and Henry VIII had loved hunting there and it had formed an important part of both kings' western itinerary. Henry VII had spent over £4,000 on re-roofing the ancient medieval hall, rebuilding the entrance gateway and modernizing the royal lodgings. Henry VIII also made alterations and

Woodstock Manor, as depicted by Peter Stent in a woodcut of 1653. It shows the gatehouse with an exaggerated great archway, while in the background are the thirty-five steps leading up to the great hall.

extensions, so, by the time Elizabeth was incarcerated there, the royal lodgings were the largest of any house outside the Thames valley.

There were two courtyards, the outer one approached by a gatehouse. In the middle of this court was a fountain fed by a natural spring in the park. The royal lodgings, sited in a second court, were unusual because both the king and the queen had great halls – the king's was really big, approached by a flight of thirty-five stairs. The lodgings were also unusual because both suites, in addition to the standard outer rooms, had private drawing rooms. The queen's bedroom was linked by the privy chamber to the king's drawing room so that the king could privately sleep with the queen if he wished.[21]

Preparations were made for the arrival of the princess: the queen's stables were repaired for her horses; five glaziers worked for a week on repairing windows; bedsteads, benches and tables were mended for the guards; and the whole place was given a thorough clean. Ominously, the single largest item of expenditure (other than mending the roof) was some 37s spent on locks and bolts for the doors.[22]

Princess Elizabeth was assigned the queen's lodgings and so had a presence, privy, withdrawing and bedchamber. At first she was refused a cloth of estate in her presence chamber – both an insult and another of

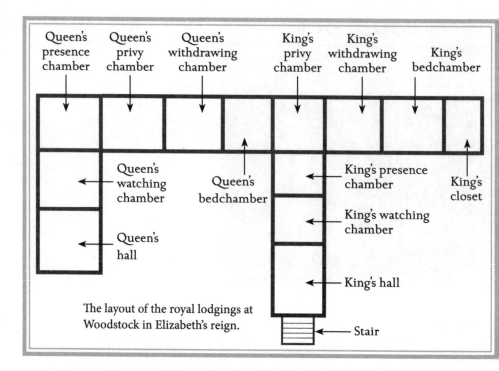

The layout of the royal lodgings at Woodstock in Elizabeth's reign.

the multitude of ambiguities that continued to surround her situation. Guards were stationed in her watching chamber, with more in the king's chambers at the other end. An ancient royal manor wasn't an ideal place to confine anyone, because the queen's rooms had several staircases and many windows: Elizabeth's jailer complained that only three doors could be securely locked. As a consequence, additional guards were stationed around the building and on the rising ground surrounding the house.

Woodstock was a summer hunting manor, never used in winter, and so, as July 1554 turned into August, it was becoming clear that the house needed repair if Elizabeth was to remain any longer. Windows were draughty, roof tiles had slipped and, it was pointed out, the wood store was nearly empty. A list of urgent requirements was sent to court, but decisions were not hastily taken and by November jailed and jailers alike were desperate to leave and get closer to London. But no recall came: Mary was far too busy with her husband and her pregnancy to want Elizabeth at court, so she sat by the fire embroidering cushions in silver

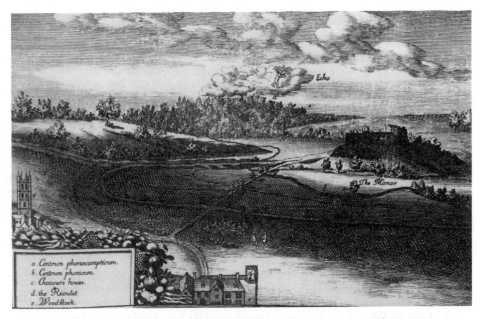

The ruins of Woodstock Manor, as illustrated by Dr Robert Plot in 1677. The rising ground on which Elizabeth's guards were stationed can be seen encircling the manor.

and gold thread. Yet as the birth neared, the call finally came and, as we have seen, at the end of April 1555 Elizabeth was summoned to Hampton Court to witness the birth of Mary's child.[23]

As I have related, Mary died at St James's in November 1558 and Elizabeth was told at Hatfield, where she had been based since 1555, that she was now queen. That very day she chose the two men who were to be the key relationships in her life: Robert Dudley, who became the Earl of Leicester in 1564, and William Cecil, who became Lord Burghley in 1571. Dudley, who had been locked up in the Tower with the rest of his family for their instigation of the Lady Jane Grey fiasco, had eventually been released and pardoned. His reward for a long friendship with Elizabeth was the post of Master of the Horse. This, one of the three great household offices, was the most personal to the monarch. The master was in charge of the queen's logistics and her stables, and, in this role, was glued to her side, the only man officially sanctioned to touch her person. Cecil, some twelve years older than Elizabeth, had served both the Duke of Somerset and the Duke of Northumberland but, because of his evangelical sympathies, retired from major political posts under Mary and, in 1550, became Elizabeth's surveyor. Having won her absolute trust in all matters of business, in 1558 he secured the most important political and administrative appointment, as her Secretary.

The royal etiquette of death was long-established and precise. While the dead monarch remained unburied, the shadow of their household and government prevailed and, in the house where they died, the rhythms of royal life continued to beat. Guards stood in the outer chamber, cooks toiled in the kitchens, food was served to an empty table on bended knee, and the canopy of state was reverenced as if the monarch were sitting beneath it.[24] All household appointments remained live and it was only when the chief officers snapped their white staves of office in two and placed them in the burial vault that they had discharged their last duty. Then the monarch's reign was over and their household dissolved. The strange undead status of a deceased monarch was one of the reasons why the new sovereign entered Whitehall only after their predecessor's funeral and their own coronation: Edward VI and Mary I had both taken up possession of their principal palace only when they had become crowned sovereigns.

Elizabeth thus, like her predecessors, entered London and made straight for the Tower. Six days later she moved to her own house, Somerset Place, where she remained for eighteen days, holding fifteen meetings of her new council, and it was not until three days before Christmas that she finally entered Whitehall as queen.[25]

The English monarchy was a male institution, but Mary's short reign had recalibrated some of the well-established structures of the masculine court. In particular she had depoliticized her privy chamber, staffing it with women, pushing politics out from her private rooms into the council chamber. Elizabeth therefore did not have to invent any new mechanism in 1558; she simply appointed her own women to her inner privy chamber (now known as the Bedchamber) and two gentlemen and a handful of grooms in the privy chamber. Her council would be only half the size of Mary's, and met under the secretaryship of Elizabeth's right-hand man, William Cecil. The new queen had promised to rule through her council, which is, in fact, what she did for four and a half decades, but at first this seemed like a temporary expedient because Elizabeth, like Mary, was expected to marry. In the interim there was the ruling Privy Council and, at court, a symbolic consort's side in the former queen's lodgings presided over by whoever was the senior nobleman present.[26]

A New Sort of Religion

Marriage was to be a big issue for Elizabeth, but on coming to the throne her first and most pressing problem was religion. Everybody was watching to see how this would be settled and, immediately, what she would do in her own chapel. In March 1559 John Jewel, Regius Professor of Divinity at Oxford University, returned from Zürich, where he and a number of prominent English Protestants had been exiled during Queen Mary's reign. The following month, eager and impatient for reform, he wrote to his close friend and mentor Peter Martyr, claiming that, in many places, the Mass was not being celebrated and that 'If the queen herself would but banish it from her private chapel, the whole thing might easily be got rid of. Of such importance among us are the examples of princes. For whatever is done after the example of the sovereign, the people, as you well know, suppose to be done rightly'.[27]

He need not have fretted, because within a week of her accession Elizabeth had replaced the papist dean of her chapel with a religious moderate and, at Christmas, walked out of the Whitehall chapel in protest at what she regarded as the idolatrous actions of the presiding bishop.[28] Her preference was for a blend of traditional religion and reformed practice, which came to characterize the Anglican Church. Though the injunctions of Edward VI had banned the use of crucifixes and 'torches, candles, tapers or images of wax' from the communion table, Elizabeth required two candlesticks and a crucifix in the royal chapel. She also ordered the communion table to be placed like an altar and hung with a cloth of gold frontal, making it indistinguishable from a stone altar.[29] This caused her chapel to be regarded with deep disapproval by the evangelicals. Thomas Sampson, one of Edward VI's most celebrated

Windsor Castle, the Chapel Royal in the upper ward. This sketch by Hollar shows the chapel after it had been roughly treated by Parliamentarian soldiers in the Civil War. Yet it does show the fittings installed by Elizabeth in 1570–71. The balcony on the north side was added in 1633–4.

preachers, who had been in exile under Queen Mary, wrote in despair to Peter Martyr in January 1560, 'Oh! My father, what can I hope for, when the ministry of the word is banished from court? While the crucifix is allowed, with lights burning before it? . . . the crucifix and candles are retained at court alone. And the wretched multitude are not only rejoicing at this, but will imitate it of their own accord'.[30]

For Elizabeth the ornaments on the communion table were as important for their aesthetic effect as their theological significance. While the beauty of holiness had some value, the magnificence of the chapel was, in her view, essential. For the christening of the granddaughter of the King of Sweden in the chapel at Whitehall, a big public event, the table was groaning with basins, plate and rich ornaments, as well as two great candlesticks with lit tapers. It was also surrounded by ten hanging lamps and on a shelf above it were twenty-one gold candlesticks with lit tapers. At Christmas the royal chapels were richly hung with cloth of gold and other rich textiles, and special displays of plate were set up.[31]

We have visual record of only one of Elizabeth's chapels, the household chapel she remodelled at Windsor in 1570–71. This remained as it had been completed by Edward III in the 1360s; it was in very poor condition and the ceiling was in danger of collapse. The whole existing

Elizabeth Regina.

S. PARALIPOM. 6.
Domine Deus Israel, non est similis tui Deus in cœlo & in terra, qui pacta custodis & misericordiam cum servis tuis, qui ambulant coram te in toto corde suo.

Richard Day's *A Booke of Christian Prayers and Meditations*, published in 1569, shows Elizabeth on the frontispiece. She is kneeling in her privy closet, which is hung with cloth of gold fringed at the bottom. Around her lie her sword and sceptre, showing her as a Christian prince. The prayers in the book were certainly commissioned by the queen and, indeed, some may have been written by her.

interior was stripped out and a new ceiling (to the old profile) installed, painted and gilded with Tudor roses. The walls were filled with plain panelling decorated with Corinthian pilasters and a frieze. The holyday closets at the west end were raised up on six columns and contained bay windows looking down into the body of the chapel; above them was a large royal coat of arms. This was a very different sort of royal chapel. Gone were big tapestries covering the walls and gone were any symbols other than royal heraldry.[32]

Elizabeth had no intention of reinstating the lavish liturgy of her father's court, but like Edward she found that reformed worship was not a good complement to the magnificence of majesty. In particular, the loss of the processions that had formed such an important element of display in Henry's and Mary's courts was a problem. So, from quite early on in her reign, Elizabeth appropriated the secular procession to chapel established by Henry VIII and made it into one of the key ceremonials at court.[33]

Late on Sunday mornings, just before dinner, the queen would attend the Chapel Royal – a visitor to court, Baron Waldstein, saw her coming forth from her privy chamber at Greenwich in July 1600. The appointed hour was 10am and, as they waited for the queen, the presence chamber was packed with courtiers and aristocrats:

> Then, dressed in white and silver, the maids of Honour . . . made ready for the entrance of the queen and of those who were to escort her to the chapel. A procession came first, led by the Chancellor carrying a gold-embroidered purse bearing the royal insignia, and a Knight of the garter holding a sword before him, and Secretary Cecil following; then she herself, glittering with the glory of majesty . . . At her entry everyone knelt.

The queen processed to chapel, where she remained for twenty minutes to hear prayers, then returned in procession to the privy chamber. The route from the privy chamber to the chapel was lined by the Yeomen of the Guard holding their halberds; as she passed between them, the queen would stop and speak to courtiers, suitors, even ambassadors, who fell to their knees as she passed and sought her attention.[34]

Some houses had plans that facilitated such a procession better than others. Thomas Platter, a visitor to the court in 1599, observed the queen in her chapel procession at Richmond. Here a gallery ran along one side of the inner court, leading to the chapel. Outside, in the courtyard, stood an expectant crowd and, as the queen walked along the gallery, she looked out at her subjects, who dropped to their knees and were then bidden to rise by a wave of the royal hand.[35]

Elizabeth also harnessed the Garter ceremonies of St George's Day for their display potential. Edward VI had been very uncomfortable with the retention of St George as the patron of the Order of the Garter and had intended to secularize it. Mary, however, was happy to restore the full ecclesiastical procession that accompanied the St George's Day feasts. Under Elizabeth, controversially, the whole staff of the Chapel Royal processed with the queen. The choir and dean of the chapel wore copes of cloth of gold – vestments otherwise banned – and processed, singing, round the precincts of the court; at Whitehall this was around the Preaching Place. No cross was carried, but a 'book', probably the Bible, was held aloft. Following the Chapel were the heralds in their tabards and the Knights of the Garter in their robes. This was as magnificent as the Elizabethan court got, and for many the commemoration of a saint by the royal chapel in full vestments was symbolic of the queen's betrayal of the evangelical cause.[36]

Processions were important, but so was another public expression of monarchical piety – preaching. The Preaching Place at Whitehall retained its function after Mary's death and both Elizabeth and James I heard sermons there regularly, in particular during Lent.[37] The Preaching Place was open to anyone who wished to come – there were no restrictions – and the audience was probably made up of more merchants and citizens than courtiers. Don Diego Guzmán de Silva, the Spanish ambassador, described the queen's attendance at the Preaching Place on Ash Wednesday 1565 at the start of the Lent sermons: 'she went to a great courtyard where on occasions such as this the sermon is preached, so that people on all side may hear as great crowds go, although the queen tells me that more go to see her than hear the sermon'.[38] The Mantuan ambassador attended a sermon in the presence of the queen in February 1559 and estimated 'the congregation consisting of more than 5,000 persons'. He reported that he 'was surprised at the concourse of people who madly flocked to hear such vain things'.[39]

So, as well as forging and establishing a new form of secular etiquette at court, Elizabeth created the new ceremonies for a Protestant court by appropriating elements of traditional religion and bending them to her needs.

✦XIII✦

ELIZABETH

GLUT

HENRY VIII LEFT HIS CHILDREN AN architectural time bomb. Many of the vast collection of buildings he had amassed had been built quickly, the king impatiently waiting to move in, so corners had been cut, green oak had been substituted for seasoned timbers, and mortar and plaster had not been allowed to cure properly. These shortcuts left a horrible maintenance legacy. For instance, many roofs had low pitches and were covered in lead, the lead sheets being laid on roof boards that were generally of oak. Seasoned oak is inert, but green oak gives out acids that can attack the lead and, in due course, corrode it so that it leaks. The building accounts show that Henry's workmen, unable to get enough seasoned oak, used green and, to reduce the risk of corrosion, laid moss on top of the oak boards to keep the acids away from the lead. This was no substitute for doing the job properly and the consequences of royal haste gradually became apparent as roofs began to leak.

In the latter part of Henry's reign it had been calculated that £1,200 a year was needed properly to maintain the standing houses – in other words the big sprawling complexes in and around London. Maintaining the further-flung houses was not budgeted for in advance, but money was always found before a royal visit. Under Edward VI these visits dried up and so a royal carpenter, Thomas Cropper, was sent out to assess the condition of the more remote houses, draw plans and specify repairs. But nothing was done, principally because money was short. The Edwardian regime, through debt, war and lack of financial discipline, was bankrupt; as a consequence, over the whole period 1547–58 only £36,137 3s 1¾d was spent on the royal houses. On average this was around £3,200 a year – over the last seven years of Henry VIII's reign annual expenditure on Whitehall alone was averaging £3,500, so the scale of slow-down was massive.[1]

With works at a low ebb, the peripheral offices that had managed construction under Henry were abolished and maintenance was centralized in the Scotland Yard office under the then surveyor Lawrence Bradshaw. Bradshaw grouped the royal residences into districts, each of which had a clerk to oversee it: thus the London and Westminster clerk, Thomas Maye, was responsible for the Tower, Westminster, Baynard's Castle and St James's.[2]

Under Elizabeth, the Surveyors of the Queen's Works were given their instructions by a small group of privy councillors led by the Lord Treasurer, William Paulet, Marquess of Winchester, and the queen's Secretary, William Cecil, Lord Burghley. Winchester was an extraordinary survivor who had also served as Treasurer under Elizabeth's siblings. He was also an ambitious builder, creating a fine Thames-side mansion at Chelsea that became a favourite stopping-off place for the queen on her way west, and a huge residence at Basing, one of the largest built in a reign famous for many vast houses. Burghley, the queen's all-seeing, all-controlling Secretary, was interested in everything, especially architecture, and was to build the largest and most extravagant houses of his age at Burghley in Lincolnshire and Theobalds (pronounced 'Tibbalds') in Hertfordshire.[3]

While Burghley and Winchester were the official custodians of the royal houses, Robert Dudley, the Earl of Leicester, as the queen's closest friend and confidant, Master of the Horse, and one of the greatest cultural patrons of his day, also had a say.[4] All three properly understood what was involved in maintaining huge houses and put in hand a series of detailed surveys ascertaining what needed to be done both in terms of maintenance and for the queen's pleasure. Their surviving summary paints a catastrophic picture of the royal housing stock: Guildford was a fair house all in decay; Woking, without help, would be past remedy; Dartford was utterly decayed; and, without repair, Beaulieu would be 'in worst case than any house now her grace has'.[5] The larger houses were in better condition and those the queen intended to use immediately were examined in greater detail. In preparation for Elizabeth's first progress, Winchester personally went upriver to Hampton Court in June 1559. On the 22nd he wrote a long letter to Burghley outlining the problems he had found and listing ten tasks to be undertaken that summer. This was typical of similar surveys undertaken at Windsor, Woodstock and elsewhere, both in its precision and in the fact that, in due course, all these things were done.[6]

In the end Winchester and Burghley were clear that the queen simply had too many houses. Under Edward twelve had been disposed of and Mary had sold three (including Nonsuch) and given away another three. But Elizabeth still inherited well over fifty residences, so various attempts were made to identify the ones that she really needed. In 1561 a general survey of royal houses, castles, manors and ex-monastic houses was ordered. The task was to identify those 'which may well be spared and not needful for our access' and to sell, lease or, if all else failed, demolish them. Not much seems to have come of this comprehensive approach, so in February 1564 Winchester wrote to Burghley suggesting that the queen might manage with only seventeen houses. These would be eight standing houses in the Thames valley: Whitehall, St James's, Greenwich, Eltham, Richmond, Oatlands, Hampton Court and Windsor; then a small number of progress houses: in Kent Otford; in Essex Beaulieu; to the north of London the two houses of her childhood, Enfield and Hatfield; a western progress house at Woodstock; Ampthill in Bedfordshire; and Grafton, Collyweston and Fotheringhay in Northamptonshire. This list was still perhaps considered too long, for the following year it was stated that the queen would be regularly using only twelve.[7]

In practice, Elizabeth was extremely reluctant to give up any. Throughout her reign she granted away only four houses, including the extremely large Beaulieu and her former nursery house at Ashridge. Two further houses she leased, including her mother's old house at Hanworth near Hampton Court. Those that she didn't use much she would rather see fall down than alienate. At least five houses collapsed into a pile of rubble through neglect: these included the huge Manor of the More that

Henry had acquired from Wolsey and another of her childhood homes, Enfield.

ELIZABETH THE BUILDER

But the story of royal building in the Elizabethan era was not simply one of neglect. In the first years of Elizabeth's reign, up until 1564, the Treasury was at full stretch financing military operations in France and Scotland – the bill amounted to some £700,000; but after peace was concluded the Crown, although heavily in debt, had a freer hand and money was finally made available to the Office of Works. In 1564 there was also a new surveyor, Lewis Stockett, a joiner by trade, but also an able administrator charged by Burghley and Winchester to instil efficiency and economy. Stockett's receipts rose from £3,800 a year to over £9,000 before declining, four years later, to slightly below the former level. In 1572, after the death of Winchester, the purse strings were tightened again and more than a decade of frugality followed. However, in the last decade of the reign spending once more increased, not only at the Office of Works but at the Wardrobe, as the most important royal houses were overhauled.[8]

Could it be said that Elizabeth enjoyed building like her father? There has long been a perception that she had little interest in architecture. Indeed, her own Lord Keeper, Sir Nicholas Bacon, persuading parliament of the frugality of their monarch, emphasized the way she refrained from 'superfluous and sumptuous buildings of delight' and how the 'gorgeous, sumptuous superfluous buildings of times past be, for the realm's good, by her majesty in this time, turned into necessary buildings and upholdings'. But this was only a comparative comment, for no monarch until George IV would equal the architectural megalomania of Henry VIII. In fact, Elizabeth did build, and took a personal interest in architecture, but, as there is no record of her voicing an opinion on the subject, we have to turn to the evidence of the buildings and the documents to glean her views.[9]

The first thing to note is that Elizabeth liked to put her name on things she built. Of course both Henry VII and Henry VIII had covered

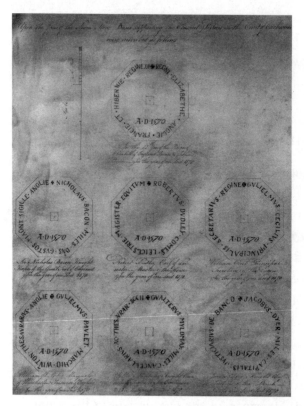

When the Westminster Exchequer building was demolished in 1823 these were the inscriptions discovere on the stone bases of the timber columns there. The names include t Earl of Leicester, William Cecil and the Earl of Winchester.

their buildings with coats of arms, badges and initials, but Elizabeth more self-consciously and deliberately labelled her works with her initials and often the date. At Hampton Court a new bay window and coach house were given a date and her initials; at Windsor her new gallery had her initials on it; at the Tower her works were dated and signed; and at Westminster there was a plaque commemorating the queen laying a foundation stone, the first instance of this that has been recorded. Most extraordinary, though, were the inscriptions ordered to be carved on the pillar bases of the Elizabethan Court of the Exchequer at Westminster, which recorded the names and titles of the queen and each of her eight Barons of the Exchequer with the date 1570. All this suggests a sense of pride in making additions to her father's buildings.[10]

One of the reasons, perhaps, that the Elizabethan extensions were so carefully labelled is that often they were indistinguishable from the Henrician work to which they were joined. At Hampton Court in 1570, a new privy kitchen was built. It was a large and impressive brick structure

Queen Elizabeth's privy kitchen at Hampton Court. Built over half a century after the original kitchens, the queen's architects took trouble to blend in the design of the chimneys with the earlier kitchens, providing a homogeneous view from the north.

on the north side of the house near the other kitchens. Though it was built eighty years after the first kitchens on the site, it was in exactly the same style to ensure it blended in. Likewise, at Whitehall, the addition of a first floor on the low gallery was not conceived as a new structure but was decorated with black-and-white grotesque-work to blend in with the rest of the building. At Westminster, the new Exchequer building, which will be described below, was also carefully matched to Henry VIII's earlier structure. So Elizabeth and her architects went out of their way to preserve the homogeneity of Henry's houses, only discreetly leaving a plaque recording their work.[11]

This might suggest that the queen was conservative in her architectural tastes. It is certainly true that great care was taken to

Queen Elizabeth added a bay window at Hampton Court in 1568, part of which survives. It has been rebuilt but retains its date stone. On the right is the later wing built by Sir Christopher Wren.

redecorate many of her father's interiors at Greenwich and Whitehall in the 1590s, but there was also new work. Particularly prominent was the construction of at least seven new fountains. These elaborate structures were luxury items, not part of the yearly slog of repair that dominated the lives of the Elizabethan royal architects. Elizabeth must have asked for them, and must have chosen their designs.

The first was at Windsor, built in 1558 as part of the completion of a new water-supply project begun under Edward VI. We have a crude image of it (see drawing opposite), which shows an octagonal or hexagonal basin with columns supporting an ogee dome. A gap of ten years separates this structure from a spurt of fountain building around 1570. The first of these, started in 1567, was at Greenwich in the inner court and it was spectacular. Raised on a hexagonal base, with carved marble panels, there were twenty-four 9-foot-high Doric columns supporting a timber roof topped with a lion. Inside, a jet of water fell into a small basin and ran into a larger one below it. Then in 1570 a fountain was built at Whitehall in the new orchard; it comprised two marble bowls with brass columns

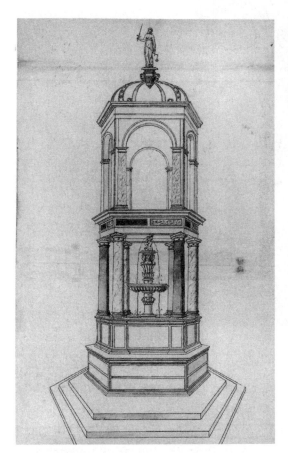

Pen-and-wash drawing of the Elizabethan fountain in Fountain Court, Hampton Court. The accounts suggest that this design was slightly modified in the making.

and what were probably engraved brass sundials. Next came the Hampton Court fountain, finished in 1591; this cost the colossal sum of £1,000 because it was carved of marble and topped with a gilt copper figure of Justice. By the turn of a concealed cock, jets of water could be squirted at bystanders. A second fountain followed at Greenwich and another at Richmond.[12]

In 1595–6 the queen bought a particularly lovely one from William Brooke, Baron Cobham. He was a great connoisseur who had just laid out spectacular gardens at his house, Cobham Hall in Kent. Elizabeth paid £20 for a fountain 'of white marble and of 5 pieces viz a base, one round pillar, one bowl fluted, one figure of a woman with a base under her feet to stand', surely a bargain for the queen. So proud of this

Robert Pinckney and William Hawthorne's chimneypiece in Queen Elizabeth's privy gallery at Windsor Castle, 1584.

acquisition was she that – in true style – with 'oil colours and gilding with fine gold in oil her majesties letters, the date of her reign and of our lord God embossed with lead on the new fountaine'.[13]

This is important, for it not only tells us that the queen liked the sight and sound of running water (and thought squirting unsuspecting courtiers funny), it also tells us about her taste, because all these fountains were built using the classical language of architecture in a correct and ambitious way. This accords with the single surviving piece of interior decoration from her private rooms – a chimneypiece carved by Robert Pinckney at Windsor Castle in 1584. This superb piece of masonry can be seen by those lucky enough to gain entry to the Royal Library – not only is the quality of the carving of the very finest, but the proportions and composition are much more sophisticated than the jumble of motifs that were so fashionable under Henry VIII.[14]

There is one other thing that illuminates the queen's architectural tastes – the work she commissioned at Greenwich in 1582–3. This project, executed at a cost of some £3,000, was the largest and architecturally most ambitious of her reign, but unfortunately we have no picture of it, only the terse summaries in the enrolled building accounts. Greenwich was Elizabeth's birthplace and her favourite residence. We have already seen that she adorned it with fountains and, in Chapter XVI, her work in the gardens will be described. In 1582–3 the inner, fountain, court was transformed, as if by magic, from a fifteenth-century brick courtyard into an elegant stone-faced classical piazza. No stone was used and the walls of the courtyard were rendered and lined out to make them look like ashlar, then a stucco cornice was run round the court, the windows given stucco architraves, and classical mouldings were applied to gable ends, porches and string courses. Timber window casements were painted to look like stone. On one side, the lower part of the courtyard was given a covered cloister like that at the Preaching Place in Whitehall. It was roofed with lead and supported by nine turned pillars, and the balustrade above had 105 balusters made to look like stone. With the fountain titivated and the court repaved in Kentish ragstone, it must have looked startlingly different from the rest of the house. But this was, literally, at the centre of the queen's life, the place where, apart from Whitehall, she spent the most time, so these improvements must have been really important to her.[15]

What did the inner court at Greenwich look like when it was finished? The effect that the queen was trying to achieve was of a stone building

The south elevation of the outer court at Somerset House; watercolour by William Moss, 1776. Although done many years after its prime, this painting shows the terrace, or colonnade, on the entrance front of Somerset Place. A very similar structure was built at Greenwich in 1582–3.

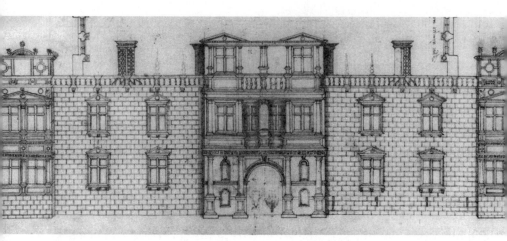

John Thorpe, elevation of the Strand front of Somerset Place, drawn in 1610–11. It is likely that the effect of the inner court at Greenwich was very similar to this, but achieved using stucco.

like Somerset Place. This was Elizabeth's first London house, site of her very first architectural commission. The great mansion, begun by Protector Somerset and left unfinished at his fall, was one of the first in London to attempt to assemble the elements of classical architecture into a coherent whole. In 1553 when Elizabeth took it over, she commissioned the completion of the Protector's scheme. A seventeenth-century drawing of the Strand elevation suggests that the stone façade had its masonry joints visibly picked out and the window architraves and pediments contrasted with this. As far as we can tell from the accounts, this is the effect achieved at Greenwich in the 1580s. Moreover, on one side of the courtyard of Somerset Place was a terrace very similar to the one built at Greenwich and, again, perhaps its inspiration.[16]

However closely, or not, the work at Greenwich was based on Somerset Place, the legitimate question remains, how much was this rather sophisticated architectural decoration the personal taste of the queen and how much was due to the taste of her privy councillors, especially Burghley and her favourite, the Earl of Leicester? Burghley was unquestionably the best-informed and most prolific patron of architecture in England and a very exacting client; Leicester too was an enthusiastic builder and connoisseur. The interaction of these two with their queen at Windsor in 1570 throws light on royal taste.

At Windsor Castle works were under the control of an administrator, Humphrey Mitchell, and here Burghley worked with Leicester, who was Constable, on new schemes and maintenance projects. In 1532, on the south side of the castle, Henry VIII had erected a massive timber terrace which was, by 1570, very dilapidated. Leicester and Burghley ordered it to be rebuilt in stone. When this 94-foot-long and 33-foot-high structure was completed, Mitchell was told that Leicester and Burghley didn't like it and that the top was to be rebuilt with a balustrade and the whole thing extended with various other embellishments. After he had spent £1,000 doing as he was told, the finished work faced a new barrage of criticism from 'our lady the queen' and Mitchell was ordered to replace more newly built parapet and make further substantial extensions. This was the last straw: Mitchell submitted a letter of resignation, claiming that his 'knowledge in these arts is little'. It was refused, and Leicester instead appointed an architect, Henry Hawthorne, to give Mitchell technical advice. This only partially reassured Mitchell, and when he was ordered to build a substantial new gallery and banqueting house for the queen he wrote to Burghley saying 'if her majesty will have the gallery and banqueting house go forward I beseech you to cause Henry Hawthorn to make perfect plans of them . . . that there may not be any alterations after they are finished, for I have found by experience (by doing and undoing) things have grown very expensive . . .'[17]

Changes of royal mind were indeed expensive and as far as we can tell Hawthorne and other Elizabethan surveyors certainly came into contact with the queen, though we have no suggestion that she, like her father, would sketch out what she wanted built. When her surveyor Robert Adams died in 1595, the queen not only expressed sorrow at his death but hoped that all his plans and drawings might be passed over to Burghley for safekeeping.[18]

Without doubt Elizabeth had developed architectural preferences. In the early 1570s Leicester suggested that she should extend and modernize her house at Grafton in Northamptonshire as a base for hunting. The job was given to Leicester's architect William Spicer, who built the queen a new privy lodging in 1573–5 at a cost of nearly £2,000. Elizabeth arrived at the completed house with Leicester in June 1575 and was clearly delighted with what she saw, as Leicester wrote to Burghley on the 28th:

> I will let your lordship understand such news as we have, which is only and chiefly of her majesty's good health . . . and for her liking of this house, I assure your Lordship that she never came to [a] place in her life that she likes better or commends more . . . The House likes her well and her own lodging especially. She thinks her cost well bestowed – she says if it had been five times as much.

As the improvements had been Leicester's idea, he had an interest in saying the queen liked them; nevertheless, she had clearly expressed delight at what had been built.[19]

Not everything, though, was to her liking. Visiting Lord Burghley at Theobalds, Elizabeth complained that a room prepared for her was not large enough, so he had to enlarge it and have repainted the elaborate mural of oak trees and coats of arms that had just been finished. On a visit to Sir Thomas Gresham at his house at Osterley during 1576, she commented that a courtyard they were passing 'would appear more handsome if divided by a wall in the middle'. Her comment was preserved for us, as the super-rich Gresham ordered that a wall be erected overnight and so, when the queen rose the next morning, her suggestion had become a reality, one wit observing that 'any house is easier divided than united'.[20]

WESTMINSTER, WHITEHALL AND WOOING

The notion that Elizabeth was destined to be the Virgin Queen is one that was, of course, born of hindsight and entrenched by romanticism. When she came to the throne in 1558 she was only twenty-five; she was young, good-looking, healthy and the most eligible monarch in Europe. Everybody expected her to marry. Twice her heart led her to the point of commitment; first in 1560 with Robert Dudley, the Earl of Leicester, who we would today say was the love of her life; and second with Francis, Duke of Anjou, to whom she was attracted in 1579. In addition to these potential husbands of choice, under intense pressure from her council and from parliament she took serious steps towards a union with two others – Archduke Charles of Austria and Henry, Duke of Anjou, older brother of Francis and the future Henry III of France.

For any match to be acceptable to the Privy Council, to parliament and to the population at large, it had to fulfil two crucial criteria: first it had to produce a Protestant heir to the English throne, and second, it had to avoid war with the Protestant Low Countries, England's principal trading partner. As most eligible princes were Catholic, this meant that any marriage treaty would be the product of long and complex negotiation. Such diplomacy was generally conducted by envoys (extraordinary ambassadors) sent specially for the occasion. Since the reign of Henry VII these ambassadors were not mere negotiators on behalf of their masters; they were given the rank of the sovereign they represented, an elevation in status that led to an equivalent elaboration of etiquette. Across Europe there developed a set protocol for dealing with the arrival, accommodation and departure of ambassadors and for how audiences would be conducted with monarchs and discussions held with councillors.

At first, under Henry VIII, Greenwich played host to the major extraordinary embassies, but later in his reign both Hampton Court and Whitehall took the leading role. The mechanisms for ambassadorial receptions were not rigidly set by the king, but on arrival diplomats were normally greeted by one of the twenty-five Gentlemen Pensioners at a convenient location to the east of London and from here would be escorted in a cavalcade to the City of London, then to Whitehall. Diplomacy continued against a background of feasting, hunting, plays and other entertainments and, when the party finally left, all the principals would be showered with gifts of plate and precious stones.[21]

By 1558 Westminster was definitively the centre of all major diplomatic ceremonial and this was one of the main reasons why, during

Elizabeth's reign, more was spent here on building than anywhere else. Westminster had always been a unique place; a township where national and local concerns mixed and melded at the gates of the principal palace of English kings and their coronation church. I have explained that Henry VIII had given extra dimension to this by seizing control of all the levers of power in the city. What happened over the succeeding years consolidated the Crown's stranglehold over Westminster. The establishment of permanent facilities for the House of Commons under Edward ensured that Westminster became the official home of parliament, and the suppression of Church assets allowed aristocrats to buy property in Westminster and along the Strand, establishing themselves in large houses close to court.

It should be no surprise, then, that early in Elizabeth's reign William Cecil, Lord Burghley, was made High Steward of Westminster, the most powerful post in the city. As such he selected Westminster's MPs and, as chief minister, appointed all the key posts at the abbey. The reason controlling Westminster was of vital importance was, of course, that it was a bustling settlement containing the destitute as well as the super-rich. Maintaining order and control was key to the safety and comfort of the queen – and to her health, as densely occupied places bred plague and other diseases. The first of a number of proclamations was issued in 1580 attempting to limit development in Westminster to prevent overcrowding and slums.[22]

Control over Westminster was one side of the coin; the other was making it better reflect the majesty of the Elizabethan monarchy. Between 1560 and 1565, over £9,000 was spent at Whitehall finishing works left incomplete at the death of Henry VIII; over the following two years a further £3,000 was spent on a series of improvements and refinements, mainly in the royal lodgings. Then followed a huge reconstruction at the old Palace of Westminster. By suppressing St Stephen's College, creating a permanent home for the Commons, and building offices for record-keeping, Edward VI had resolved the long-term use for the palace. Now, as England's official administrative and parliamentary headquarters, it was felt that proper offices should be built for the various departments

Westminster Palace, showing the west end of Westminster Hall on the left and on the right the red-brick Office of Augmentations built by Henry VIII in 1537–8; between them is the stone Exchequer building built by Elizabeth, harmonizing the elevations of the old palace. By 1793, when William Capon drew this view, various sheds and walls had been built in front of the Tudor buildings.

that administered the Crown finances. In 1565 Elizabeth herself laid the foundation stone of these, including a large new Treasury building, a number of courts and the repair and redecoration of many older buildings. In all, the cost was just over £12,000, making this by far the most expensive building work of the reign.

Unquestionably, part of the motivation for all this was a more efficient administration of Crown business, but aesthetic effect was as significant. Ever since the fire of 1511, the Palace of Westminster had been an architectural mess. The new buildings regularized this: the new Court of Exchequer, for instance, built between Westminster Hall and Henry VIII's Court of Augmentations, copied exactly the elevation of Henry's building, providing an elegance and coherence previously completely lacking.

There were other improvements: Henry VII's chapel was scaffolded, its pinnacles strengthened, beasts re-carved and the roof re-leaded. In 1568 the Queen's Bridge – the main landing stage that provided royal access to Westminster from the river – was rebuilt. A huge coat of arms was erected, as were four massive posts topped with 5-foot-high heraldic beasts – a dragon, a lion, a greyhound and, apparently, a tiger – each bearing a tall, gilded iron vane. With this refinement, Westminster as a whole was equipped to be the glittering centre of the capital. Processions to and from parliament and the abbey from Whitehall were now undertaken against a carefully conceived architectural background: visiting ambassadors were in no doubt about the splendour and sophistication of Elizabeth's rule.[23]

One of the first major embassies to appreciate the new glories of Westminster was the Duke of Montmorency's in 1572. The duke had been sent to England both for the ratification of a treaty and to open negotiations about a possible marriage with Francis, Duke of Anjou and Alençon. Montmorency, who was an experienced soldier and a consummate politician, knew the English court, having been sent over in 1559 to ratify the peace treaty of Cateau-Cambrésis. The 1559 embassy had been low key, but when he returned in 1572 not only had Westminster been spruced up, but a canvas banqueting house had been built for his reception on ground to the east of the Preaching Place.[24]

Against the odds, the marriage negotiations continued and, in 1579, Anjou arrived in England in disguise to woo the forty-five-year-old queen in person. To avoid anti-French demonstrations, Elizabeth wanted the visit kept secret and so they stayed away from Whitehall, spending most of the ten-day visit at Richmond. On 23 August Elizabeth hosted a grand ball, where she secreted Anjou behind a hanging and danced for him, coyly waving as she did. A secret as great as this could not be kept and soon it was common knowledge that the queen was clandestinely wooing a Catholic prince. Although the visit provoked vocal opposition in London, Elizabeth was persuaded of the political and diplomatic merits of a marriage treaty with France and in mid-April 1581 a huge official and public embassy of more than 500 French arrived in England to prepare the way for marriage.[25]

In preparation, Whitehall had been a building site since the start of the year. First there was the construction of a huge new gallery. Henry VIII had built a 400-foot single-storey long gallery along the east side of the great gardens, decorated with a series of history paintings depicting his coronation and favourite houses. In 1581 Elizabeth added a second storey to this, creating a magnificent first-floor passage to Princess Mary's old lodgings on the riverfront (now known as the Prince's Lodging). These were the most magnificent rooms at Whitehall other than the king's and queen's apartments themselves. It is likely that the new long gallery, soon to be known as the Matted Gallery, was an addition to make the entrance to the prince's lodgings more impressive. Elizabeth perhaps intended these to be set aside for a future visit by Anjou. On the waterfront nearby, a new garden was laid out to improve the view from the east-facing windows of the gallery.

Although Whitehall had a number of large buildings, the queen believed that there was nothing large or modern enough to be the centrepiece of her entertainment of the French, so she ordered Thomas Graves, her Surveyor of the Works, to design and construct a new banqueting house for their visit. This was constructed on the site of the earlier canvas hall next to the Preaching Place. It was 122 feet long and 44 feet wide, raised up on a basement; the walls were framed in timber but covered in canvas painted in imitation of stone. It had 292 glass windows and the roof inside was hung with holly and ivy, mistletoe, rosemary and bay, 'with all manner of strange fruits as pomegranates, oranges, pumpkins, cucumbers, grapes, carrots with such other like, spangled with gold and most richly hanged'. For the spectators there were ten steps or stages so that people could get a good view of the entertainments. Graves was given only three months in which to design and construct this elaborate building. To do so he had 375 men working day and night, two of them breaking their legs in the process.

The embassy was accompanied by lavish feasting, dancing, plays and entertainment in the tiltyard, cockpit, tennis courts and bowling alleys. In between times, there was some hard negotiation. It was soon followed by a second, official, visit by the duke. During his three-month trip he visited Richmond again, but probably stayed in the queen's side at Whitehall. Frames were made for maps, suggesting that his rooms were helpfully provided with an English geography lesson. During this stay, he and the queen seem to have genuinely fallen for each other. Elizabeth famously nicknamed him her frog – a reference to his diminutive size and pockmarked face. At one point she was seen to kiss him on the mouth and declare her intention to marry him. Rings were exchanged and everything looked set for a happy conclusion, but the English barons were unsettled by the match. Leicester, Walsingham, Hatton and others all wanted the queen to cool her passion. Cool it she did, breaking off the engagement and saying goodbye to her French prince.[26]

The duke departed, but the banqueting house remained. Remarkably, this temporary structure, with a bit of patching up, survived twenty-five years until James I decided to take it down and replace it. Its substantial brick foundations were excavated in 1964 beneath the present Whitehall banqueting house, the only surviving physical remains of Elizabeth's romance with the man she called her frog.

GETTING ABOUT

Elizabeth was always on the move and she, no less than her predecessors, recognized the River Thames as the transport gyratory of England. It was fundamental to national prosperity as the principal conduit for trade; for defence, as a place to supply and manufacture warships; for diplomacy, as the entry point for foreign dignitaries; and, for the royal family, its main means of conveyance. All the principal royal houses were sited on the Thames, allowing rapid river transport by barge between them. Elizabeth's grandfather, Henry VII, cannot have been the first monarch to appreciate the possibilities of river travel for ceremonial, but, as in so much, he was responsible for building the magnificence of monarchy into the everyday round of royal life. At the end of his very first progress, in June 1486, the royal barges returning to London from Sheen were met at Putney by those of the richest citizens, the livery companies and the Lord Mayor, who accompanied the royal party to Westminster. From that point on all the major events of the reign were marked by waterborne processions, a practice continued by Henry VIII.[27]

Fundamental to all this and, more importantly, to the everyday business of conveying the royal family up- and downriver, were the royal barges. In 1532 Henry VIII made Whitehall their headquarters and there, in a long, narrow dock dug in Scotland Yard, a small flotilla of barges was maintained and sometimes stored. Together there were enough to form the core of a remarkable armada of thirty rich barges, which in 1522 met the Emperor Charles V at Gravesend and rowed him to Greenwich. On the way from Greenwich to Whitehall cannons on the wharf and walls of the Tower of London would fire a salute at the passing royal barge.

The royal barges were furnished and decorated by the Great Wardrobe and were not only beautiful but comfortable. A visitor who admired Elizabeth's barge pulled up on a slipway on the south bank of the Thames in 1593 described it as having 'two splendid cabins beautifully ornamented with glass windows, painting and gilding'. In front of these was the area of the oarsmen in their liveries, up to thirty of them on a large barge.

A boat trip on the river was an agreeable pastime. In summer 1539 Henry VIII 'took his barge at Whitehall and rowed up to Lambeth and had his drums and fifes playing and so rowed up and down the Thames an hour'. Elizabeth also liked these aquatic musical excursions, which were sometimes accompanied by fireworks. In 1536 a new barge was made, the Whitehall dock was enlarged and a large superstructure erected over it. The king's Barge Master, and his oarsmen, had offices and storerooms nearby. Here were kept the braziers on which sweet herbs were burned on board to hide the smells of the river; here were the liveries worn by the oarsmen and the tailored covers of cloth and leather that were used to store the boats and keep rain off their occupants.[28]

The Barge Masters not only had to navigate, but had to master the tides. As already noted, until the eighteenth century the Thames was tidal at least as far as Hampton Court and often as far as Windsor. As a result, on removing days, court officials had to plan their departure and arrivals carefully; catching the tide made travel many times faster than attempting

Cardinal Wolsey travelling to Greenwich by barge, from an illustrated copy of
Dr Stephen Bateman's edition of George Cavendish's *Life of Wolsey*, 1578. The barge,
with its fabric-covered wooden hoops, is approaching the royal landing stage with
posts topped with heraldic beasts.

to struggle against it. It was for this reason that in 1541 Henry VIII
installed a clock at Hampton Court that showed the time of high tide at
London Bridge. It was designed by Nicholas Kratzer, a German
mathematician, astronomer and horologist, who settled in England and
was appointed Royal Astronomer by Henry VIII. It was made by the
French clockmaker Nicholas Oursain, who was subsequently official
clock-keeper at Hampton Court with the substantial wage of 4d a day.

The huge tidal variation, which could be as much as 23 feet, left large
areas of muddy foreshore in front of the royal houses twice a day. This
often meant that it was impossible to disembark at the architecturally
pretentious watergate that led directly to the royal lodgings. And in
March 1558 the tide was so low that it was possible to walk across the
river. At such times barges would take the royal family as far upriver as
they could and they would then ride the rest of the way. Even then, long
timber bridges had to be built out into the mud flats to ensure a dignified
disembarkation.

In winter the Thames was prone to freezing upstream of London Bridge due to its narrow arches restricting the flow. On these occasions the royal family, courtiers and ambassadors had to resort to horseback. Moving from Whitehall to Greenwich by horse was not easy in Henry VIII's reign; it was easier to cross the Thames by horse ferry at Westminster than ride through the City and cross at London Bridge. In December 1578 the ice was so thick that the barges carrying the players for the Christmas revels at court could not move downriver to Greenwich and two horses had to be hired.[29]

Despite these problems, from the early Middle Ages anyone with any means travelled around London by river. But the 1550s saw a revolution which had far-reaching impact. The invention of the horse-drawn carriage was a holy grail – for centuries people had been trying to devise a passenger vehicle that could be drawn by a horse at a trot without pulverizing its occupants. In the 1550s well-travelled English diplomats and aristocrats began to import a new type of carriage originating from Hungary. Instead of the passenger compartment resting directly on axles, the new Pomeranian coach was slung on leather braces, giving a smoother and more comfortable ride.

In around 1555 Giovanni Michiel, the Venetian ambassador to Mary's court, brought to England a coach from Italy. The queen must have coveted it, for the ambassador was asked by Susan Tonge, Mary's Mistress of the Robes, whether he might present it to the queen. Unable to refuse, this lavish vehicle, complete with harness and horses, was handed over as a gift. When the queen ordered one of her own, Susan Tonge was given the Italian one as a hand-me-down. In July 1556 Mary took a barge across the Thames to Lambeth Palace. There her coach was waiting for her and she set off surrounded by mounted courtiers for Eltham, where she must have been the first monarch to give a royal wave from a coach to the 10,000 people who, it was reported, turned out to welcome her. That December she was driven in her coach from St James's to Whitehall; there she walked through the palace and exited on the waterside, boarded her barge and was rowed to Westminster. Presumably she did not take the coach all the way in order to make her arrival at Westminster, by river, more ceremonious.[30]

Under Elizabeth, any coyness shown by Mary in using coaches for formal entrées was forgotten. Several new models were commissioned; the one the queen had made in 1564 cost £401 in the days when a luxurious travelling wagon could be bought for £78. Covered in blue velvet with gold braid on the outside, it was lined with blue and purple silk and the queen was made comfortable by four purple velvet pillows. All this luxury was no guarantee of a smooth ride, however, for in 1568 the French ambassador heard Elizabeth complain of bruises she had got the previous day due to her coach being driven too fast. Nevertheless, by 1573 the queen was travelling as far afield as Canterbury by coach, so things must have become smoother.[31]

For a few years people noted the queen's novel use of coaches, but soon the contemporary records cease describing how Elizabeth travelled. So to map the increasing use of coaches we have to turn to a rather unusual form of evidence. As the queen passed through various towns on her travels, church bells would be rung to welcome her and a small reward would be paid by a royal official to the bellringers. The harbingers enforced this with some ferocity. In June 1563 a number of churches were shut until the churchwardens paid a fine for not ringing their bells as the queen passed on her way to Greenwich. From 1570 the churchwardens' accounts in Kingston-upon-Thames show that Elizabeth increasingly travelled to Hampton Court by coach. For instance, in 1571 the bells were rung eight times, but on only one of these occasions was it the royal barge that carried the queen.

So during Elizabeth's reign there was a revolution in royal transport – and this had a huge impact on royal houses, and on London itself. As the queen amassed carriages, so did her courtiers; the Earl of Leicester, for instance, ordered a new coach in 1585. The new development brought about a dramatic change in the way the queen and her courtiers approached royal houses. Although the watergates were still used, carriages now drove through the gatehouses and pulled up in front of the great halls, disgorging courtiers in the heart of the house. Traffic congestion ensued, as did squabbles about precedence and access. The courtyards of several royal houses were paved, or repaved, to allow for the tightly turning iron-shod wheels of carriages.

Elizabeth riding in procession through London in around 1588, shown on a playing card, the 4 of spades.

Queene Eliz:Riding in Tri=umph through London in a: Chariot drawn by two Hor=fes and all ÿ Companies_attending her w.ᵗʰ their Baners

In 1585 Elizabeth was observed making her entrance into the paved inner court of St James's in a carriage:

The queen sat in an open gilt carriage under a canopy of red velvet, embroidered with gold and pearls. In the front and back parts of the carriage were fastened three plumes of various colours; four brown horses royally attired were harnessed to the carriage, the coachman was clad in red velvet with the queen's crest and the rose, silver gilt in front and on his back. She sat alone in the carriage being clad in a white robe.

Behind the carriage rode the Earl of Leicester as Master of the Horse, then came twenty-four ladies-in-waiting, all mounted, followed by fifty Yeomen of the Guard. Next in procession came two empty carriages, 'a gilt carriage embroidered with gold and silver, but not equal to the queen's carriage, and another vehicle ornamented with yellow nails'. These empty coaches demonstrate that by the 1580s carriages were already huge status symbols used to impress the crowds with the queen's splendour.[32]

The proliferation of coaches led to a dramatic improvement in the road network round London. Henry VIII had passed laws requiring parishes to maintain roads in their area, but in 1555 came an Act that required parishes formally to survey the state of their roads and appoint persons to mend them. Fines were imposed on people who refused to meet their obligations. The weakness of this otherwise far-sighted measure was that heavily used routes might be the responsibility of very small communities. So, as well as vigorously ringing bells for the queen as she passed through Kingston, its inhabitants had the upkeep of roads for the royal coach. In 1598 the chamberlain of Kingston paid 21d to mend the road to smooth the elderly queen's passage from Sir Thomas Cecil's house at Wimbledon to Nonsuch. Eventually the solution for the most used road, from Whitehall out to Fulham and on to Richmond, was to privatize it. This is the origin of King's Road, a private royal artery that originally could be used by ordinary people only with a special pass.[33]

Modern coaches and well-kept roads shrank the Thames valley. A coachman might make 12mph on the best stretches of road from London to Richmond and Hampton Court; further afield, with less good surfaces, he still might make 6mph. As a result, it was possible for the queen to go out to Richmond or Greenwich for dinner by road and return the same evening. More importantly, she was less confined to the Thames-side mansions than before.

Carriages called for different types of horses. Of course, they needed to be suitable for harness work but, even more important, they needed to match, because much of the effect of a fine coach was in the splendour of the horseflesh. Elizabeth's reign was thus notable for the extension of stables and the construction of coach houses. The first coach house was, inevitably, for Whitehall, built in the royal mews at Charing Cross and completed in 1568. It is long gone, but the one at Hampton Court, built in 1570, still survives. It was of fourteen bays and measures 16 × 75 feet, with a great central archway complete with a stone plaque above it that reads 'Elizabethe Regina 1570'.[34]

By the 1570s, the largest houses had more stables than ever. At Greenwich there were nine: the king's stable (182 feet long); the coach stable (much smaller at 50 feet); the four-horse stable (20 feet); the Hobbies stable (120 feet); the Barbary horse stable (20 feet); the queen's double stable (62 feet); the Moyle stable (3 feet); the surveyor's stable (14 feet) and the Master of the Horse's stable (50 feet). This last belonged to the Earl of Leicester, who held the position for thirty years. So large grew his responsibilities that, in 1577, the Office of Works gave up responsibility for the scores of stable buildings, coach houses, barns and the royal mews, and the earl took control of them himself. It was a massive operation: in 1585 the queen had 40 coursers, 24 geldings, 6 litter mules and 15 coach horses, and in 1590 the wages of its staff alone came to £2,100 a year.[35]

✦XIV✦

HOME AND AWAY

On the Move

THE ANNUAL ROUND OF ELIZABETH'S LIFE was not materially different from her father's. During the winter months the court was itinerant, oscillating between the standing houses in the Thames valley, the queen moving by coach or sometimes barge between them. Whitehall was her most frequently used residence, followed (in order) by the country manors of Greenwich, Richmond and Hampton Court. If she went to stay at one of these, it was usually from Whitehall; rarely would she travel from Hampton Court or Richmond directly to Greenwich or vice versa. Visits to Hampton Court, which were mainly autumnal, would often be combined with trips to Windsor or Oatlands. At Windsor the queen loved to hunt, but the castle also provided a refuge in times of trouble or plague in London.

In the summer the queen would frequently leave the Thames valley on progress. In forty-four years she embarked on twenty-three annual progresses; these, like her father's, typically started in July and ended in late September, lasting around fifty days. Her travels took her as far west as Bristol, east to Norwich and as far north as Staffordshire. Yet most of her time was spent in the south, and in half of her progresses she barely moved out of a 50-mile radius from London. In fact, the people of Surrey, the county she visited most, complained that though it was the 'least and most barren' of counties, 'it is the most charged of any, by reason that her majesty lies in or about the shire continually, and thereby it is charged with continual removes and carriage of coals, wood and other provisions to the court . . . also by my lord treasurer for the repair of her majesties houses'. They were right; there were eleven royal houses

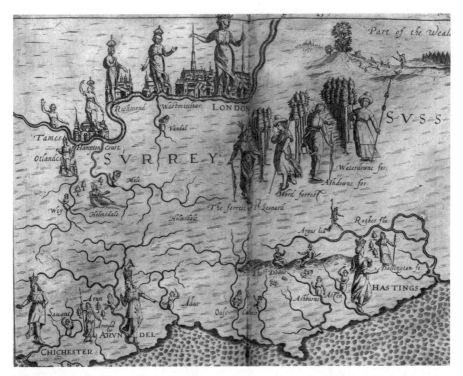

William Hole's map of the River Thames with the royal houses of Westminster, Richmond, Hampton Court and Oatlands. This is an illustration from Michael Drayton's *Poly-Olbion*, an epic poem describing England and Wales, first published in 1612. The royal houses on the Thames appear as crowned maidens.

in the county by 1547 and Elizabeth spent 42 per cent of the nights of her reign there.[1]

Much of this could have been said of Henry VIII, the key difference being that, after 1530, on progress he stayed in his own houses over 90 per cent of the time; in contrast, Elizabeth preferred to stay with her courtiers – around 80 per cent of nights on progress she was somebody's guest. In 1561 the royal progress into Essex, Suffolk and Hertfordshire lasted sixty-eight days, during which Elizabeth visited eighteen private houses and two towns but stayed at only four royal houses. Although there was a hard core of privy councillors whom she visited regularly, in all some 420 of her subjects had their monarch under their roof for a night or more over the reign. Having the court to stay was a mixed blessing. The queen was, of course, a guest, but she was also technically the host and, as she stepped over the threshold, her hosts became guests in their own homes. When in 1591 Elizabeth stayed at Cowdray House in Sussex, she was theatrically presented with a golden key to the house and invited to enter and 'possess all'.[2]

Burghley and Winchester disliked progresses. They were expensive, time-consuming to organize, they disrupted business and created chaos as itineraries changed due to the queen's whims and outbreaks of plague. In February 1593 Elizabeth was vacillating over whether to move from Windsor or not. One of the Earl of Essex's men, Anthony Standen, described the chaotic scene as relayed to him by one of the carters:

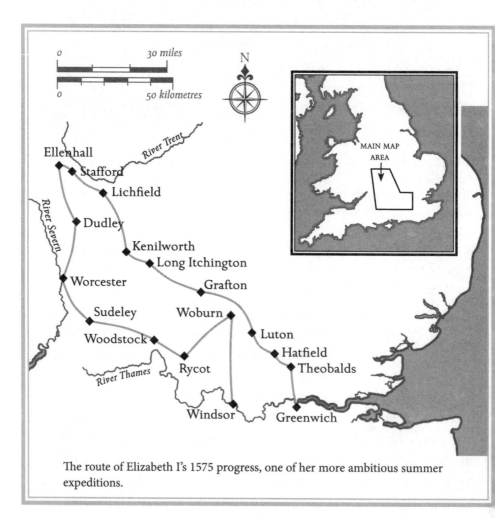

The route of Elizabeth I's 1575 progress, one of her more ambitious summer expeditions.

three times he had been at Windsor with his cart to carry away, upon summons of a remove, some part of the stuff of her majesty's wardrobe; and when he had repaired there once, twice and the third time, that the remove held not, clapping his hand to his thigh said these words 'Now I see' said the carter, 'that the queen is a woman as well as my wife'. Which words being overheard by her majesty, who then stood at a window, she said, 'what villain is this' and so sent him three angels [gold coins] to stop his mouth.

On another occasion, in December 1602, half the court had already removed from Whitehall and the carriages were on the road to Richmond when the queen decided not to go, but to stay where she was.[3]

While the bureaucrats hated progresses, Leicester loved them. He had, in all probability, been responsible for introducing Elizabeth to the pleasures of the hunt soon after her accession. He was not only Master of the Horse but was appointed, in 1572, Master of the Royal Buckhounds and these two posts gave him a monopoly over the queen's outdoor pursuits. There is little evidence that as a princess Elizabeth hunted, or even that she could ride side-saddle – the essential prerequisite to the chase. Leicester wrote to the Earl of Sussex after her first true progress ended in 1560, 'the queen's majesty is now become a great huntress and does follow it daily'; he continued that she needed suitable horses and not the ambling geldings she had previously ridden. By 1572 she had acquired some of the fanaticism of her father, and the French ambassador, who was with her on progress, reported that she had chased a stag well into the night and as a result had retired exhausted with a nasty stomach upset.[4]

Leicester was a brilliant horseman and, with the queen, hunted fearlessly, Elizabeth sometimes riding pillion behind him on the same horse. Windsor was one of their favourite hunting grounds: the Spanish ambassador, Don Diego Guzmán de Silva, was given a tour of the park by Leicester in August 1565 and, after seeing the queen hunt, noted that she 'went so hard that she tired everybody out, and as [for] the ladies and courtiers who were with her they were all put to shame. There was more

work than pleasure in it for them'. Elizabeth was still hunting when she was seventy and continued to shoot deer from a standing until her last months.

Like her predecessors, the queen liked to move from a larger house to hunt at a smaller one nearby. In 1597 she rode over to Enfield from Theobalds and had dinner there; the park had been set up with toils (hunting nets) and after dinner the queen shot deer from a standing, before returning to Theobalds in the evening. We know exactly how good a shot Elizabeth was because of the survival of the careful record made of the deer in Kenilworth Park by one of Leicester's estate officers. On her brief visit in 1568, for instance, she killed seven stags in the paddock, her hounds had two bucks in the chase, another fifteen bucks were shot by bow and her hound had one more. Not a bad record.[5]

Facing page left: 'Queen Elizabeth Hawking', from George Turberville, *The booke of Falconrie*, 1575.

Facing page right: Queen Elizabeth being entertained to a picnic while hunting. Woodcut entitled 'Of the place where and how an assembly should be made in the presence of a prince', from George Gascoigne, *The Noble Art of Venerie or Hunting*, 1575.

Left: The queen being presented with a knife for the disembowelling of a stag, also from Gascoigne's *Noble Art of Venerie*.

In 1563 Elizabeth gave Leicester Kenilworth Castle, a magnificent royal fortress sited amongst the best hunting country in the Midlands. This was an extraordinarily lavish gift, for the castle was not only vast and in a heart-stoppingly beautiful setting, but it was one of the most prestigious royal castles in England, exceeded only by the Tower and Windsor. In August 1566 the queen decided to stay there with the earl on her progress. While still a royal possession, Henry VIII had favoured Kenilworth and had made some improvements, but it remained more fortress than residence and Leicester, writing to Elizabeth in 1570, called it, tongue-in-cheek, her 'old ill lodging'.[6] By this stage, however, he had already laid plans for major improvements and, when the queen paid a brief day visit to the castle in 1568, work was under way to build a new tower especially for her. In 1575, when she returned to the castle, Leicester presented Elizabeth with the finished building – a palace within a palace for the queen.[7]

Kenilworth Castle as it was in 1620, a nineteenth-century print based on a sketch of a lost painting. To the right is the great Norman keep that contained a single vast chamber. The Earl of Leicester balanced it on the far left by his new tower containing the queen's lodgings. The range joining the two was built by Henry VIII. The clock that stopped at 2pm during Elizabeth's visit can be seen on the face of the keep.

Unfortunately, this remarkable building was partially destroyed during the Civil War, but, in 2014, while I was running English Heritage, which now looks after the castle, we decided to put back the floors and a staircase in the tower and it suddenly became possible to walk again in the rooms that Leicester built for Elizabeth and to understand how the building worked during a progress.

The parade of state rooms leading off the great hall contained, as usual, a guard chamber, presence chamber, privy chamber and withdrawing chamber. It was in these fine rooms that the queen publicly presided. On one side, the withdrawing chamber led to a gallery that stretched over the entrance front with views on both sides to the two courts. It led at its far end to the massive Norman keep, in which there was a single gaunt chamber. On the other side of the withdrawing room a door led to the new tower.

There is no handy inventory or plan that shows how these rooms were used, but it is most likely that off the withdrawing chamber was Elizabeth's bedchamber and beyond this were two closets and a back

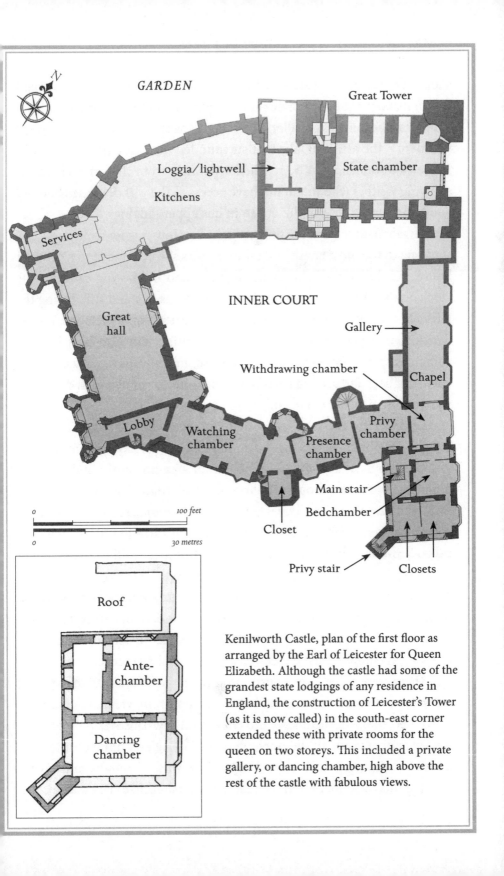

GARDEN

Great Tower

N

Loggia/lightwell →

State chamber

Kitchens

Services

INNER COURT

Great hall

Gallery →

Withdrawing chamber

Chapel

Lobby

Watching chamber

Presence chamber

Privy chamber

Main stair

Bedchamber

0 ——— 100 feet
0 ——— 30 metres

Closet

Privy stair

Closets

Roof

Ante-chamber

Dancing chamber

Kenilworth Castle, plan of the first floor as arranged by the Earl of Leicester for Queen Elizabeth. Although the castle had some of the grandest state lodgings of any residence in England, the construction of Leicester's Tower (as it is now called) in the south-east corner extended these with private rooms for the queen on two storeys. This included a private gallery, or dancing chamber, high above the rest of the castle with fabulous views.

stair. This was all very standard for a royal house. The nice refinement was that above the bedchamber and closets was another floor, comprising a top chamber and a sky gallery. From here there were incredible views of the mere – the artificial lake that surrounded the castle on its west side. These two rooms could be reached separately from the privy chamber, allowing visitors who might not have access to the withdrawing chamber and bedchamber to visit the queen in her upper lodgings.

Elizabeth arrived at the finished house in July 1575 for a nineteen-day stay, one of the most lavish and famous visits she ever made to a courtier house. As she entered the castle to the sound of blasting cannons the clock on the great tower was stopped – time was to stand still during the fairytale reception. Entertainment was non-stop and included music, dancing, masques, plays, acrobats and hunting, but also bear-baiting, aquatic displays, fireworks and, of course, many elaborate feasts. Forty barrels of beer and sixteen barrels of wine were consumed each day of the visit, not to mention ten oxen.[8]

Leicester set the tone, and others followed. In 1564 when Burghley bought Theobalds it was a modest moated manor house conveniently located a day's ride from Greenwich in an area north of London richly populated with royal houses. Before Burghley made any improvements, Elizabeth came over on a day trip to inspect it; it may even have been her encouragement that caused him to begin transforming it into what he called 'a monument to her Majesty's bountifulness'. In the six years after 1567 he spent £10,000 making it into the largest private house in England, and certainly the most expensively built. Nothing Elizabeth constructed in her entire reign was anything like as large, modern or extravagant. But, since Burghley's riches flowed entirely from the queen (and they both knew it), the house must be seen as a quasi-royal residence.

There were three large courts, as at the largest royal residences – an outer service courtyard that led to the first court, in which was the most celebrated room in the house: the Green Gallery. This was painted with the coats of arms of all the noble families of England hung on fifty-two trees, in between which were England's towns, boroughs and rivers. Leaving this introduction to the realm, visitors reached the middle court containing the great hall, the chapel and the great chamber. The great chamber provided a fanfare for the rooms of state beyond. According to a visitor in 1592, in here there was 'a very high rock of all colours, made of real stones out of which gushes a splendid fountain that falls into a large circular bowl or basin supported by two savages'. The ceiling was decorated with the signs of the zodiac, with a mechanical sun that moved across the sky. It was on the south side of this court that Elizabeth liked to stay. Here, on the second floor of the house, with panoramic views of the gardens, she had a withdrawing chamber, bedchamber and a privy gallery, where, apparently, she dined. Her presence chamber was on the ground floor, far beneath.[9]

Theobalds, because of its location, and because of its owner, occupied a pivotal place in the queen's itinerary – she visited more than a dozen times. Nothing now remains of the house, so we cannot accurately reconstruct the rooms in which she stayed; however, Burghley's house in Lincolnshire, Burghley House, not only exists but there is a Jacobean plan of the first-floor rooms. Although Elizabeth never visited Burghley House it was fully the intention that she should, and so here we can get a sense of the rooms that must have existed at Theobalds – and the arrangement was very similar. In the inner court at Burghley a huge triumphal gateway formed the entrance to a ground-floor great hall, which would have been used as a guard chamber. A magnificent flight of stairs, like the great stair at Windsor Castle, led up to a presence chamber, beyond which was the queen's privy chamber. The royal bedchamber and closet were beyond, sited next to a back stair, after which came the long gallery served by many small closets and bay windows. On the floor above was an upper privy gallery reached by the back stairs and this in turn gave access to the roof walks with views over the park and gardens.[10]

Kenilworth, Theobalds and Burghley were exceptional in the provision they made for the monarch. Most houses, even great ones, were infrequently visited by the court and then often only with great difficulty. We do not know whether Elizabeth was being ironic when she complained to Sir Nicholas Bacon that his very large and modern house at Gorhambury was too small, but we do have his witty reply: 'Madam,

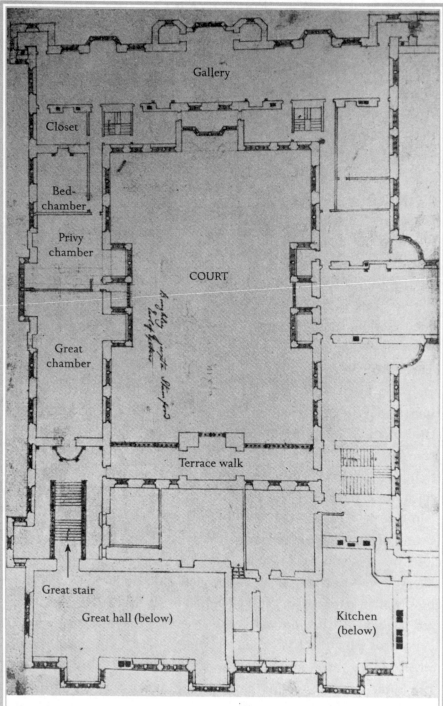

Labels within the image:

Gallery

Closet

Bed-chamber

Privy chamber

COURT

Great chamber

Terrace walk

Great stair

Great hall (below)

Kitchen (below)

Burghley House in the sixteenth century. Although Elizabeth never made it to Burghley, this house, like Theobalds, was built to entertain the queen. Because an early plan survives, we know how Lord Burghley arranged the principal rooms. It is noticeable that the gallery was enormous and must have been intended as the queen's principal chamber when she stayed.

The courtyard of Burghley House, from a drawing made by John Haynes in 1755 before it was altered in the nineteenth century. It shows the spectacular entrance to the state rooms up a staircase under the central arch. Roundels in the central tower contained heads of great monarchs and the queen's supposed ancestors. The balconies on either side were perhaps grandstands for welcoming the queen or for her to watch performances in the courtyard below.

my house is well, but it is you that have me too great for my house'. Bacon was rich enough to make special arrangements for the royal visit, but each year the Office of Works would survey private houses to be visited in order to make minor alterations at the queen's expense. The 1573 progress took her to Surrey, Kent and Sussex, and at five of the houses she visited it was judged that there was insufficient provision for her clothes; rooms were therefore converted into wardrobes and cupboards were built. But the sums spent on people's houses were never large: in 1581, 49s 9d was spent at Cobham Hall, 8s 6d at Wanstead, and 75s 6d at Loughborough Hall. The most common alterations were arrangements to hang the queen's cloth of estate and the changing of locks, which was done on all the doors of the queen's inner rooms wherever she stayed.[11]

Even with the aid of the Office of Works, receiving the court on progress was nerve-racking. An experienced court hand, Michael Hickes, one of Burghley's secretaries, asked one of his fellow secretaries at court to get some tips from the Lord Chamberlain when 'the resplendence of her majesties royal presence and princely aspect' threatened to come to his house at Ruckholt in Essex. He thought he had 'no convenient place to entertain some of the majesties necessary servants'. He was advised, in that case, to move his family out and 'leave the house to the queen'. Elizabeth seems to have been quite happy with Ruckholt when she stayed for two days in the autumn of 1597, but, faced with his sovereign's presence, Hickes was struck dumb with terror during his welcome speech on the steps of his mansion.[12]

Another courtier, Sir John Puckering, who was expecting the queen to arrive at his place in Kew in August 1594, made a careful list of seventeen considerations he had to bear in mind. Number 16 was 'great care to be had, and conference with the gentlemen ushers, how her majesty, may be lodged, for her best ease and liking, far from heat or noise of any office near her lodging and how her bed chamber may be kept free from any noise near it'.[13]

Full and careful consultation with the gentlemen ushers, as Puckering suspected, was the key to a successful visit. This is what happened before the queen's arrival at Hengrave Hall in Suffolk during her great progress to Norwich in 1578. Hengrave had been built by Sir Thomas Kitson, an extremely wealthy London merchant, at exactly the same time as the royal house at Bridewell, and had cost the same amount. Kitson had died in 1540 and it was his son, also Thomas, who welcomed Queen Elizabeth on 27 August. The house was big, with over fifty rooms clustered round a central courtyard. The great hall on the north of the house had a hammerbeam roof and, from here, a large processional stair led up to the principal lodgings on the first floor on the west side. There was a great chamber, a bedchamber with an 'inner chamber' next to it and an 'upper garret' over it. This abutted the chapel, which was ingeniously tucked into one arm of the gatehouse.

Before Elizabeth arrived at Hengrave, one of her gentlemen ushers arrived to check all was ready. Though the house was very well appointed,

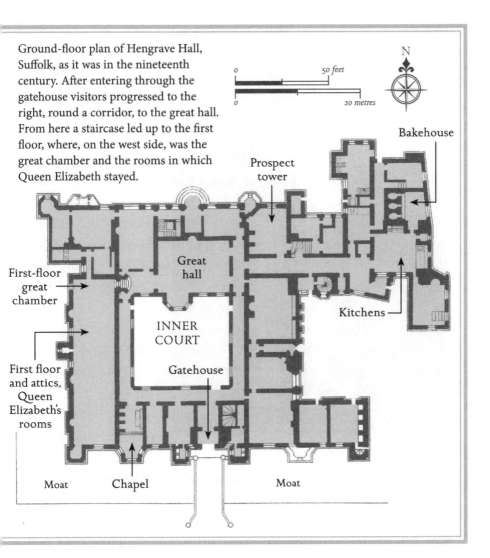

Ground-floor plan of Hengrave Hall, Suffolk, as it was in the nineteenth century. After entering through the gatehouse visitors progressed to the right, round a corridor, to the great hall. From here a staircase led up to the first floor, where, on the west side, was the great chamber and the rooms in which Queen Elizabeth stayed.

0   50 feet

0   20 metres

N

Bakehouse

Prospect tower

Great hall

First-floor great chamber

Kitchens

INNER COURT

First floor and attics, Queen Elizabeth's rooms

Gatehouse

Moat   Chapel   Moat

he decided that a temporary banqueting house should be erected so that the queen could retire after dinner and enjoy sweetmeats with the family. An inventory of the house taken in 1603 reveals that the bedroom the queen occupied, chosen by the usher, was still then called Queen Elizabeth's Chamber. It was incredibly richly furnished, with a bed of black velvet embroidered with cloth of gold and yellow taffeta curtains fringed in black. There were black-and-gold chairs and table carpet to match; the floor was covered with three luxurious rugs that matched those on the window seats. The walls were hung with six pieces of tapestry. This was very likely the suite of furnishings that the queen herself

The entrance front of Hengrave Hall, Suffolk, visited by Elizabeth I in summer 1578.

had used. Such rooms were memorialized and shown to visitors for generations afterwards. The cloth of estate Elizabeth had used at Kimberley House in Norfolk a few days before her visit to Hengrave was kept at the house until the twentieth century, when it went to the Burrell Collection in Glasgow (see plate section).

In his hospitality Kitson was, like most of his contemporaries, competitive and was judged to have exceeded his local rivals; his after-dinner entertainment was a 'show representing the fairies' that culminated with the presentation of a 'rich jewel' to the queen.[14]

A house like Hengrave, and certainly Theobalds or Kenilworth, was furnished by its owner for the queen. Most other houses were furnished by the royal Wardrobe in advance of her arrival. For the long and ambitious progress of 1572, when the queen went as far as Warwickshire, the Wardrobe carried four beds, four bolsters and eight pillows, half a dozen chairs, a dozen stools, a couple of canopies of state and several close stools. Beautifully made leather cases protected the royal furnishings from the knocks and bumps of the wardrobe carts. The bed cases were of red leather lined with red cotton and had sturdy locks to prevent tampering. A crimson velvet-covered box with its custom-made leather carrying case transported the queen's nightclothes.[15]

In preparation for the winter progress of 1582, when the queen went down to the south coast to say farewell to the Duke of Anjou, a remarkable folding bed of carved and gilded walnut was made, together with two pairs of curtains, one of figured velvet and one pair of damask. It was topped with six plumes of ostrich feathers. The bed broke down and could be carried in two leather cases for the hangings and a wooden chest for the timber and ironwork; other large items, such as the frames for canopies of state, were sometimes made with folding sections.[16]

The Elizabethan court was better prepared and more professional on progress than Henry VIII's. Wolsey had been continually worried about vandalism and theft when the king stayed with courtiers; apparently door locks, tables, benches and cupboards were either stolen or destroyed by his retinue and large quantities of food and drink spirited away. The gentlemen ushers were therefore ordered to make inventories of the houses before the court arrived and compensation was paid when items were proved to have gone missing. After the progress of 1526, for instance, the king had to pay out £8 1s.[17]

If Elizabethan courtiers were better behaved, this did not mean that having the queen to stay was any cheaper. Sir William Petre hosted the court at his house, Ingatestone Hall in Essex, between 19 and 22 June 1561. Some weeks before their arrival, Petre went shopping. His most expensive outlay was some extra plate: a large gilt basin, four gilt cups and a large gilt jug. Meanwhile, Lady Petre took control of the interior decoration, ordering new green taffeta curtains for the windows and having their best wall hangings sent down from their London house. Their workmen erected sheds and workhouses for the royal servants and kitchen staff, and the cellars were filled with beer, ale and wine. On the eve of the court's arrival servants were sent out to procure food, including 6 cygnets, 12 dozen quails, 5 dozen chickens, 30 herons, 693 eggs, a stag and a salmon. More food came from Petre's estate, including rabbits, doves, fish and all the cereals. In total, his steward calculated the visit (including gifts for the queen and tips for her staff) cost £136. It was expensive for the queen too – the royal account book shows an outlay of more than £216 for the visit.[18]

The progress was not all fun, for the business of government had to continue and privy councillors found themselves dragged round the country holding meetings in houses where the queen stayed. Often there was no room for them and they had to lodge nearby. After the death of Winchester in 1572 there was a Cabinet reshuffle in which Burghley became Lord Treasurer and Sir Francis Walsingham became Secretary. As an evangelical, Walsingham rather disapproved of the expense and frivolity of court life, preferring more bookish interests. He was amongst the foremost complainers of government on the hoof, writing, on progress in 1575, that he knew nothing of what was going on, 'being lodged as I am far off from the court, and having no great disposition to repair there but drawn by special occasion.'[19]

Key to maintaining effective government was communication between court and capital. For this purpose Henry VIII had maintained messengers who rode between houses. They wore royal livery and carried their papers in special boxes rather like a ministerial red box today. In a busy year they might make around 700 trips, but to be effective they needed new horses every 20 miles, or even more frequently on difficult terrain. Thus a system was built up whereby fresh beasts were kept at posts a set distance apart and, in 1512, Sir Brian Tuke was appointed Master of the Posts to supervise this. The first permanent post route was to Dover, allowing messages to be sent rapidly to the coast and on to Calais. In Mary's reign this was formalized into a system of standing posts that allowed messages also to be sent from London north to Berwick and west to Portsmouth. A letter written in London could now reach York in fifty-five hours and Berwick in eighty. This system created the infrastructure that supported the Elizabethan progresses. The royal messengers, or posts, used the so-called standing posts as a trunk system to which branches would be attached as the court perambulated. So, during the 1587 progress to Norwich, which was off the standing (or ordinary) post route, special stages had to be laid at a cost of £50.[20]

A post messenger riding with his horn and his bag. Title page of Nicholas Breton's 1602 book *A Poste with a Packet of Madde Letters.*

The post system, together with the proliferation of carriages, explains the extensive programme of stable building during Elizabeth's reign. The supply of horses depended partly on private enterprise, but royal stables were sited strategically across the country to serve progresses and the post. Stables were positioned at Sheen and Chertsey to serve the south-west of London and at St Albans and Waltham for the north. At Reading, in 1570, a very large timber-framed stable was built from 100 large oak trees at a cost of £1,000. Reading was a key point servicing the queen's westward travels and the new stable was 162 feet long, with three aisles probably stabling around fifty horses. Considering the modest investment in the queen's own houses, the construction of such splendid stables shows the importance of communication networks to the Elizabethan regime.[21]

LODGING THE COURT

While the royal family always had first claim on accommodation either in royal or courtier houses, provision was always made for at least some of the household. Of these, the servants in the Lord Steward's department were the most plainly housed. They slept communally in rooms and garrets above their workhouses. In the larger royal houses they got simple timber-framed beds with webbing bases, but on progress they often had to sleep on palliasses on the floor. Where there was no space, tents would be erected near the royal kitchens; a visitor to the court at Oatlands in 1602 saw the 'common servants of the court set up their tents like a military camp'. Courtiers fared much better. At the top of the list were the monarch's body servants. While they were on duty they slept at their stations and used facilities provided for them in the monarch's own rooms; when not on duty many had their own lodgings.[22]

In Henry VIII's reign the Groom of the Stool always had rooms next to the sovereign – Henry Norris had a room next to the king's closet at Greenwich and at Whitehall he stayed in the privy gallery itself. His successor, Sir Thomas Heneage, had lodgings at Hampton Court directly below the privy chamber. The privilege of rooms close to Henry's was afforded to a select group of other courtiers, including, at various times, George Boleyn, Lord Rochford and Thomas Howard, Duke of Norfolk, whose room was next to the king's bathroom at Hampton Court. Rooms so close to the king's were small and the Groom of the Stool normally had larger lodgings in the outer court, where he could keep his wardrobe, papers and his servants. The most important people had lodgings in almost every house – the Duke of Norfolk had rooms in at least nine houses, including all the greater ones in the Thames valley.[23]

Elizabeth's ladies occupied most of the rooms formerly belonging to Henry's Privy Chamber. Lady Mary Sidney, the Earl of Leicester's sister, found that after a temporary absence from court her rooms close to Elizabeth's had been re-allocated and she was given a small, cold room remote from the queen. She wrote to the Lord Chamberlain, the Earl of Sussex, who was responsible for the allocation of rooms: 'Her majesty hath commanded me to come to the court and my chamber is very cold and my own hangings very scant and nothing warm'; because she had been ill she dared not 'venture to lie in so cold a lodging without some further help'. She begged for the loan of hangings from the Great Wardrobe, which she promised to return when the weather got warmer. The Lord Chamberlain, who was, in fact, her brother-in-law, had no desire for her to be close to the queen where she could advance Leicester's career and refused all help.[24]

It is difficult to generalize about how many rooms were available for

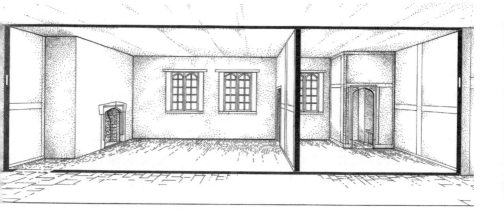

Diagram of one of the double lodgings at Hampton Court in the Base Court. These were spartan, whitewashed boxes that had to be furnished at the expense of the occupant. See page 218. Drawing by Daphne Ford.

courtiers, as the size of houses varied so much. But we do know that Base Court at Hampton Court, which had been built by Wolsey in 1515–22 as guest accommodation, contained forty lodgings, some single and some double. The double rooms were the most desirable and were allocated to senior courtiers such as the Groom of the Stool, the Master of the Horse and the Lord Privy Seal. Base Court was quite innovative, in that the lodgings were all entered off a gallery (or corridor) rather than individually from outside. The outer room had a fireplace in it, windows looking outside and an internal window bringing borrowed light from the corridor. Beyond this there was an inner room, unheated, with a garderobe in a small enclosure. The lodgings were pretty stark. When a courtier arrived the walls were bare plaster and it was expected that the occupant would bring his own hangings, furniture and bedding.[25]

In 1525 Henry Courtenay, Marquess of Exeter, one of Henry VIII's closest friends and a member of the Privy Chamber, had to pay for rushes to be spread on the floor of his rooms at Windsor Castle and bought hooks to hang his tapestries. That summer he spent £10 3s 4d on moving his bed, wall hangings and bedding between houses and paying carpenters to 'dress' his room. His wife was with him for much of the time, and on progress he brought along between thirteen and sixteen servants – officially someone of his rank was allowed eight. These probably included his chaplain, a gentleman, a couple of yeomen and some grooms to look after his rooms. When the court was at Greenwich he paid for six beds for his servants in an inn, The Angel. Servants were hard to lodge, horses sometimes even more so. Exeter hired stables at Greenwich on a permanent basis to avoid the hassle of finding stabling; when he stayed at Windsor he had to pay to stable fifty-one horses, eighteen for himself and his yeomen and thirty-three for his gentlemen.[26]

Exeter was important but he was not in the league of the Earl of Leicester. In every royal house he had lodgings close to the queen. At Greenwich, for instance, he had chambers on the riverfront and his bedroom had a balcony on the roof where he had supper.[27] His rooms were richly furnished with his own tapestries and furniture: in November 1584, when the earl moved his stuff from Hampton Court to St James's, eight men spent two days transporting it in nine carts at a cost of 9s 6d. Whilst in residence, more items would be sent upriver from his houses in London or Wanstead in Essex. These included things such as his armour, candles, a close stool, leashes and collars for his hounds, plus a new pair of shoes for a servant.

Leicester was accompanied at court by an entourage. During the seven weeks that he was at Hampton Court in 1560 he paid for the beds of four gentlemen and nine yeomen, his surveyor of stables and three other named servants. It is unclear where they stayed, but their allowances, 12d a week for the gentlemen and 8d for the yeomen, presumably bought them lodgings at a nearby inn.[28]

Lodgings in large houses were normally provided with a garderobe in a small closet off one of the inner rooms. These generally had a wooden seat on top of a brick shaft that ended in a brick-lined pit. The pits had to be emptied by hand by a court official called the Gong Scourer, 'gong' being a euphemism for a garderobe. The work was unpleasant, as the brick chamber had to be opened and small boys set to work inside with spades and then scrubbing brushes; when it was clean the bricklayers would seal the pit up again.[29]

Famously, the queen's godson Sir John Harington claimed to have devised the 'flushing close stool', an invention he published in 1596 in his book *The Metamorphosis of Ajax*. His claim has to be treated with scepticism, as modern archaeology at the royal manor of Eltham has shown that a flushing garderobe with a lead cistern activated by a sluice was installed there in Henry VIII's reign. Yet Harington's particular contraption seems to have been built at least at Richmond if his witty epigram entitled 'To the ladies of the queen's privy chamber at the making of their perfumed privy at Richmond' is anything to go by. The lodgings of important courtiers who did not have built-in garderobes were issued with close stools. These were not as lavish as the queen's, but were leather-covered boxes with seats upholstered in a coarse woollen twill with tin chamber pots inside.[30]

For the many staff who did not have lodgings with their own facilities there was the common house of easement, or the common jakes (yet another euphemism). Most houses had these and the outside walls of the one built by Henry VIII at Hampton Court survive. This monster WC had fourteen seats on two levels and discharged into a flushed culvert rather

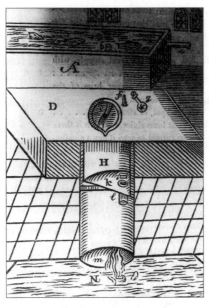

A	Cistern, including fish
B	Washer
C	Overflow pipe
D	Seat
E	Pipe from the cistern
F	Screw
G	Flushing lever
H	Pipe below seat
I	Stopper
K	Current
L	Sluice
M	Vault into which it discharges

Sir John Harington's *New Discourse of a Stale Subject, called the Metamorphosis of Ajax.* Subtitled 'How unsavoury places may be made sweet, noisome places made wholesome, filthy places made clean. Published for the common benefit of builders, house-keepers, and house-owners.' An early flushing lavatory designed for the ladies at Queen Elizabeth's court.

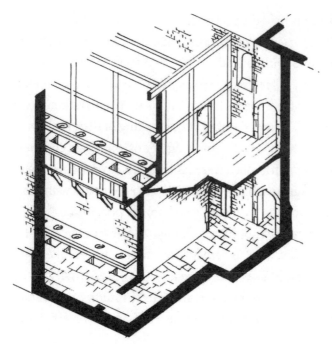

The arrangement at the Hampton Court Great House of Easement. Seats were arranged on two levels and both discharged into a drain that was flushed into the Thames. See page 218. Drawing by Daphne Ford.

than a sealed pit. In the big houses in the Thames valley there was always a temptation to go in a dark corner rather than to find the common jakes. In September 1547 the Privy Council issued an order forbidding courtiers to 'make water' in the precincts of the court. More practical measures were already in place, including painting large, red 'No Pissing' crosses on the walls of the courts and, more helpfully, providing lead-lined pissing places and strategically stationing pissing pots at the foot of well-used staircases. For the Yeomen of the Guard, who were not allowed out of the watching chamber, there were either discreet garderobes or tin chamber pots.[31]

To modern eyes, life at court seems cramped and overcrowded, and in a sense it was. But Tudor life was lived much more in the open than life today, and those with lodgings at court with their own servants, efficient sanitary arrangements, regular meals and access to the monarch were lucky. Even the lowliest servants lived in conditions better than many ordinary citizens. Court was not to everyone's taste, but for those who enjoyed it the material comforts were more than adequate and the opportunities for advancement were legion.

· XV ·

THE ELIZABETHAN ROYAL
LODGINGS

Life in the Outer Rooms

The outer rooms of elizabeth's houses were supervised by the gentlemen ushers, assisted by the grooms of the chamber and the pages. Yeomen ushers kept the doors and the Yeomen of the Guard stood in the watching chamber, while the Gentlemen Pensioners stood in the presence chamber. The moment the queen left the privy chamber the pensioners, in their black uniforms and bearing gleaming axes, lined the rooms and galleries through which she passed. If she decided to go out and take her horse, the pensioners would flank her as she mounted.

Following the example of her father, Elizabeth used the great hall and the watching chamber as a communication route or for formal ceremonial; occasionally the court might gather for a religious ceremony, such as the Maundy washing of poor men's feet, which required a larger space than the chapel. There was one exception to this – the increasing use of the outward chambers for plays. From earliest times monarchs and their courts were entertained by music and drama, but it was not until the reign of Henry VIII that a permanent infrastructure was established for managing the large number of plays, masques and jousts at court. In 1534 a department of the household was formed with responsibility for what were known as the revels, and the man in charge, from 1544, was known as the Master of the Revels. As the setting of most revels depended on textiles and paint, the department grew out of the Great Wardrobe located in the City, but, as a separate entity, it soon required additional space. The suppression of the monasteries supplied this and, in the last year of Henry's reign, London Blackfriars became the HQ for the new Revels Department.

The first Master of the Revels was Sir Thomas Cawarden, a protégé of Thomas Cromwell and a fervent evangelical. He had superb organizational skills and managed large projects such as the construction of a temporary banqueting house in Hyde Park for the reception of a French embassy in 1551. He was also chief court impresario, creating the costumes and scenery for theatrical events. As Edward VI slipped into his final illness in January and February 1553, Cawarden put on five masques to distract the ailing boy: 'a Mask of Greek Worthies; a Mask of Medyoxes, being half death, half man; a Mask of Bagpipes; A Mask of Cats and a Mask of Tumblers going upon their hands with their feet upward.'[1]

Near to the Thames, the new stores and workshops at Blackfriars were ideally located for ferrying equipment up- and downstream, particularly to Greenwich, where the vast majority of Edward VI's and Mary's revels took place. The extensive premises, with several very large rooms, allowed scenery and other props to be prefabricated and tested before being erected at court. A visit to Blackfriars in Edward VI's reign would have been a remarkable sight: here craftsmen were not working on luxury goods for the court as they did in the Wardrobe, but on the stuff of fantasy and comedy. At Shrovetide 1549 work was under way on the costumes and props for a strongly anti-papal play. In the workshops lay brightly coloured papal vestments; paper crowns for a king and a pope in gold, silver, green and red; a dragon with seven heads to serve as the beast from the Book of Revelation; wigs and false beards, including some with bald patches to serve as tonsures for monks; costumes for hermits; and banners with 'writing' on them.[2]

In 1572 the Revels moved their headquarters to another former monastic site, the Priory of St John of Jerusalem at Clerkenwell. This had been one of the most important and lavish of all ecclesiastical properties in London. Though it had a church and cloister, it was really a palatial residence with a great hall and a fine series of state chambers. St John's had been the last of all the London monastic suppressions and Henry VIII reserved the site with the thought that it might serve as a residence for Princess Mary. Indeed, before her accession, she did sometimes stay there. What made it the obvious choice as the headquarters for the Elizabethan Revels Department was not its convenience as a manufacturing centre (Blackfriars, on the river, was much better suited for this), but the great state chambers, which were similar in scale to those at the royal houses and were therefore ideal rehearsal rooms.[3]

Rehearsals took place in the hall and great chamber, which were set up with scenery and props. The larger rooms were also used as painting workshops, especially for the bigger pieces of canvas scenery that were painted attached to large wooden frames. The former prior's house also contained workshops, as well as lodgings for children who were used in many masques, so they could learn 'their parts and gestures'. At Shrovetide 1574 nine children were required for a masque at Hampton Court where they, their costumes and scenery, were taken in a barge and two wherries. When they arrived, the queen could not decide whether she wanted to see the play and so they had to be billeted in Kingston overnight. They performed the next day and when they got back to St John's on Ash Wednesday, some of them 'being sick and cold and hungry', they were given a good supper in front of the fire before taking their shilling in reward and going home.[4]

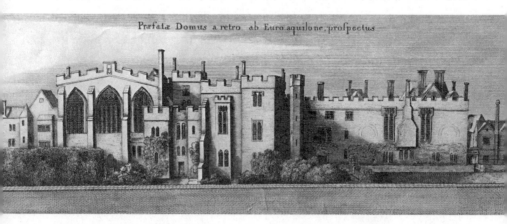

The former Priory of St John of Jerusalem at Clerkenwell, depicted by Wenceslaus Hollar in 1661. For most of Elizabeth's reign this was the headquarters of the royal Revels Department. The chancel of the church can be seen on the left; the building to its right was the former mansion of the prior, used from 1572 as the rehearsal rooms and workshops of the Revels.

Under Elizabeth, plays, tragedies and triumphs were always staged over the twelve days of Christmas and, most importantly, on Twelfth Night. At Shrovetide a smaller festival of plays was also often arranged. In the 1560s Christmas was most frequently held at Whitehall, where the great hall would be set up as a theatre with a 'broad stage' for the whole festive period.[5] During the 1570s Elizabeth often spent Christmas at Hampton Court, and here new daises were constructed beneath the cloth of estate in the great chamber and elsewhere, and staging was made for the seats of the ladies of honour and other courtiers. Elaborate scenery was installed and wires stretched across the hall from which to hang oil lamps.[6] At Shrovetide 1573 two plays and a masque were held at Hampton Court, and the following year four plays were performed at Christmas. Over Christmas and New Year 1576–7 six plays were acted by the Earl of Warwick's servants, the Lord Howard's servants, the Earl of Leicester's men, the choir boys of St Paul's Cathedral, the choir boys of Windsor and the Chapel Royal, and the Lord Chamberlain's Men.[7]

At Richmond theatrical events were more intimate and the great chamber was used rather than the hall. Here the accounts of the Office of Works describe the construction of a mini-theatre: 'making new halpaces [platforms] there for the queen's majesty's use and a new stage 14ft square for the players to play on and halpaces for the lords and ladies to sit on and 3 other halpaces for the people to stand on'. At Greenwich in 1590 staging was set up in the great chamber on the queen's side for plays at Shrovetide; as the staging and scenery put a room out of use for some days, using the redundant and empty queen's side seems like a sensible option. Plays and revels were an expensive item because, as well as the Revels Department, the Office of Works was involved in staging events and often the Great Wardrobe supplied items too. Costs could be as high as £2,000 a year – higher if there was a special occasion. The queen also enjoyed plays while she was on progress and, on occasions when her hosts were not providing the entertainment, the Revels Department had to transport scenery, costumes and players to wherever she was staying.[8]

Plays generally took place after supper, in winter by artificial light, and often ended with dancing by members of the court. When the music stopped guests were invited into the presence chamber for a void or banquet; such an event was described by the Spanish ambassador who had sat through a long play in English in March 1565 and was ushered into the presence chamber at midnight: 'they had spread a very large table,' he wrote, 'with many sorts of cakes, confitures, and preserves, and in one part of it there were herrings and other small fishes in memory of the principle of Lent'. When invited by the queen to help himself, the poor ambassador refused, exhausted, and watched as the apparently wide-awake queen retreated to her privy lodgings.[9]

The presence chamber was the focus of the queen's interaction with the court. The most formal of interviews would take place in here, in full view of everyone: visiting dignitaries would be received and formal speeches of welcome made. The luckiest ones would later be dined in the same room by senior courtiers and privy councillors. The more formal recreations of the court were also held in the presence chamber: tables were set up for playing cards and courtiers might listen to music or dance. The French ambassador, who saw dancing in the presence chamber at Greenwich in 1598, reported that Elizabeth took 'such pleasure in it that when her maids dance she follows the cadence with her head hand and foot. She rebukes them if they do not dance to her liking, and without doubt is a mistress of the art'. One Mr Palmer, who was judged by some to be the best dancer of the time, was prised away from his partner and danced with the ailing queen on St Stephen's Day 1602.[10]

Unlike Henry VIII, Elizabeth did not like to dine in public and so a bizarre ceremony was enacted in the presence chamber each day. The Yeomen of the Guard carried in trestle tables and then, with much bowing and solemnity, the cloth was spread and the table laid, with food, wine and ale set out. A lady-in-waiting, with more genuflecting, would give various dishes to a guard to taste (in case of poison) and then dishes were paraded into the privy chamber next door, where the queen would decide which ones she wanted before eating them privately with her ladies. All the time the servers and guards treated the empty table and canopy of state as if the queen herself were sitting there.

Only on the most important feast days would this rule be broken, and then an even grander table would be set up with large quantities of silver gilt, plate, salts, jugs and goblets. Musicians would gather and start to play, then the queen would enter and sit beneath the canopy and the senior officers of the court would come and stand either side of her. Dishes would be paraded into the room in procession and service was on bended knee. The queen was a stickler for proper service and when one of her younger ladies, Lady Margaret Howard, was not ready with a cup at dinner she was called an ungracious flouting wench and was sent away. If the queen ushered someone over for conversation, they would converse with her on their knees. On such a feast day the queen would leave the table after dinner, people would speak to her (on their knees) and then dancing would begin.[11]

It was because Elizabeth disliked eating in public that the privy lodgings increasingly contained specialized spaces for her to take her meals. There were small dining chambers at many houses, including Whitehall. At Greenwich there was a breakfast room – very useful, as

William Rogers, Queen Elizabeth in her privy chamber, c.1593–5. This remarkably detailed engraving shows the queen in an extraordinarily lavish dress standing on a carpet by a window. Behind her is a canopy of state over a stepped dais. On the dais is an X-frame chair of estate with a fat cushion. On this lies another jewelled cushion on which is an open book.
The window surround has a strong architectural frame and the upper part of the casement may have had glass designed to diffuse the bright sun.

Elizabeth was a late riser and once told the Earl of Hertford, 'I am no morning woman'. Here she could start the day slowly and in privacy with her ladies. These new eating rooms were connected by stairs to the privy kitchens below.[12]

During the half century between the establishment of the privy chamber as Henry VII's inner sanctum and its crowning as Henry VIII's principal reception chamber, the room had moved from a place of intimate privacy to one of state ceremonial. In the 1540s, as I have described, Henry VIII had liberally invited people into his privy lodging. Elizabeth did no such thing – access was regulated and, as a result, the privy chamber became the most important room in any house. This was the room where people got close to the queen, the place where the principal ceremonial of Elizabethan England was enacted. As a consequence, at Richmond, where the state rooms were quite small and dated from Henry VII's time, she enlarged her privy chamber by making her privy closet (private chapel) next door smaller.

The queen spent most of her time in the privy chamber. This is where she would dine in private, where she would listen to music, read and converse with her ladies and where male members of the court were invited to see her privately. Foreign emissaries would be ushered in for intimate conversations – the French ambassador the Sieur de Maisse found her in the Whitehall privy chamber having the spinet played to her, and she told him that she was listening to a pavanne and that she loved music. [13]

THE ELIZABETHAN BEDCHAMBER

The rooms behind the closed door of the Elizabethan privy chamber formed part of the ultra-private bedchamber. This was not a single room, but the complex of chambers and closets that had formed Henry VIII's secret lodgings. Here was a feminine world presided over by four Ladies of the Bedchamber, one of whom was the chief, or first, lady, who inherited one of the jobs of the Henrician Groom of the Stool – waiting upon the queen as she sat on her close stool. The groom's other Henrician tasks, financial and administrative, were not passed on to the first lady and remained in the hands of men in the privy chamber without. Assisting the ladies were seven or eight gentlewomen of the privy chamber and four chamberers. In addition, there were six maids of honour – aristocratic teenagers who were not formally part of the privy chamber, but were ornaments to the queen in private and public. They were under the strict eye of the Mother of the Maids, who presided over the dormitory they slept in. Outside this magic circle of a score of ladies was a contingent of honorific ladies, who could be called upon when required. Finally there was the important post of Mistress of the Robes, who was assisted by various Wardrobe staff, including the laundresses.[14]

The royal bedchamber was a populous place and the queen was never alone; when she was accused of conducting an improper relationship with Leicester she pointed out that 'she could never understand how any single person could be displeased, seeing that she was always surrounded by her ladies of the bedchamber and maids of honour, who at all time could see whether there was anything dishonourable between her and her master of the horse'.[15]

At Whitehall Elizabeth used the same rooms as Henry VIII, including the bedchamber in which he died – a room known as the Dark Bedchamber as it had only a single window. At Richmond too she seems to have used her father's rooms; but at Greenwich the queen had an official 'standing' bedchamber and a private one beyond. At Hampton Court, early in her reign she moved her bedroom, giving it a new bay window overlooking the garden. Later she moved the room several more times and we learn of a 'red' bedchamber, a 'white' bedchamber, a 'middle' bedchamber and, by 1595-6, an 'old' bedchamber.[16]

All these bedrooms had adjacent stool rooms. Elizabeth's close stools, like Henry VIII's, were timber boxes with lids covered in crimson or black velvet, trimmed with ribbon and fringe and gilt nails and embroidered with the letters ER. The seats had cotton stuffing and the pans inside were of pewter. Each stool had a linen-lined leather carrying case to fit. It seems that Elizabeth was particularly fastidious about her close stools, as improbably large orders were placed for her personal use every year,

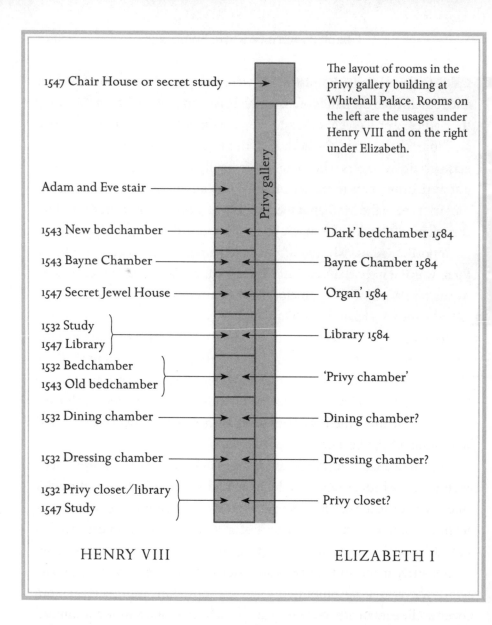

1547 Chair House or secret study ———→

The layout of rooms in the privy gallery building at Whitehall Palace. Rooms on the left are the usages under Henry VIII and on the right under Elizabeth.

Privy gallery

Adam and Eve stair ———→

1543 New bedchamber ———→ ←——— 'Dark' bedchamber 1584

1543 Bayne Chamber ———→ ←——— Bayne Chamber 1584

1547 Secret Jewel House ———→ ←——— 'Organ' 1584

1532 Study
1547 Library } ———→ ←——— Library 1584

1532 Bedchamber
1543 Old bedchamber } ———→ ←——— 'Privy chamber'

1532 Dining chamber ———→ ←——— Dining chamber?

1532 Dressing chamber ———→ ←——— Dressing chamber?

1532 Privy closet/library
1547 Study } ———→ ←——— Privy closet?

HENRY VIII   ELIZABETH I

which suggests that they were used for only a short time before being thrown away.[17] Unlike Henry VIII, whose groom stood by him when he relieved himself, Elizabeth retreated inside a tent when she sat on hers. In her stool rooms there was a canopy over the close stool supported by an iron frame with a gilded topknot; the top and valance were made of cloth of gold striped with crimson silk and the curtains of crimson sarsenet (a light silk). These buttoned up at the front to enclose the queen completely. This special stool canopy had a leather carrying case to make it portable.[18]

Psyche Served in her Bath, after Francesco Salviati, c.1530. This engraving gives a good impression of what a Tudor 'Turkish' bath would have been like. There is a stove in the corner, a bathtub and a pool; a bed can be glimpsed round the corner.

Most of the larger houses had bathrooms close to the main bedchamber. By the end of Henry's reign bathrooms were not small panelled hideaways, such as that built at Hampton Court in 1530. They were large and luxurious Turkish-style baths containing sunken pools. One such was excavated in the 1930s at Whitehall, lined with tiles and entered by three steps. They were heated by large glazed ceramic stoves stoked by coal. The remains of one of these stoves were excavated at Whitehall near the sunken bath and many of the panels bore the royal arms. The larger bathrooms, like those at Whitehall, Beaulieu and Greenwich, contained beds set into the walls and hung with curtains of richly coloured fabric; the bathrooms at Windsor were panelled in mirror glass and an upstairs bathroom at Whitehall had a shell grotto with a water fountain. There were large supplies of bathrobes and towels, as well as a selection of textiles for lining baths. Elizabeth used her father's baths at the main residences, but the bath at Greenwich was rebuilt for her in the late 1580s. The queen enjoyed bathing and on progress there was often no suitable place for her to do so, so she had a travelling bath made of iron that moved with her.[19]

Sunken bath built for Henry VIII, as revealed on the ground floor of Whitehall Palace in the 1930s.

Reconstruction of the large green glazed stove erected in Henry VIII's 'Turkish' bath at Whitehall in the late 1530s. Fragments of this stove were excavated in the 1930s and are now on show in the British Museum.

In most houses, immediately beneath the queen's privy chamber was the Wardrobe of the Robes. Elizabeth loved to dress up. On her death there were more than 1,900 items of clothing, including dresses, doublets, petticoats, cloaks and gloves, in her wardrobe. These were objects of great value, all but the undergarments being of extremely valuable textile embroidered with gold and silver thread and stitched with pearls and precious stones. No wonder the Wardrobe employed a dedicated locksmith.[20]

The Wardrobe of the Robes was part of the Great Wardrobe and, as with furniture and hangings, it had central depositories as well as the smaller wardrobes at individual houses for everyday use. The main reserve stores were at the Tower of London, Whitehall and Somerset Place. These wardrobes were manned and supervised the whole time. Protection from mice, moths and damp meant that fires were lit, and the places regularly fumigated. However, large quantities of clothes were also stored at the most regularly used standing houses in the Thames valley. Here the everyday work of preparing them for the queen was undertaken. Poles from which to hang garments were erected, cords strung across rooms for drying, firepans and other devices for ironing clothes were supplied, sweet powder was sprinkled over and around stored items. At Richmond the royal wardrobe grew to such a size that cupboards had to be built round the windows and up to the ceiling to accommodate it all. The queen's laundress washed her underclothes, which included ruffs, smocks, petticoats and cuffs – all of which prevented the sovereign's body from coming into contact with the rich fabric of her outer clothes. These were simply brushed – a brushing table was supplied for the Greenwich wardrobe in 1580.[21]

Access to her inner rooms was a favour that Elizabeth used to great effect. In 1584 Sir James Melville came as an envoy from the Scottish court to smooth the tense relationship between Elizabeth and Mary, Queen of Scots. The queen received him at Hampton Court for nine days and was determined to show off her talents, knowing Melville would report them, in detail, to Mary. He was thus treated to the most remarkable staged access to Elizabeth in her privy lodgings. Late one evening, after supper, she invited Melville into her bedchamber. They were not alone: in the far corner of the room were Burghley and Leicester. The queen led Melville to a cabinet in which were several portraits that she kept wrapped in paper with the names of the sitters written in her own hand. By candlelight, she showed him first Leicester's portrait, then a portrait of the Queen of Scots. She then showed him a ruby 'great like a racket ball'. Melville asked that Elizabeth send Mary either the painting of Leicester or the ruby as a present. Elizabeth refused both, but gave him a diamond instead. On another occasion, after dinner with Lord Hunsdon, Melville was taken to a 'quiet gallery' and posted outside a door to one of the queen's rooms to hear her play the virginals. After a time Melville audaciously drew aside the tapestry covering the door and, seeing that Elizabeth had her back to him, entered. After a few moments the queen saw him and rose, as Melville thought, to chastise him. In fact she then sat down on a cushion and, calling Lady Stafford from the next room to join them, invited the Scottish lord to do the same. Melville had a series of other encounters with Elizabeth, including several in the privy garden, a favourite place for early-morning audiences. The same technique of granting privileged access had been used by the queen during her courtship with the Duke of Anjou when his close friend and servant arrived at court to negotiate the marriage treaty. Elizabeth had warmed to this Frenchman and, at one point, allowed him to come into her bedchamber where he 'took' a nightcap and a handkerchief as trophies for the duke.[22]

Only once do we learn of an unauthorized incursion into the queen's bedroom. This took place at Nonsuch in September 1599. After the death of Leicester in 1588 his stepson, Robert Devereux, Earl of Essex, became the focus of the queen's affections. This elegant and energetic man, in his early twenties, was incredibly ambitious and, in the late 1580s and 1590s, led a number of high-profile military expeditions that won him fame, glory and the deepening affection of the queen. But his ambition grated and his pride and petulance won him enemies and turned the queen from him. Following an unsuccessful expedition to put down rebellion in Ireland, he made a truce with the Irish without Elizabeth's authorization. Knowing he was in deep trouble, he made the journey from Dublin to London in just four days, arriving at Nonsuch at 10am on 28 September. That morning, 'my Lord of Essex lighted at court gate in post, and made all haste up to the presence, and so to the privy chamber, and staid not until he came to the queen's bedchamber, where he found the queen newly up, her hair about her face'. The queen, without her wig or make-up, was both horrified and embarrassed, and the court was aghast: 'tis much wondered at here, that he went so boldly to her majesty's presence, she not being ready and he being so full of dirt and mire'. The next day Essex was called before the Privy Council and amongst the charges against him was his 'overbold going yesterday to her majesty's presence to her bedchamber'.[23]

Essex's incursion was both a breach of security and an affront to the queen's modesty. Elizabeth was intensely vain and, as she aged, more time each day was devoted to creating a mask of youthfulness.[24] But in the crowded court it was inevitable that she would be glimpsed *déshabillé*. In July 1565, while Leicester was giving a tour of Windsor Castle to a group of visiting ambassadors, Elizabeth, disturbed by the shouting of

Leicester's fool, appeared at the window of her bedchamber only in her nightgown. Later, dressed, the queen confronted the earl and his fool in anger. More than a decade later, in 1578, she was furious about a similar incident. Gilbert Talbot, the son of the Earl of Shrewsbury, was walking in the tiltyard at Greenwich at 8am. Glancing up, he saw the queen at a window 'and she was greatly ashamed thereof, for that she was unready, and in her nightstuff; so when she saw me after dinner, as she went to walk, she gave me a great phylypp on the forehead'.[25]

It was for this reason that at a number of residences rails were erected outside sensitive parts of the house to keep prying eyes away. Particularly vulnerable was the bedchamber at Oatlands, which, uniquely, faced into the outer court. Here stout rails were erected at a distance from its windows to stop people peering in. At Greenwich, rails were erected along the riverfront to keep the public away from the windows of the council chamber and the queen's holyday closet above the chapel. The rooms for the maids of honour at Whitehall, which were on the ground floor facing the privy garden, were similarly railed off.[26]

For large parts of Elizabeth's reign the Privy Council was anxious about the queen's security. They had good cause, as she was the centre of a number of plots and coups, both planned and executed. There were two issues. The first was one of majesty – how to balance access to the queen with security; how to allow her to come into contact with her people without exposing her to undue risk. The second was one of architecture: the royal houses, especially Whitehall, Greenwich and Hampton Court, were warrens of passages and staircases with back stairs and byways to the queen's inner chambers. Controlling this was incredibly problematic. A memo to the queen drawn up by Burghley soon after her accession set out the problem: 'if it may please your majesty to give order who shall take the charge of the backdoors to your chamberers chambers where laundresses, tailors, wardrobers, and such use to come; and that the same doors may be duly attended upon as becomes, but not to stand open but upon necessity'.

On a number of occasions regulations were tightened. The queen was horrified to hear of the murder of Mary, Queen of Scots' Secretary

David Rizzio by a gang of Scots nobles in the queen's bedchamber at the Palace of Holyroodhouse. At the English court all keys to the privy lodgings were withdrawn and everyone who wanted access had to enter from the privy chamber. After the Armada, with further waves of Spanish invasion anticipated, Burghley published sweeping restrictions on foreigners and on access to the court. Two staff of the chamber, with a clerk of the household, were to vet everyone coming to court and their servants. A place was to be set up outside each residence where petitioners were, in future, to come and leave their requests; none of these were to be allowed further without a special licence. Even more drastically, the harbingers and guard were to search for possible malefactors in an area of 2 miles around the court.[27]

Guards, locks and regulations were all very well, but the fundamental issue was that people who were known to the court could gain access easily. In 1601, when the queen's sometime favourite the Earl of Essex attempted a coup against the government, one of his captains was apprehended by guards at the very door of the privy chamber. Under interrogation he admitted that he had been trying to break in at suppertime, for at that time the queen was 'attended with a few ladies and such as that are known at court and have credit might easily come to the privy chamber door without suspicion'. The fact was that if you were known to the guards and the ushers it was possible to enter the royal lodgings and even gain access to the privy chamber.[28]

BUILDING THE PRIVY LODGINGS

By the end of Henry VIII's reign almost every royal residence had a privy gallery entered from the king's or queen's bedroom or closet. Indeed the fundamental private, or privy, unit within a Tudor royal house was a bedroom, closet and gallery. At Windsor the royal bedchamber had been built by Henry VII and, although there were two handsome rooms above it, probably used as a library, there was no other private accommodation the queen and her ladies could use. This is why, in 1576, the queen asked Burghley to organize a new gallery for her and the Office of Works architect Henry Hawthorne was instructed to prepare a number of options for her to look at. This was in response to the earlier farce of the Windsor terrace project, described in Chapter XIII, where everyone kept changing their minds. The option finally chosen not only provided a gallery and closets for the queen, it linked her bedchamber with the lodgings of the Earl of Leicester, the castle's constable.[29]

The new gallery was 100 feet long and 15 feet wide and terminated, at its west end, in a giant bay window, next to which was the door that communicated with Leicester's rooms. On the north side of the gallery was a square closet with a fireplace and bay window looking out towards Eton and the north. The floors beneath this contained a large staircase built round a solid newel. The stair did not come up to the queen's gallery, but was linked to it by a secret stair built into the wall that connected with the gallery through a hidden door in the bay window.

This was a very ingenious piece of planning. The secret stair allowed the queen to leave her lodgings and go down to the terrace, where she could mount her horse and ride out into the park. The stair also had another purpose. On the other side of the gallery, on the ground floor, accessed from the inner court, was an anteroom in which people could wait to be ushered up secretly to the queen's gallery. There had been back stairs before in many royal houses, but never had one been planned so carefully and integrated into the plan of the building so skilfully. Burghley was a master at this. In his own houses the queen's lodgings were serviced by secret stairs that allowed people to come and go to her inner chambers. Francis Bacon, the future Lord Chancellor and a nephew of Burghley, thought such devices allowed his uncle to 'walk invisible' at court.[30]

In July 1600, with the court away from Windsor, a young Moravian nobleman was shown the gallery and tells us that it contained a couch on which Elizabeth sat to consult privately with her ministers. Thanks to the records of Sir John Finet, James I's Master of Ceremonies, we learn that James used the royal lodgings at Windsor much as Elizabeth had done. When the Landgrave of Hesse came to see the king, he entered 'by the door of the Terras staires into the presence', so using the Elizabethan back stair.[31]

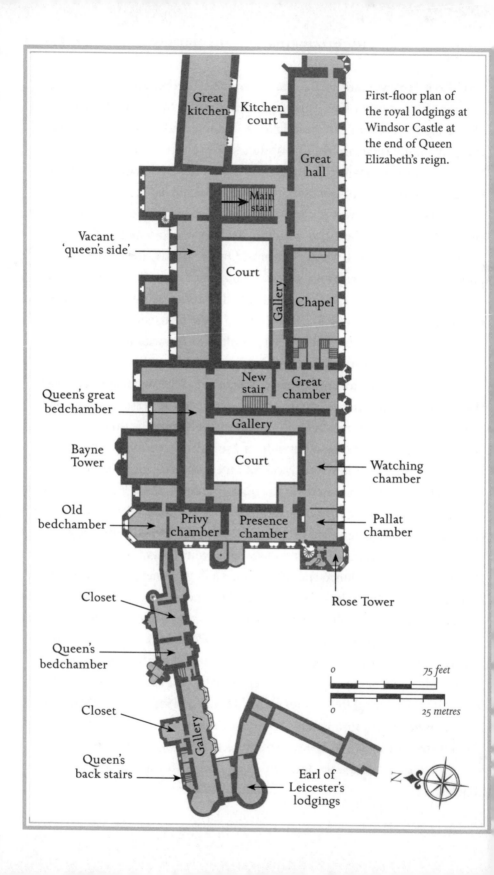

Great kitchen

Kitchen court

Great hall

First-floor plan of the royal lodgings at Windsor Castle at the end of Queen Elizabeth's reign.

Main stair

Vacant 'queen's side'

Court

Gallery

Chapel

New stair

Great chamber

Queen's great bedchamber

Gallery

Bayne Tower

Court

Watching chamber

Old bedchamber

Privy chamber

Presence chamber

Pallat chamber

Rose Tower

Closet

Queen's bedchamber

Closet

Gallery

Queen's back stairs

Earl of Leicester's lodgings

0   75 feet

0   25 metres

N

The new privy gallery was not only a place for business, it was also for private recreation. Roger Ascham, Elizabeth's former schoolmaster, would come to Windsor and read Greek and Latin texts with her; he claimed that 'beside her perfect readiness in Latin, Italian, French and Spanish, she readeth now here at Windsor more Greek everyday than some prebendary of this church doth read Latin in a whole week'.[32] This, and her work translating Boethius's *de Consolatione Philosophiae*, which she started at Windsor in 1593, is likely to have been undertaken in her gallery – a room linked to the rooms above her bedchamber and which probably contained her library.[33]

One of Hawthorne's plans shows a doorway between the end of the gallery and the room above the archway of the middle gate – part of the constable's lodgings. This link with Leicester's quarters had always been the intention. However, the money ran out before the constable's lodgings were incorporated into the scheme.[34] While this might have been the official reason for the halt in works, there was another, less mundane. In December 1584 Elizabeth sent Leicester to the Netherlands, where, the following January, he became Governor General. This was no banishment, for on September 27th he had spent the evening with the queen at Windsor and, the next morning, had written to Cecil: 'Mr Secretary, I find her majesty very desirous to keep me, she makes the cause only the doubtfulness of her own self ... She used very pitiful words to me of her fear she shall not live & wold not have me from her'.[35]

As the queen reluctantly parted with her favourite, work on the constable's lodgings stopped. For three years nothing happened and then, in 1588, in preparation for Leicester's return, work resumed, building a fine new entrance hall, staircase and other new rooms on the south side of the gate. However, it was all too late, for, with his health fatally weakened by his time in the Netherlands, Leicester died in September 1588 before his lodgings were complete. In 1590 Lord Howard of Effingham became constable, so it is very unlikely that a direct connection was ever made between the constable's lodging and the queen's bedchamber. [36]

Although the gallery was remodelled in the 1830s, when it was converted into the royal library, it is the only room from the hundreds of

Queen Elizabeth's gallery at Windsor Castle, built in 1582–4, the only Elizabethan royal interior to retain anything of its original character. Even so, it was converted into a library for King William IV and its walls are lined with bookcases and the original ceiling replaced by a copy.

Elizabethan royal interiors that gives some impression of what they were like. The original ceiling was very innovative – instead of making a fret of shallow timber batons enriched with low-relief decoration in timber (as in Henry VII's tower, shown on page 44), the whole ceiling was moulded out of plaster, creating a much more harmonious composition that flowed, in white, unifying the whole space. This was one of the first plaster ceilings in England and one that was widely copied. The fireplace, carved by the London joiner and carver Robert Pinckney, was a masterpiece that has already been mentioned.[37]

What is notable is how little the architecture of the interiors of Elizabethan royal residences changed during her long reign. In 1567–70 a new chimney with the queen's arms was installed at Whitehall and a new great portal to the presence chamber built at Greenwich. New windows were put in the presence chambers at Greenwich and Whitehall in

1580–81; the bedchamber at Greenwich was given a new frieze and cornice the following year. This was the sum total of Elizabethan improvements until the mid-1590s when, as will be explained, the queen felt that some of her father's interiors were in need of redecoration.[38]

The hard architecture of Elizabethan royal interiors was softened and enriched by textiles, which formed the principal decorative element. There were tapestries, of course, but it was the silks and velvets that gave these rooms their rich appearance. In big rooms like the Windsor gallery there were floor-to-ceiling curtains, hung from metal rods over the windows and creating splashes of bright colour. Increasingly galleries, in particular, were hung with paintings, for which richly carved and gilded frames were made. Paintings, too, had their own curtains hung from neat rails fixed to the walls above them.[39]

Smaller and more intimate closets were hung with silk and velvet. In 1596 Elizabeth had a room she called her 'cabinet' redecorated at Greenwich. The walls were hung with panes of yellow, crimson and light blue velvet, with white satin embroidery on the borders. The velvet field was embroidered with gold and twisted braid of gold and silver. A matching suite of five cloth-of-gold cushions was supplied, and long, yellow damask window curtains.[40] Textiles, of course, fade and wear out, so it might be expected that the queen spent more on soft furnishings than on the hard architectural elements. But even here there is a strong sense of frugality. Good housekeeping was a feminine quality much admired by the Tudors, and the Elizabethan court, much more than its predecessors, was prepared to recycle, mend and re-use. In 1563 the Wardrobe was ordered to use a gown 'of black velvet embroidered very richly with borders of damask and Venice gold' that had belonged to Edward VI and cut it up to be used to upholster a square stool and two matching cushions. Old canopies of state and cushions were taken from store and patched, given new fringes and extra stuffing to make them usable. The royal bed-maker pulled apart pillows and quilts, washed and dried the wool, carded it and put it back inside. Old beds were taken apart for their feathers and used to stuff new pillowcases. Old quilts were given new covers.[41]

No detailed financial accounts survive from the queen's personal expenditure, but a summary of ten years of money disbursed from her chamber shows that, apart from jewellery – which was by far her greatest outlay – and clothes, what she spent on the interior of her houses was minimal. Indeed in the late 1560s, after a spurt of expenditure on maintaining her residences, she personally ordered a stay on all works, and this was in a period when royal finances were improving.[42]

FIRE AND WATER

In the sixteenth century a preoccupation for everyone, rich or poor, was keeping warm. By Henry VIII's reign all royal rooms had fireplaces and the necessity to exclude draughts with shutters and curtains was well understood. Most courtier lodgings had fireplaces too; hardly a single room at a house like Hampton Court was without means of heating. Wood supplied by the royal woodyard was burnt on iron fire dogs, and charcoal from the scullery was delivered to the kitchens and sometimes to the royal lodgings. Courtiers with Bouche of Court (as explained on page 161) had a daily allowance of firewood, but so many fires burning at once was a hazard and fire buckets painted with the queen's arms, the date and the name of the house were distributed in case of emergency.[43]

Early sixteenth-century London had suffered a fuel crisis. By the middle of Henry VIII's reign it had become clear that it was impossible to sustain the City on the basis of burning timber. Various measures were enacted to preserve timber, but the court did not set a good example. It was a voracious consumer of firewood and the royal purveyors had the right to take logs from suppliers in London and mark people's trees for firewood in the countryside. So unpopular was this that in the end an agreement was reached with the City Corporation limiting the amount the court could purvey for each residence. Still the amounts required were enormous – some 9,000 cartloads a year.[44]

The answer was, of course, coal, and by the reign of Queen Mary London was already importing huge quantities from the north-east of England. William Harrison, in his 1577 description of England, told how the use of coal had spread from the forge to the kitchen and thence to the hall. However, for many the problem was that their chimney flues were suitable only for burning timber – coal smoke is heavier than wood smoke and a coal-burning chimney requires a strong draught. Not only that, but coal requires a grate in order to burn efficiently. Therefore switching to fossil fuel demanded physical changes to people's houses.[45]

Elizabeth was not a lover of coal smoke, but the greater calorific value of coal and its improved availability meant that it was increasingly used at court, first in stoves and braziers and then in fire grates. Coal baskets lined with leather and coal buckets made their appearance in royal rooms in Elizabeth's reign and grates were ordered for fireplaces. Large fire screens were placed in front of the fire to save the queen from the ferocity of direct heat.[46]

In winter Elizabeth particularly liked Richmond, as the royal lodgings, compactly arranged in a stone tower, could be kept warm easily. In the great hall there had been a hearth in the centre of the room, for ceremonial effect rather than heat, and so in 1578–9 a proper fireplace with a flue was inserted. Other country houses were less easy to keep warm. In February 1594, while the queen was at Hampton Court, she ordered three new curtains for the windows in her lodgings in the hope that she might keep out the cold. In the summer curtains were drawn over the mouths of the chimneypieces to keep out draughts.[47]

Supplying the royal houses with water was, in theory, easier than fuel. Since the Middle Ages conduits had supplied running fresh water and, during the reign of Henry VIII, almost every major residence was given a new water-supply system. One of these conduits, built in the 1540s at Hampton Court, survives and the neat brick-built conduit houses on Kingston Hill can still be glimpsed over garden walls driving into Kingston from London. Because Tudor monarchs were always afraid of poisoning, the conduit houses were given stout doors and heavy locks; brambles were planted round the heads to deter people from coming close. At Greenwich a fence was built round the spring in Blackheath where Queen Elizabeth's water was sourced. [48]

At Windsor, set high up on a scarp, water supply had always been problematic and Henry VIII built a long terrace containing water tanks to collect run-off from the castle roofs. The system never worked well and in Edward VI's reign work started on a conduit that ran to the castle from Blackmore Park, 5 miles away in Winkfield. The supply came into the upper court, to a fountain, then into settling tanks from where it was piped to the rest of the castle. The fountains at Hampton Court and Greenwich, likewise, were not just decorative: they performed the important task of helping to regulate the water supply for the kitchens and royal lodgings, allowing water round the clock, whether it was being drawn for use or not.[49]

✦XVI✦

THE LAST DECADES

Turning Point

W HEN THE DUKE OF ANJOU LEFT England in early February 1582, Elizabeth's life reached a turning point. It had been her last courtship, and she knew it. She was fifty and all hope of marriage and children was now gone. It was clear to everyone that an heir to the throne would not come from her womb but through an act of nomination, one that she resolutely refused to make. If Anjou's departure was a personal watershed, the defeat of the Spanish Armada six years later was a national one. While the Elizabethan regime had faced numerous political, military and economic challenges, a sense of shared purpose and common history kept the Privy Council together and the government effective despite the queen's unpredictability. By the late 1580s her government was aging, but the queen refused to refresh the council, the nobility or those around her at court. The 1590s were difficult years: the country was at war; there was drought, famine and disease; the economy was hit by inflation, falling wages and high taxation; in Parliament there was anxiety about social disorder; and the politics of the court were complex and strained.

At the centre of this was an old woman who was tired and lonely, and who resolutely refused to confront her mortality or the destiny of the country over which she ruled. The manufactured image of a virgin queen ordained by God to usher in a golden age of peace and prosperity remained unchanging in the face of Elizabeth's physical decline. An unsympathetic observer, the Jesuit priest Father Anthony Rivers, reporting on goings-on at court in March 1603, said that 'it was commonly observed this Christmas that her Majesty, when she came to be seen, was continually painted, not only all over her face but her very neck and breast also, and that the same was in some places half an inch thick.'[1]

During the 1590s, as reality and ideal moved further apart, Elizabeth not only used face paint to bolster an image of eternal youth and glory but increasingly emphasized her personal magnificence through her surroundings. John Clapham, an historian and one of Lord Burghley's household, wrote about the queen soon after her death. He observed that 'in her latter time, when she showed herself in public, she was always magnificent in apparel, supposing happily thereby, that the eyes of her people, being dazzled by the glittering aspect of these accidental ornaments would not so easily discern the marks of age and decay of natural beauty'. He was right – the evidence shows that during the late 1580s and 1590s the setting of the court became more lavish and ceremony and pageantry increasingly elaborate and formal.[2]

One of the most prominent manifestations of this was the rising importance of what became known as the Accession Day Tilts. Stimulated by the 1570 papal bull excommunicating Elizabeth and absolving any would-be assassin of her murder, and by her recovery from an attack of smallpox at Hampton Court in 1572, Elizabeth's accession day, 17 November, became a day of national rejoicing and celebration. Across the nation bells were rung, bonfires were lit, guns were fired and, on their knees, the faithful people of England blessed Elizabeth as their gift from the Almighty. In due course special service books were produced, collecting together psalms, readings and prayers suitable for the commemoration of such a significant national feast. At court, during the 1570s, the day was taken as an excuse for young courtiers to joust in the queen's honour. In the 1580s these informal tournaments were transformed into a court spectacular, becoming nothing less than the most important day in the court calendar.

The Accession Day Tilts were held at Whitehall, the ceremonial heart of the kingdom, and the place where the largest numbers could appreciate them. The event marked the start of the winter season and the drawing in of the nights. Before the return of the court to Whitehall, the Office of Works would have been labouring for weeks setting up the tiltyard with staging for the spectators and an elaborate prefabricated pavilion for the judges. The queen could observe from the tiltyard gallery – an extension of the privy gallery reached through the Whitehall gatehouse over the street. Here, under the gallery's gilded ceiling, the wardrobe laid out chairs, carpets and cushions, creating a luxurious and comfortable royal box. Courtiers took their specially assigned seats below the windows of the gallery and punters paid 12d or more for a place in the stands. The jousters, almost all members of the queen's band of Gentlemen Pensioners, were accompanied by their servants in livery or fancy dress and ascended the stairs at the end of the gallery to deliver a speech to the queen and present their coats of arms painted on wooden shields. Afterwards, the shields were kept by Elizabeth and hung in the Water Gallery, the passage leading to her privy landing stage. To each one was attached a dedication, and these cheesy and sycophantic verses were carefully recorded by foreign visitors: 'Thou art the light from whom others take their brilliance' is a typical example.[3]

The lavishness of these occasions was matched by a revival of opulence on progress. During the difficult 1580s, Elizabeth's summer perambulations were confined to a series of stays in houses close to

Drawing of the judges' pavilion and tiltyard at Whitehall made by the heralds at the College of Arms.

London, particularly in Surrey, but in 1591 she returned to the ambitious sort of progress that she had enjoyed in the 1570s, taking the court through Sussex into Hampshire and on to Portsmouth and Southampton; she even contemplated a visit to the Isle of Wight. The entertainments and hospitality were some of the most lavish and expensive of her reign and marked a new phase in the bolstering of the queen's image. But things had changed: some courtiers were markedly reluctant to have the queen to stay – they could see no long-term benefit in the huge financial outlay.[4]

Most of the lavish building for tilts and in progress-time was ephemeral, or at least temporary, but the reality was that by the early 1580s the permanent infrastructure of the queen's principal residences was getting very shabby. Twenty years of tight-fisted Elizabethan maintenance had not burnished the fading splendour of Henrician interiors. The dominant figure in the Office of Works, after the death of the surveyor Lewis Stockett in 1579, was Thomas Fowler, not an architect or designer but a meticulous administrator. Before Burghley promoted him to be Paymaster of the Works on Stockett's death, Fowler had been in the more junior post of Comptroller for twenty years, so he was a master of the arcane details of Tudor accounting practice. Over the sixteen years he was at the helm of the royal works, he kept the purse strings tightly drawn. His average expenditure was around £4,100 a year; there were a few projects, already noted in this book, but Fowler was principally there to safeguard against architectural extravagance and waste.

His death in 1595 coincided with the upsurge of magnificence at court and a determination, probably on the queen's part, to rejuvenate the once splendid interiors at her main houses. Special extra issues had been made by the Exchequer in the last two years of Fowler's life, but, after his death, the regular expenditure at the Office of Works shot up and stayed nearly £1,000 a year higher than during his tenure.[5]

Though the increase in outlay tells part of the story, the whole picture is revealed only by looking at the account rolls for the last decade of the queen's reign. Carefully dissecting these, and the meticulous accounts of the Great Wardrobe, it can be seen that Fowler's death was followed by a concerted campaign to redecorate the principal interiors of the royal houses. At Greenwich the presence chamber and privy chamber were redecorated and then completely 'new made' in 1599–1600; then, in 1601–2, the presence chamber ceiling with its forty-two pendants was regilded and the flat ground painted with the very valuable blue paint known as bice. At Richmond, too, the main state rooms were redecorated and gilded; even at Whitehall the privy chamber was regilded. The Great Wardrobe was engaged in the programme of refurbishment and at all the main houses large sets of new furniture were made. In Richmond, in particular, in 1601 there was a vast programme of refurnishing, some of the details of which we shall come to.[6]

Anthonis van den Wyngaerde, view of the south front of Hampton Court from the river, 1558. On the right is the watergate, a massive brick-covered landing stage. The south front of the house can be seen behind the gardens. At the top is the great hall and to the left the great gatehouse. The plan on page 406 identifies the various elements.

GARDENS

One of the areas in which the queen showed particular interest in her old age was gardens. None of the major Tudor royal residences was without a garden and the largest and most important houses –Whitehall, Hampton Court, Greenwich and Richmond – had extensive and elaborate ones. Gardens are ephemeral and, without drawings or paintings, almost impossible to visualize today. Yet thanks to Anthonis van den Wyngaerde, a Flemish topographical artist who came to England at the start of Elizabeth's reign, we have a magnificent series of drawings that accurately depict the Elizabethan gardens at Hampton Court. These had been laid out by Henry VIII in the 1530s and were meticulously maintained through the Tudor era.

In the early 1990s, when I was Curator of the Historic Royal Palaces, I led what is still probably the most ambitious garden archaeology project ever to be undertaken in England. This was a major excavation on the site

of the Hampton Court privy garden – not, as it happens, to find the Tudor garden, but to restore the seventeenth-century one that replaced it. Almost all of the Tudor garden had been scraped away by King William III's builders, but we did find some of it and we did focus closely on the evidence for it in the documents and drawings.

The gardens on the south front were divided into three compartments by high brick walls faced with earthen banks. The privy garden was the largest of these, divided into squares by 180 wooden posts topped with heraldic beasts, 96 stanchions and 960 yards of rail painted in white and green chevrons. The squares were, according to an Elizabethan visitor, 'filled with red brick-dust, some with white sand and some with green lawn very much resembling a chess board'.[7] The effect was designed to be seen either from the first- and second-floor long galleries or from the raised banks on the garden's periphery. Once the visitor descended into the flat of the garden, they could appreciate twenty brass sundials and the violets, strawberries, roses, mint, sweet williams, gillyflowers and primroses planted round the edges of the squares. Closer to the building, and around the walls, were some small trees, including damsons.[8]

Privy gardens were an extension of the monarch's privy lodgings. At all the major houses, private stairs led down from the privy lodgings to the privy garden, and at Hampton Court ground-floor lodgings opened directly on to it. Just as in the privy lodgings, access was restricted to only a very small number of trusted household officials who had keys to the garden gate. A painting of Elizabeth I by Marcus Gheeraerts the Elder shows her in front of one of her privy gardens with a Yeoman of the Guard at the gate ensuring that only those permitted had access (see plate section). Elizabeth would regularly give audiences in her gardens; on one such occasion at Oatlands in 1602 a visiting foreign duke was led to the privy garden where he was brought to the queen by several lords, and there they knelt on the grass while the queen addressed them.[9]

To the south of the privy garden was the Mount. This was essentially a huge mound of earth topped with a two-storey circular banqueting house used for banquets – small-scale after-dinner refreshments of the most succulent sweet delicacies. As it was so far from the privy kitchen it contained its own subterranean cellars and kitchen. Though it was designed for more intimate repasts, when Henry and Jane Seymour arrived at Hampton Court as man and wife in May 1537 a buffet was set up in it to display the king's plate, which suggests some degree of formality. The entrance was reached by a spiral path that curled its way round the mount, lined by rosemary and sixteen more heraldic beasts on poles. In the surrounding garden were yew, bay and holly trees brought from the charterhouse at Richmond and cut into shapes. The Duke of Nájera, visiting Hampton Court in 1544, saw topiary in the form of 'monsters', which in 1599 were described as being 'all manner of shapes, men and women, half men and half horse, sirens, serving maids with baskets'.[10]

The third part of the southern gardens was the Pond Yard. Here there were three ponds set in a matrix of low walls with stone pillars supporting forty heraldic beasts holding shields. Planted round them were hawthorn, hazel and privet hedges, white roses, woodbine and hops. At first the ponds were filled from the Thames with buckets – a very slow process – but soon a well was dug with a mechanical pump and water was drawn from there. Although ornamental, the ponds also had a practical purpose as ponds for breeding and storing fish. Fresh flowing water was kept running, as the overflow from the water-supply system was directed into them from the cisterns, running first through the fountain in Fountain Court. From here sluices could be opened to let the water drain into the Thames.[11]

These gardens, executed over six or seven years and carefully maintained by all three of Henry's successors, were integrated with the architecture of the house. The various compartments were like additional courtyards, each extending the crenellated skyline, gleaming with gilded vanes and domes, towards the Thames. It was a uniquely English product, quite unlike anything being made in France, but perhaps closer to the urban gardens of the Burgundian dukes.[12]

We don't know who designed the first gardens at Hampton Court but, at least initially, Henry VIII continued to employ Wolsey's gardener, John Chapman, as his chief designer; Edmund Griffith (or Gryffin), who was in charge of creating the Mount garden, replaced him in 1533. One of

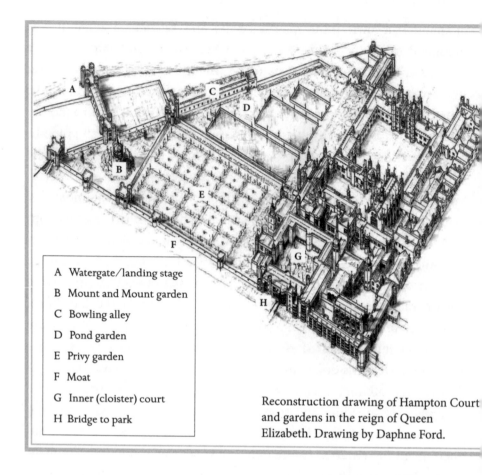

A Watergate/landing stage

B Mount and Mount garden

C Bowling alley

D Pond garden

E Privy garden

F Moat

G Inner (cloister) court

H Bridge to park

Reconstruction drawing of Hampton Court and gardens in the reign of Queen Elizabeth. Drawing by Daphne Ford.

Griffith's assistants, advisors or possibly designers seems to have been a mysterious French priest who had a key to the king's garden and planted some of the Mount. Yet the gardeners can have played only a partial role in the design – the Office of Works architects must have designed the framework. [13]

Edward VI was very interested in gardening, and it is noticeable that all the royal gardens received special care and attention during his reign. When the young king was whisked away from Hampton Court by the Duke of Somerset in 1549, one of his complaints was that Windsor Castle, where he was confined, had no garden. In May 1548 a warrant was issued to Lawrence Bradshaw, Surveyor of the Works, to undertake £28 18s worth of improvements and alterations in the great and Mount gardens at Hampton Court and to institute a new programme of weeding and maintenance.[14]

The chance survival of the book of monthly accounts kept by Hugh Braderton, the keeper of Edward VI's and Mary I's gardens at Hampton Court, gives a vivid sense of the effort and expense that went into keeping these high-maintenance gardens in top condition. In October 1552 the hedges were cut and the borders trimmed, while five weeders worked for ten days; the following month there were six weeders and they worked for eighteen days. In December Braderton presented no bill, but in January work began in earnest on cleaning the gravel paths, and in February on digging the beds. In March eighteen days were spent in pruning the hedges and trees before sowing began in April. The accounts for May and June are much busier, with a great deal of weeding and tidying of beds. In all, Braderton's bill for October 1552–June 1553 amounted to £13 14s 3d.[15]

Elizabeth too was enthusiastic about gardens and, in 1583, a French gardener, John Markye, was appointed to review the planting at Hampton Court. This he did, with a small team of assistants (including an interpreter), over a period of three years. His bill survives, listing the purchase of timber poles to make arbours, box plants for hedging, several holly trees, a bay tree, a 'musk tree', lavender plants, double primroses and daisies. The bill came to a substantial £420 in total.[16]

Whereas Henry VIII completed his gardens at Hampton Court, at Whitehall his children inherited work in progress. Henry had relocated the privy garden to the north of the privy gallery and, as we have seen, created a cloister round it that was intended for court processions and was later converted, by Edward VI, into the Preaching Place. Thus, when Elizabeth came to the throne, there was no privy garden at Whitehall, so in 1561 she started the process of reorganizing the gardens to create one. She wanted to revert to the original arrangement of a private royal garden on the south of the privy gallery, approached by the Adam and Eve staircase. So she moved the orchard that had been planted there into a new compartment to the far south of the gardens and re-established a privy garden close to her lodgings.

The new garden was seen by a foreign visitor in 1585:

> In it there are thirty-four high, painted, various animals of wood with gilt horns placed upon columns. On these columns are, further, banners with the Queen's coats of arms. In the centre of the garden is a beautiful fountain and thereto a large gnomon which shows the hours in thirty different ways. Between the herbaceous plants that are set in the garden there are beautiful, pleasant grassy walks. The plants are artistically set out in various ways and surrounded by hedges trimmed in the form of seats.

This description suggests that, as well as being fascinated by the sundial, the visitor was probably spared the full effect of the fountain, for another visitor tells us that 'water from it, squirting up through concealed pipes, soaks people standing near'.[17]

In 1580, in preparation for the reception of the Duke of Anjou, Elizabeth laid out a pretty new garden on the riverside in front of the queen's long gallery and south of the privy bridge. After levelling the ground and preparing it, workmen were paid for 'making of borders and setting and sowing divers kinds of trees and herbs to bring it to full perfection of a garden'. This garden was later used as an aviary and it may be that the queen, who was fond of birds, was the first to use it for the purpose. At Richmond, too, improvements were made for the reception of the French: bays, sweet briar and jasmine were planted in new borders and new walks were made in the 'pineapple garden'.[18]

But it was at Greenwich where the queen made the most improvements in her old age. She enjoyed picnicking and sitting in the gardens, particularly those to the north of the old friary. Here a little room with fireplaces was made for the winter enjoyment of the orchard and, in 1589, a 'great seat' was made under her favourite mulberry tree to be used in summer 'when we sup abroad'. Supported on a brick base, this had carved and painted human figures and four pillars to support a canopy. The seat was covered in lead so it could be left outside the year round. Nearby was a standing where she could enjoy the view of the garden and in 1593 she took delivery of a new canopy for it. It was made of carnation-coloured camlet lined with white sarsenet decorated with flowers and trimmed with lace fringe. It had curtains of crimson-and-white striped taffeta.[19]

TURKISH DELIGHTS

In the last year of Elizabeth's life John Harington, her godson, called the queen 'a lady shut up in a chamber from all her subjects and most of her servants, and seen seldom but on holy days'. John Clapham, the Elizabethan historian, suggested that 'she came abroad more seldom to make her presence the more grateful and applauded by the multitude, to whom things rarely seen are in a manner new'. Whatever her motivation, it is certainly the case that in the last years of her life the queen was increasingly reclusive, spending most of her time in her privy lodgings and coming forth into the public rooms only on Sundays.[20] From 1574 it is increasingly apparent that the way these rooms were furnished was changing. Already incorporating Turkish-style bathing arrangements, the queen's bedchamber and secret lodgings became more and more Ottoman in appearance. This, perhaps, should not be a matter of surprise, as the Tudor period almost exactly coincided with the high point of power and influence of Ottoman Turkey, particularly under Süleyman (1520–66), whom Europeans called 'The Magnificent'. From the reign of Henry VII onwards the Turk became a subject of both fascination and unease, one that was already reflected in the 1520s at Windsor Castle.

In the mid-1520s Henry VIII commissioned a large wall mural in the presence chamber at Windsor, the subject of which was the Siege of Rhodes. There had been two sieges of the island base of the Knights of St John of Jerusalem; famously, they won the first in 1480 but, in 1522, at a second siege, they capitulated to the Turks and withdrew to Crete. Henry's new mural showed this defeat at the hands of the Turkish navy. We have no image of the painting and do not know the artist, but whoever got the commission probably copied one of the many woodcuts of the siege – perhaps one by the prolific German engraver Sebald Beham.[21]

Although there was a certain horror and disapproval of Muslims, especially Turks, the Tudors were impressed by their military achievements and interested in their customs, social life, dress, diet and furnishings: in fact, Henry VIII hung a full-length portrait of Süleyman at Whitehall and liked to dress up in Turkish fancy dress. Venice was, at first, the conduit through which Ottoman luxuries flowed to northern Europe, but, as a result of the political and economic isolation caused by Elizabeth's excommunication, England signed a trading agreement with the Ottoman sultan Murad III in 1581. This gave English merchants preferential trading status amongst the nations of the west. A decade later, perhaps a thousand Elizabethan merchants, diplomats, sailors and craftsmen were trading with the Islamic world around the Mediterranean, from Marrakesh to Constantinople, and, after the defeat of the Spanish

The siege of Rhodes was an extremely popular subject in Henry VIII's reign. We do not know what the mural of the siege at Windsor looked like, but it almost certainly will have followed one of the published engravings of the event, perhaps that of Hans Sebald Beham, done in 1522, as seen here.

Armada, the links with the Islamic world became more strongly political as the opportunities to align England and the North African Ottoman states against Spain became evident.[22]

A fascinating aspect of this economic and political alliance was the relationship that Elizabeth was able to forge with the sultana, Murad III's wife. Letters were written and gifts exchanged. On the advice of the English ambassador, the sultana sent Elizabeth 'a suit of princely attire being after the Turkish fashion', with 'an upper gown of cloth of gold very rich, an under gown of cloth of silver, and a girdle of Turkey work, rich and faire'. Elizabeth was to respond by sending an organ and an English-made coach worth £600, still a relative novelty in England.[23]

While monarchs traded gifts, so merchants, diplomats and artists began to take an interest in Ottoman design and, as early as 1527, pattern books of Islamic designs were being published; in 1548 one was issued in London. These designs mixed and melded with streams of grotesque ornament from fifteenth-century Italy, as well as with native Gothic influences, and were applied to metalwork architectural decoration and especially textiles.[24]

It was Ottoman textiles that had the greatest impact on the Tudor court. The first to be imported to England in any volume were carpets. At first knotted pile carpets (as opposed to woven textiles) were rare and generally used as coverings for furniture rather than being placed on the floor. In the early sixteenth century such carpets, made in the Near East, came to England through Venice, and we know that Wolsey had to haggle hard to get a delivery of Turkish carpets for Hampton Court. By 1547 there were around 800 carpets in the various royal houses, half of which came from Turkey. Around fifty or sixty were large carpets used under canopies of state and on the floors of the king's innermost rooms, but most were for covering cupboards, tables, window sills and other timber and stone surfaces.[25]

The late Elizabethan court began to use these Ottoman textiles very differently. Though Henry VIII had both carpets and cushions, it is not clear that he used them in the Ottoman way to recline on the floor. Elizabeth, however, did, and increasingly she adopted a semi-recumbent

Engraving from Thomas Geminus, *Morysse and Damashin renewed and increased, very profitable for Goldsmythes and Embroiderars*, London, 1548. This is an example of one of the collections of Ottoman designs that began to be published towards the end of Henry VIII's reign.

posture both in public and private. From around 1574 it is noticeable that the queen was ordering very large numbers of cushions and carpets: that year 32 embroidered cushions 'of tissue, cloth of gold, velvet and satin lined with satin and leather' were ordered, plus another 26 cushions; there were also 4 great carpets, 6 demi-carpets and 50 small carpets, all Turkish. Other carpet orders were even larger: on one occasion a huge job lot of 100 carpets was delivered.[26]

Carpets were routinely laid on the floor of the privy chamber and sometimes in the presence chamber and on these were stacked cushions for the queen to recline on. Courtiers or ambassadors who wished to speak to her knelt at her side. In 1581 a canopy of state was made to match cushions of white embroidered satin and, a few years later, for the first time, a new cloth of estate, embroidered with the queen's arms, garter and crown imperial, was made and, instead of a chair of estate to match it, twelve matching cushions were supplied for the queen to recline on. The set also included seven side chairs, six square stools and two footstools for elsewhere in the room. The cushions were set on a very low and wide

Ottoman-style chair, almost like a day bed. In 1601 we have a description of one of these: 'a great chair of timberwork a yard wide with two wings to the elbows'. It was covered with peach-coloured cloth of silver fringed with silver and silk and upholstered with down pillows. A canopy of the same material was constructed, and matching were two square stools, a footstool and six cushions. A visitor to Nonsuch in 1599 saw the queen on a low chair just like this; she was 'sat down on a seat covered with red damask and cushions embroidered in gold thread, and so low was the chair that the cushions almost lay on the ground, and there was a canopy above, fixed very ornately to the ceiling'.[27]

When the French ambassador, the Sieur de Maisse, was brought to Whitehall to see the queen in 1597, he was ushered into the presence chamber where 'there was a cushion made ready' for him. On this he lounged until the time was ready for him to enter the privy chamber. The queen was in here on a 'low chair' under the canopy. This apparent informality was nothing of the sort. The cushions, carpets and canopies, though in Ottoman style, were as much revered objects as the formal, stiff chairs that they had replaced. One day, we learn from an Elizabethan letter-writer, 'some young gentlemen being more bold than well-mannered, did stand on the carpet of the cloth of estate, and did almost lean on the cushions. Her Highness found fault with my lord chamberlain and vice chamberlain, and with the gentleman ushers for suffering such disorders'.[28]

The late Elizabethan court, though for some a stifling place presided over by an intemperate, vain and fussy old woman, was at its most exotic and decadent in its last decade. The houses had never looked more glitzy or been so richly furnished, court entertainments had never been so spectacular, progresses never so lavish and the queen was herself, for better or worse, a remarkable spectacle. Though visibly aging, Elizabeth was healthy and energetic right to the last months of her life, though by then many had started to look to Scotland and to her yet unnamed heir, King James VI.

Epilogue

It was in the inner lodgings at Richmond that Elizabeth died. Her last days were observed and recorded by her godson, Robert Carey, who arrived at court in early March 1603 and was admitted into Elizabeth's drawing room on a Saturday evening. He found her lying on cushions on the floor in a state of deep depression. Asked where she would like to worship the following morning, she said the great closet, which was duly prepared. The next morning she did not want to rise and asked that the privy closet next to the privy chamber be made ready. Cushions were laid at the door of the closet and the queen lay there listening to the service. For four days and nights she remained on cushions on the floor before she was persuaded to take to her bed. When asked what was wrong, the queen reportedly said, 'I am not sick, I feel no pain, and yet I pine away'; it was as if she had given up on life. Neither eating nor drinking, she became speechless and by 24 March she was dead. The lineal descent of princes from Henry VII, which had continued in one family for 117 years, was cut off with the thread of her life.[1]

It had been a long time since a monarch had died, but everyone knew the routine. Elizabeth, like her siblings, was not dead until her body was in the tomb. The full machinery of the household continued to operate until her funeral cortège, half a mile long, had reached Westminster and her chief officers had broken their wands of office and thrown them on top of the coffin. By this time King James was well on his way to London, his thoughts far from the doleful events in Westminster Abbey.

Despite the passing of fifty-six years since the death of Henry VIII, when James VI and I arrived in London he inherited most of the residences that had been bequeathed by Henry to his son. Some, as we have seen, had been sold, demolished or just abandoned, but the principal manors sprawled on the banks of the Thames like little gilded towns set in their pleasure grounds. These places, built by the father, had been tended, extended and improved by his younger daughter.

In this book I have tried to show that Elizabeth, who has not had a reputation as a builder, was actually a connoisseur of fine architecture and interior decoration. Though her building works did not match in scale those of her father, they did not need to. She did not require more houses; what she needed to do was adapt them to her taste and to the changing requirements of the times. Her remodelling of the inner court at Greenwich, the construction of a privy gallery and chapel at Windsor, her substantial works at Whitehall and Westminster, the rebuilding of Grafton House, her remodelling of Woking House, the massive programme of stable and coach-house construction, the creation and remodelling of gardens and her passion for fountains represent a substantial architectural opus.

This is why England was a land of milk and honey to the thirty-seven-year-old king of Scots. His residences in Scotland were still like those of Henry VII, and in most houses he lived in just three great tapestry-hung rooms. As he made his way south, staying in the mansions of Elizabethan courtiers, he began to get a sense of what he would find in London, but nothing could have prepared him for the size and splendour of Whitehall, Hampton Court, Greenwich and Richmond.

In 1603 England had a royal family again: James brought with him his Danish queen, Anne, the nine-year-old Prince Henry, his three-year-old brother Charles, and their sister, Princess Elizabeth, aged seven. Each required their own establishment and in particular James urgently needed to resolve the question of the queen's household. He asked Burghley's son, Sir Robert Cecil, to look into the rights and privileges of a queen of England. Based on his research in the state archives, Cecil proposed that Anne's jointure should be modelled on that of Katharine of Aragon, the last royal princess to marry an English king. In all, Anne's settlement was worth a handsome £6,376 a year. None of the estates held by Katharine was now available: the Tudor queens' London residence, Baynard's Castle, for instance, had fallen out of royal use before the end of Henry VIII's reign. Cecil had therefore to propose alternatives. In

London he suggested that the queen use Somerset Place, which, though a little old-fashioned, was the obvious choice.[2]

The Office of Works' focus, though, was on the queen's lodgings in the major residences. These rooms had last been used regularly by Philip of Spain, and before that by Queen Katherine Parr. The queen's side at Eltham was renovated, as James seems to have preferred that at first to Greenwich; but later Greenwich was modernized too. Work also went ahead at Whitehall to bring the queen's rooms into use. In 1603 Prince Henry was lodged at St James's, the house built by Henry VIII for the heir to the throne. When, in 1610, he was created Prince of Wales, he was granted Richmond, Woodstock and a house at Byfleet; new work was commissioned at Richmond almost immediately. The following year Queen Anne was granted Oatlands as her country seat and she started major renovations there.

But it wasn't only architecture and its rich trimmings that James inherited. He took on a whole new way of life, a court system that had been developed and refined from the time of Henry VII onwards. The royal houses had been designed to facilitate and enhance the formality and magnificence of the Tudor court – they were a building type as specialized as any cathedral or fortress. James had to come to terms with this, and it wasn't easy. As much as the riches of England dazzled him, so did the stifling formality and etiquette of the court frustrate him. In 1607 he commissioned two new informal residences at Newmarket and Royston from where he could hunt and where, in the evening, he could retire to his study with his books.

James did like splendour and grandeur: he bought Theobalds as a royal residence and commissioned a great new stone banqueting house in Whitehall, but, like Elizabeth, he never commissioned a new house or entirely rebuilt an old one. His son, Charles I, was also an architectural enthusiast and enjoyed redecorating and modernizing his houses; but, like James, he never built a new one. Thus, as England plunged into a bloody civil war in the 1640s, the royal family were still living in houses built more than a century before by the first two Henrys. Whatever might be said about the quality of their legacy, nobody could doubt its longevity.

Notes

L&P Hen. VIII   *Letters and Papers, Foreign and Domestic, of the reign of Henry VIII,*
                    1509–1547, ed. J. S. Brewer *et al.,* 21 vols and addenda (1862–1932)

NUL   Nottingham University Library

RPTE   S. J. Thurley, *The Royal Palaces of Tudor England: Architecture and Court*
         Life 1460–1547 (New Haven and London, 1993)

State Papers   *State Papers Published under the Authority of Her Majesty's Commission,*
                   King Henry VIII, 11 vols (London, 1830–52)

Stat. Realm   *Statutes of the Realm,* ed. A. Luders, T. E. Tomlins, J. Raithby *et al.,* 11 vols
                  (1810–28)

TNA   The National Archives

I A GRAND INHERITANCE

[1] E. Impey (ed.), *The White Tower* (New Haven and London, 2008), pp. 150–2; A. Keay, *The Crown Jewels* (London, 2011), pp. 20–2; J. Ashbee, *The Jewel Tower* (London, 2013), pp. 19–28.

[2] J. Ashdown-Hill, *The Last Days of Richard III* (Stroud, 2010), pp. 48–61.

[3] C. Skidmore, *Bosworth: The Birth of the Tudors* (London, 2013), pp. 283–313; G. Foard and A. Curry, *Bosworth 1485: A Battlefield Rediscovered* (Oxford, 2013), pp. 179–97.

[4] *HKW,* i, pp. 266–7; J. M. Luxford, 'The Collegiate Church as Mausoleum', in C. Burgess and M. Heale (eds), *The Late Medieval English College and its Context* (Woodbridge, 2008), pp. 128–9.

[5] J. Schofield, *St Paul's Cathedral Before Wren* (Swindon, 2011), pp. 163–5, 324–5; D. J. Guth, 'Richard III, Henry VII and the city: London politics and the "Dun Cowe"', in R. A. Griffiths and J. W. Sherborne (eds), *Kings and Nobles in the Later Middle Ages: a tribute to Charles Ross* (Gloucester, 1986), pp. 185–204.

[6] C. L. Kingsford, 'Historical Notes on Medieval London Houses', *London Topographical Record,* x (1916), pp. 59–62; *HKW,* iv, pp. 50–2.

[7] R. A. Griffiths and R. S. Thomas, *The Making of the Tudor Dynasty* (Gloucester, 1985), pp. 32–5.

[8] T. F. Tout, *Chapters in the Administrative History of Medieval England,* iv (Manchester, 1928), pp. 405–12; D. Keene, 'Wardrobes in the City: Houses of Consumption, Finance and Power', in M. Prestwich, R. Britnell and R. Frame (eds), *Thirteenth Century England,* vii (Woodbridge, 1999), pp. 63–4; *HKW,* ii, pp. 980–1.

[9] A. R. Martin, *Franciscan Architecture in England* (Manchester, 1937), pp. 176–204.

[10] M. K. Jones and M. G. Underwood, *The King's Mother: Lady Margaret Beaufort, Countess of Richmond and Derby* (Cambridge, 1992), pp. 51–2.

[11] A. V. Antonovics, 'Henry VII, King of England, "By the Grace of Charles VIII of France"', in Griffiths and Sherborne (eds), *Kings and Nobles,* pp. 169–84.

[12] Henry VII's movements, as described in this and subsequent chapters, are taken from the excellent scholarly itinerary in L. L. Ford, 'Conciliar Politics and Administration in the Reign of Henry VII' (unpublished PhD thesis, University of St Andrews, 2001), pp. 205–83.

[13] F. Taylor and J. S. Roskell (eds), *Gesta Henrici Quinti: The Deeds of Henry V*

(Oxford, 1975), pp. 12–13; C. Given-Wilson, *The Royal Household and the King's Affinity: Service, Politics and Finance in England, 1360–1413* (New Haven and London, 1986), pp. 29–35.

[14] C. T. Allmand, *Henry V* (London, 1992), pp. 272–7; *HKW*, i, pp. 265–8.

[15] *HKW*, ii, pp. 994–1002; R. Cowie and J. Cloake, 'An archaeological survey of Richmond Palace, Surrey', *Post-Medieval Archaeology*, xxxv (2001), pp. 6–16.

[16] J. Harvey, *English Medieval Architects: a Biographical Dictionary down to 1550*, rev. edn (Gloucester, 1984), pp. 330–1; J. A. A. Goodall, *Warkworth Castle and Hermitage* (London, 2006), p. 17; A. Emery, *Greater Medieval Houses of England and Wales*, i (Cambridge, 1996), pp. 144–50.

[17] C. L. Kingsford, 'On Some London Houses of the Early Tudor Period', *Archaeologia*, lxxi (1921), pp. 21–50.

[18] S. J. Thurley, 'Whitehall Palace and Westminster 1400–1600: a royal seat in transition', in D. R. M. Gaimster and P. Stamper (eds), *The Age of Transition: the Archaeology of English Culture 1400–1600* (Oxford, 1997), pp. 93–4.

[19] *HKW*, i, pp. 494–504.

[20] E. Cavell (ed.), *The Heralds' Memoir, 1486–1490: Court Ceremony, Royal Progress and Rebellion* (Donington, 2009), p. 98.

[21] Jones and Underwood, *The King's Mother*, p. 74.

[22] M. Prestwich, *Edward I* (London, 1988), pp. 134–69; M. Morris, *A Great and Terrible King: Edward I and the Forging of Britain* (London, 2008), pp. 144–5; G. Matthew, *The Court of Richard II* (London, 1968), pp. 21–31.

[23] N. Saul, *Richard II* (New Haven and London, 1997), pp. 327–33.

[24] Matthew, *Court of Richard II*, pp. 21–52.

[25] C. M. Barron, 'Richard II: Image and Reality', in D. Gordon (ed.), *Making and*

Meaning: The Wilton Diptych (London, 1993), pp. 13–19.

[26] J. Munby, R. Barber and R. Brown, *Edward III's Round Table at Windsor: The House of the Round Table and the Windsor Festival of 1344* (Woodbridge, 2007), pp. 38–65.

[27] S. Brindle (ed.), *Windsor Castle: a thousand years of a royal palace* (London, forthcoming)

[28] Given-Wilson, *Royal Household*, pp. 22–3.

[29] G. L. Harriss, 'The Court of the Lancastrian Kings', in J. Stratford (ed.), *The Lancastrian Court: Proceedings of the 2001 Harlaxton Symposium* (Donington, 2003), pp. 1–18; J. Watts, 'Was there a Lancastrian Court?', in Stratford (ed.), *Lancastrian Court*, pp. 253–71; R. A. Griffiths, 'The King's Court During the Wars of the Roses: Continuities in an Age of Discontinuities', in R. A. Griffiths (ed.), *King and Country: England and Wales in the Fifteenth Century* (London, 1991), pp. 11–32; D. A. L. Morgan, 'The House of Policy: The Political Role of the Late Plantagenet Household, 1422–1485', in D. R. Starkey (ed.), *The English Court: From the Wars of the Roses to the Civil War* (London, 1987), pp. 25–70.

[30] Descriptions of Edward IV's court can be found in 'The Record of Bluemantle Pursuivant, 1471–1472', in C. L. Kingsford (ed.), *English Historical Literature in the Fifteenth Century* (Oxford, 1913), pp. 382–5; M. Letts (ed.), *The Travels of Leo of Rozmital through Germany, Flanders, England, France, Spain, Portugal and Italy, 1465–1467*, Hakluyt Society, 2nd ser., cviii (1957), pp. 45–56.

II THE LABOURS OF HERCULES

[1] M. Whiteley, 'The Courts of Edward III of England and Charles V of France: A Comparison of their Architectural Setting and Ceremonial Functions', in N. Saul (ed.), *Fourteenth Century England*, i (Woodbridge, 2000), pp. 153–66.

[2] C. M. Barron, 'Introduction: England and the Low Countries, 1327–1477', in C. M.

Barron and N. Saul (eds), *England and the Low Countries in the Late Middle Ages* (Stroud, 1995), pp. 2–12.

3 A. F. Sutton and P. W. Hammond, *The Coronation of Richard III: the extant documents* (Gloucester, 1983), pp. 47–87; M. A. Hayward, *The Great Wardrobe Accounts of Henry VII and Henry VIII*, London Record Society, xlvii (2012), pp. xviii–xxii, xxvi–xxxviii.

4 T. P. Campbell, *Henry VIII and the Art of Majesty: Tapestries at the Tudor Court* (New Haven and London, 2007), pp. 67–76.

5 See for instance TNA E101/414/6, f. 23v, concerning preparations for the progress in 1496.

6 Ford, 'Conciliar Politics', Appendix 1. For the first fifteen years of the reign, Ford identified Henry's location for 60% of nights. I have therefore averaged out the figures, and thus details given here are approximate in detail but accurate in conclusion.

7 J. Gairdner, *Memorials of King Henry the Seventh* (London, 1858), pp. 309–27.

8 A. Hewerdine, *The Yeomen of the Guard and the Early Tudors: The Formation of a Royal Bodyguard* (London, 2012), pp. 5–19, 45–69.

9 S. Cunningham, *Henry VII* (London, 2007), pp. 74–80.

10 Impey (ed.), *The White Tower*, pp. 161–2.

11 To aid comprehension here, the room 'privy chamber' is given in lower case, while the household department 'Privy Chamber' is given upper-case initials.

12 D. R. Starkey, 'Intimacy and Innovation: the Rise of the Privy Chamber, 1485–1547', in Starkey (ed.), *English Court*, pp. 71–5; D. Grummitt, 'Household, Politics and Political Morality in the Reign of Henry VII', *Historical Research*, lxxxii (2009), pp. 398–402.

13 A. R. Myers, *The Household of Edward IV: The Black Book and the Ordinance of 1478*

(Manchester, 1959), pp. 19–20. The myth of Burgundian influence on the English court, postulated by the present author, amongst others, in the 1990s, has now been definitively slain. See J. Duindam, 'The Burgundian-Spanish legacy in European court life: a brief reassessment and the example of the Austrian Habsburgs', *Publications du Centre Européen d'Etudes Bourguignonnes*, xlvi (2006), pp. 203–20; D. R. Starkey, 'Henry VI's Old Blue Gown: The English Court under the Lancastrians and Yorkists', *The Court Historian*, iv (1999), pp. 1–28; M. G. A. Vale, 'An Anglo-Burgundian Nobleman and Art Patron: Louis de Bruges, Lord of la Gruthuyse and Earl of Winchester', in Barron and Saul (eds), *England and the Low Countries*, pp. 115–31.

14 TNA E36/214, f. 17.

15 The details of the visit are taken from the following sources: BL Cotton MS Vesp. C XII, printed in full in R. R. Tighe and J. E. Davis, *Annals of Windsor, being a History of the Castle and Town, with some account of Eton and places adjacent*, i (London, 1858), pp. 434–4; A. F. Pollard, *The Reign of Henry VII from Contemporary Sources*, i (London, 1913), pp. 263–81; Gairdner, *Memorials*, pp. 283–302; D. Hay (ed.), *The Anglica Historia of Polydore Vergil, A.D. 1484–1537*, Camden Society, 3rd ser., lxxiv (1950), pp. 137–9.

16 B. P. Wolffe, *The Royal Demesne in English History: The Crown Estate in the Governance of the Realm from the Conquest to 1509* (London, 1971), p. 204.

17 D. Grummitt, 'Henry VII, Chamber Finance and the "New Monarchy": some new evidence', *Historical Research*, lxxii (1999), pp. 229–43.

18 S. B. Chrimes, *Henry VII* (London, 1972), pp. 216–8.

19 *HKW*, ii, pp. 999–1000; iv, pp. 222–3.

20 TNA E101/414/16, f. 10v; A. H. Thomas and I. D. Thornley (eds), *The Great Chronicle of London* (London, 1938), p. 286, and, in more detail, *Cal. SP. Milan*, p. 347; Cowie and Cloake, 'Richmond Palace', p. 34.

21 The key primary texts for Sheen are G. Kipling (ed.), *The Receyt of the Ladie Kateryne*, Early English Text Society, cclxxxxvi (1990), pp. 70–4; the parliamentary survey of 1649, TNA E317/SURREY/46, printed in W. H. Hart, 'The Parliamentary Surveys of Richmond, Wimbledon, and Nonsuch, in the county of Surrey', *Surrey Archaeological Collections*, v (1871), pp. 76–85. The earliest list of the rooms in the tower dates from 1538–9; NUL MS, Ne O 2, ff. 217v–218.

22 TNA E101/415/3, ff. 64v, 75v; E. Jeffery (ed.), *The Antiquarian Repertory*, ii (London, 1808), p. 190.

23 Campbell, *Art of Majesty*, pp. 76–100; Hayward, *Great Wardrobe Accounts*, pp. xxxviii–li, 28–9.

24 For this and my general points below, see J. L. Laynesmith, *The Last Medieval Queens: English Queenship 1445–1503* (Oxford, 2004).

25 A. R. Myers, *Crown, Household and Parliament in Fifteenth Century England* (London, 1985), pp. 252–4, 258–9.

26 Laynesmith, *Medieval Queens*, p. 236.

27 'ERP', pp. 91–2; N. H. Nicolas, *Privy Purse Expenses of Elizabeth of York: Wardrobe Accounts of Edward the Fourth* (London, 1830), pp. 20, 26, 80, 102.

28 TNA E36/214, f. 150v; *HKW*, iv, pp. 50–2.

29 Elizabeth's itinerary, compiled from her Privy Purse expenses, is conveniently printed in A. N. Okerlund, *Elizabeth of York* (Basingstoke, 2009), p. 188. Henry VII's itinerary is in Ford, 'Conciliar Politics', pp. 205–83.

30 *Cal. SP. Span.*, i, p. 11; Laynesmith, *Medieval Queens*, pp. 227–8.

31 *Cal. SP. Milan*, p. 323.

32 Jeffery (ed.), *Antiquarian Repertory*, i, pp. 313–4.

33 *ibid.*, pp. 304–5; K. Staniland, 'Royal Entry into the World', in D. Williams (ed.), *England in the Fifteenth Century: Proceedings of the 1986 Harlaxton Symposium* (Woodbridge, 1987), pp. 297–313.

34 R. A. Griffiths, 'The Burials of King Henry VI at Chertsey and Windsor', in N. Saul and T. Tatton-Brown (eds), *St George's Chapel, Windsor: History and Heritage* (Wimborne Minster, 2010), pp. 100–7.

35 *HKW*, iii, pp. 308–13.

36 TNA E101/415/3 f. 44v; C. S. L. Davis, 'Tudor: What's in a Name?', *History*, lxxxxvii (2012), pp. 24–42.

37 R. Pynson, *The Traduction and Marriage of the Princess* (London, 1500); *Cal. SP. Span.*, i, pp. 264–5.

38 TNA E101/415/3, ff. 51, 56v, 62.

39 Kipling (ed.), *Receyt of Ladie Kateryne*, pp. 44–5.

40 *ibid.*, pp. 69, 71.

41 Gairdner, *Memorials*, p. 302.

III GOD AND MAMMON

1 V. K. Henderson, 'Rethinking Henry VII: The Man and his Piety in the Context of the Observant Franciscans', in D. L. Biggs, S. D. Michalove and A. C. Reeves (eds), *Reputation and Representation in Fifteenth Century Europe* (Leiden, 2004), pp. 317–47.

2 For instance TNA E101/414/16, ff. 4v, 24v, 25v, 44, 56v; E101/414/6, ff. 61, 66, 70v, 75, 84.

3 The progress of building is summarized in *HKW*, iii, pp. 195–6; BL Add. MS 59899, ff. 48–9; *Cal. Papal Regs*, xviii, p. 23.

4 H. H. Drake (ed.), *Hasted's History of Kent, Part 1* (London, 1886), pp. 87–8; *HKW*, iii, pp. 195–6; C. Thomas, B. Watson and J. Bowsher, 'The Mendicant Houses of Medieval London. An Archaeological Review', in N. Rogers (ed.), *The Friars in Medieval Britain* (Harlaxton Medieval Studies xix, 2010), pp. 285–8; O. Millar (ed.), *The Tudor, Stuart and Early Georgian Pictures in the Collection of Her Majesty the Queen* (London, 1963), pp. 52–3. There is a payment for a painted tabernacle for

Richmond in BL Add. MS 59899, ff. 11, 19v. For Richmond's conventual buildings, see *Cal. Papal Regs*, xviii, p. 23.

5 N. Saul (ed.), *St George's Chapel Windsor in the Fourteenth Century* (Woodbridge, 2005), p. 75; R. Bowers, 'The Music and Musical Establishment of St George's Chapel in the Fifteenth Century', in C. Richmond and E. Scarff (eds), *St George's Chapel, Windsor, in the Late Middle Ages*, Historical Monographs relating to St George's Chapel, Windsor Castle, xvii (Windsor, 2001), p. 172.

6 For this, see the manual of royal chapel ceremonial written by William Say, Dean of the Royal Chapel in 1449: W. Ullmann (ed.), *Liber Regie Capelle: A Manuscript in the Biblioteca Publica, Evora*, Henry Bradshaw Society, lxxxxii (London, 1961), esp. pp. 64–5.

7 F. L. Kisby, '"When the King Goeth a Procession": Chapel Ceremonies and Services, the Ritual Year, and Religious Reforms at the Early Tudor Court, 1485–1547', *Journal of British Studies*, xl (2001), pp. 60–3; F. L. Kisby, 'Religious Ceremonial at the Tudor Court: Extracts from royal household regulations', in I. W. Archer *et al.* (eds), *Religion, Politics and Society in Sixteenth-Century England*, Camden Society, 5th ser., xxii (2003), pp. 1–33.

8 N. Beckett, 'Henry VII and Sheen Charterhouse', in B. Thompson (ed.), *The Reign of Henry VII: Proceedings of the 1993 Harlaxton Symposium* (Stamford, 1995), pp. 117–32.

9 F. L. Kisby, 'The early Tudor Household Chapel, 1485–1547' (unpublished PhD thesis, University of London, 1996), pp. 129–37.

10 J. Burtt, 'Charter of Henry VII to the Franciscan Friars at Greenwich, and an Inedited Seal of the Warden', *Archaeological Journal*, xxiii (1866), p. 56. The Queen wanted to be buried in the friars' church at Greenwich. *L&P Hen. VIII*, x, no. 40.

11 K. Rawlinson, 'The English Household

Chapel, c.1100–c.1500: An Institutional Study' (unpublished PhD thesis, University of Durham, 2008), p. 271; W. Page (ed.), *The Victoria History of the County of Kent*, ii (1926), p. 194; E. Hall, *Chronicle Containing the History of England* (London, 1809), pp. 305–6.

12 *L&P Hen. VIII*, v, no. 941; A. G. L'Estrange, *The Palace and the Hospital; or Chronicles of Greenwich*, i (London, 1886), pp. 242–6; D. Knowles, *The Religious Orders in England*, iii (Cambridge, 1979), pp. 206–11; R. Brown (ed.), *Four Years at the Court of Henry VIII*, ii (London, 1854), p. 260. This last work does not state that the friary was the location of the event, but the description would hardly suggest that it could have all taken place in the palace chapel.

13 *HKW*, ii, pp. 684–5.

14 A. Richardson, 'Greenwich's First Royal landscape: the Lost Palace and Park of Humphrey Duke of Gloucester', *Southern History*, xxxiv (2012), pp. 51–72; Drake (ed.), *Hasted's Kent*, p. 56; *HKW*, ii, pp. 949–50; C. Williams (ed.), *Thomas Platter's Travels in England, 1599* (London, 1937), p. 226.

15 P. Dixon, *Excavations at Greenwich Palace* (London, 1972), pp. 9–14; Cowie and Cloake, 'Richmond Palace', p. 34.

16 BL Add. MS 59899, ff. 15, 18, 24, 27v, 35v, etc.

17 T. P. Smith, *The Medieval Brickmaking Industry in England 1400–1450*, British Archaeological Reports, cxxxviii (Oxford, 1985), pp. 4–8; J. A. A. Goodall, 'Henry VI's Court and the Construction of Eton College', in L. Keen and E. Scarff (eds), *Windsor: Medieval Archaeology, Art and Architecture of the Thames Valley*, British Archaeological Association Transactions, xxv (Leeds, 2002), pp. 254–7; J. A. A. Goodall, 'A Medieval Masterpiece: Herstmonceux Castle, Sussex', *The Burlington Magazine*, cxlvi (2004), pp. 516–25.

18 Although work started in May 1500, a

plan, or 'platt' as it was then known, was only provided by him two and a half years later, so must have been for a subsequent phase of work, as, by then, much of the river range must have been completed.

19 This is brilliantly analysed, with an appendix giving the provenance of the relevant household ordinances, in Starkey, 'Old Blue Gown'. My description of the king's day is informed by 'Household Regulations for Henry VIII, 4 February 1526', which in reality reproduce a missing Henry VII order of 1494–1501. The original is in College of Arms, MS Arundel XVII/2 and it is printed in Jeffery (ed.), Antiquarian Repertory, ii, p. 190.

20 TNA E101/413/11, f. 37.

21 G. Bernard, 'The Rise of Sir William Compton, Early Tudor Courtier', English Historical Review, xcvi (1981), pp. 754–8.

22 J. Gairdner (ed.), Letters and Papers Illustrative of the Reigns of Richard III and Henry VII, i (London, 1861), pp. 391–3.

23 BL Add. MS 59899, ff. 33, 48, 77, 79v, 36v, 30v; TNA E101/414/6, ff. 41, 87, 9, 59; E101/414/16, f. 18v; E101/414/6, f. 59; E36/214, f. 31; E101/414/6, ff. 13v, 15v; E101/414/16, f. 10v.

24 RPTE, pp. 34–6; 'ERP', pp. 85–91.

25 TNA E36/215, f. 151v.

26 TNA E101/415/3; E36/214, f. 84; E36/214, f. 166; Grummitt, 'Henry VII, Chamber Finance and the "New Monarchy": some new Evidence', pp. 238–9. I am grateful to Dr David Starkey for discussion on these points.

IV FATHER AND SON

1 D. R. Starkey, Henry: Virtuous Prince (London, 2008), pp. 234–56; T. Penn, Winter King: The Dawn of Tudor England (London, 2011), pp. 333–46.

2 R. Shoesmith and A. P. Johnson (eds), Ludlow Castle: Its History and Buildings (Almeley, 2000), pp. 69–70.

3 J. Priestley, Eltham Palace (Chichester, 2008), pp. 51–62.

4 'ERP', pp. 38–45, summarized in RPTE, pp. 18–31; F. M. Nichols (ed.), The Epistles of Erasmus from his Earliest Letters to his Fifty-First Year, i (London, 1901), pp. 200–1.

5 Paraphrase from the Spanish original in G. Mattingly, Catherine of Aragon (London, 1950), p. 92; Hart, 'Parliamentary Surveys', p. 78.

6 N. Machiavelli, Lettere Familiari, ed. E. Alvisi (Florence, 1883), p. 293.

7 D. R. Starkey, 'King Henry and King Arthur', in J. P. Carley and F. Riddy (eds), Arthurian Literature XVI (Woodbridge, 1998), pp. 171–96.

8 S. Anglo, Spectacle, Pageantry, and Early Tudor Policy (Oxford, 1969), pp. 98–117; A. R. Young, Tudor and Jacobean Tournaments (London, 1987), pp. 22–7, 43–50.

9 TNA E36/215, f. 227.

10 TNA E36/215, ff. 16v, 24v, 30, 39, 65, 72, 83, 97v.

11 TNA E36/215, ff. 230, 236, 257v, 260, 264v, 276v; E36/216, ff. 17, 24, 34, 66v; E36/215, ff. 257v, 260, 264v, 276v, 282, 284; E36/216, ff. 79v, 83.

12 A. Williams and A. de Reuck, The Royal Armoury at Greenwich, 1515–1649: A History of its Technology (London, 1995), pp. 26–31, 43–51.

13 The king had previously temporarily set the area up for feats of arms. Hall, Chronicle, p. 515; TNA E36/216, ff. 14v, 19v.

14 Hall, Chronicle, p. 635.

15 L&P Hen. VIII, iv, no. 4676.

16 L&P Hen. VIII, xvi, no. 1130.

17 N. H. Nicolas, The Privy Purse Expenses of King Henry the Eighth from November MDXXIX to December MDXXXII (London, 1827), pp. 47, 171.

18 RPTE, p. 192; Nicolas, Privy Purse Henry VIII, pp. 7, 19, 28, 35, 39, 43, 45, 50, 68, 70, 154, 156, 167, 288; J. P. Hore, The History of

the Royal Buckhounds (Newmarket, 1895), pp. 28–52.

[19] G. Richardson, 'Hunting at the Courts of Francis I and Henry VIII', *The Court Historian*, xviii (2013), pp. 127–41; A. MacGregor, *Animal Encounters: Human and Animal Interaction in Britain from the Norman Conquest to World War I* (London, 2012), pp. 110–95.

[20] S. J. Gunn, 'The Courtiers of Henry VII', *English Historical Review*, cviii (1993), p. 25.

[21] *RPTE*, p. 193; *Cal. SP. Span.*, iv (ii), no. 765 (p. 212); Nicolas, *Privy Purse Henry VIII*, pp. 157, 38, 15; J. Cummins, *The Hound and the Hawk: The Art of Medieval Hunting* (London, 1988), pp. 202–3.

[22] *HKW*, iv, pp. 90–1, 160–1, 349–51; J. Bond and K. Tiller, *Blenheim: Landscape for a Palace* (Oxford, 1987), pp. 22–51.

[23] There is also one instance suggesting that the king's council was in charge of repairs at Greenwich. TNA E36/215, f. 160v.

[24] See Oxford DNB entry for Wolsey for estimates of his wealth.

[25] S. J. Thurley, 'The Domestic Building Works of Cardinal Wolsey', in S. J. Gunn and P. G. Lindley (eds), *Cardinal Wolsey: Church, State and Art* (Cambridge, 1991), pp. 76–81.

[26] See S. J. Thurley, *Hampton Court Palace: A Social and Architectural History* (New Haven and London, 2004), pp. 33–4, 41.

[27] *L&P Hen. VIII*, iii, nos 700, 825. For an analysis of the authorship of the design, see 'ERP', pp. 132–8. More conveniently, see the summary in Thurley, 'Domestic Works of Wolsey', pp. 94–6. Also, see the analysis of the works in G. Richardson, *The Field of Cloth of Gold* (New Haven and London, 2013), pp. 52–67, and J. Munby, 'The Field of Cloth of Gold: Guînes and the Calais Pale Revisited', *English Heritage Historical Review*, ix (2014), pp. 30–63.

[28] Campbell, *Art of Majesty*, pp. 143–55.

[29] H. S. Cobb, 'Descriptions of the State Opening of Parliament, 1485–1601: A Survey', *Parliamentary History*, xviii (1999), pp. 303–15.

[30] 'ERP', pp. 104–22, summarized in *RPTE*, pp. 40–2; A. W. Clapham, 'On the Topography of the Dominican Priory of London', *Archaeologia*, lxiii (1912), pp. 57–84.

[31] *L&P Hen. VIII*, iii, no. 1451 (20); *HKW*, iv, pp. 172–4; 'ERP', pp. 122–6, summarized in *RPTE*, pp. 44–5.

V NEW PASSIONS

[1] My account follows D. R. Starkey, *Six Wives: The Queens of Henry VIII* (London, 2003). For an alternative view, see G. W. Bernard, *Anne Boleyn: Fatal Attractions* (New Haven and London, 2010).

[2] *Cal. SP. Span.*, iii (ii), p. 276; *L&P Hen. VIII*, iv, no. 3318.

[3] *L&P Hen. VIII*, iv, nos 5016, 4005, 4251 (p. 1871).

[4] *L&P Hen. VIII*, iv, no. 5063; M. S. Byrne, *The Letters of King Henry VIII* (London, 1968), pp. 82–3; H. Savage (ed.), *The Love Letters of Henry VIII* (London, 1949), pp. 38–9; *L&P Hen. VIII*, iv, no. 5016 (p. 2177).

[5] See my account of the excavations in S. J. Thurley, *Whitehall Palace: An Architectural History of the Royal Apartments, 1240–1698* (New Haven and London, 1999), pp. x–xiv.

[6] My account of Whitehall is dispersed over a number of publications. The east side is covered in Thurley, *Whitehall Palace: An Architectural History*; the west side is covered in H. J. M. Green and S. J. Thurley, 'Excavations on the West Side of Whitehall 1960–2 Part I: From the Building of the Tudor Palace to the Construction of the Modern Offices of State', *Transactions of the London and Middlesex Archaeological Society*, xxxviii (1987), pp. 59–130; the key plan of the palace is analysed in S. J. Thurley, *The Whitehall Palace Plan of 1670*, London Topographical Society, cliii (London, 1998); and other sources are published in S. J. Thurley, *The Lost Palace of Whitehall*, Royal Institute of British Architects Exhibition

Catalogue (London, 1998; repr. 1999). A summary of all these appears in S. J. Thurley, *Whitehall Palace: The Official Illustrated History* (London, 2008).

7 N. Samman, 'The Henrician Court during Cardinal Wolsey's ascendancy c.1514–1529' (unpublished PhD thesis, University of Wales, 1988), p. 235 n. 64; *Cal. SP. Ven.*, vi (iii), Appendix, no. 79.

8 G. Rosser and S. J. Thurley, 'Whitehall Palace and King Street, Westminster: The Urban Cost of Princely Magnificence', *London Topographical Record*, xxvi (1990), pp. 57–77; M. Everett, *The Rise of Thomas Cromwell: Power and Politics in the Reign of Henry VIII* (New Haven and London, 2015), pp. 67–98.

9 W. D. Hamilton (ed.), *A Chronicle of England During the Reigns of the Tudors from A.D. 1485 to 1559 by Charles Wriothesley, Windsor Herald*, i, Camden Society, new ser., xi (1875), p. 22.

10 Starkey, *Six Wives*, pp. 439–43.

11 Nicolas, *Privy Purse Henry VIII*, p. 281.

12 BL Sloane MS 2495, ff. 13–13v names the place where they were married as 'the high chamber over the west gate'; N. Pocock (ed.), *A Treatise on the Pretended Divorce between Henry VIII and Catharine of Aragon, by Nicholas Harpsfield, LL.D., Archdeacon of Canterbury*, Camden Society, new ser., xxi (1878), pp. 234–5. For the timing, see Starkey, *Six Wives*, pp. 474–5.

13 'ERP', pp. 161–7; *L&P Hen. VIII*, v, no. 1467.

14 Nicolas, *Privy Purse Henry VIII*, pp. 278–9; *Cal. SP. Span.*, iv (ii), no. 1033; *L&P Hen. VIII*, v, no. 1685.

15 E. Ives, *The Life and Death of Anne Boleyn* (Oxford, 2004), pp. 172–5; Bod. Lib. Rawlinson MS. D 775, f. 218v.

16 Hall, *Chronicle*, p. 805; Hamilton (ed.), *Wriothesley's Chronicle*, i, p. 22.

17 For the following, see D. R. Starkey, 'The King's Privy Chamber 1485–1547' (unpublished PhD thesis, University of

Cambridge, 1973), summarized in Starkey, 'Intimacy and Innovation', pp. 71–118.

18 G. Walker, 'The "expulsion of the minions" of 1519 Reconsidered', *Historical Journal*, xxxii (1989), pp. 1–16.

19 Thurley, *Whitehall Palace: An Architectural History*, pp. 21–2, 50.

20 R. Strong, *The Artist and the Garden* (New Haven and London, 2000), pp. 17–20.

21 Thurley, 'Whitehall Palace and Westminster', pp. 93–104.

22 Hall, *Chronicle*, p. 816; G. H. Gater and F. R. Hiorns (eds), *Trafalgar Square and Neighbourhood (St Martin-in-the-Fields, Part III)*, Survey of London, xx (London, 1940), pp. 7–14.

23 The following is based on Green and Thurley, 'Excavations on the West Side of Whitehall'; *RPTE*, pp. 182–91.

24 Kipling (ed.), *Receyt of Ladie Kateryne*, pp. 73–4; BL Cott. MS Vesp. C XII, f. 285v.

25 *Cal. SP. Ven.*, ii, no. 1287; Nicolas, *Privy Purse Henry VIII*, p. 36.

26 T. Fuller, *Anglorum Speculum, or the Worthies of England in Church and State* (London, 1684), p. 804.

27 R. Graziani, 'Sir Thomas Wyatt at a Cockfight, 1539', *Review of English Studies*, new ser., xxvii (1976), p. 301.

28 Nicolas, *Privy Purse Henry VIII*, pp. 273, 275, 280.

29 Cobb, 'State Opening', pp. 306–8; D. Dean, 'Image and Ritual in the Tudor Parliaments', in D. E. Hoak (ed.), *Tudor Political Culture* (Cambridge, 1995), pp. 243–71.

VI TOWN AND COUNTRY

1 S. J. Thurley, 'Henry VIII and the Building of Hampton Court: A Reconstruction of the Tudor Palace', *Architectural History*, xxxi (1988), pp. 1–57; S. J. Thurley, 'The Sixteenth-Century Kitchens at Hampton Court', *Journal of the British Archaeological Association*,

cxliii (1990), pp. 1–28; Thurley, *Hampton Court*.

2 For the above see Thurley, *Hampton Court*, pp. 16–41.

3 *ibid.*, p. 41.

4 *HKW*, iii, pp. 25–45.

5 Hall, *Chronicle*, pp. 674, 689; J. G. Nichols (ed.), *The Chronicle of Calais in the Reigns of Henry VII and Henry VIII to the year 1540*, Camden Society, xxxv (1846), pp. 125–9; *HKW*, iii, pp. 346–7; iv, pp. 375–7.

6 *L&P Hen. VIII*, iii (ii), p. 1547.

7 'ERP', pp. 98–104, summarized in *RPTE*, pp. 39–40; TNA SP1/201/784, transcribed in J. Dent, *The Quest for Nonsuch* (London, 1962), pp. 284–5.

8 *HKW*, iii, pp. 7–13.

9 TNA E36/251, p. 164; E36/252, p. 413; M. A. Hayward, *Dress at the Court of King Henry VIII* (Leeds, 2007), pp. 283–4.

10 *HKW*, iii, pp. 5–45.

11 For the whole of this section, see Thurley, *Hampton Court*, pp. 45–9; *RPTE*, pp. 145–61; Thurley, 'Kitchens at Hampton Court'. Some additional detail is provided in P. Brears, *All the King's Cooks: The Tudor Kitchens of King Henry VIII at Hampton Court Palace* (London, 2011).

12 *Cal. SP. Span.*, i, no. 204 (p. 163).

13 D. L. Hamilton, 'The Household of Queen Katharine Parr' (unpublished PhD thesis, University of Oxford, 1992), pp. 13–15, 44–7, 54, 58, 80.

14 Thurley, 'Kitchens at Hampton Court'; P. Brears, *Cooking and Dining in Medieval England* (Totnes, 2008), pp. 35–46.

15 *RPTE*, pp. 150–60; C. M. Woolgar, *The Great Household in Late Medieval England* (New Haven and London, 1999), pp. 90–3; *Cal. SP. Span.*, Supplement, p. 22.

16 *State Papers*, viii, pp. 507–8: *L&P Hen. VIII*, xvi, nos 368, 369, 449, 436.

17 TNA E36/215, ff. 96v, 262v; Nicolas, *Privy Purse Henry VIII*, pp. 33, 39, 46, 48, 50, 53,

55, 58, 62, 66, 71, 74, 95, 109, 141, 160, 169, 178, 226, 253, 254. For the king's medical history, see F. Chamberlin, *The Private Character of Henry the Eighth* (London, 1932). For his girth, see Hayward, *Dress at Court*, p. 6.

18 *RPTE*, p. 160.

19 For what follows see Thurley, *Hampton Court*, pp. 49–50 and *RPTE*, pp. 135–6.

20 *RPTE*, pp. 141–2.

21 Thurley, *Hampton Court*, p. 56.

22 *ibid.*, pp. 54–61, 92–5.

23 B. Dix and S. Parry, 'The Excavation of the Privy Garden', in S. Thurley (ed.), *The King's Privy Garden 1689–1995* (Apollo Magazine, 1990), pp. 85–7.

24 Samman, 'Henrician Court', pp. 283–312.

25 *Cal. SP. Span.*, Further Supplement, p. 153.

26 *L&P Hen. VIII*, iv, Appendix, no. 206.

27 *RPTE*, pp. 45–6; *L&P Hen. VIII*, x, no. 601 (p. 245).

28 *State Papers*, i (i), pp. x–xiv.

VII To Have and to Hold

1 J. Guy, 'Thomas Cromwell and the Intellectual Origins of the Henrician Revolution', in J. Guy (ed.), *The Tudor Monarchy* (London, 1997), pp. 213–21.

2 W. C. Richardson, *History of the Court of Augmentations 1536–1554* (Baton Rouge, 1961), pp. 325, 346–50; *HKW*, iv, pp. 288–9.

3 J. C. K. Cornwall, *Wealth and Society in Early Sixteenth Century England* (London, 1988), pp. 28–9, 130–1, 143–4.

4 *L&P Hen. VIII*, vii, no. 143.

5 *HKW*, iv, pp. 3–7; *L&P Hen. VIII*, i (i), no. 94 (35); Hall, *Chronicle*, p. 650.

6 *L&P Hen. VIII*, xv, no. 954.

7 J. G. Nichols (ed.), *Narratives of the days of the reformation, chiefly from the manuscripts of John Foxe the martyrologist: with two contemporary biographies of Archbishop*

Cranmer, Camden Society, lxxvii (1860), p. 266.

[8] 'ERP', pp. 240–69, summarized in *RPTE*, pp. 56–8.

[9] *L&P Hen. VIII*, ii (ii), no. 4034.

[10] *RPTE*, pp. 1–10.

[11] 'ERP', pp. 317–73, summarized in *RPTE*, pp. 67–73.

[12] I owe this observation to the late David Bowie, as I have never been on tour with a rock band.

[13] *RPTE*, pp. 70–2; F. Madden, *Privy Purse Expenses of the Princess Mary, Daughter of King Henry VIII, afterwards Queen Mary* (London, 1831), pp. 61, 64.

[14] See the papers of William Thynne, Clerk of the Kitchen, BL Add. MS 9835, ff. 2, 111–111v, 23v; *Cal. SP. Ven.*, xviii, no. 517; *L&P Hen. VIII*, xvi, no. 1489 (p. 703). The 1589 cart list is BL Lansdowne MS 59, no. 25; TNA E36/216, f. 9v.

[15] BL Add. MS 9835, f. 13; J. E. Jackson, 'Wulfhall and the Seymours', *Wiltshire Archaeological and Natural History Magazine*, xv (1875), p. 170.

[16] *L&P Hen. VIII*, iii (i), no. 851.

[17] *L&P Hen. VIII*, iii (i), no. 1286 (ii); W. Jerdan (ed.), *Rutland Papers: Original Documents illustrative of the Courts and Times of Henry VII and Henry VIII*, Camden Society, xxi (1842), p. 83; *Household Ordinances*, p. 240.

[18] Account of the progress in *Cal. SP. Span.*, vi (i), no. 163 (p. 327); *L&P Hen. VIII*, xvi, nos 1011, 1088, 1130, 1183; *L&P Hen. VIII*, xvi, no. 677; R. W. Hoyle and J. B. Ramsdale, 'The Royal Progress of 1541, the North of England, and Anglo-Scottish Relations, 1534–1542', *Northern History*, 41 (2004), pp. 263–5; C. J. Sansom, 'The Wakefield Conspiracy of 1541 and Henry VIII's Progress to the North Reconsidered', *Northern History*, 45 (2008) pp. 217–38.

[19] I. Roberts, *Pontefract Castle. Archaeological Excavations 1982–86*, (West

Yorkshire Archaeology Service, 2002), pp. 59–70.

[20] Gunn, 'Courtiers of Henry VII', pp. 45–6; *L&P Hen. VIII*, x, no. 226 (33–4); iii (i), nos 1262 (20), 581 (14).

[21] TNA E101/631/25, f. 6.

[22] *RPTE*, pp. 83–4; TNA LC5/36 p. 269.

[23] A. Keay, *The Elizabethan Tower of London: The Haiward and Gascoyne plan of 1597*, London Topographical Society, clviii (London, 2001), p. 42.

[24] *RPTE*, pp. 74–5; D. R. Starkey (ed.), *The Inventory of King Henry VIII*, i (London, 1998), p. 355 (nos 14147–8); Campbell, *Art of Majesty*, pp. 245–8; *L&P Hen. VIII*, xvi, no. 1489 (p. 706).

[25] BL Add. MS 71009, f. 19v; R. S. Sylvester (ed.), *The Life and Death of Cardinal Wolsey by George Cavendish*, Early English Text Society, ccxliii (London, 1959), p. 71; *L&P Hen. VIII*, xvi, no. 380 (f. 147); *RPTE*, pp. 74–5; M. A. Hayward, 'Repositories of Splendour: Henry VIII's wardrobes of the Robes and Beds', *Textile History*, xxix (1998), pp. 134–56.

[26] Jeffery (ed.), *Antiquarian Repertory*, ii, p. 204.

[27] Starkey, 'King's Privy Chamber', p. 274; TNA E36/252, p. 589; E36/251, p. 14; University of Nottingham Newcastle MS Neo2 f. 217v; Bodleian Library Rawlinson MS D 775 f. 38.

[28] Hayward, *Dress at Court*, pp. 147–53.

[29] *RPTE*, p. 75; Hayward, *Dress at Court*, pp. 151–3.

VIII Room Service

[1] G. R. Elton, *The Tudor Revolution in Government* (Cambridge, 1953), pp. 382–97.

[2] *Household Ordinances*, p. 160.

[3] Thurley, *Hampton Court*, pp. 51–4.

[4] Nicolas, *Privy Purse Henry VIII*, p. 191; M. A. Hayward (ed.), *The 1542 Inventory of Whitehall: The Palace and its Keeper*, i, (London, 2004), p. 29.

[5] Brown (ed.), *Four Years*, ii, p. 204.

[6] *RPTE*, pp. 113–20.

[7] 'ERP', pp. 308–12, summarized in *RPTE*, p. 118. See also L. R. Shelby, *John Rogers: Tudor Military Engineer* (Oxford, 1967), pp. 24–48.

[8] *RPTE*, pp. 120–2; Hewerdine, *Yeomen of the Guard*, pp. 45–69.

[9] *RPTE*, pp. 122–5; Hall, *Chronicle*, p. 688; M. A. Hayward, 'Symbols of Majesty: Cloths of Estate at the Court of Henry VIII', *Furniture History*, xli (2005), pp. 1–11.

[10] Brown (ed.), *Four Years*, i, pp. 85–6.

[11] Brown (ed.), *Four Years*, ii, p. 98. See also *L&P Hen. VIII*, iv (ii), p. 1399.

[12] F. Madden (ed.), 'Narrative of the visit of the Duke de Nájera to England in the year 1543–4; written by his Secretary, Pedro de Gante', *Archaeologia*, xxiii (1831), p. 351.

[13] *RPTE*, pp. 136–41.

[14] D. R. Starkey, 'Representation through Intimacy: A Study in the Symbolism of Monarchy and Court Office in Early Modern England', in J. Guy (ed.), *The Tudor Monarchy* (London, 1997), pp. 42–77.

[15] *RPTE*, pp. 139–41.

[16] 'ERP', ii, fig. 123; *HKW* iv, pp. 6–7.

[17] S. Foister, *Holbein in England* (London, 2006), pp. 63–102.

[18] K. van Mander, *The lives of the illustrious Netherlandish and German Painters*, ed. H. Miedema, 6 vols (1996), i, p. 145.

[19] Hayward (ed.), *Inventory of Whitehall*, ii, p. 15, no. 237; Starkey (ed.), *Inventory of Henry VIII*, i, p. 418, no. 16922.

[20] G. B. Harrison and R. A. Jones (eds), *A Journal of All that was accomplished by Monsieur de Maisse, Ambassador in England from King Henry IV to Queen Elizabeth, Anno Domini 1597* (London, 1931), pp. 23, 26–7.

[21] M. S. Byrne (ed.), *The Lisle Letters*, iii (London, 1981), p. 396.

[22] Thurley, *Hampton Court*, pp. 54–61, 65–6.

[23] *L&P Hen. VIII*, i (i), no. 94 (35).

[24] J. G. Nichols (ed.), 'Inventories of the Wardrobes, Plate, Chapel Stuff, etc. of Henry Fitzroy, Duke of Richmond, and of the Wardrobe Stuff at Baynard's Castle of Katharine, Princess Dowager', *Camden Miscellany III*, Camden Society, lxi (1855), pp. 23–41.

[25] Starkey (ed.), *Inventory of Henry VIII*, i, p. 434 (nos 17637–8); *L&P Hen. VIII*, xv, no. 541; iii (i), no. 152; iv (i), no. 1704; *Cal. SP. Ven.*, iv, no. 105 (pp. 57–8); Madden (ed.), 'Duke de Nájera', pp. 350–4.

[26] *L&P Hen. VIII*, vi, no. 613; Bernard, *Anne Boleyn: Fatal Attractions*, pp. 186–7.

[27] Starkey, *Six Wives*, pp. 564–9, 663–81.

[28] BL Add. MS 71009, f. 20; *Cal. SP. Span.*, viii, no. 204.

[29] Thurley, *Hampton Court*, pp. 65–8.

IX The New Look

[1] M. A. Hayward, *Rich Apparel: Clothing and the Law in Henry VIII's England* (Farnham, 2009), pp. 17–39.

[2] J. Fortescue, *The Governance of England*, ed. C. Plummer (Oxford, 1885), p. 125.

[3] T. Astle, *The Will of King Henry VII* (London, 1775), p. 6.

[4] Sylvester (ed.), *Cavendish's Wolsey*, p. 72.

[5] Nichols (ed.), *Chronicle of Calais*, pp. 54–7.

[6] S. J. Thurley, *The Building of England: How the History of England Has Shaped Our Buildings* (London, 2013), pp. 206–8.

[7] H. S. London, *Royal Beasts* (East Knoyle, 1956); TNA E36/244, p. 78.

[8] P. R. Moore, 'The Heraldic Charge against the Earl of Surrey, 1546–47', *English Historical Review*, cxvi (2001), pp. 557–83.

[9] A. Payne, 'Sir Thomas Wriothesley and his Heraldic Artists', in M. P. Brown and S. McKendrick (eds), *Illuminating the Book: Makers and Interpreters: Essays in honour of Janet Backhouse* (London, 1998), pp. 143–61.

[10] For what follows, see *RPTE*, pp. 85-96.

[11] Thurley, *Building of England*, pp. 210-12; Foister, *Holbein in England*, p. 94.

[12] H. Vogtherr, *Ein Frembds und wunderbars Kunstbüchlein* (Strasbourg, 1538).

[13] BL Add. MS 34809.

[14] Thurley, *Hampton Court*, pp. 22-6.

[15] Campbell, *Art of Majesty*, comprehensively deals with the topic of Henry's tapestries.

[16] *ibid.*, pp. 177-87, 238-41, 205-7.

[17] *RPTE*, pp. 207-233.

[18] *ibid.*, pp. 102-10. On Armstrong, see S. T. Bindoff, 'Clement Armstrong and His Treatises of the Commonweal', *Economic History Review*, xiv (1944), pp. 64-73; E. H. Shagan, 'Clement Armstrong and the godly commonwealth: radical religion in early Tudor England', in P. Marshall and A. Ryrie (eds), *The Beginnings of English Protestantism* (Cambridge, 2002), pp. 60-83.

[19] *RPTE*, pp. 86-98

[20] *HKW*, iii, p. 18; L. F. Salzman, *Building in England down to 1540: A Documentary History* (Oxford, 1952), p. 38; D. Knoop and G. P. Jones, *The Medieval Mason*, 3rd edn (Manchester, 1967), pp. 80-5; Harvey, *English Mediaeval Architects*, pp. 210-13.

[21] Thurley, *Hampton Court*, p. 72.

[22] TNA E36/243, f. 217; E36/239, f. 120; E36/239, f. 415.

[23] TNA E36/251, p. 50; Bodleian Library MS Vet.E1b.6; Bodleian Library MS Eng. hist. b. 192/1, f. 75; TNA E36/252, pp. 637, 641.

X GRAND FINALE

[1] *L&P Hen. VIII*, iii (i), nos 491, 528, 579; iii (ii), app. no. 20.

[2] Madden, *Privy Purse Mary*, pp. xxii-xxxii; *L&P Hen. VIII*, iii (ii), no. 3375 (4).

[3] B. A. Murphy, 'The Life and Political Significance of Henry Fitzroy, Duke of

Richmond, 1525-1536' (unpublished PhD thesis, University of Wales, Bangor, 1999), pp. 96-8, 243-4.

[4] W. R. B. Robinson, 'Princess Mary's Itinerary in the Marches of Wales 1525-1527: a Provisional Record', *Historical Research*, lxxi (1998), pp. 233-52; *HKW*, iii, pp. 277-8; *L&P*, iv (i) no. 1577 (3).

[5] Bod. Lib. Rawlinson MS D 775, f. 115v; Nicolas, *Privy Purse Henry VIII*, pp. 40, 41, 131; *Stat. Realm*, iii, p. 688.

[6] *Cal. SP. Span.*, iv (ii), nos 1144 (p. 839), 1161 (pp. 882-3), 1164 (p. 894), 1165 (p. 898); *Cal. SP. Span.*, vi, no. 4; Bod. Lib. Rawlinson MS D 776, ff. 242-246v; P. F. Robinson, *Vitruvius Britannicus: History of Hatfield House, illustrated by Plans, Elevations and Internal Views* (London, 1833), p. 5, plate 1; *L&P Hen. VIII*, vi, nos 1528, 1558 (p. 629); *L&P Hen. VIII*, vii, no. 440; *State Papers*, i (i), p. 415.

[7] *RPTE*, p. 79; *L&P Hen. VIII*, xi, no. 860; J. L. McIntosh, *From Heads of Household to Heads of State: The Preaccession Households of Mary and Elizabeth Tudor, 1516-1558* (New York, 2009), pp. 37-49.

[8] Thurley, *Hampton Court*, pp. 69-70.

[9] *ibid.*, pp. 68, 77.

[10] *RPTE*, pp. 81-2; Nichols (ed.), 'Inventories of Fitzroy', pp. 1-21.

[11] *L&P Hen. VIII*, xix (i), no. 864; xix (ii), no. 4.

[12] TNA PROB2/199; Bod. Lib. MS Film 308, f. 252; Bod. Lib. Rawlinson MS D 781, ff. 188-207.

[13] Starkey, *Six Wives*, p. 660; *RPTE*, p. 79.

[14] Thurley, *Whitehall Palace*, pp. 58-9; Madden, *Privy Purse Mary*, pp. 22, 38, 76, 88, 98-9, 113, 168; Starkey (ed.), *Inventory of Henry VIII*, i, nos 15203-58 (pp. 376-80).

[15] J. Guy, *The Children of Henry VIII* (Oxford, 2013), pp. 99, 107; *L&P Hen. VIII*, xix (i), no. 780.

[16] F. L. Kisby, 'Kingship and the Royal Itinerary: A Study of the Peripatetic

Household of the Early Tudor Kings 1485–1547', *The Court Historian*, iv (1999), p. 34; S. J. Thurley, 'The Cloister and the Hearth: Wolsey, Henry VIII and the Early Tudor Palace Plan', *Journal of the British Archaeological Association*, clxii (2009), pp. 187–9; Thurley, *Hampton Court*, p. 64.

[17] S. J. Thurley, 'The Impact of Royal Landholdings on the County of Surrey, 1509–1649', in J. Cotton, G. Crocker and A. Graham (eds), *Aspects of Archaeology and History in Surrey* (Guildford, 2004), pp. 155–68.

[18] Richardson, *Court of Augmentations*, p. 3 n. 3, pp. 133–4.

[19] *APC*, ii, pp. 190–2. See also *APC*, i, pp. 239–40.

[20] Starkey (ed.), *Inventory of Henry VIII*, i, no. 12953; E. Lodge, *Illustrations of British History, Biography and Manners in the reigns of Henry VIII, Edward VI, Mary, Elizabeth and James I*, i (London, 1791), p. 5; *L&P Hen. VIII*, xxi (ii), no. 22.

[21] *L&P Hen. VIII*, vii, no. 419 (25); xv, no. 144 (2); xvi, no. 503 (25); xix (i), no. 141 (65); *RPTE*, p. 78.

[22] *L&P Hen. VIII*, xx (ii), nos 236, 240, 247, 252, 267, 270, 278, 290, 779, 786, 795, 800, 809, 814; xxi (ii), nos 408, 413, 459, 547.

[23] R. Poulton, with A. Cook, S. J. Thurley *et al.*, *Excavations at Oatlands Palace, 1968–73 and 1983–4*, Spoil Heap Publications Monograph 3 (Woking, 2010), pp. 9–10, 158–73.

[24] Madden, *Privy Purse Mary*, pp. 124, 151.

[25] J. Loach, *Edward VI* (New Haven and London, 1999), p. 9.

[26] W. K. Jordan (ed.), *The Chronicle and Political Papers of King Edward VI* (Ithaca, 1966), p. 3; Loach, *Edward VI*, pp. 11–16.

[27] See Dent, *Quest for Nonsuch*; *HKW*, iv, pp. 179–201.

[28] M. Biddle, '"Makinge of moldes for the walles" – The Stuccoes of Nonsuch: materials, methods and origins', in R.

Frederiksen and E. Marchand (eds), *Plaster Casts: Making, Collecting and Displaying from Classical Antiquity to the Present* (Berlin, 2010), p. 110.

[29] 'ERP', pp. 277–97, summarized in *RPTE*, pp. 60–5.

[30] TNA E351/3234–6.

[31] J. G. Nichols (ed.), *Literary Remains of King Edward the Sixth*, i (London, 1857; repr. New York, 1964), pp. xxvii–xxx.

[32] J. C. Turquet, 'The Inner Court of Nonsuch Palace' (unpublished PhD thesis, University of London, 1983).

[33] Nichols (ed.), *Literary Remains*, i, pp. xcvi–xcvii.

[34] S. J. Thurley, *Somerset House: The Palace of England's Queens 1551–1692*, London Topographical Society, clxviii (London, 2009), pp. 21–6.

[35] M. H. Cox and P. Norman (eds), *Neighbourhood of Whitehall*, vol. 1 *(The Parish of St Margaret, Westminster, Part II)*, Survey of London, xiii (London, 1930), pp. 20, 261–2.

[36] K. Sharpe, *Selling the Tudor Monarchy: Authority and Image in Sixteenth-Century England* (New Haven and London, 2009), pp. 163–9; W. Kuyper, *The Triumphant Entry of Renaissance Architecture into the Netherlands: The Joyeuse Entrée of Philip of Spain into Antwerp in 1549; Renaissance and Mannerist Architecture in the Low Countries from 1530 to 1630* (Alphen aan den Rijn, 1994), pp. 59, 62.

[37] Thurley, *Whitehall Palace*, pp. 61–2; Madden (ed.), 'Duke de Nájera', p. 354.

[38] F. J. Furnivall (ed.), *Harrison's Description of England in Shakspere's Youth: Being the Second and Third Books of his Description of Britaine and England, edited from the First Two Editions of Holinshed's Chronicle, A.D. 1577, 1587* (London, 1877), pp. 267–9, 270; W. Thomas, *The Pilgrim: A Dialogue on the Life and Actions of King Henry the Eighth*, ed. J. A. Froude (London, 1861), p. 79.

[39] J. Guy, *Henry VIII: The Quest for Fame* (London, 2014), p. 52.

[40] *Cal. SP. Span.*, vi (i), p. 473; *L&P Hen. VIII*, xvii, no. 124 (p. 51); Hall, *Chronicle*, p. 724; *L&P Hen. VIII*, v, no. 1187.

[41] Starkey (ed.), *Inventory of Henry VIII*, i, no. 10647; *L&P Hen. VIII*, x, no. 1231.

[42] J. O. Halliwell (ed.), *Letters of the Kings of England*, i (London, 1848), p. 15.

XI KING EDWARD'S GODLY COURT

[1] The standard history of the reign is Loach, *Edward VI.*

[2] Nichols (ed.), *Literary Remains*, i, pp. cclxvii–cccv.

[3] *Cal. SP. Dom. Edw. VI*, nos 39, 234; Nichols (ed.), *Literary Remains*, i, pp. xcvi–xcvii, cx, 53, 59; S. Alford, *Kingship and Politics in the Reign of Edward VI* (Cambridge, 2002), p. 76 n. 52.

[4] *Cal. SP. Span.*, ix, p. 332; Robinson (ed.), *Original Letters*, ii, p. 648; Haynes, *Collection of State Papers*, p. 108; Jordan, *Chronicle of Edward VI*, p. 19; S. Brigden (ed.), 'The Letters of Richard Scudamore to Sir Philip Hoby, September 1549–March 1555', *Camden Miscellany XXX*, Camden Society, 4th ser., xxxix (1990), pp. 107–8.

[5] D. E. Hoak, 'The King's Privy Chamber, 1547–1553', in D. J. Guth and J. W. McKenna (eds), *Tudor Rule and Revolution: Essays for G. R. Elton from his American Friends* (Cambridge, 1982), pp. 91–4; D. E. Hoak, *The King's Council in the Reign of Edward VI* (Cambridge, 1976), pp. 199–201; *APC*, iii, pp. 29–30.

[6] Jordan, *Chronicle of Edward VI*, p. 100; Hamilton (ed.), *Wriothesley's Chronicle*, ii, pp. 63–4.

[7] *APC*, ii, pp. 105, 171, 412; *APC*, iii, pp. 56, 381; TNA E351/2932.

[8] *APC*, iii, p. 56; TNA E351/3326; Gater and Hiorns (eds), *Trafalgar Square*, pp. 7–14; Jordan, *Chronicle of Edward VI*, p. 137

[9] J. Murphy, 'The illusion of decline: the Privy Chamber, 1547–1558', in Starkey (ed.), *English Court*, pp. 129–30. Sir Richard Blount's account of the duties of a gentleman usher in the reign of Edward VI is in Jeffery (ed.), *Antiquarian Repertory*, iv, pp. 648–51. This, for perhaps the first time, uses the term 'bedchamber' in an institutional sense.

[10] Jordan, *Chronicle of Edward VI*, pp. 72–3.

[11] Thurley, *Whitehall Palace: An Architectural History*, p. 67 sets out the basic evidence. The archaeological evidence for this chamber post-dating the cloister (which was completed in 1547) is unequivocal and the building was certainly in existence by 1549. It is thus likely to have been built immediately on Edward's accession. The first time the room is identified as a council chamber in the written record is in 1584; however, the need for a new council chamber for the council of regency must have existed in 1547, and I here suggest that this was the original purpose of this building. For Somerset's architectural interests see Thurley, *Somerset House*, pp. 21–3.

[12] TNA E351/3224; TNA E351/3241; TNA E351/543; Hoak, *King's Council*, pp. 160–2; *APC*, ii, pp. 106, 188, 316.

[13] *Cal. SP. Span.*, x, p. 493; Jordan, *Chronicle of Edward VI*, p. 76; Alford, *Kingship and Politics*, pp. 162–70; Nichols (ed.), *Literary Remains*, ii, pp. 489–90.

[14] A. Hawkyard, 'From Painted Chamber to St Stephen's Chapel: The Meeting Places of the House of Commons at Westminster until 1603', in C. Jones and S. Kelsey (eds), *Housing Parliament: Dublin, Edinburgh and Westminster* (Edinburgh, 2002), pp. 76–84; *APC*, ii, pp. 188, 316, 106.

[15] R. Rex, 'The Religion of Henry VIII', *The Historical Journal*, lvii (2014), pp. 1–32.

[16] S. J. Thurley, 'Religion at the Tudor Court', in S. Hoppe and K. de Jong (eds), *Court Residences as Places of Exchange in Late Medieval and Early Western Europe 1400–1700* (Turnhout, forthcoming).

[17] Thurley, *Hampton Court*, p. 63; *L&P Hen. VIII*, xiv (ii), no. 163.

[18] Thurley, *Hampton Court*, pp. 63–4; Thurley, 'The Cloister and the Hearth: Wolsey, Henry VIII and the Early Tudor Palace Plan', pp. 187–90.

[19] J. F. Merritt, *The Social World of Early Modern Westminster: Abbey, Court and Community, 1525–1640* (Manchester, 2005), pp. 25–7, 72–3; T. F. Shirley, *Thomas Thirlby: Tudor Bishop* (London, 1964), pp. 34–5.

[20] Hayward (ed.), *Inventory of Whitehall*, i, p. 35; ii, p. 228; L. Monnas, 'The Splendour of Royal Worship', in Starkey (ed.), *Inventory of Henry VIII*, ii (London, 2012), pp. 300–2; J. P. Carley, *The Books of King Henry VIII and his Wives* (London, 2004), p. 24.

[21] E. Duffy, *The Stripping of the Altars: Traditional Religion in England c.1400–c.1580* (New Haven and London, 1992), pp. 450–2.

[22] W. H. Frere and W. M. Kennedy (eds), *Visitation Articles and Injunctions of the Period of the Reformation*, ii, Alcuin Club Collections, xv (London, 1910), pp. 158–65, 213–27; M. F. Bond (ed.), *The Inventories of St George's Chapel, Windsor Castle, 1384–1667*, Historical Monographs relating to St George's Chapel, Windsor Castle, vii (Windsor, 1947), pp. 13–22.

[23] A. Hiver de Beauvoir (ed.), *Papiers des Pot de Rhodes: 1529–1648* (Paris, 1864), p. 76; Thurley, *Hampton Court*, p. 80.

[24] J. H. Primus, *The Vestments Controversy: An Historical Study of the Earliest Tensions within the Church of England in the Reigns of Edward VI and Elizabeth* (Kampen, 1960), p. 64, n. 23, and see pp. 3–86.

[25] Loach, *Edward VI*, pp. 149–51.

[26] D. MacCulloch, *Thomas Cranmer: A Life* (New Haven and London, 1996), pp. 138–9, 149–52; Thurley, *Whitehall Palace*, pp. 67–8; J. Stow, *Annales, or a Generall Chronicle of England* (London, 1631), p. 595.

[27] J. Foxe, *Actes and Monuments of these Latter and Perillous Dayes, Touching Matters of the Church . . .* (London, 1563), p. 1483.

[28] G. E. Corrie (ed.), *Sermons by Hugh Latimer, sometime Bishop of Worcester* (Cambridge, 1844), p. 204.

[29] Jordan, *Chronicle of Edward VI*, pp. 137–9; TNA E101/426/8; Nichols (ed.), *Literary Remains*, i, p. 81; ii, p. 490; *HKW*, iv, pp. 508–14.

[30] *Cal. SP. Span.*, x, pp. 565–6; Jordan, *Chronicle of Edward VI*, p. 137.

[31] Hamilton (ed.), *Wriothesley's Chronicle*, ii, p. 83.

XII QUEENS REGNANT

[1] *Cal. SP. Span.*, xi, pp. 167, 183, 188, 190, 192.

[2] *ibid.*, pp. 220-1 (also p. 240 and pp. 252-3).

[3] *ibid.*, pp. 214, 238, 252.

[4] *Stat. Realm*, iv (i), p. 222.

[5] *Cal. SP. Span.*, xiii, pp. 30–4.

[6] *Cal. SP. Dom. Edw. VI*, no. 557; Nichols (ed.), *Literary Remains*, i, p. cxi; Hamilton (ed.), *Wriothesley's Chronicle*, ii, pp. 60–1.

[7] *Cal. SP. Span.*, xiii, pp. 23, 31, 45.

[8] *Cal. SP. Span.*, x, pp. 5–6.

[9] *Cal. SP. Span.*, xi, pp. 169, 188, 210; Hamilton (ed.), *Wriothesley's Chronicle*, ii, p. 128; S. Duncan, ' "He to be Intituled Kinge": King Philip of England and the Anglo-Spanish Court', in C. Bean and M. Taylor (eds), *The Man behind the Queen: Male Consorts in History* (New York, 2014), p. 67.

[10] *CPR 1554-5*, p. 103. See also D. M. Loades, *Mary Tudor: A Life* (Oxford, 1989), p. 256.

[11] B. Webb, *Mary Tudor* (London, 1935), p. 309.

[12] *Cal. SP. Span.*, xiii, no. 178.

[13] *Cal. SP. Ven.*, vi (i), no. 174; Loades, *Mary Tudor*, pp. 248–53.

[14] *Cal. SP. Ven.*, vi (i), nos 116, 150.

[15] J. G. Nichols (ed.), *The Diary of Henry*

Machyn, Citizen and Merchant-Taylor of London, From A.D. 1550 to A.D. 1563, Camden Society, xlii (1848), p. 139.

[16] McIntosh, *From Heads of Household,* pp. 201–17; Viscount Strangford (ed.), 'Household Expenses of the Princess Elizabeth during her residence at Hatfield, October 1, 1551, to September 30, 1552', *Camden Miscellany II,* Camden Society, lv (1853), pp. 43–4.

[17] Thurley, *Somerset House,* pp. 27–30.

[18] Nichols (ed.), *Machyn's Diary,* p. 37; D. R. Starkey, *Elizabeth: Apprenticeship* (London, 2001), pp. 112–24.

[19] TNA E351/3330.

[20] Foxe, *Actes and Monuments,* fol. 1712; J. G. Nichols (ed.), *The Chronicle of Queen Jane, and of Two Years of Queen Mary,* Camden Society, xlviii (1850), pp. 70–1; C. R. Manning (ed.), 'State Papers Relating to the Custody of the Princess Elizabeth at Woodstock in 1554', *Norfolk Archaeology,* iv (1855), pp. 141–2.

[21] *HKW,* iv, pp. 349–54; BL Lansdowne MS 313, pp. 319–48; TNA E317/Oxon/12; Williams (ed.), *Platter's Travels,* pp. 220–2.

[22] TNA E 101/670/2.

[23] Manning (ed.), 'State Papers', pp. 163, 202, 216–7, 224–5; Williams (ed.), *Platter's Travels,* pp. 213, 220–22.

[24] *Cal. SP. Span. Eliz.,* i, no. 1 (p. 3).

[25] *Cal. SP. Ven.,* vi (ii), no. 743 (p. 836); Nichols (ed.), *Machyn's Diary,* p. 120; Starkey, *Elizabeth: Apprenticeship,* p. 256.

[26] J. M. Richards, 'Examples and Admonitions: What Mary Demonstrated for Elizabeth', in A. Hunt and A. Whitelock (eds), *Tudor Queenship: The Reigns of Elizabeth and Mary* (Basingstoke, 2010), pp. 31–45; P. Wright, 'A Change in Direction: The Ramifications of a Female Household, 1558–1603', in Starkey (ed.), *English Court,* pp. 147–72.

[27] H. Robinson (ed.), *The Zurich Letters, comprising The Correspondence of Several English Bishops and Others with some of The Helvetian Reformers during the early part of The Reign of Queen Elizabeth,* i (Cambridge, 1842), pp. 18, 55.

[28] R. Bowers, 'The Chapel Royal, the First Edwardian Prayer Book, and Elizabeth's Settlement of Religion, 1559', *The Historical Journal,* xliii (2000), p. 322.

[29] J. Strype, *Annals of the Reformation and Establishment of Religion and other various occurrences in the Church of England during Queen Elizabeth's Happy Reign,* new edn, i (i) (Oxford, 1824), pp. 297–8; Nichols (ed.), *Machyn's Diary,* p. 266; TNA LC5/34, p. 315; LC5/36, p. 165.

[30] Robinson (ed.), *Zurich Letters,* i, p. 63.

[31] J. Leland, *Joannis Lelandi Antiquarii De Rebus Britannicis Collectanea,* ed. T. Hearne, ii (London, 1774; repr. Farnborough, 1970), pp. 691–2; G. von Bülow, 'Journey through England and Scotland made by Lupold von Wedel in the years 1584 and 1585', *Transactions of the Royal Historical Society,* new ser., ix (1895), p. 262.

[32] TNA E351/3204; SP12/81, no. 62; G. W. Groos (ed.), *The Diary of Baron Waldstein* (London, 1981), pp. 141; Williams (ed.), *Platter's Travels,* p. 211; TNA E351/3335.

[33] S. J. Thurley, 'Religion at the Tudor Court', in S. Hoppe and K. de Jong (eds), *Court Residences as Places of Exchange in Late Medieval and Early Western Europe 1400–1700* (Turnhout, forthcoming).

[34] Groos (ed.), *Waldstein's Diary,* pp. 73–81; W. B. Rye, *England as Seen by Foreigners in the days of Elizabeth and James the First* (London, 1865), pp. 104–5; Bülow, 'Wedel's Journey', pp. 250–1.

[35] Williams (ed.), *Platter's Travels,* p. 228.

[36] Nichols (ed.), *Machyn's Diary,* pp. 232, 257, 280–1.

[37] P. E. McCullough, *Sermons at Court: Politics and Religion in Elizabethan and Jacobean Preaching* (Cambridge, 1998), p. 47.

[38] *Cal. SP. Span. Eliz.,* i, no. 286.

[39] Cal. SP. Ven., vii, no. 23.

XIII Elizabeth

[1] TNA E101/474/19, f. 3; HKW, iii, pp. 56, 75.

[2] TNA E101/474/19.

[3] HKW, iii, p. 77.

[4] E. Goldring, Robert Dudley, Earl of Leicester and the World of Elizabethan Art: Painting and Patronage at the Court of Elizabeth I (New Haven and London, 2014), pp. 167–235.

[5] TNA SP12/4, no. 57.

[6] TNA SP12/4, no. 55; SP12/4, no. 56. See also SP12/6, no. 25.

[7] TNA C66/972, m.31d; BL Harl. MS 6990, ff. 42–3; TNA E351/3203.

[8] F. C. Dietz, English Public Finance 1558–1641, ii (London, 1964), pp. 16–39.

[9] T. E. Hartley (ed.), Proceedings in the Parliaments of Elizabeth I, i (Leicester, 1981), pp. 85, 186.

[10] Thurley, Hampton Court, pp. 85–6; Brindle (ed.), Windsor Castle: a thousand years of a royal palace; E351/3203; see also Williams (ed.), Platter's Travels, p. 212.

[11] Thurley, Hampton Court, pp. 84–6; Thurley, Whitehall Palace: An Architectural History, p. 73.

[12] TNA E351/3204–5; Thurley, Hampton Court, p. 87.

[13] TNA E351/3230.

[14] TNA AO1/2477/258; AO3/1243.

[15] TNA E351/3217.

[16] Thurley, Somerset House, pp. 27–30.

[17] TNA SP12/119, no. 31

[18] T. Fuller, Anglorum Speculum, or the Worthies of England in Church and State (London, 1684), p. 471; HMC, Salisbury, v, p. 378; HKW, iii, pp. 94–5.

[19] Cal. SP. Dom., Addenda, 1566–79, pp. 339–40; TNA E351/3337–8; BL Harl. MS 6992, f. 11.

[20] J. G. Nichols, Progresses and Public Processions of Queen Elizabeth, i, (London, 1787), p. 205; Fuller, Anglorum Speculum, Middlesex, p. 177

[21] S. J. Thurley, 'Architecture and Diplomacy: Greenwich Palace under the Stuarts', The Court Historian, xi (2006), pp. 125–6. See also Madden (ed.), 'Duke de Nájera', pp. 350–5.

[22] Merritt, Social World of Westminster, pp. 72–3, 188–94.

[23] TNA E351/3203–4.

[24] TNA E351/3206.

[25] Cal. SP. Span. Eliz., ii, nos 592–3.

[26] TNA E351/3215–6; Thurley, Whitehall Palace, pp. 68–73; R. Holinshed, The Third Volume of the Chronicles (London, 1587), p. 1315. On the Anjou courtship, see S. Doran, Monarchy and Matrimony: The Courtships of Elizabeth I (London, 1996), pp. 154–94.

[27] D. R. Starkey, 'London, Flower of Cities All: Royal Ritual and the River', in S. Doran and R. J. Blyth (eds), Royal River: Power, Pageantry and the Thames (London, 2012), pp. 10–13.

[28] P. Hentzner, Paul Hentzner's travels in England, during the reign of Queen Elizabeth, trans. Horace Earl of Orford (London, 1797), p. 29; RPTE, pp. 75–6; Nichols (ed.), Machyn's Diary, pp. 196, 200, 234. Queen Elizabeth built another covered barge house in 1597–99; TNA E351/3233–4.

[29] 'ERP', pp. 360–4; Nichols (ed.), Machyn's Diary, pp. 21, 168; TNA E351/3213–4; E351/3218; A. Feuillerat (ed.), Documents relating to the Office of the Revels in the time of Queen Elizabeth (London, 1908), p. 298.

[30] Cal. SP. Ven., vi (ii), no. 884 (p. 1084); J. Stow, A Survey of London, ed. C. L. Kingsford, ii (Oxford, 1908), pp. 282–3; Nichols (ed.), Machyn's Diary, pp. 110, 122.

[31] J. Munby, 'Queen Elizabeth's Coaches: The Wardrobe on Wheels', Antiquaries

Journal, lxxxiii (2003), pp. 311–67; R. Straus, *Carriages and Coaches: Their History and Their Evolution* (London, 1912).

[32] Harrison and Jones (eds), *Maisse's Journal*, p. 36; Bülow, 'Wedel's Journey', pp. 256–7. See also Williams (ed.), *Platter's Travels*, p. 225.

[33] Kingston Borough Archives KG2/3 (1567–1681), p. 18; KD5/1/1 (1567–1637) p. 195, and pp. 185, 196; TNA E351/3203, 3217; S. Adams (ed.), *Household Accounts and Disbursement Books of Robert Dudley, Earl of Leicester, 1558–1561, 1584–1586*, Camden Society, 5th ser., vi (1995), pp. 273, 434; *HKW*, v, p. 459.

[34] Thurley, *Hampton Court*, p. 85; *RPTE*, pp. 69–70; TNA E351/3202–5.

[35] TNA E351/3341; *HKW*, iii, p. 80.

XIV Home and Away

[1] Thurley, 'Impact of Royal Landholdings', pp. 155–66.

[2] M. H. Cole, *The Portable Queen: Elizabeth I and the Politics of Ceremony* (Amherst, 1999), pp. 1–34; E. Goldring, F. Eales, E. Clarke and J. E. Archer (eds), *John Nichols's The Progresses and Public Processions of Queen Elizabeth I: A New Edition of the Early Modern Sources*, iii (Oxford, 2014), p. 552.

[3] T. Birch, *Memoirs of the Reign of Queen Elizabeth*, i (London, 1754), pp. 154–5; Goldring et al. (eds), *Nichols's Progresses*, iv, p. 210.

[4] BL Cott. MS Titus B XIII, f. 17; S. Adams, '"The Queenes majestie . . . is now become a great huntress": Elizabeth I and the Chase', *The Court Historian*, xviii (2013), pp. 143–58, 161.

[5] *Cal. SP. Span. Eliz.*, i, no. 314 (p. 466); *Cal. SP. Dom.*, 1601–3, p. 232; F. H. Mares (ed.), *The Memoirs of Robert Carey* (Oxford, 1972), pp. 43–4; Goldring et al. (eds), *Nichols's Progresses*, iv, pp. 129–30; Adams, 'The Queenes majestie', p. 160.

[6] TNA SP15/17, f. 83, transcribed in A. Keay and J. Watkins (eds), *The Elizabethan*

Garden at Kenilworth Castle (London, 2013), pp. 174–5.

[7] R. K. Morris, '"I was never more in love with an olde howse nor never newe worke coulde be better bestowed": The Earl of Leicester's remodelling of Kenilworth Castle for Queen Elizabeth I', *Antiquaries Journal*, lxxxix (2009), pp. 241–305. However, I differ from Richard in the identification of some of the rooms.

[8] Goldring et al. (eds), *Nichols's Progresses*, ii, pp. 233–332.

[9] J. Summerson, 'The Building of Theobalds, 1564–1585', *Archaeologia*, xcvii (1959), p. 121; HMC, *Salisbury*, xiii, pp. 110–11.

[10] J. Husselby, 'The Politics of Pleasure: William Cecil and Burghley House', in P. Croft (ed.), *Patronage, Culture and Power: The Early Cecils* (New Haven and London, 2002), pp. 21–45; J. Summerson, *The Book of Architecture of John Thorpe in Sir John Soane's Museum*, Walpole Society, xl (Glasgow, 1966), p. 61; Groos (ed.), *Waldstein's Diary*, pp. 81–7

[11] Works at courtier houses are mentioned almost every year in the Elizabethan works' accounts. My examples can be found in: TNA E351/3208, f. 8v; E351/3216, f. 17; E351/3235, f. 14; E351/3236, f. 12v; E351/3227, f. 10v.

[12] A. G. R. Smith, *Servant of the Cecils: The Life of Sir Michael Hickes, 1543–1612* (London, 1977), p. 108.

[13] Goldring et al. (eds), *Nichols's Progresses*, iii, pp. 741–2.

[14] Z. Dovey, *An Elizabethan Progress: The Queen's Journey into East Anglia, 1578* (Stroud, 1996), pp. 104–9; J. Gage, *The History and Antiquities of Hengrave, in Suffolk* (London, 1822), pp. 21–32; J. G. Nichols, *The Progresses and Public Processions of Queen Elizabeth*, ii (London 1788), p. 215.

[15] TNA LC5/34, pp. 175–6, 316.

[16] TNA LC5/35, p.308.

[17] Household Ordinances p. 145; TNA E101/419/13, f. 32.

[18] F. G. Emmison, Tudor Secretary: Sir William Petre at Court and Home (London, 1961), pp. 237–43.

[19] BL Harl. MS 6992, no. 8, f. 15; Cole, Portable Queen, p. 37.

[20] M. Brayshay, Land Travel and Communications in Tudor and Stuart England: Achieving a Joined-up Realm (Liverpool, 2014), pp. 267–8, 272–304, 309–14, 347–50.

[21] TNA E351/3204–5; R. Baxter, The Royal Abbey of Reading (Woodbridge, 2016), pp. 149–52.

[22] G. von Bülow and W. Powell (eds), 'Diary of the Journey of Philip Julius, Duke of Stettin-Pomerania, through England in the year 1602', Transactions of the Royal Historical Society, new ser., vi (1892), p. 51.

[23] RPTE, pp. 128–9.

[24] BL Cott. MS Vesp. F xii, f. 179a.

[25] Thurley, Hampton Court, pp. 17–32.

[26] Samman, 'Henrician Court', pp. 73–9.

[27] TNA E351/3220; Cal. SP. Span. Eliz., i, pp. 178–9.

[28] Adams, Household Accounts, pp. 80–3, 143–5, 181, 183, 185, 194, 196.

[29] RPTE, pp. 174–6.

[30] G. Kilroy, The Epigrams of Sir John Harington (Farnham, 2009), p. 124; TNA LC5/35, p. 10.

[31] RPTE, pp. 173–5; TNA LC5/35, p. 311.

XV THE ELIZABETHAN ROYAL LODGINGS

[1] HMC, Seventh Rep., p. 606.

[2] E. K. Chambers, Notes on the History of the Revels Office under the Tudors (London, 1906), pp. 5–19; A. Feuillerat (ed.), Documents relating to the Revels at Court in the time of King Edward VI and Queen Mary (Louvain, 1914), pp. 6–8, 32, 39–43.

[3] B. Sloane and G. Malcolm, Excavations at the Priory of the Order of the Hospital of St John of Jerusalem, Clerkenwell, London (London, 2004), pp. 224–5, 227–228.

[4] E. K. Chambers, The Elizabethan Stage, i (Oxford, 1923), pp. 223–4; Feuillerat, Office of Revels Elizabeth, pp. 179, 277, 218–9.

[5] TNA E351/3237, and also see E351/3203; E351/3212.

[6] TNA E351/3227.

[7] P. Cunningham (ed.), Extracts from the Accounts of the Revels at Court in the Reigns of Queen Elizabeth and King James I (London, 1842), pp. 62, 68, 87–8, 95, 98, 101, 113; APC, xxiv, p. 102; APC, xxiii, p. 205.

[8] TNA E351/3223, and see also E351/322–5; Cunningham (ed.), Extracts from the Accounts of the Revels, p. 225.

[9] Cal. SP. Span. Eliz., i, no. 286.

[10] Mares (ed.), Carey's Memoirs, pp. xiv, 30; Williams (ed.), Platter's Travels, p. 192; Bülow and Powell (eds), 'Diary of the Journey of Philip Julius, Duke of Stettin-Pomerania, through England in the year 1602', Transactions of the Royal Historical Society, new ser., vi (1892), p. 53; Harrison and Jones (eds), Maisse's Journal, p. 95; A. Collins, Letters and Memorials of State in the reigns of Queen Mary, Queen Elizabeth, King James, [. . .], 2 vols (London, 1746), p. 262.

[11] Williams (ed.), Platter's Travels, pp. 194–5; Groos (ed.), Waldstein's Diary, p. 81; Bülow, 'Wedel's Journey', pp. 262–4; John Harrington, Nugae Antiquae, ed. P. T. Vernon (London, 1804), i, p. 233. Harrison and Jones (eds), Maisse's Journal, pp. 35–6.

[12] TNA E351/3225; HMC, Bath, iv, p. 186.

[13] Collins, Letters and Memorials of State in the reigns of Queen Mary, Queen Elizabeth, King James, [. . .], p. 54; TNA E351/3210. Harrison and Jones (eds), Maisse's Journal, p. 55.

[14] Wright, 'Change in Direction', pp. 150–1.

[15] Baron Breuner to the Emperor Ferdinand, 6 August 1559. V. von Klarwill

(ed.), *Queen Elizabeth and some Foreigners, being a series of hitherto unpublished letters from the archives of the Hapsburg family* (London, 1928), pp. 114–5.

[16] TNA E351/3217; Thurley, *Hampton Court*, p. 86.

[17] TNA LC5/33, p. 78. Four were ordered in 1563 (LC5/33, p. 78), four in 1569 (LC5/34, p. 84), six in 1572 (LC5/34, p. 175), six in 1574 (LC5/34, p. 317) and another six the same year (LC5/35, p. 8). In 1581 she ordered fifteen (LC5/35, p. 309).

[18] *L&P Hen. VIII*, iv (ii), no. 4005; xiv (ii), no. 153; TNA LC5/35, pp. 9, 309.

[19] *RPTE*, pp. 170–1; Thurley, *Whitehall Palace*, pp. 149–61; Groos (ed.), *Waldstein's Diary*, p. 51; TNA E351/3224, 3236; TNA LC5/33, f. 91.

[20] J. Arnold, *Queen Elizabeth's Wardrobe Unlock'd* (Leeds, 1988), p. 174; BL Egerton MS 2806, ff. 32v, 81v, 228v, 120v, 154v.

[21] Arnold, *Elizabeth's Wardrobe*, pp. 227–8, 232–4; TNA E351/3214; E351/3234; E351/3205.

[22] J. Melville, *Memoirs of his own life, by Sir James Melville of Halhill, MDXLIX–MDXCIII*, ed. T. Thompson (Edinburgh, 1827), pp. 115–26; William Camden, annals p. 1579.

[23] A. Collins, *Letters and Memorials of State in the reigns of Queen Mary, Queen Elizabeth, King James, [. . .]*, ii (London, 1746), pp. 127–9.

[24] A. Whitelock, *Elizabeth's Bedfellows: An Intimate History of the Queen's Court* (London, 2013), pp. 190–1.

[25] *Cal. SP. Span. Eliz.*, i, p. 465; Lodge, *Illustrations*, ii, p. 170.

[26] TNA E351/3222.

[27] C. C. Jones, *Court Fragments; or Recollections of Royalty from the Death of Rufus, in 1100, to that of the Cardinal York*, ii (London, 1828), pp. 43–4; *Cal. SP. Span. Eliz.*, i, p. 621; P. L. Hughes and J. F. Larkin (eds), *Tudor Royal Proclamations*, iii (New Haven and London, 1969), pp. 134–6.

[28] T. B. Howell, *A Complete Collection of State Trials and Proceedings for High Treason and other Misdemeanors from the Earliest Period to the year 1783*, i (London, 1816), cols. 1403–10; TNA SP12/278/61, ff. 104r–106v.

[29] TNA SP12/81, no. 62; SP12/89, no. 48.

[30] Husselby, 'Politics of Pleasure', p. 40.

[31] Groos (ed.), *Waldstein's Diary*, p. 141; J. Finet, *Finetti Philoxensis* (London, 1656), p. 114.

[32] R. Ascham, *The Schoolmaster* (London, 1909), pp. 66–7.

[33] Nichols, *Progresses and Processions*, iii, p. 564n.

[34] S. Brindle (ed.), *Windsor Castle: a thousand years of a royal palace* (London, forthcoming); TNA SP12/223, no. 6.

[35] TNA SP 12/182/41.

[36] TNA SP12/223, no. 6; *HKW* portfolio plan iv.

[37] M. Girouard, *Elizabethan Architecture: Its Rise and Fall, 1540–1640* (New Haven and London, 2009), pp. 188, 190; C. Gapper, 'Plasterers and Plasterwork in City, Court and Country c.1530–c.1640' (unpublished PhD thesis, University of London, 1998), chap. 2; TNA AO1/2477/258; AO3/1243.

[38] TNA E351/3204, 3215, 3217.

[39] TNA E351/3232–3; LC5/35, p. 313.

[40] TNA LC5/37 pp. 83–6.

[41] TNA LC5/33, p. 78; LC5/33, p. 121; LC5/34, pp. 84, 132.

[42] BL Harl. Roll AA 23; BL Lansdowne MS 11, no. 49 (f. 113).

[43] TNA E351/3227.

[44] A. Woodworth, 'Purveyance for the Royal Household in the Reign of Queen Elizabeth', *Transactions of the American Philosophical Society*, xxxv (1945), pp. 69–70.

[45] L. Withington (ed.), *Elizabethan England: From "A Description of England" by William Harrison* (London, 1876), p. 145; J. Hatcher,

The History of the British Coal Industry: Vol. 1: Before 1700 (Oxford, 1993), pp. 32–55.

[46] J. U. Nef, *The Rise of the British Coal Industry*, i (London, 1932), p. 198; Groos (ed.), *Waldstein's Diary*, p. 153; TNA LC5/33, pp. 78, 93, 176; LC5/34, pp. 48, 179: Harrison and Jones (eds), *Maisse's Journal*, p. 26.

[47] TNA E351/3213; LC5/37, p. 4; LC5/37, p. 241.

[48] *RPTE*, pp. 163–7; Thurley, *Hampton Court*, pp. 26, 87; TNA E351/3232.

[49] *HKW*, iii, pp. 317–8.

XVI THE LAST DECADES

[1] H. Foley (ed.), *Records of the English Province of the Society of Jesus*, i (London, 1877), p. 8.

[2] E. P. Read and C. Read (eds), *Elizabeth of England: Certain Observations Concerning the Life and Reign of Queen Elizabeth by John Clapham* (Oxford, 1951), p. 86.

[3] TNA E351/3216, ff. 7v–8; R. Strong, *The Cult of Elizabeth: Elizabethan Portraiture and Pageantry* (London, 1977), pp. 129–62; Bülow, 'Wedel's Journey', p. 235; Williams (ed.), *Platter's Travels*, p. 164. It should be noted that a new tiltyard was built at Greenwich in 1577–8; TNA E351/3212.

[4] Cole, *Portable Queen*, pp. 33–4; J. Guy, *Elizabeth: The Forgotten Years* (London, 2016), pp. 145–60.

[5] *HKW*, iii, pp. 87–103.

[6] TNA E351/3230–37.

[7] Williams (ed.), *Platter's Travels*, p. 200.

[8] TNA E36/241, pp. 42, 39, 410; E36/243, p. 320; E36/237, pp. 306, 148; E36/241, pp. 250, 267, 280; E36/237, p. 42; Nicolas, *Privy Purse Henry VIII*, p. 255.

[9] Strong, *Artist and the Garden*, pp. 24–6; Bülow, 'Wedel's Journey', pp. 51–2.

[10] Thurley, *Hampton Court*, p. 93; Williams (ed.), *Platter's Travels*, p. 200. This feature was also noted by Baron Waldstein on his visit in 1600; Groos (ed.), *Waldstein's Diary*, p. 147.

[11] TNA E36/240, pp. 502, 582; E36/243, p. 222; E36/237, f. 745; E36/237, pp. 520, 532, 751; E36/239, p. 412; E36/243, p. 640; E36/244, pp. 28, 417; E36/243, pp. 366, 639; C. K. Currie, 'Fishponds as Garden Features, c.1550–1750', *Garden History*, xviii (1990), pp. 22–46.

[12] R. Strong, 'The Renaissance Garden in England Reconsidered', *Garden History*, xxvii (1999), p. 4; Thurley, *Hampton Court*, pp. 89–92.

[13] J. H. Harvey, *Early Nurserymen* (London, 1974), p. 30; TNA E36/243, pp. 267, 277.

[14] P. F. Tytler, *England under the reigns of Edward VI and Mary*, ii (London, 1839), p. 242; *APC*, ii, pp. 188, 306; iii, p. 311.

[15] Surrey History Centre MS LM709/1.

[16] TNA E351/3362; E351/3218–19.

[17] TNA E351/3203, 3204–5; Klarwill (ed.), *Elizabeth and some Foreigners*, p. 319. The beasts were repainted in 1577–8; TNA E351/322; Groos (ed.), *Waldstein's Diary*, p. 59.

[18] TNA E351/3215, 3227; E351/3216.

[19] TNA E351/3234; E351/3236; LC5/36, p. 267; LC5/37, p. 242.

[20] Read and Read (eds), *Elizabeth of England*, p. 86; J. Harington, *A Tract on the Succession to the Crown (A.D. 1602)*, ed. C. R. Markham (London, 1880), p. 51.

[21] J. Rowlands, *The Age of Dürer and Holbein. German Drawings 1400–1550* (London, 1988), pp. 122–3.

[22] Hall, *Chronicle*, p. 513; Starkey (ed.), *Inventory of Henry VIII*, i, p. 240 (no. 10728); N. Matar, *Turks, Moors and Englishmen in the Age of Discovery* (New York, 1999), p. 34; G. MacLean and N. Matar, *Britain and the Islamic World* (Oxford, 2011), pp. 198–202; P. Frankopan, *The Silk Roads: A New History of the World* (London, 2015), pp. 245–9.

[23] L. Jardine, 'Gloriana Rules the Waves: Or, the Advantage of Being Excommunicated (and a Woman)', *Transactions of the Royal*

Historical Society, 6th ser., xiv (2004), pp. 209–22.

24 T. Geminus, Morysse and Damashin renewed and increased, very profitable for Goldsmythes and Embroiderars (London, 1548).

25 D. King, 'From the Exotic to the Mundane: carpets and coverings for tables, cupboards, window seats and floors', in Starkey (ed.), Inventory of Henry VIII, ii, pp. 131–43; J. M. Sweetman, The Oriental Obsession: Islamic Inspiration in British and American Art and Architecture, 1500–1920 (Cambridge, 1987), pp. 10–16.

26 TNA LC5/34, p. 316; LC5/35, p. 310; LC5/37, p. 4.

27 TNA LC5/35, pp. 7, 309–10; LC5/36, p. 58; LC5/37, p. 238; Bülow, 'Wedel's Journey',

p. 264; Harrison and Jones (eds), Maisse's Journal, pp. 22–3; Williams (ed.), Platter's Travels, p. 192; Mares (ed.), Carey's Memoirs, p. 57.

28 Harrison and Jones (eds), Maisse's Journal, pp. 22–3; T. Wright (ed.), Queen Elizabeth and Her Times, ii (London, 1838), p. 174.

EPILOGUE

1 Mares (ed.), Carey's Memoirs, pp. 57–60; Read and Read (eds), Elizabeth of England, p. 98.

2 HMC Salisbury XV, p. 348, printed in Lodge, Illustrations, iii, pp. 206–212.

BIBLIOGRAPHY

Adams, S. (ed.), *Household Accounts and Disbursement Books of Robert Dudley, Earl of Leicester, 1558–1561, 1584–1586,* Camden Society, 5th ser., vi (1995)

Adams, S., ' "The Queenes majestie . . . is now become a great huntress": Elizabeth I and the Chase', *The Court Historian,* xviii (2013), pp. 143–64

Alford, S., *Kingship and Politics in the Reign of Edward VI* (Cambridge, 2002)

Allmand, C. T., *Henry V* (London, 1992)

Anglo, S., *Spectacle, Pageantry, and Early Tudor Policy* (Oxford, 1969)

Antonovics, A. V., 'Henry VII, King of England, "By the Grace of Charles VIII of France" ', in R. A. Griffiths and J. W. Sherborne (eds), *Kings and Nobles in the Later Middle Ages: a tribute to Charles Ross* (Gloucester, 1986), pp. 169–84

Arnold, J., *Queen Elizabeth's Wardrobe Unlock'd* (Leeds, 1988)

Ascham, R., *The Schoolmaster* (London, 1909)

Ashbee, J., *The Jewel Tower* (London, 2013)

Ashdown-Hill, J., *The Last Days of Richard III* (Stroud, 2010)

Auerbach, E., *Tudor Artists: A Study of Painters in the Royal Service and of Portraiture on Illuminated Documents from the Accession of Henry VIII to the Death of Elizabeth I* (London, 1954)

Barron, C. M., 'Richard II: Image and Reality', in D. Gordon (ed.), *Making and Meaning: The Wilton Diptych* (London, 1993), pp. 13–19

Barron, C. M., 'Introduction: England and the Low Countries, 1327–1477', in C. M. Barron and N. Saul (eds), *England and the Low Countries in the Late Middle Ages* (Stroud, 1995), pp. 1–28

Baxter, R., *The Royal Abbey of Reading* (Woodbridge, 2016)

Beckett, N., 'Henry VII and Sheen Charterhouse', in B. Thompson (ed.), *The Reign of Henry VII: Proceedings of the 1993 Harlaxton Symposium* (Stamford, 1995), pp. 117–32

Bernard, G., 'The Rise of Sir William Compton, Early Tudor Courtier', *English Historical Review,* xcvi (1981), pp. 754–77

Bernard, G. W., *Anne Boleyn: Fatal Attractions* (New Haven and London, 2010)

Biddle, M., ' "Makinge of moldes for the walles" – The Stuccoes of Nonsuch: materials, methods and origins', in R. Frederiksen and E. Marchand (eds), *Plaster Casts: Making, Collecting and Displaying from Classical Antiquity to the Present* (Berlin, 2010), pp. 99–117

Bindoff, S. T., 'Clement Armstrong and His Treatises of the Commonweal', *Economic History Review*, xiv (1944), pp. 64–73

Birch, T., *Memoirs of the Reign of Queen Elizabeth*, 2 vols (London, 1754)

Bond, J., and K. Tiller, *Blenheim: Landscape for a Palace* (Oxford, 1987)

Bond, M. F. (ed.), *The Inventories of St George's Chapel, Windsor Castle, 1384–1667*, Historical Monographs relating to St George's Chapel, Windsor Castle, vii (Windsor, 1947)

Bowers, R., 'The Chapel Royal, the First Edwardian Prayer Book, and Elizabeth's Settlement of Religion, 1559', *The Historical Journal*, xliii (2000), pp. 317–44

Bowers, R., 'The Music and Musical Establishment of St George's Chapel in the Fifteenth Century', in C. Richmond and E. Scarff (eds), *St George's Chapel, Windsor, in the Late Middle Ages*, Historical Monographs relating to St George's Chapel, Windsor Castle, xvii (Windsor, 2001), pp. 171–214

Brayshay, M., 'Long-distance royal journeys: Anne of Denmark's journey from Stirling to Windsor in 1603', *Journal of Transport History*, xxv (2004), pp. 1–21

Brayshay, M., *Land Travel and Communications in Tudor and Stuart England: Achieving a Joined-up Realm* (Liverpool, 2014)

Brears, P., *Cooking and Dining in Medieval England* (Totnes, 2008)

Brears, P., *All the King's Cooks: The Tudor Kitchens of King Henry VIII at Hampton Court Palace* (London, 2011)

Brigden, S. (ed.), 'The Letters of Richard Scudamore to Sir Philip Hoby, September 1549–March 1555', *Camden Miscellany XXX*, Camden Society, 4th ser., xxxix (1990), pp. 67–148

Brindle, S. (ed.), *Windsor Castle: a thousand years of a royal palace* (London, forthcoming)

Brown, R. (ed.), *Four Years at the Court of Henry VIII*, 2 vols (London, 1854)

Bülow, G. von, and W. Powell (eds), 'Diary of the Journey of Philip Julius, Duke of Stettin-Pomerania, through England in the year 1602', *Transactions of the Royal Historical Society*, new ser., vi (1892), pp. 1–67

Bülow, G. von, 'Journey through England and Scotland made by Lupold von Wedel in the years 1584 and 1585', *Transactions of the Royal Historical Society*, new ser., ix (1895), pp. 223–70

Burtt, J., 'Charter of Henry VII to the Franciscan Friars at Greenwich, and an Inedited Seal of the Warden', *Archaeological Journal*, 23 (1866), pp. 54–9

Byrne, M. S., *The Letters of King Henry VIII* (London, 1968)

Byrne, M. S. (ed.), *The Lisle Letters*, 6 vols (London, 1981)

Campbell, T. P., *Henry VIII and the Art of Majesty: Tapestries at the Tudor Court* (New Haven and London, 2007)

Carley, J. P., *The Books of King Henry VIII and his Wives* (London, 2004)

Cavell, E. (ed.), *The Heralds' Memoir, 1486–1490: Court Ceremony, Royal Progress and Rebellion* (Donington, 2009)

Chamberlin, F., *The Private Character of Henry the Eighth* (London, 1932)

Chambers, E. K., *Notes on the History of the Revels Office under the Tudors* (London, 1906)

Chambers, E. K., *The Elizabethan Stage*, 4 vols (Oxford, 1923)

Chrimes, S. B., *Henry VII* (London, 1972)

Clapham, A. W., 'On the Topography of the Dominican Priory of London', *Archaeologia*, lxiii (1912), pp. 57–84

Cobb, H. S., 'Descriptions of the State Opening of Parliament, 1485–1601: A Survey', *Parliamentary History*, xviii (1999), pp. 303–15

Cole, M. H., *The Portable Queen: Elizabeth I and the Politics of Ceremony* (Amherst, 1999)

Collins, A., *Letters and Memorials of State in the reigns of Queen Mary, Queen Elizabeth, King James, [. . .]*, 2 vols (London, 1746)

Cornwall, J. C. K., *Wealth and Society in Early Sixteenth Century England* (London, 1988)

Corrie, G. E. (ed.), *Sermons by Hugh Latimer, sometime Bishop of Worcester* (Cambridge, 1844)

Cowie, R., and J. Cloake, 'An archaeological survey of Richmond Palace, Surrey', *Post-Medieval Archaeology*, xxxv (2001), pp. 3–52

Cox, M. H., and P. Norman (eds), *Neighbourhood of Whitehall*, vol. 1 *(The Parish of St Margaret, Westminster, Part II)*, Survey of London, xiii (London, 1930)

Cummins, J., *The Hound and the Hawk: The Art of Medieval Hunting* (London, 1988)

Cunningham, P. (ed.), *Extracts from the Accounts of the Revels at Court in the Reigns of Queen Elizabeth and King James I* (London, 1842)

Cunningham, S., *Henry VII* (London, 2007)

Currie, C. K., 'Fishponds as Garden Features, c.1550–1750', *Garden History*, xviii (1990), pp. 22–46

Davis, C. S. L., 'Tudor: What's in a Name?', *History*, lxxxxvii (2012), pp. 24–42

Dean, D., 'Image and Ritual in the Tudor Parliaments', in D. E. Hoak (ed.), *Tudor Political Culture* (Cambridge, 1995), pp. 243–71

Dent, J., *The Quest for Nonsuch* (London, 1962)

Dietz, F. C., *English Public Finance 1558–1641*, 2 vols, 2nd edn (London, 1964)

Dix, B., and S. Parry, 'The Excavation of the Privy Garden', in S. Thurley (ed.), *The King's Privy Garden 1689–1995* (Apollo Magazine, 1990), pp. 79–115

Dixon, P., *Excavations at Greenwich Palace* (London, 1972)

Doran, S., *Monarchy and Matrimony: The Courtships of Elizabeth I* (London, 1996)

Dovey, Z., *An Elizabethan Progress: The Queen's Journey into East Anglia, 1578* (Stroud, 1996)

Drake, H. H. (ed.), *Hasted's History of Kent, Part 1* (London, 1886)

Duffy, E., *The Stripping of the Altars: Traditional Religion in England c.1400–c.1580* (New Haven and London, 1992)

Duindam, J., 'The Burgundian-Spanish legacy in European court life: a brief reassessment and the example of the Austrian Hapsburgs', *Publications du Centre Européen d'Etudes Bourguignonnes*, xlvi (2006), pp. 203–20

Duncan, S., '"He to be Intituled Kinge": King Philip of England and the Anglo-Spanish Court', in C. Bean and M. Taylor (eds), *The Man behind the Queen: Male Consorts in History* (New York, 2014), pp. 55–80

Elton, G. R., *The Tudor Revolution in Government* (Cambridge, 1953)

Emery, A., *Greater Medieval Houses of England and Wales*, 3 vols (Cambridge, 1996–2006)

Emmison, F. G., *Tudor Secretary: Sir William Petre at Court and Home* (London, 1961)

Everett, M., *The Rise of Thomas Cromwell: Power and Politics in the Reign of Henry VIII* (New Haven and London, 2015)

Feuillerat, A. (ed.), *Documents relating to the Office of the Revels in the time of Queen Elizabeth* (London, 1908)

Feuillerat, A. (ed.), *Documents relating to the Revels at Court in the time of King Edward VI and Queen Mary* (Louvain, 1914)

Finet, J., *Finetti Philoxensis* (London, 1656)

Foard, G., and A. Curry, *Bosworth 1485: A Battlefield Rediscovered* (Oxford, 2013)

Foister, S., *Holbein in England* (London, 2006)

Foley, H. (ed.), *Records of the English Province of the Society of Jesus*, 7 vols in 8 (London, 1877–84)

Ford, L. L., 'Conciliar Politics and Administration in the Reign of Henry VII' (unpublished PhD thesis, University of St Andrews, 2001)

Fortescue, J., *The Governance of England*, ed. C. Plummer (Oxford, 1885)

Foxe, J., *Actes and Monuments of these Latter and Perillous Dayes, Touching Matters of the Church . . .* (London, 1563)

Frankopan, P., *The Silk Roads: A New History of the World* (London, 2015)

Frere, W. H., and W. M. Kennedy (eds), *Visitation Articles and Injunctions of the Period of the Reformation*, 3 vols, Alcuin Club Collections, xiv–xvi (London, 1910)

Fuller, T., *Anglorum Speculum, or the Worthies of England in Church and State* (London, 1684)

Furnivall, F. J. (ed.), *Harrison's Description of England in Shakspere's Youth: Being the Second and Third Books of his Description of Britaine and England, edited from the First Two Editions of Holinshed's Chronicle, A.D. 1577, 1587* (London, 1877)

Gage, J., *The History and Antiquities of Hengrave, in Suffolk* (London, 1822)

Gairdner, J., *Memorials of King Henry the Seventh* (London, 1858)

Gairdner, J. (ed.), *Letters and Papers Illustrative of the Reigns of Richard III and Henry VII*, 2 vols (London, 1861–3)

Gapper, C., 'Plasterers and Plasterwork in City, Court and Country c.1530–c.1640' (unpublished PhD thesis, University of London, 1998)

Gater, G. H., and F. R. Hiorns (eds), *Trafalgar Square and Neighbourhood (St Martin-in-the-Fields, Part III)*, Survey of London, xx (London, 1940)

Geminus, T., *Morysse and Damashin renewed and increased, very profitable for Goldsmythes and Embroiderars* (London, 1548)

Girouard, M., *Elizabethan Architecture: Its Rise and Fall, 1540–1640* (New Haven and London, 2009)

Given-Wilson, C., *The Royal Household and the King's Affinity: Service, Politics and Finance in England, 1360–1413* (New Haven and London, 1986)

Goldring, E., *Robert Dudley, Earl of Leicester and the World of Elizabethan Art: Painting and Patronage at the Court of Elizabeth I* (New Haven and London, 2014)

Goldring, E., F. Eales, E. Clarke and J. E. Archer (eds), *John Nichols's The Progresses and Public Processions of Queen Elizabeth I: A New Edition of the Early Modern Sources*, 5 vols (Oxford, 2014)

Goodall, J. A. A., 'Henry VI's Court and the Construction of Eton College', in L. Keen and E. Scarff (eds), *Windsor: Medieval Archaeology, Art and Architecture of the Thames Valley*, British Archaeological Association Transactions, xxv (Leeds, 2002), pp. 247–63

Goodall, J. A. A., 'A Medieval Masterpiece: Herstmonceux Castle, Sussex', *The Burlington Magazine*, cxlvi (2004), pp. 516–25

Goodall, J. A. A., *Warkworth Castle and Hermitage* (London, 2006)

Gordon, D. (ed.), *Making and Meaning: The Wilton Diptych* (London, 1993)

Graziani, R., 'Sir Thomas Wyatt at a Cockfight, 1539', *Review of English Studies*, new ser., xxvii (1976), pp. 299–303

Green, H. J. M., and S. J. Thurley, 'Excavations on the West Side of Whitehall, 1960–2. Part I: From the Building of the Tudor Palace to the Construction of the Modern Offices of State', *Transactions of the London and Middlesex Archaeological Society*, xxxviii (1987), pp. 59–130

Griffiths, R. A., and R. S. Thomas, *The Making of the Tudor Dynasty* (Gloucester, 1985)

Griffiths, R. A., 'The King's Court During the Wars of the Roses: Continuities in an Age of Discontinuities', in R. A. Griffiths (ed.), *King and Country: England and Wales in the Fifteenth Century* (London, 1991), pp. 11–32

Griffiths, R. A., 'The Burials of King Henry VI at Chertsey and Windsor', in N. Saul and T. Tatton-Brown (eds), *St George's Chapel, Windsor: History and Heritage* (Wimborne Minster, 2010), pp. 100–7

Groos, G. W. (ed.), *The Diary of Baron Waldstein* (London, 1981)

Grummitt, D., 'Henry VII, Chamber Finance and the "New Monarchy": some new evidence', *Historical Research*, lxxii (1999), pp. 229–43

Grummitt, D., 'Household, Politics and Political Morality in the Reign of Henry VII', *Historical Research*, lxxxii (2009), pp. 393–411

Gunn, S. J., 'The Courtiers of Henry VII', *English Historical Review*, cviii (1993), pp. 23–49

Guth, D. J., 'Richard III, Henry VII and the city: London politics and the "Dun Cowe"', in R. A. Griffiths and J. W. Sherborne (eds), *Kings and Nobles in the Later Middle Ages: a tribute to Charles Ross* (Gloucester, 1986), pp. 185–204

Guy, J., 'Thomas Cromwell and the Intellectual Origins of the Henrician Revolution', in J. Guy (ed.), *The Tudor Monarchy* (London, 1997), pp. 213–33

Guy, J., *The Children of Henry VIII* (Oxford, 2013)

Guy, J., *Henry VIII: The Quest for Fame* (London, 2014)

Guy, J., *Elizabeth: The Forgotten Years* (London, 2016)

Hall, E., *Chronicle Containing the History of England* (London, 1809)

Halliwell, J. O. (ed.), *Letters of the Kings of England*, 2 vols (London, 1848)

Hamilton, D. L., 'The Household of Queen Katharine Parr' (unpublished PhD thesis, University of Oxford, 1992)

Hamilton, W. D. (ed.), *A Chronicle of England During the Reigns of the Tudors from A.D. 1485 to 1559 by Charles Wriothesley, Windsor Herald*, 2 vols, Camden Society, new ser., xi (1875), xx (1877)

Harington, J., *A Tract on the Succession to the Crown (A.D. 1602)*, ed. C. R. Markham (London, 1880)

Harrington, J., *Nugae Antiquae*, ed. P. T. Vernon, 2 vols (London, 1804)

Harrison, G. B., and R. A. Jones (eds), *A Journal of All that was accomplished by Monsieur de Maisse, Ambassador in England From King Henry IV to Queen Elizabeth, Anno Domini 1597* (London, 1931)

Harriss, G. L., 'The Court of the Lancastrian Kings', in J. Stratford (ed.), *The Lancastrian Court: Proceedings of the 2001 Harlaxton Symposium* (Donington, 2003), pp. 1–18

Hart, W. H., 'The Parliamentary Surveys of Richmond, Wimbledon, and Nonsuch, in the county of Surrey', *Surrey Archaeological Collections*, v (1871), pp. 75–156

Hartley, T. E. (ed.), *Proceedings in the Parliaments of Elizabeth I*, 3 vols (Leicester, 1981–95)

Harvey, J., *English Medieval Architects: a Biographical Dictionary down to 1550*, rev. edn (Gloucester, 1984)

Harvey, J. H., *Early Nurserymen* (London, 1974)

Hatcher, J., *The History of the British Coal Industry: Vol. 1: Before 1700* (Oxford, 1993)

Hawkyard, A., 'From Painted Chamber to St Stephen's Chapel: The Meeting Places of the House of Commons at Westminster until 1603', in C. Jones and S. Kelsey (eds), *Housing Parliament: Dublin, Edinburgh and Westminster* (Edinburgh, 2002), pp. 62–84

Hay, D. (ed.), *The Anglica Historia of Polydore Vergil, A.D. 1484–1537*, Camden Society, 3rd ser., lxxiv (1950)

Haynes, S. (ed.), *A Collection of State Papers relating to Affairs in the Reigns of King Henry VIII, King Edward VI, Queen Mary and Queen Elizabeth, from the Year 1542 to 1570 . . . now remaining at Hatfield House* (London, 1740)

Hayward, M. A., 'Repositories of Splendour: Henry VIII's wardrobes of the Robes and Beds', *Textile History*, xxix (1998), pp. 134–56

Hayward, M. A. (ed.), *The 1542 Inventory of Whitehall: The Palace and its Keeper*, 2 vols (London, 2004)

Hayward, M. A., 'Symbols of Majesty: Cloths of Estate at the Court of Henry VIII', *Furniture History*, xli (2005), pp. 1–11

Hayward, M. A., *Dress at the Court of King Henry VIII* (Leeds, 2007)

Hayward, M. A., *Rich Apparel: Clothing and the Law in Henry VIII's England* (Farnham, 2009)

Hayward, M. A., *The Great Wardrobe Accounts of Henry VII and Henry VIII*, London Record Society, xlvii (2012)

Henderson, V. K., 'Rethinking Henry VII: The Man and his Piety in the Context of the Observant Franciscans', in D. L. Biggs, S. D. Michalove and A. C. Reeves (eds), *Reputation and Representation in Fifteenth-Century Europe* (Leiden, 2004), pp. 317–47

Hentzner, P., *Paul Hentzner's travels in England, during the reign of Queen Elizabeth*, trans. Horace, Earl of Orford (London, 1797)

Herbert, T., *Memoirs of the Two Last Years of the Reign of Charles I* (London, 1813)

Hewerdine, A., *The Yeomen of the Guard and the Early Tudors: The Formation of a Royal Bodyguard* (London, 2012)

Hiver de Beauvoir, A. (ed.), *Papiers des Pot de Rhodes: 1529–1648* (Paris, 1864)

Hoak, D. E., *The King's Council in the Reign of Edward VI* (Cambridge, 1976)

Hoak, D. E., 'The King's Privy Chamber, 1547–1553', in D. J. Guth and J. W. McKenna (eds), *Tudor Rule and Revolution: Essays for G. R. Elton from his American Friends* (Cambridge, 1982), pp. 87–108

Holinshed, R., *The Third Volume of the Chronicles* (London, 1587)

Hore, J. P., *The History of the Royal Buckhounds* (Newmarket, 1895)

Howell, T. B., *A Complete Collection of State Trials and Proceedings for High Treason and other Misdemeanors from the Earliest Period to the year 1783*, 21 vols (London, 1816)

Hoyle, R. W., and J. B. Ramsdale, 'The Royal Progress of 1541, the North of England, and Anglo-Scottish Relations, 1534–1542', *Northern History*, 41 (2004), pp. 263–5

Hughes, P. L., and J. F. Larkin (eds), *Tudor Royal Proclamations*, 3 vols (New Haven and London, 1964–9)

Hunt, A., and A. Whitelock (eds), *Tudor Queenship: The Reigns of Elizabeth and Mary* (Basingstoke, 2010)

Husselby, J., 'The Politics of Pleasure: William Cecil and Burghley House', in P. Croft (ed.), *Patronage, Culture and Power: The Early Cecils* (New Haven and London, 2002), pp. 21–45

Impey, E. (ed.), *The White Tower* (New Haven and London, 2008)

Ives, E., *The Life and Death of Anne Boleyn* (Oxford, 2004)

Jackson, J. E., 'Wulfhall and the Seymours', *Wiltshire Archaeological and Natural History Magazine*, xv (1875), pp. 140–207

Jardine, L., 'Gloriana Rules the Waves: Or, the Advantage of Being Excommunicated (and a Woman)', *Transactions of the Royal Historical Society*, 6th ser., xiv (2004), pp. 209–22

Jeffery, E. (ed.), *The Antiquarian Repertory*, 4 vols (London, 1807–9)

Jerdan, W. (ed.), *Rutland Papers: Original Documents illustrative of the Courts and Times of Henry VII and Henry VIII*, Camden Society, xxi (1842)

Jones, C. C., *Court Fragments; or Recollections of Royalty from the Death of Rufus, in 1100, to that of the Cardinal York*, 2 vols (London, 1828)

Jones, M. K., and M. G. Underwood, *The King's Mother: Lady Margaret Beaufort, Countess of Richmond and Derby* (Cambridge, 1992)

Jordan, W. K. (ed.), *The Chronicle and Political Papers of King Edward VI* (Ithaca, 1966)

Keay, A., *The Elizabethan Tower of London: The Haiward and Gascoyne Plan of 1597*, London Topographical Society, clviii (London, 2001)

Keay, A., *The Crown Jewels* (London, 2011)

Keay, A., and J. Watkins (eds), *The Elizabethan Garden at Kenilworth Castle* (London, 2013)

Keene, D., 'Wardrobes in the City: Houses of Consumption, Finance and Power', in M. Prestwich, R. Britnell and R. Frame (eds), *Thirteenth Century England*, vii (Woodbridge, 1999), pp. 61–80

Kilroy, G., *The Epigrams of Sir John Harington* (Farnham, 2009)

King, D., 'From the Exotic to the Mundane: carpets and coverings for tables, cupboards, window seats and floors', in D. R. Starkey (ed.), *The Inventory of King Henry VIII*, ii, (London, 2012) pp. 131–43

Kingsford, C. L. (ed.), *English Historical Literature in the Fifteenth Century* (Oxford, 1913)

Kingsford, C. L., 'Historical Notes on Medieval London Houses', *London Topographical Record*, x (1916), pp. 59–62

Kingsford, C. L., 'On Some London Houses of the Early Tudor Period', *Archaeologia*, lxxi (1921), pp. 17–54

Kipling, G. (ed.), *The Receyt of the Ladie Kateryne*, Early English Text Society, cclxxxxvi (1990), pp. 70–4

Kisby, F. L., 'The early Tudor Household Chapel, 1485–1547' (unpublished PhD thesis, University of London, 1996)

Kisby, F. L., 'Kingship and the Royal Itinerary: A Study of the Peripatetic Household of the Early Tudor Kings 1485–1547', *The Court Historian*, iv (1999), pp. 29–39

Kisby, F. L., ' "When the King Goeth a Procession": Chapel Ceremonies and Services, the Ritual Year, and Religious Reforms at the Early Tudor Court, 1485–1547', *Journal of British Studies*, xl (2001), pp. 44–75

Kisby, F. L., 'Religious ceremonial at the Tudor court: Extracts from royal household regulations', in I. W. Archer *et al.* (eds), *Religion, Politics and Society in Sixteenth-Century England*, Camden Society, 5th ser., xxii (2003), pp. 1–33

Klarwill, V. von (ed.), *Queen Elizabeth and Some Foreigners, being a series of hitherto unpublished letters from the archives of the Hapsburg family* (London, 1928)

Knoop, D., and G. P. Jones, *The Medieval Mason*, 3rd edn (Manchester, 1967)

Knowles, D., *The Religious Orders in England*, 3 vols (Cambridge, 1948–59; repr. 1979)

Kuyper, W., *The Triumphant Entry of Renaissance Architecture into the Netherlands: The Joyeuse Entrée of Philip of Spain into Antwerp in 1549; Renaissance and Mannerist Architecture in the Low Countries from 1530 to 1630* (Alphen aan den Rijn, 1994)

Laynesmith, J. L., *The Last Medieval Queens: English Queenship 1445–1503* (Oxford, 2004)

Leland, J., *Joannis Lelandi Antiquarii De Rebus Britannicis Collectanea*, ed. T. Hearne, 6 vols (London, 1774; repr. Farnborough, 1970)

L'Estrange, A. G., *The Palace and the Hospital; or Chronicles of Greenwich*, 2 vols (London, 1886)

Letts, M. (ed.), *The Travels of Leo of Rozmital through Germany, Flanders, England, France, Spain, Portugal and Italy, 1465–1467*, Hakluyt Society, 2nd ser., cviii (1957)

Loach, J., *Edward VI* (New Haven and London, 1999)

Loades, D. M., *Mary Tudor: A Life* (Oxford, 1989)

Lodge, E., *Illustrations of British History, Biography and Manners in the reigns of Henry VIII, Edward VI, Mary, Elizabeth and James I*, 3 vols (London, 1791)

London, H. S., *Royal Beasts* (East Knoyle, 1956)

Luxford, J. M., 'The Collegiate Church as Mausoleum', in C. Burgess and M. Heale (eds), *The Late Medieval English College and its Context* (Woodbridge, 2008), pp. 110–39

MacCulloch, D., *Thomas Cranmer: A Life* (New Haven and London, 1996)

MacGregor, A., *Animal Encounters: Human and Animal Interaction in Britain from the Norman Conquest to World War I* (London, 2012)

MacLean, G., and N. Matar, *Britain and the Islamic World* (Oxford, 2011)

Machiavelli, N., *Lettere Familiari*, ed. E. Alvisi (Florence, 1883)

Madden, F., *Privy Purse Expenses of the Princess Mary, Daughter of King Henry VIII, afterwards Queen Mary* (London, 1831)

Madden, F. (ed.), 'Narrative of the visit of the Duke de Nájera to England in the year 1543–4; written by his Secretary, Pedro de Gante', *Archaeologia*, xxiii (1831), pp. 344–57

Manning, C. R. (ed.), 'State Papers Relating to the Custody of the Princess Elizabeth at Woodstock in 1554', *Norfolk Archaeology*, iv (1855), pp. 133–231

Mares, F. H. (ed.), *The Memoirs of Robert Carey* (Oxford, 1972)

Martin, A. R., *Franciscan Architecture in England* (Manchester, 1937)

Matar, N., *Turks, Moors and Englishmen in the Age of Discovery* (New York, 1999)

Matthew, G., *The Court of Richard II* (London, 1968)

Mattingly, G., *Catherine of Aragon* (London, 1950)

McCullough, P. E., *Sermons at Court: Politics and Religion in Elizabethan and Jacobean Preaching* (Cambridge, 1998)

McIntosh, J. L., *From Heads of Household to Heads of State: The Preaccession Households of Mary and Elizabeth Tudor, 1516–1558* (New York, 2009)

Melville, J., *Memoirs of his own life, by Sir James Melville of Halhill, MDXLIX–MDXCIII*, ed. T. Thompson (Edinburgh, 1827)

Merritt, J. F., *The Social World of Early Modern Westminster: Abbey, Court and Community, 1525–1640* (Manchester, 2005)

Millar, O. (ed.), *The Tudor, Stuart and Early Georgian Pictures in the Collection of Her Majesty the Queen* (London, 1963)

Monnas, L., 'The Splendour of Royal Worship', in D. R. Starkey (ed.), *The Inventory of King Henry VIII*, ii (London, 2012), pp. 295–333

Moore, P. R., 'The Heraldic Charge against the Earl of Surrey, 1546–47', *English Historical Review*, cxvi (2001), pp. 557–83

Morgan, D. A. L., 'The House of Policy: The Political Role of the Late Plantagenet Household, 1422–1485', in D. R. Starkey (ed.), *The English Court: From the Wars of the Roses to the Civil War* (London, 1987), pp. 25–70

Morris, M., *A Great and Terrible King: Edward I and the Forging of Britain* (London, 2008)

Morris, R. K., ' "I was never more in love with an olde howse nor never newe worke coulde be better bestowed": The Earl of Leicester's remodelling of Kenilworth Castle for Queen Elizabeth I', *Antiquaries Journal*, lxxxix (2009), pp. 241–305

Munby, J., 'Queen Elizabeth's Coaches: The Wardrobe on Wheels', *Antiquaries Journal*, lxxxiii (2003), pp. 311–67

Munby, J., R. Barber and R. Brown, *Edward III's Round Table at Windsor: The House of the Round Table and the Windsor Festival of 1344* (Woodbridge, 2007)

Munby, J., 'The Field of Cloth of Gold: Guînes and the Calais Pale Revisited', *English Heritage Historical Review*, ix (2014), pp. 30–63

Murphy, B. A., 'The Life and Political Significance of Henry Fitzroy, Duke of Richmond, 1525–1536' (unpublished PhD thesis, University of Wales, Bangor, 1999)

Murphy, J., 'The illusion of decline: the Privy Chamber, 1547–1558', in D. R. Starkey (ed.), *The English Court: From the Wars of the Roses to the Civil War* (London, 1987), pp. 119–40

Myers, A. R., *The Household of Edward IV: The Black Book and the Ordinance of 1478* (Manchester, 1959)

Myers, A. R., *Crown, Household and Parliament in Fifteenth Century England* (London, 1985)

Nef, J. U., *The Rise of the British Coal Industry*, 2 vols (London, 1932)

Nichols, F. M. (ed.), *The Epistles of Erasmus from his Earliest Letters to his Fifty-First Year*, 3 vols (London, 1901)

Nichols, J. G., *The Progresses and Public Processions of Queen Elizabeth*, 3 vols (London, 1787–1805)

Nichols, J. G. (ed.), *The Chronicle of Calais in the Reigns of Henry VII and Henry VIII to the year 1540*, Camden Society, xxxv (1846)

Nichols, J. G. (ed.), *The Diary of Henry Machyn, Citizen and Merchant-Taylor of London, From A.D. 1550 to A.D. 1563*, Camden Society, xlii (1848)

Nichols, J. G. (ed.), *The Chronicle of Queen Jane, and of Two Years of Queen Mary*, Camden Society, xlviii (1850)

Nichols, J. G. (ed.), *Narratives of the days of the reformation, chiefly from the manuscripts of John Foxe the martyrologist: with two contemporary biographies of Archbishop Cranmer*, Camden Society, lxxvii (1860)

Nichols, J. G. (ed.), 'Inventories of the Wardrobes, Plate, Chapel Stuff, etc. of Henry Fitzroy, Duke of Richmond, and of the Wardrobe Stuff at Baynard's Castle of Katharine, Princess Dowager', *Camden Miscellany III*, Camden Society, lxi (1855)

Nichols, J. G. (ed.), *Literary Remains of King Edward the Sixth*, 2 vols (London, 1857; repr. New York, 1964)

Nicolas, N. H., *The Privy Purse Expenses of King Henry the Eighth from November MDXXIX to December MDXXXII* (London, 1827)

Nicolas, N. H., *Privy Purse Expenses of Elizabeth of York: Wardrobe Accounts of Edward the Fourth* (London, 1830)

Okerlund, A. N., *Elizabeth of York* (Basingstoke, 2009)

Page, W. (ed.), *The Victoria History of the County of Kent*, 3 vols (London, 1908–32)

Payne, A., 'Sir Thomas Wriothesley and his Heraldic Artists', in M. P. Brown and S. McKendrick (eds), *Illuminating the Book: Makers and Interpreters: Essays in honour of Janet Backhouse* (London, 1998), pp. 143–61

Penn, T., *Winter King: The Dawn of Tudor England* (London, 2011)

Pocock, N. (ed.), *A Treatise on the Pretended Divorce between Henry VIII and Catharine of Aragon, by Nicholas Harpsfield, LL.D., Archdeacon of Canterbury*, Camden Society, new ser., xxi (1878)

Pollard, A. F., *The Reign of Henry VII from Contemporary Sources*, 3 vols (London, 1913–14)

Poulton, R., with A. Cook, S. J. Thurley *et al.*, *Excavations at Oatlands Palace, 1968–73 and 1983–4*, Spoil Heap Publications Monograph 3 (Woking, 2010)

Prestwich, M., *Edward I* (London, 1988)

Priestley, J., *Eltham Palace* (Chichester, 2008)

Primus, J. H., *The Vestments Controversy: An Historical Study of the Earliest Tensions within the Church of England in the Reigns of Edward VI and Elizabeth* (Kampen, 1960)

Pynson, R., *The Traduction and Marriage of the Princess* (London, 1500)

Rawlinson, K., 'The English Household Chapel, c.1100–c.1500: An Institutional Study' (unpublished PhD thesis, University of Durham, 2008)

Read, E. P., and C. Read (eds), *Elizabeth of England: Certain Observations Concerning the Life and Reign of Queen Elizabeth by John Clapham* (Oxford, 1951)

Rex, R., 'The Religion of Henry VIII', *The Historical Journal*, lvii (2014), pp. 1–32

Richards, J. M., 'Examples and Admonitions: What Mary Demonstrated for Elizabeth', in A. Hunt and A. Whitelock (eds), *Tudor Queenship: The Reigns of Elizabeth and Mary* (Basingstoke, 2010), pp. 31–45

Richardson, A., 'Greenwich's First Royal landscape: the Lost Palace and Park of Humphrey Duke of Gloucester', *Southern History*, xxxiv (2012), pp. 51–72

Richardson, G., 'Hunting at the Courts of Francis I and Henry VIII', *The Court Historian*, xviii (2013), pp. 127–41

Richardson, G., *The Field of Cloth of Gold* (New Haven and London, 2013)

Richardson, W. C., *History of the Court of Augmentations 1536–1554* (Baton Rouge, 1961)

Roberts, I., *Pontefract Castle. Archaeological Excavations 1982–86* (West Yorkshire Archaeology Service, 2002)

Robinson, H. (ed.), *The Zurich Letters, comprising The Correspondence of Several English Bishops and Others with some of The Helvetian Reformers during the early part of The Reign of Queen Elizabeth*, 2 vols. (Cambridge, 1842–5)

Robinson, H. (ed.), *Original Letters Relative to the English Reformation*, 2 vols (Cambridge, 1846–7)

Robinson, P. F., *Vitruvius Britannicus: History of Hatfield House, illustrated by Plans, Elevations and Internal Views* (London, 1833)

Robinson, W. R. B., 'Princess Mary's Itinerary in the Marches of Wales 1525–1527: a Provisional Record', *Historical Research*, lxxi (1998), pp. 233–52

Rosser, G., and S. J. Thurley, 'Whitehall Palace and King Street, Westminster: The Urban Cost of Princely Magnificence', *London Topographical Record*, xxvi (1990), pp. 57–77

Rye, W. B., *England as Seen by Foreigners in the days of Elizabeth and James the First* (London, 1865)

Salzman, L. F., *Building in England down to 1540: A Documentary History* (Oxford, 1952)

Samman, N., 'The Henrician Court during Cardinal Wolsey's ascendancy c.1514–1529' (unpublished PhD thesis, University of Wales, 1988)

Sansom, C. J., 'The Wakefield Conspiracy of 1541 and Henry VIII's Progress to the North Reconsidered', *Northern History*, 45 (2008) pp. 217–38

Saul, N., *Richard II* (New Haven and London, 1997)

Saul, N. (ed.), *St George's Chapel Windsor in the Fourteenth Century* (Woodbridge, 2005)

Savage, H. (ed.), *The Love Letters of Henry VIII* (London, 1949)

Schofield, J., *St Paul's Cathedral Before Wren* (Swindon, 2011)

Shagan, E. H., 'Clement Armstrong and the godly commonwealth: radical religion in early Tudor England', in P. Marshall and A. Ryrie (eds), *The Beginnings of English Protestantism* (Cambridge, 2002), pp. 60–83

Sharpe, K., *Selling the Tudor Monarchy: Authority and Image in Sixteenth-Century England* (New Haven and London, 2009)

Shelby, L. R., *John Rogers: Tudor Military Engineer* (Oxford, 1967)

Shirley, T. F., *Thomas Thirlby: Tudor Bishop* (London, 1964)

Shoesmith, R., and A. P. Johnson (eds), *Ludlow Castle: Its History and Buildings* (Almeley, 2000)

Skidmore, C., *Bosworth: The Birth of the Tudors* (London, 2013)

Sloane, B., and G. Malcolm, *Excavations at the Priory of the Order of the Hospital of St John of Jerusalem, Clerkenwell, London* (London, 2004)

Smith, A. G. R., *Servant of the Cecils: The Life of Sir Michael Hickes, 1543–1612* (London, 1977)

Smith, T. P., *The Medieval Brickmaking Industry in England 1400–1450*, British Archaeological Reports, cxxxviii (Oxford, 1985)

Staniland, K., 'Royal Entry into the World', in D. Williams (ed.), *England in the Fifteenth Century: Proceedings of the 1986 Harlaxton Symposium* (Woodbridge, 1987), pp. 297–313

Starkey, D. R., 'The King's Privy Chamber 1485–1547' (unpublished PhD thesis, University of Cambridge, 1973)

Starkey, D. R., 'Intimacy and Innovation: the Rise of the Privy Chamber, 1485–1547', in D. R. Starkey (ed.), *The English Court: From the Wars of the Roses to the Civil War* (London, 1987), pp. 71–118

Starkey, D. R. (ed.), *The English Court: From the Wars of the Roses to the Civil War* (London, 1987)

Starkey, D. R., 'Representation through Intimacy: A Study in the Symbolism of Monarchy and Court Office in Early Modern England', in J. Guy (ed.), *The Tudor Monarchy* (London, 1997), pp. 42–77

Starkey, D. R., 'King Henry and King Arthur', in J. P. Carley and F. Riddy (eds), *Arthurian Literature XVI* (Woodbridge, 1998), pp. 171–96

Starkey, D. R. (ed.), *The Inventory of King Henry VIII*, 2 vols (London, 1998–2012)

Starkey, D. R., 'Henry VI's Old Blue Gown: The English Court under the Lancastrians and Yorkists', *The Court Historian*, iv (1999), pp. 1–28

Starkey, D. R., *Elizabeth: Apprenticeship* (London, 2001)

Starkey, D. R., *Six Wives: The Queens of Henry VIII* (London, 2003)

Starkey, D. R., *Henry: Virtuous Prince* (London, 2008)

Starkey, D. R., 'London, Flower of Cities All: Royal Ritual and the River', in S. Doran and R. J. Blyth (eds), *Royal River: Power, Pageantry and the Thames* (London, 2012), pp. 10–17

Stow, J., *Annales, or a Generall Chronicle of England* (London, 1631)

Stow, J., *A Survey of London*, ed. C. L. Kingsford, 2 vols (Oxford, 1908)

Strangford, Viscount (ed.), 'Household Expenses of the Princess Elizabeth during her residence at Hatfield, October 1, 1551, to September 30, 1552', *Camden Miscellany II*, Camden Society, lv (1853)

Stratford, J. (ed.), *The Lancastrian Court: Proceedings of the 2001 Harlaxton Symposium* (Donington, 2003)

Straus, R., *Carriages and Coaches: Their History and Their Evolution* (London, 1912)

Strong, R., *The Cult of Elizabeth: Elizabethan Portraiture and Pageantry* (London, 1977)

Strong, R., 'The Renaissance Garden in England Reconsidered', *Garden History*, xxvii (1999), pp. 2–9

Strong, R., *The Artist and the Garden* (New Haven and London, 2000)

Strype, J., *Annals of the Reformation and Establishment of Religion and other various occurrences in the Church of England during Queen Elizabeth's Happy Reign*, 4 vols, new edn (Oxford, 1824)

Summerson, J., 'The Building of Theobalds, 1564–1585', *Archaeologia*, xcvii (1959), pp. 107–26

Summerson, J., *The Book of Architecture of John Thorpe in Sir John Soane's Museum*, Walpole Society, xl (Glasgow, 1966)

Sutton, A. F., and P. W. Hammond, *The Coronation of Richard III: the extant documents* (Gloucester, 1983)

Sweetman, J. M., *The Oriental Obsession: Islamic Inspiration in British and American Art and Architecture, 1500–1920* (Cambridge, 1987)

Sylvester, R. S. (ed.), *The Life and Death of Cardinal Wolsey by George Cavendish*, Early English Text Society, ccxliii (London, 1959)

Taylor, F., and J. S. Roskell (eds), *Gesta Henrici Quinti: The Deeds of Henry V* (Oxford, 1975)

Thomas, A. H., and I. D. Thornley (eds), *The Great Chronicle of London* (London, 1938)

Thomas, W., *The Pilgrim: A Dialogue on the Life and Actions of King Henry the Eighth*, ed. J. A. Froude (London, 1861)

Thurley, S. J., 'Henry VIII and the Building of Hampton Court: A Reconstruction of the Tudor Palace', *Architectural History*, xxxi (1988), pp. 1–57

Thurley, S. J., 'The Sixteenth-Century Kitchens at Hampton Court', *Journal of the British Archaeological Association*, cxliii (1990), pp. 1–28

Thurley, S. J., 'English Royal Palaces, 1450–1550' (unpublished PhD thesis, University of London, 1991)

Thurley, S. J., 'The Domestic Building Works of Cardinal Wolsey', in S. J. Gunn and P. G. Lindley (eds), *Cardinal Wolsey: Church, State and Art* (Cambridge, 1991), pp. 76–102

Thurley, S. J., *The Royal Palaces of Tudor England: Architecture and Court Life 1460–1547* (New Haven and London, 1993)

Thurley, S. J., 'Whitehall Palace and Westminster 1400–1600: a royal seat in transition', in D. R. M. Gaimster and P. Stamper (eds), *The Age of Transition: the Archaeology of English Culture 1400–1600* (Oxford, 1997), pp. 93–104

Thurley, S. J., *The Whitehall Palace Plan of 1670*, London Topographical Society, cliii (London, 1998)

Thurley, S. J., *The Lost Palace of Whitehall*, Royal Institute of British Architects Exhibition Catalogue (London, 1998; repr. 1999)

Thurley, S. J., *Whitehall Palace: An Architectural History of the Royal Apartments, 1240–1698* (New Haven and London, 1999)

Thurley, S. J., *Hampton Court Palace: A Social and Architectural History* (New Haven and London, 2004)

Thurley, S. J., 'The Impact of Royal Landholdings on the County of Surrey, 1509–1649', in J. Cotton, G. Crocker and A. Graham (eds), *Aspects of Archaeology and History in Surrey* (Guildford, 2004), pp. 155–68

Thurley, S. J., 'Architecture and Diplomacy: Greenwich Palace under the Stuarts', *The Court Historian*, xi (2006), pp. 125–33

Thurley, S. J., *Whitehall Palace: The Official Illustrated History* (London, 2008)

Thurley, S. J., 'The Cloister and the Hearth: Wolsey, Henry VIII and the Early Tudor Palace Plan', *Journal of the British Archaeological Association*, clxii (2009), pp. 179–95

Thurley, S. J., *Somerset House: The Palace of England's Queens 1551–1692*, London Topographical Society, clxviii (London, 2009)

Thurley, S. J., *The Building of England: How the History of England Has Shaped Our Buildings* (London, 2013)

Thurley, S. J., 'The Tudors and Stuarts', in S. Brindle (ed.), *Windsor Castle: a thousand years of a royal palace* (London, forthcoming)

Thurley, S. J., 'Religion at the Tudor Court', in S. Hoppe and K. de Jong (eds), *Court Residences as Places of Exchange in Late Medieval and Early Western Europe 1400–1700* (Turnhout, forthcoming)

Tighe, R. R., and J. E. Davis, *Annals of Windsor, being a History of the Castle and Town, with some account of Eton and places adjacent*, 2 vols (London, 1858)

Tout, T. F., *Chapters in the Administrative History of Medieval England*, 6 vols (Manchester, 1920–33)

Turquet, J. C., 'The Inner Court of Nonsuch Palace' (unpublished PhD thesis, University of London, 1983)

Tytler, P. F., *England under the reigns of Edward VI and Mary*, 2 vols (London, 1839)

Ullmann, W. (ed.), *Liber Regie Capelle: A Manuscript in the Biblioteca Publica, Evora*, Henry Bradshaw Society, lxxxxii (London, 1961)

Vale, M. G. A., 'An Anglo-Burgundian Nobleman and Art Patron: Louis de Bruges, Lord of la Gruthuyse and Earl of Winchester', in C. M. Barron and N. Saul (eds), *England and the Low Countries* (Stroud, 1995), pp. 115–31

Vogtherr, H., *Ein Frembds und wunderbars Künstbüchlein* (Strasbourg, 1538)

Walker, G., 'The "expulsion of the minions" of 1519 Reconsidered', *Historical Journal*, xxxii (1989), pp. 1–16

Watts, J., 'Was there a Lancastrian Court?', in J. Stratford (ed.), *The Lancastrian Court: Proceedings of the 2001 Harlaxton Symposium* (Donington, 2003), pp. 253–71

Webb, B., *Mary Tudor* (London, 1935)

Whiteley, M., 'The Courts of Edward III of England and Charles V of France: A Comparison of their Architectural Setting and Ceremonial Functions', in N. Saul (ed.), *Fourteenth Century England*, I (Woodbridge, 2000), pp. 153–66

Whitelock, A., *Elizabeth's Bedfellows: An Intimate History of the Queen's Court* (London, 2013)

Williams, A., and A. de Reuck, *The Royal Armoury at Greenwich, 1515–1649: A History of its Technology* (London, 1995)

Williams, C. (ed.), *Thomas Platter's Travels in England, 1599* (London, 1937)

Withington, L. (ed.), *Elizabethan England: From "A Description of England" by William Harrison* (London, 1876)

Wolffe, B. P., *The Royal Demesne in English History: The Crown Estate in the Governance of the Realm from the Conquest to 1509* (London, 1971)

Woodworth, A., 'Purveyance for the Royal Household in the Reign of Queen Elizabeth', *Transactions of the American Philosophical Society*, xxxv (1945), pp. 1–89

Woolgar, C. M., *The Great Household in Late Medieval England* (New Haven and London, 1999)

Wright, P., 'A Change in Direction: The Ramifications of a Female Household, 1558–1603', in D. R. Starkey (ed.), *The English Court: From the Wars of the Roses to the Civil War* (London, 1987), pp. 147–172

Wright, T. (ed.), *Queen Elizabeth and Her Times*, 2 vols (London, 1838)

Young, A. R., *Tudor and Jacobean Tournaments* (London, 1987)

Acknowledgements

This book has been thirty years in the making and so I have long and deep debts as well as more immediate ones.

In 1995 I was one of five who founded the Society for Court Studies at a party in the Whitehall Banqueting House. The scholars I have met through the Society, and the friends I have made there, have taught me a huge amount about the study of courts, just as my colleagues, first at Historic Royal Palaces, then at the Museum of London and English Heritage, have taught me about royal buildings. Many of the ideas in this book I first tested out in lectures given in my role as Visiting Professor of the Built Environment at Gresham College. I would like to thank my audiences there for their stimulating and illuminating feedback.

For much of what is in this book I have already acknowledged individuals in my previous, more specialized, accounts listed in the Bibliography, but I must record the assistance of those who, in particular, have helped me in this enterprise. In no particular order I would like to thank Rob Poulton for his help with Oatlands and Woking; Stephen Brindle and Brian Kerr for a long and fruitful relationship on the history and archaeology of Windsor Castle; Michael Turner for his continuing thoughts on St James's; Julian Bowsher for sharing his researches into Greenwich; Edward Impey for his thoughts on the Tower and on medieval royal houses more generally; Jeremy Ashbee and Tim Tatton Brown for discussion about Westminster; Martin Biddle for Nonsuch; Julian Munby for his illuminating work on the Field of Cloth of Gold and carriages; Clare Gapper for her thoughts on plasterwork; Tom Campbell for continuing to open my eyes to the significance of tapestry; and Steve Gun for his generous advice on Henry VII.

I would like to thank Jonathan Mackman for spending many patient hours checking references for me, and George Bernard, who read the book at draft stage and took great care to provide an expert and challenging commentary which has helped me much improve it. For more than twenty-five years I have enjoyed the company and insights of David Starkey, with whom I have discussed many aspects of this book; I'd like to thank him in particular for sharing with me his current thoughts about Henry VII.

My editor at Transworld, Susanna Wadeson, and my copy-editor, Brenda Updegraff, have much improved this book. Phil Lord has made it look beautiful, with the expert help of Liane Payne, who redrew many of my bad plans and hunted down elusive pictures. Clare Murphy has (again) helped me with many illustrations. Finally, I want to thank Anna Keay, my wife, who has shared my passion for palaces and courts for more than twenty years, for reading the book as I wrote it and being my most insightful critic and most powerful inspiration.

PICTURE ACKNOWLEDGEMENTS

Every effort has been made to contact copyright holders. Any we have omitted are invited to get in touch with the publishers.

COLOUR PLATES, Section 1

Page 1: Tower of London: © British Library Board, All Rights Reserved/ Bridgeman Images
Page 2: *(above)* Talbot Shrewsbury Book: © British Library Board, All Rights Reserved/Bridgeman Images; *(below)* October from *Les Très Riches Heures du duc de Berry*: Musée Condé, Chantilly
Page 3: *(above)* Royal Manor of Richmond, attributed to Wenceslaus Hollar: By kind permission of the Society of Antiquaries of London; *(below left)* Henry VIII at prayer: St George's Chapel Archive, Windsor; *(below right) The Family of Henry VII*: © Her Majesty Queen Elizabeth II, 2016/Bridgeman Images
Page 4: *(above)* Reconstruction of Whitehall Palace by Stephen Conlin: © Stephen Conlin; *(below)* Field of Cloth of Gold: © Her Majesty Queen Elizabeth II, 2016/Bridgeman Images
Page 5: *(above)* Two details from *The Family of Henry VIII*: © Her Majesty Queen Elizabeth II, 2016/Bridgeman Images; *(below)* Hans Holbein portrait of unknown man, possibly James Nedeham: Kunsthistorisches Museum, Vienna, Austria/Bridgeman Images
Page 6: *(above)* Wolsey Closet, Hampton Court: Historic Royal Palaces; *(below)*

Hans Holbein, Whitehall Mural: © Her Majesty Queen Elizabeth II, 2016/ Bridgeman Images
Page 7: *(above)* Royal lock from Beddington Place: © Victoria and Albert Museum, London; *(middle)* Hendrick Danckerts, East front of Hampton Court: © Her Majesty Queen Elizabeth II, 2016/ Bridgeman Images; *(below)* Sir Thomas Wriothesley, Record of arms: College of Arms
Page 8: *(above)* David and Bathsheba from story of David tapestry: Musée National de la Renaissance, Ecouen, France/Peter Willi/Bridgeman Images; *(below)* St Paul before King Herod Agrippa detail from story of St Paul tapestry: Detroit Institute of Arts, USA/ Bridgeman Images

COLOUR PLATES, Section 2

Page 1: Chapel ceiling, Hampton Court: Historic Royal Palaces/James Brittain
Page 2: Hampton Court great hall: Historic Royal Palaces/Robin Forster
Page 3: *(above)* Detail from John Norden map showing Ditton House: British Library, London, UK; *(below)* Whitehall Palace from the river, anonymous painting, Royal Collection Trust/© Her Majesty Queen Elizabeth II 2017
Page 4: *(above)* Georg Hoefnagel painting of Nonsuch: Christie's; *(below)* Prince Edward at Hunsdon: © Her Majesty Queen Elizabeth II, 2016/Bridgeman Images

Page 5: *(above)* Family of Henry VIII at Whitehall Palace: © Her Majesty Queen Elizabeth II, 2016/Bridgeman Images; *(below) The Somerset House Conference, 1604*: National Portrait Gallery, London/ Pictures from History/Bridgeman Images

Page 6: *(above)* Hans Eworth, Mary I and Philip II of Spain: Trustees of the Bedford Estate, Woburn Abbey, UK/Bridgeman Images; *(below)* Detail from John Norden, Survey of Windsor Forest: British Library, London, UK

Page 7: *(above)* Cloth of estate for Elizabeth I, Kimberley, Norfolk: Burrell Collection; *(below)* Elizabeth I receiving Dutch emissaries: © Museumslandschaft Hessen Kassel/Bridgeman Images

Page 8: *(above)* Marcus Gheeraerts the Elder, Elizabeth I: Portland Collection, Harley Gallery, Welbeck Estate, Nottinghamshire/Bridgeman Images; *(below)* Elizabeth I: Hardwick Hall, Derbyshire, UK/National Trust Photographic Library/P. A. Burton/ Bridgeman Images

TEXT ILLUSTRATIONS

Page ix: Tour d'Elven: Getty Images/ BERTHIER Emmanuel/hemis.fr

Page 3: Jewel Tower, Westminster Palace: Ian Bottle/Alamy

Page 24: Reconstruction of Edward III's lodgings, Windsor: English Heritage

Page 42: Henry VII's privy tower, Windsor: Trustees of the British Library, London, UK

Page 44: Ceiling of Henry VII privy closet, Windsor: By permission of the Duke of Buccleuch and Queensberry KBE

Page 48: Anthonis van den Wyngaerde, Inner court at Sheen: Ashmolean Museum, University of Oxford, UK/Bridgeman Images

Page 53: Wenceslaus Hollar, View of Richmond: Trustees of the British Museum

Page 55: Anthonis van den Wyngaerde, Baynard's Castle: Ashmolean Museum, University of Oxford, UK/Bridgeman Images

Page 59: Wenceslaus Hollar, Bird's-eye view of Windsor: Hulton Archive/Getty Images

Page 69: Anthonis van den Wyngaerde, Richmond Friary: Ashmolean Museum, University of Oxford, UK/Bridgeman Images

Page 76: Riverfront at Greenwich, Author's reconstruction

Page 79: Henry VII at his table: Trustees of the British Library, London, UK

Page 83: Plans drawn for Henry VIII: Hatfield House, by courtesy of the Marquess of Salisbury

Page 89: Thomas Wriothesley, Deathbed of Henry VII: © British Library Board, All Rights Reserved/Bridgeman Images

Page 96: Windsor Castle gatehouse: Getty Images/Topical Press Agency/Stringer

Page 100: Anthonis van den Wyngaerde, Greenwich tiltyard and towers: Ashmolean Museum, University of Oxford, UK/ Bridgeman Images

Page 103: Dog kennels, from *The Noble Art of Venerie*: Author

Pages 112–13: *(inset)* Detail from The Agas map of London: City of London, London Metropolitan Archives

Pages 114–15: New Hall, Essex: Author

Page 121: Excavation of Whitehall Palace 1939: Author

Page 125: Detail from The Agas map of London: City of London, London Metropolitan Archives

Page 128: Bird's-eye view of Tower of London 1597: © Look and Learn/Peter Jackson Collection/Bridgeman Images

Page 134–5: *(inset)* King Street and Whitehall gates: Society of Antiquaries and Author

Pages 138–9: Anthonis van den Wyngaerde, Whitehall from the river: Ashmolean Museum, University of

Oxford, UK/Bridgeman Images
Page 144: Great close tennis play, Whitehall: Author
Page 152: Wolsey's inner court, Hampton Court: © Historic Royal Palaces
Pages 154–5: First-floor plan, Wolsey's Hampton Court: © Historic Royal Palaces
Page 160: Board of the Greencloth: Trustees of the British Library, London, UK
Pages 164–5: Plan of kitchens, Hampton Court: © Historic Royal Palaces
Page 169: Plan of Henry VIII's privy tower: © Historic Royal Palaces
Pages 172–3: East front, Hampton Court, end of Henry VIII's reign: © Historic Royal Palaces
Page 175: Plan of Elizabeth's Hampton Court gardens: © Historic Royal Palaces
Pages 206–7: Anthonis van den Wyngaerde, Hampton Court from the north: Ashmolean Museum, University of Oxford, UK/Bridgeman Images
Page 208: Wenceslaus Hollar, Kingston-upon-Hull: Author
Page 209: First-floor plan, Hull Manor House: British Library, London, UK/Bridgeman Images
Page 212: Henry VIII dining: Private Collection/Bridgeman Images
Pages 218–19: First-floor plan, Hampton Court: © Historic Royal Palaces
Pages 222–3: East front Hampton Court, 17th century: © Historic Royal Palaces
Page 230: Guilelmus de Saliceto, *De Salutate Corporis*: British Library, London, UK/Bridgeman Images
Page 231: Henry VIII's shield, detail from Cornelis Metsys engraving: British Library, London, UK/Bridgeman Images
Page 234: Perino del Vaga pattern sheet: Victoria and Albert Museum, London
Page 235: Title page by Holbein: Trustees of the British Library, London, UK
Page 236: Corinthian order, French treatise owned by Henry VIII: Trustees of the British Library, London, UK

Page 240: Henry VIII enthroned, from John Foxe, *Acts and Monuments*, 1563: Trustees of the British Library, London, UK
Page 241: Chapel Royal ceiling, St James's Palace: Author
Page 243: Interior wall design: Cliché des Musées Nationaux, Paris
Page 250: Tickenhill Manor gatehouse: The Bodleian Library, University of Oxford
Page 254: St James's gatehouse: Westminster City Archives
Page 260: *(above)* Tudor royal standing, Waltham Forest: English Heritage
Pages 260–61: Anthonis van den Wyngaerde, Oatlands: Ashmolean Museum, University of Oxford, UK/Bridgeman Images
Page 263: View and plan of Oatlands: Author
Page 266: Excavations at Nonsuch 1959: English Heritage
Page 268: Stucco panel, Nonsuch: English Heritage
Page 269: John Speed, Nonsuch: Author
Page 274: Whitehall Palace excavations 1950s: Author
Page 276: George Vertue, King Street Gate, and English Arch, Antwerp: Society of Antiquaries and Author
Page 288: Faithorne and Newcourt map of London and Westminster: © Look and Learn/Elgar Collection/Bridgeman Images
Page 291: Richard Grafton, Edward VI's council chamber: Trustees of the British Library, London, UK
Page 295: Chapel Royal processional: Trustees of the British Library, London, UK
Page 297: Hugh Latimer preaching, Preaching Place: Trustees of the British Library, London, UK
Page 311: Peter Stent, Woodstock Manor: Author
Page 313: Robert Plot, Ruins of Woodstock Manor: Author
Page 316: Chapel Royal, Windsor Castle: The Bodleian Library, University of Oxford

Page 317: Richard Day, *Booke of Christian Prayers and Meditations*, frontispiece: © Lambeth Palace Library, London, UK/ Bridgeman Images

Page 326: Westminster Exchequer columns: Westminster City Archives

Page 327: Elizabeth's privy kitchen, Hampton Court: Historic Royal Palaces

Page 328: Hampton Court bay window: Author

Page 329: Elizabethan fountain, Hampton Court: Hatfield House, by courtesy of the Marquess of Salisbury

Page 330: Chimneypiece, Windsor Castle: The Print Collector/ Getty Images

Page 331: Outer court, Somerset House: Government Art Collection

Page 332: Strand front, Somerset House: Historic Royal Palaces

Page 337: William Capon, Westminster Palace: Trustees of the British Library, London, UK, Add MS 36370 f. 211

Page 342: Cardinal Wolsey travelling by barge: The Bodleian Library, University of Oxford, MS Douce 363 fol. 052v

Page 345: Elizabeth riding in procession: © National Maritime Museum, Greenwich, London

Page 351: River Thames from *Poly-Olbion*: Author

Page 352: Map of 1575 Progress: Author

Pages 354 and 355: Three hunting prints: Trustees of the British Library, London, UK

Page 356: Kenilworth Castle 1620: Getty Images/Hulton Archive

Page 357: First-floor plan of Kenilworth Castle: English Heritage

Page 360: Plan of Burghley House: Trustees of the Sir John Soane Museum

Page 361: John Haynes, Burghley House courtyard: Burghley House Preservation Trust

Page 367: Post messenger: British Library, London, UK/Bridgeman Images

Page 369: Double lodgings, Hampton Court: Historic Royal Palaces

Page 371: Flushing close stool, John Harington, *Metamorphosis of Ajax*: Author

Page 372: Hampton Court Great House of Easement: Historic Royal Palaces

Page 376: St John of Jerusalem, Clerkenwell: Author

Page 379: William Rogers, Elizabeth I in her privy chamber: Private Collection/ Bridgeman Images

Page 383: *Psyche Served in Her Bath*: Trustees of the British Museum

Page 384: *(left)* Sunken bath, Whitehall excavations: Author; *(right)* Reconstruction of green glazed stove: Author

Page 392: Elizabeth's gallery, Windsor: Author

Page 400: Judges' pavilion and tiltyard, Whitehall: College of Arms

Pages 402–3: Anthonis van den Wyngaerde, South front, Hampton Court: Ashmolean Museum, University of Oxford, UK/Bridgeman Images

Page 406: Hampton Court gardens: Historic Royal Palaces

Page 410: Hans Sebald Beham, *Siege of Rhodes*: Photo Scala, Florence/bpk, Bildagentur fuer Kunst, Kultur und Geschichte, Berlin

Page 412: Thomas Geminus, Ottoman design: © Victoria and Albert Museum, London

PLANS AND MAPS

Plans on the following pages are copyright © Simon Thurley 2017: pages 10–11, 13, 17, 18–19, 26–7, 32–3, 40–41, 50–51, 82, 90, 93, 99, 112–13 *(main)*, 129, 134–5 *(main)*, 140, 186–7, 191, 193, 211, 258, 267, 270, 280–81, 310, 382, 390

INDEX

page numbers in *italics* refer to pages with illustrations

ABOUT THE AUTHOR

D R SIMON THURLEY IS A LEADING architectural historian, a regular broadcaster on television and radio, and was until 2015 the Chief Executive of English Heritage, the government's principal advisor on the historic environment in England. Previous posts have included Curator of the Historic Royal Palaces and Director of the Museum of London. Simon is the author of a number of books on architectural history, including *The Royal Palaces of Tudor England*, *Whitehall Palace* and *Hampton Court*. In 2013 he published a major history of English architecture for HarperCollins, *The Building of England*. Simon is married to the historian Anna Keay and lives in Norfolk.